The
CRIMINAL
EVENT

The CRIMINAL EVENT

An Introduction to Criminology

Vincent F. Sacco
Queen's University

Leslie W. Kennedy
University of Alberta

Nelson Canada

I(T)P

Published in 1994 by
Nelson Canada,
A Division of Thomson Canada Limited
1120 Birchmount Road
Scarborough, Ontario M1K 5G4

Cover photo: Comstock

Canadian Cataloguing in Publication Data

Sacco, Vincent F., 1948–
     The criminal event: an introduction to criminology

Includes bibliographical references and index.
ISBN 0-17-603504-4

1. Criminology.   2. Crime - Canada.
I. Kennedy, Leslie W., 1951– . II. Title.

HV6025.S33 1994   364   C94-930114-0

Acquisitions Editor	Charlotte Forbes
Editorial Manager	Nicole Gnutzman
Production Editor	Bob Kohlmeier
Developmental Editor	Heather Martin
Art Director	Bruce Bond

Printed and bound in Canada
1 2 3 4 (BG) 97 96 95 94

To
Tiia, Daniel, Katherin, and Ema
Ilona, Alexis, Andrea, and Grandparents

CONTENTS

■ PART II THEORIES

■ PART III THE CRIMINAL EVENT

■ PART VI RESPONSES TO CRIME

PREFACE

For a number of years we both taught introductory criminology using a fairly conventional approach. We provided definitions of crime, reviewed the important theories, talked about measurement, and then provided a discussion of correlates of crime. While this organization of a criminology course provided all of the material that an introductory student needs, it left us both feeling a bit dissatisfied. We felt that students were getting information about crime but that it was disjointed. Like a story without a theme, it became a collection of seemingly unrelated anecdotes about what different researchers were saying about how we should study crime. In talking to others who have taught introductory students, we found a similar frustration with the lack of an integrating theme in the books they were using.

We believe that introductory criminology has long paid too much attention to the different elements of crime and ignored the integrating nature of the criminal event in its entirety. In this book, we use the idea of criminal event to provide the missing theme. This theme runs through our discussion of what motivates people to commit crime, of who suffers and how, and of what we should do about this. It also allows us to look at the determinants of crime, as well as individual choice and opportunity, as part of a more complete explanation of criminal outcomes.

Further, we believe that we should look at crime in different contexts, assuming that situations can vary greatly in affecting the ways in which crime evolves. We have identified three domains of crime that guide our analysis of context: the family, leisure, and work. These domains contain most daily behaviour and have been the prime areas of study in research on crime and its consequences.

The text that appears here, then, reflects our effort to achieve the objectives laid out above. We have been careful to include the major theories in our discussion. We have also made a concerted effort to include as much contemporary research on criminality as possible. As Richard A. Wright has said, introductory criminology books have failed to reflect the current state of the research. We have tried not to fall into the trap of simply repeating old truths but have sought confirmation of our points in current empirical studies.

To recap:

- Our use of an integrating theme—that of the criminal event as a whole—enables the reader to understand crime as more than simply a collection of loosely connected elements.

- Because it is important to study crime in different contexts, we have identified three domains of crime—family, leisure, and work—and used these to guide our discussion of context.

- We give careful consideration to all of the major criminological theories.

- We use as much contemporary research as possible to inform our points of discussion.

This book was made possible through the efforts of our editor Charlotte Forbes and her marvellous colleagues at Nelson Canada. Charlotte and Developmental Editor Heather Martin showed great patience and perseverance in removing the inevitable annoyances that can get in the way of simply sitting down and writing the book. They also worked hard to get constructive feedback for us on our ideas. The reviewers provided us with countless suggestions and encouraged us to improve certain parts of the text that needed more work. We thank John Casey, Grant MacEwan Community College; Larry R. Comeau, Sheridan College; Helene A. Cummins, Wilfrid Laurier University; David Forde, University of Manitoba; Karin Kaercher, Camosun College; Carl Keane, Queen's University; David Lynes, Lakehead University; Chris McCormick, St. Mary's University; Scott Nicholls, Humber College; and Douglas M. Skoog, University of Winnipeg. We are grateful to Bob Kohlmeier for all his time and attention as our manuscript moved through its various development stages. We also appreciate the patience and dedication of Sarah Robertson, who undertook the difficult job of copy editing the manuscript.

Les Kennedy would like to thank his colleagues and support staff at the University of Alberta for their support of this work. Specifically, he would like to thank Fran Russell, Kelly McGuirk, Kerri Calvert, Joanne Milson, and Joanne Mah for their help. Also, he is grateful for the financial aid provided through the Centre for Criminological Research, which is funded through a contributions grant from the Solicitor General of Canada. Of course, special thanks go to Ilona, Alexis, and Andrea for providing perspective as well as the moral support that is needed to complete a long, intensive job of writing.

Vince Sacco would like to thank his friends and colleagues in the Department of Sociology at Queen's University. Reza Nakhaie and Ross Macmillan frequently and patiently allowed their busy schedules to be interrupted by impromptu monologues about criminal events. Roberta Hamilton, Frank Pearce, Terry Willett, and Elia Zureik, as always, provided encouragement. Wilma Bauder's help in the facilitation of the project is greatly appreciated, and Martha Roberts's technical assistance proved invaluable at several key stages. A special thanks is owed to Joan Westenhaefer, without whose help production of the manuscript would have been a stressful if not impossible task. Finally, and as always, the biggest thank you is owed to Tiia, Katherin, and Daniel.

Both of us would like to make special mention of the support that our friend Bob Silverman has provided to us over the years. In his role as colleague and mentor, he has kept us honest to the profession and committed to the field of criminology.

PART I

INTRODUCTION

CRIME, CRIMINOLOGY, AND THE PUBLIC VIEW

THE VICTIM'S WIFE WEPT. She called the decision unbelievable. Her husband was dead and she thought that she knew who was responsible. Twenty-six other men were dead as well, and their relatives too had hoped for a murder conviction against the people they held responsible. But the court, upon deciding there was insufficient evidence to support the allegations, had dismissed the case (*Globe and Mail,* 1993: A1). Compounding their grief and frustration, the families of the victims were not to find out why the men died. Who was to blame?

This case did not involve a mass murderer wielding an assault weapon and mowing down innocent bystanders in a shopping mall or targeted victims in a factory. The men died in a mine explosion at the Westray coal mine in Nova Scotia. Murder charges alleging failure to enforce proper safety standards in the workplace had been brought against Westray's mine manager and underground manager.

In a Calgary courtroom, on the same day, a teenager was given a life sentence with no parole for ten years, the maximum allowed in the sentencing of juveniles appearing in adult court. The convicted killer had stabbed a 13-year-old in an attack described by the judge in the case as "a senseless, brutal, callous, and heartless act that took place in a schoolyard where children of this nation should feel safe and be safe" (*Globe and Mail,* 1993: A3). There were concerns expressed in this case that the law is not effective enough in deterring young offenders from commiting these types of serious acts.

Meanwhile, in Edmonton, the police charged the former girlfriend of a noted photographer with aggravated assault, possessing a prohibited weapon, and uttering a death threat against another woman. The photographer claimed that he was the victim of a relationship that went sour. When he refused to sell his business to the accused, she and her new boyfriend allegedly began to threaten him and even conspired to murder him. The photographer went to the police, who, after investigating his claims, felt that they had sufficient evidence to pursue criminal charges. Not surprisingly, this case has attracted a good deal of attention from the tabloid press; the photographer plans to write a book or screenplay about his case (*Globe and Mail,* 1993: A4).

The above events appear to be very different from one another. However, there are consistent ways in which we can approach these and other crimes, ways that allow us to make sense of what happened and to put them into a broader context. While we may not be able to always understand why people do certain things, we search for the motivations behind crime by examining such factors as circumstances, characteristics of offenders and victims, and their relationship to one another. What events led up to the act? Who else was involved? Where did the event take place? What did the police do? We also want to know what was done after the events occurred to deal with their consequences. What punishment was handed down to ensure that similar events did not occur again? Thus, while the examples presented above appear as unique social events, they share many characteristics that would allow us to make sense of them as a singular group of behaviour, that is, as acts that are criminal.

In presenting an overview of explanations of crime, we introduce the student to the major theories of criminology as well as the research methods and data that are used to test hypotheses and identify trends in criminal behaviour. We also present findings from the considerable research literature, with particular emphasis on crime that occurs in the home, during leisure, and at work, those domains of activity in which most criminal activity occurs. We end with an overview of general societal responses to crime (i.e., crime prevention). Because our explanations of crime heavily influence our views of what we should do to respond to it, it is important to understand what the current program responses are and how they can be brought into line to deal more effectively with the problems we face.

Our approach to the study of crime is defined by the discipline of criminology, a school of inquiry that has gained in profile and credibility over the years. There are strong traditions that have developed within this school of thought, many of which are complementary, as we will see. Let us begin by looking at criminology as a discipline, as practised in Canada and elsewhere, before we review the various factors that influence the study of crime.

WHAT IS CRIMINOLOGY?

Criminology is a subject area that draws on a number of different disciplines as it seeks to clarify the nature of the criminal event. Through this interdisciplinary perspective, criminologists attempt to understand not only the motivations of the offender but also the nature of the circumstances leading up to the act and its consequences for the victim(s), for others in the community, and for the society at large. Criminologists are also called upon to provide insights into how we should respond to crime (e.g., through changes in policing strategies or through the development of crime-prevention programs). Finally, criminologists monitor the ways in which changes in the laws and their interpretation can affect how people behave in society and, in turn, how agents of social control respond to this behaviour.

The interdisciplinary nature of criminology means that people with quite different types of training contribute to the understanding of criminal events. Criminologists include historians, psychologists, political scientists, economists, legal scholars, and sociologists. For the most part, though, when criminology is taught at universities outside of departments of criminology, it is treated as a subdiscipline of sociology. The fact that sociology has become the major focus of criminological training in North America can be explained by the tendency of

WHAT IS IT?

Criminology

Criminology uses an interdisciplinary perspective to understand not only the motivations of the offender but also the nature of the circumstances leading up to the act and its consequences for the victim(s), for others in the community, and for the society at large. Criminologists study ways in which we should respond to crime through changes in policing strategies or through the development of crime-prevention programs. In addition, criminologists pay close attention to the ways in which changes in the law and their interpretation can affect how people behave in society and, of course, how agents of social control respond to this behaviour.

sociologists to be more involved than researchers from other disciplines in the study of social problems. As well, the major figures in the teaching of criminology, particularly in the United States, have been sociologists by training, a fact reflected in the courses that are taught in universities. The tendency in Europe, in contrast, is for criminologists to reside in law schools, which gives a more legal orientation to the research that is pursued there.

The interdisciplinary programs in criminology have been very successful in creating a focus for many people who are interested in the critical study of crime. For example, the strong emphasis in quantitative sociology on survey research has provided an important base from which criminologists have been able to launch the work that has been done in victimization surveys. Economic perspectives too, have made important contributions to the understanding of offender motivations.

The study of crime in Canada has benefited from a variety of research efforts. We draw on a great deal of this work in this book. We also introduce findings from research that has been done in other parts of the world. Some would argue that the growth of modern criminology has been strongest in the United States, particularly as a result of federal funding for research in the 1970s and 1980s in response to the problems of large-scale social disorder in American cities. More recently, the U.S. government has spent liberally on the study of drug-related crime and less liberally in other areas of research. Still, little money is spent on criminological research when compared with the amounts committed to other areas, such as medical or biophysical research. This disparity exists despite the large costs that some criminological research entails, particularly large-scale victimization surveys or longitudinal studies of offenders.

There is a great deal of interest in countries outside of North America in the study of crime. Like Canada and the United States, many of these countries have become involved in large-scale victimization surveys and some, like Britain, through the Home Office Research Unit, have promoted government agencies that apply criminological research to the development of policy on policing, community crime prevention programs, and offender programs. Again, we draw on this work in this book.

Our presentation is heavily influenced by recent thinking in criminology that places great significance on the routine nature of crime, and maintains that individual lifestyles bring offenders and victims together in time and space to create crime opportunities. The crime that results creates consequences for all parties concerned, either as a result of police intervention or the action of third parties.

Studying the crime event as a consequence of routine does not mean that we ignore the importance of criminological thinking that has been developed over the centuries to explain offender motivations or the role of punishment in deterring crime. Criminological thought goes back to the ideas of Cesare Beccaria, who wrote in the late 1700s about the need to account for the psychological reality of the offender. The state, he argued, needs to use the fear of pain to control behaviour. Beccaria's view emphasized reform of the repressive and barbaric laws of 18th-century Europe, a period in which the administration of justice was arbitrary and abusive. The standing of the person in the community had a direct impact on the treatment that he or she could expect from the courts; justice therefore was relative rather than absolute.

According to Beccaria, the degree of punishment should be sufficient to outweigh the pleasure one derives from a criminal act (Martin, Mutchnik, and Austin, 1990: 8). It was Beccaria's views, together with those of Jeremy Bentham after him, that so heavily influenced modern thinking about deterrence and punishment. The "rational man" would act to avoid punishment, hence the importance of laws that were clear both about how one should act and about the costs of deviating from lawful behaviour.

The model of "rational man" led to a view that the law could be used as an instrument of control. This assumed, however, that men and women were free to judge and all were equal in their ability to make judgments. In the late 1800s, Cesare Lombroso began to question this assumption. His basic belief was that human behaviour was determined, a view that stands in direct opposition to Beccaria's assumption that people have free will. For Lombroso, individual constitution determined responses to surroundings and was influential in creating deficiencies in human behaviour that led to criminality; thus heredity was a principal cause of criminal tendencies (Martin, Mutchnik, and Austin, 1990: 29). These assumptions led Lombroso to argue for a perspective that emphasized the development of crime types, including the born criminal, the criminal by passion, the insane criminal, and the occasional criminal.

The two perspectives that have emerged from the early influences of Beccaria and Lombroso are *classicism* and *positivism*. Current classical criminology still views the offender as rational, deterred only by the threat of punishment from legal sanction or by other informal pressures to conform. Supporters of this position argue, therefore, that laws must be invariant and punishment certain, and that formal justice is successful in eradicating crime only when its costs to the offender exceed its benefits. The research that has developed in this perspective has sought to support the view of "rational man" operating in a society in which there is consensus about what constitutes right and wrong.

Contemporary positivists argue instead that the explanations of criminality, and hence the secret to crime cessation, are found in forces outside of the offender that influence behaviour. The sociological environment of the offender provides a model for behaviour that encourages adherence to rules. But when strain arises as a consequence of unrealized expectations, or when there are strong cultural forces at work that contradict the rules, rulebreaking may occur. Those who deviate need to be reintegrated through resocialization or rehabilitation, which involves removing them from the influences of deviant others.

> **WHAT DOES IT MEAN?**
>
> ***Classical vs. Positivist***
> Classical criminology still views the offender as rational, deterred only by the threat of sanction. Positivists argue that explanations of criminality—and hence the secret to crime cessation—are found in forces outside of the offender that influence behaviour. The sociological environment of the offender provides a model for behaviour that encourages adherence to rules.

While the classicists have been very clear about the parameters of successful deterrence, the positivists have left ideas of punishment and legal threat out of their explanation of crime desistence, relying instead on arguments concerning social change. Equally, the classicists have taken at face value the neutrality of positive law, believing that it can exist outside of society and be applied equally and fairly to all individuals.

For all their differences, the various theories that fall roughly into these two schools of thought have in common a fixation on criminality rather than crime; that is to say they focus little attention on the dynamics of the criminal event itself, except as it relates to offender actions (i.e., trying to explain why an individual would act in a particular way at a particular time). It is only in recent years that the criminal event in its totality has served as a focus of criminology (Gottfredson and Hirchi, 1990).

Following from the work of the human ecologists who mapped crime, there has been an intensive investigation into the relationship between situational factors and individual lifestyles that allows us to consider at the same time motivation and structural conditions in the environment, including the deterrent effects of detection and prospective punishment. Marcus Felson, Lawrence Cohen, and David Luckenbill and others have begun to help us to understand more clearly what happens in crime events and to use our knowledge as a basis for predicting certain outcomes. Using this approach, modern criminology has emerged with a more holistic view of the crime problem.

DEFINING CRIME

Criminologists study and teach about crime, but they are not the only sources of information about this phenomenon. Through its depiction in the media and through public debate we develop particular views of what crime is, how extensive it is, and what we can do about it. These views are not always compatible with the perspectives and data supplied by criminologists.

CRIME AS LAWBREAKING

In Western society, crime is defined strictly as behaviour that breaks the law and is liable to public prosecution and punishment. In a very fundamental way, terms like "crime," "offender," and "victim" are legal concepts. An offender, for instance, is someone who is recognized as having behaved in a way that contravenes the criminal law. But the judgment that it is appropriate to label an event participant an offender, criminal, or lawbreaker may not always be straightforward. Individuals who are judged to be offenders by the law may not see themselves in this way or be regarded as such by witnesses or even victims. To a considerable degree, criminal trials are organized, state-sponsored attempts to determine who should be considered an offender.

> **WHAT IS IT?**
>
> ***Crime***
>
> In Western society, crime is defined strictly as behaviour that breaks the criminal law and is liable to public prosecution and punishment. A criminal intention *(mens rea)* without the action *(actus reus)* is not a crime.

Social events have meaning as criminal events, then, only in reference to law. As Nettler (1984: 32) states, "crime is a word, not a deed," and to label something a crime is to invoke the moral evaluation of the behaviour that is embodied in the law. Thus, the law may be understood as a form of social control that evaluates the moral nature of the behaviour in question. When we describe an act as criminal, we imply that the act is disvalued. It is a form of wrongdoing that "good people" should avoid at the risk of punishment. One of the major functions of the law is to deter people from engaging in the behaviour that the law prohibits. The law may be understood as a set of written rules that are supported by state authority and accompanied by a standardized schedule of penalties.

Even when there is a clear agreement that an offence has been committed, there may be disagreement about what to do about it. What type of offence has occurred? How much agreement exists in the community about the nature of the act and the punishment that should be applied? In a startling break from tradition, an Edmonton judge decided in early 1992 to accept a charge of second-degree murder directed against a couple who had grievously assaulted their foster child. The judge decided that, even though the child was not technically dead (parts of his brain stem were still functioning and he continued to breathe spontaneously), there was sufficient evidence to accept the view that the persistent vegetative state that resulted from his injuries should be incorporated into the legal definition of death. This judgment sparked a great deal of debate and controversy over what we might consider to be fairly straightforward, the definition of life and death.

Subsequently, the charge was changed to aggravated assault, which resulted in a conviction for the couple. John Dosseter, a bioethics expert, commented on the reduced charge. "I don't think society is ready for such an important matter (changing the definition of life and death) to be decided in such a way in the courts. The matter needs more debate and I don't think a simple court decision is going to do it" (Moysa, 1992: A1). What this means is that it is necessary for the public and lawmakers to debate the changes in the law that would recognize death as something that extends beyond its current legal definition as complete cessation of life.

In a similar way, the law is undergoing changes in how it considers actions such as murder. As illustrated in the Westray case, one does not have to wield a knife or pull the trigger on a gun to be labelled a murderer. That same case also exemplifies the difficulty of establishing motive. Did the Westray managers intend to kill? Did they know that what they did might result in death? These are among the questions that arise in cases in which neglect or incompetence have deadly consequences.

In general, the law is more concerned with crime or criminal behaviour than with criminal events (Gould, 1989). In other words, the law focuses on what offenders do (rather than on other event elements) in deciding what a crime is or when a crime occurs. From a legal standpoint, crime is largely synonymous with the actions of the offender. However, to characterize crime as an act that either is prohibited by law or constitutes failure to perform an act required by law is, in legal terms, to give it too broad a definition.

Brantingham (1991) notes that, while in Canada there are over 40,000 different federal and provincial statutes and municipal bylaws, only those offences that are defined by federal law are technically crimes. From a legal standpoint, crimes are acts that violate the criminal law. The principal piece of Canadian criminal law is the Criminal Code of Canada, a federal piece of legislation that includes most but not all of the categories of offending we normally think of as crimes (Osborne, 1991).

Legal definitions are even more specific. The fact that someone behaves in a way that appears on the surface to be inconsistent with the requirements of the Criminal Code does not mean that he or she has committed a crime. To be criminal in a legal sense, an act must be intentional (Barnhorst, Barnhorst, and Clarke, 1992). The mere physical act—what is legally known as the *actus reus*—is not enough. There must also be a willful quality to the act, what the law refers to as *mens rea* (Nettler, 1984). Moreover, to be criminal, an act must be committed in the absence of a legally recognized defence or justification (Parker, 1991). For example, while the Criminal Code defines assaultive behaviour as a crime, a particular assaultive act may not be criminal if it were accidental (rather than intentional) or committed in self-defence (and therefore legally justifiable).

All criminal law operates with some psychological model of behaviour. Judgment must be employed in controlling one's acts so that some accidents will not occur. The law has traditionally set out to make able but negligent people accountable. To do this, it has included the concept of *constructive intent*. The penalties for doing damage through negligence are usually lighter than those for being deliberately criminal, yet the term "crime" covers both. A criminal intention *(mens rea)* without the action *(actus reus)* is not a crime. Since intent is part of the definition of crime, prosecutors must establish such purpose in the actor. They sometimes try to do this by constructing the motive (Nettler, 1984). Why would the person act as he or she did? Establishing motive does not establish guilt, however, as intent and action together are required to obtain a criminal conviction.

Courts can also redefine the criteria used in judging guilt. In 1990, the Supreme Court of Canada removed some responsibility as incorporated in the idea of constructive intent. Under the previous interpretation of the law, an offender who killed someone in the midst of a robbery could be convicted of murder even if there had been no intention to kill. The Court determined that this judgment violated the Canadian Charter of Rights and Freedoms. Now, a homicide committed in the course of another crime is not automatically considered to be a case of first-degree murder.

It may be that a person acts in such a way that is beyond his or her control. This situation is covered by a judgment of competence, which may be restricted because of age, duress, self-defence, or insanity. With respect to age, in Canada, children under 12 cannot be held responsible for their own actions in the criminal sense. Children from 12 to 17 are held culpable for their actions but are judged separately from adults through the Young Offenders Act (YOA). Unlike the Juvenile Delinquents Act, which it replaced, the YOA is a body of criminal law that establishes a justice and corrections system separate and distinct from the adult system. It acknowledges that juveniles have special needs, require special legal protection, and should not be held as fully accountable as adults for violating the criminal law (Bala, 1991: 39).

Whereas the Juvenile Delinquents Act was based on a philosophy of *parens patiae* in which the state, acting as a kind of "superparent," was given wide latitude in dealing with the child, the YOA makes the rights and responsibilities of youth much more central issues (Barnhorst, Barnhorst, and Clarke, 1992). Recent notorious cases in which young offenders who committed serious crimes received light sentences under the YOA have provoked strong efforts to waive individuals who have committed serious crimes to adult court and to extend sentences such that they are served past the statutory age limit of juvenile offenders. In the stabbing case described earlier in this chapter, the offender will serve part of his sentence in juvenile detention, until he reaches 18, and the balance in an adult institution.

Individuals operating under duress may also claim that they did not intend to commit a crime and therefore are not guilty of an offence. In these cases, it must be proved that there was no chance of escape, that the threat was immediate, and that the fear was reasonable (Parker, 1991: 26). The idea that one is under duress when committing a crime is often difficult to prove. The degree of force used must be commensurate with the degree of harm the individual perceived was being directed his or her way. Duress, however, is never a defence against murder.

Self-defence involves action that is taken to protect oneself or one's property. To be defensible this action must involve reasonable force. These cases are not always straightforward, and our view of self-defence now includes actions that are taken to respond to an ongoing threat in domestic situations. Recently, the Supreme Court of Canada accepted the argument of self-defence in cases where the existence of "battered woman syndrome" can be proved. This syndrome is based on the premise that women who are in violent relationships are in a state of protracted fear, believe that their lives are in imminent danger, and at some point reach a psychological state in which they are driven to take action to protect themselves. To date, the courts have been cautious in the acceptance of this defence, restricting it to cases in which the woman was in clearly defined physical danger. Women who killed their abusive husbands while they slept have been found guilty of murder. However, as a result of the Supreme Court ruling, women who shoot their husbands in response to physical violence may be declared innocent of the charge of murder (Silverman and Kennedy, 1993).

When it comes to proving insanity, it is incumbent upon the defence to prove a state of insanity; the prosecution is not required to prove sanity. Putting the onus on the defence has the effect of restricting the extent to which one can declare that limited capacity to form intent has resulted from mental breakdown.

BOX 1.1   THE INSANITY DEFENCE IN CANADA

Being acquitted of a crime by reason of insanity is not a ticket to freedom.

Despite what the public may think, perhaps only one in 100 murderers is judged insane, says Dr. Herb Pascoe, a forensic psychiatrist at Alberta Hospital, Edmonton.

And for that small percentage, an insanity verdict can be a more severe punishment than serving a fixed jail sentence. Most jail terms have endings, but there are no guarantees of freedom for an individual judged insane.

Pascoe estimates that at any one time, there are 35 to 40 people in the province who have been acquitted of an offence by reason of insanity.

He optimistically predicts only one-third will leave hospital and remain out. Even for those, the road to recovery and release is arduous.

"You can expect one-third of the patients will do very well and gradually will work their way out of the hospital to resume a useful place in the community," says Pascoe. Another third will stay the same or their conditions will worsen, and the conditions of the last third will go up and down.

"For all the publicity insanity trials get, the number of acquittals is very, very small," he says. "About one out of every 100 murders results in an acquittal by reason of insanity.

"It's a small number but, of course, when it happens it's pretty gruesome, sadistic stuff."

The Criminal Code allows for an insanity verdict if the person, when he committed the offence, was "in a state of natural imbecility or (had) disease of the mind to an extent that (rendered) him incapable of appreciating the nature and quality of an act or omission or of knowing that an act or omission (was) wrong."

The code continues: "A person who has specific delusions, but is in other respects sane, shall not be acquitted on the ground of insanity unless the delusions caused him to believe in the existence of a state of things that, if it existed, would have justified or excused his act or omission."

Following an acquittal by reason of insanity, the person is remanded to Alberta Hospital on a lieutenant-governor's warrant.

He will be kept at the hospital until a review board, consisting of a Court of Queen's Bench justice, two psychiatrists, a lawyer and lay person, recommend the warrant be cancelled.

"We don't want to take chances," says Justice Neil Primrose, board chairman. "A person under certain circumstances could be dangerous.

"But generally, the rehabilitation and recovery of patients has been very good, in my experience.

"There are all sorts of safeguards and we are very conservative," says Pascoe. "Things do not happen in a hurry. If a patient makes good progress it will still be several years before he will be allowed out."

The review board meets twice a year in Edmonton and reviews all patients committed on a lieutenant-governor's warrant.

The members hear recommendations from attending psychiatrists, social workers and psychologists. Only the board has the power to recommend a patient be given certain liberties or freedoms, such as ground passes, weekends with family or special outings under strict supervision.

If a patient does exceedingly well, he may eventually be allowed to work during the day and live at the hospital at night.

If all goes well, the patient may eventually be given a conditional discharge on the warrant, and finally an absolute discharge.

Until that time patients can be brought back to hospital at any sign of trouble.

"Most of the patients here appear to be a lot more together than a member of the public would think," says Dr. Maggie Tweddle, a consultant forensic psychiatrist.

"But if they were so obviously crazy, they wouldn't be so dangerous.

"I wouldn't dare let some of these people out without the warrant for several years," says Tweddle. "We have a responsibility to the patient and to the community.

"We're treading a pretty narrow line between doing what is best for the patient and dealing with society. It's certainly a challenge."

Source: Joanne Munro, "Insanity-based acquittal rarely route to early freedom," *Edmonton Journal*, September 6, 1983, p. B1.

The legal system plays an important role in managing criminal events. It may appear from a distance that legal definitions of crime are immutable, determined by clear-cut rules of evidence in establishing guilt or innocence. In reality, this is not the case. Legal response can be and is heavily influenced by circumstance, public tolerance, and judicial discretion. Police and courts apply the law not only to fight crime and punish criminals but also to reduce social conflict. Any study of crime needs to account for behaviour that is disorderly or dangerous but not yet unlawful. Alternative or informal legal responses create the outside limits of criminality by redefining criminal justice responses to misbehaviour.

Law is only one form of social control (Black, 1976). Social life is also regulated by informal expectations about how people should and should not behave. Whether we call these expectations etiquette, professionalism, or simply good taste, people evaluate the morality of each other's behaviour and respond accordingly through a variety of means. Gossip, ridicule, and ostracism are forms of social control that involve less formal social processes than do legal forms. When actions are classified as crimes, much more is implied than the mere condemnation of the behaviour. Calling an act a crime suggests strong emotional parallels between this act and other acts that bear the same label. The label also implies that the problem will be processed in a particular way, and that specific state agencies will assume responsibility for solving it. In other words, to label a particular wrongdoing a crime is to confer the ownership of the problem in question to the police, the courts, and other criminal justice agencies (Gilsinan, 1990).

If a problem is defined as one that involves an uninformed public acting on the basis of incomplete or incorrect information, then educational experts might be expected to provide the solutions to the problem. If a problem is defined as one that results from some medical condition, then mental or physical health sciences will dominate efforts at problem amelioration. However, when behaviour is deemed criminal, the issue will likely be surrendered to law enforcement and crime-prevention specialists. It is evident that these alternative views are associated with dramatically different consequences. As Gusfield (1989) notes, it makes a real difference whether we see social problems as involving people who are troubled or people who are troublesome.

CRIME AND MORALITY

The idea of crime starts with some conception of proper behaviour that is based on an accepted form of morality. Society sets out general rules detailing what is permissible or normative behaviour. Morals change whether we want them to or not, and accompanying the changes are variations in the content of crime. "The broad boundaries of offenses against property, person, and 'society' remain fairly steady, but the criminal content within these boundaries varies" (Nettler, 1984: 2). What we define as normative behaviour is affected by our reactions to behaviour as morality evolves over time.

A related question emerges when addressing the forces that bring about changes in public beliefs about morality. A question posed by Jack Gibbs ("With what frequency must a type of act occur before it is considered a norm?") (Gibbs, 1981: 14) can be asked with reference to delinquent or criminal behaviour. Suppose that large parts of the society partake in what is considered to be criminal behaviour. Does the fact that the behaviour is widespread make it normative? Obviously, this depends on the degree of harm being done and on the willingness of the society to retaliate against this harm. For example, violence in the American West was commonplace during the settlement years. The behaviour of gunslingers appeared to be normative, but was it acceptable? Clearly, the strong demand by inhabitants of these settlements for law enforcement indicates that they wanted the violence to be curtailed. Criminologists must assess how legal and moral definitions of crime coincide with the circumstances that people face, circumstances that evolve into events that demand enforcement and result in labelling individuals as criminal.

Emile Durkheim (1964) suggested that crime itself is normative in society. By this he meant that there are no societies that exist without crime, and that crime in fact identifies for members of a society the acceptable boundaries of behaviour. Defining and punishing criminals are means by which society illustrates what people can and cannot do.

Our approach to the study of crime takes into account the issues related to its normalcy, particularly in our review of the impact that changes in law have on definitions of criminality. But the definitions that victims and offenders themselves bring to criminal situations (definitions that we measure in victimization surveys, reports on crime, action by public-interest groups, and reports in the media) heavily influence how we react to and what we do about crime. The perspective that we offer in this book questions the recent tendency in positivist criminology to isolate one or two characteristics of individuals as a way of increasing our precision in predicting their criminal tendencies or identifying a "criminal type." Theories of crime evolve out of our classifications of the social forms and factors associated with criminal behaviour (Cain and Kulscar, 1981–82: 386). We believe that this type of theory building is preclusive in that it sets up artificial borders around different aspects of crime and discourages criminologists from looking at the social bases of crime, that is, crime as it evolves out of social interaction and affects social structures.

The artificial boundaries placed around crime actually change through continuous negotiation of what constitutes criminal behaviour, both in the ways individuals respond to criminal behaviour and in the ways the criminal justice system tries to control it. While positivist approaches certainly simplify the number of things we have to consider in our assessment of the cases brought before us, they ignore the complexity of the criminal event—its precursors, the circumstances that prevail during the act, and its aftermath.

CLAIMSMAKING

Some writers refer to the processes by which laws are passed or legal reforms are initiated as claimsmaking (Best, 1990; Spector and Kitsuse, 1977). In the claimsmaking process, groups offer assertions about the existence of some problem that requires a policy solution. They then attempt to gain public support for these claims and to attract the attention of public officials and the mass media. Howard Becker describes the claimsmaker as a "moral entrepreneur" who is best exemplified by the crusading reformer. According to Becker (1963), there is "some evil which profoundly disturbs" these reformers, who believe that "nothing can be right in the world until rules are made to correct it" (147–148).

In the early stages, the claims may reflect a narrow set of relatively private interests (Pfuhl, 1986; Ross and Staines, 1972). Claimsmakers may regard themselves as representing those who have been victimized by the condition or who feel directly threatened by it (Weeks et al., 1986). However, claims may also be issued by state agencies seeking to expand their mandates or by professional groups seeking to enhance their status. It has been argued, for example, that American

> ### WHAT DOES IT MEAN?
>
> *Claimsmaker*
> Howard Becker (1963) describes the claimsmaker as a "moral entrepreneur" who is best exemplified by the crusading reformer. According to Becker, there is "some evil which profoundly disturbs" these reformers, who believe that "nothing can be right in the world until rules are made to correct it" (147–148).

marijuana laws find their origin not in widespread public concern about drug use, but in the claimsmaking activities of the Federal Bureau of Narcotics (Becker, 1963; Reasons, 1976). More recently, researchers have argued that the pressure for the passage of computer crime laws has largely resulted from the crusading efforts of computer crime "experts," who, in publicizing the issue, were able to gain recognition for themselves and their work (Hollinger and Lanza-Kaduce, 1988).

Joel Best (1990) argues that, in terms of legislative and other policy-making bodies, claimsmakers may be described as being either insiders or outsiders. Insiders include political lobbyists, representatives of powerful professional organizations, or members of government, all of whom have relatively direct access to those who make public policy. By contrast, outsiders have no such direct access and must rely to a greater extent on efforts that take their message to the general public. In so doing, outsiders hope to enlist members in their cause.

Spector and Kitsuse (1977) offer a four-stage model of the claimsmaking process. In Stage 1, groups attempt to argue that some condition is harmful and that public action (perhaps the passage of new laws) is necessary. In Stage 2, the problem is recognized by some official agency. The result may be an official investigation (e.g., a royal commission or parliamentary hearings). Stage 3 is characterized by the re-emergence of claims and demands, either by the original group or by others who express dissatisfaction with the official response to the problem. The fourth and final stage involves a rejection by claimsmakers of the official response (or lack of response) to the problem. Spector and Kitsuse acknowledge that this "natural history" model may not precisely describe all efforts to mobilize the public response to crime or other social problems. The manner in which any specific claimsmaking process unfolds will depend on several factors, two of which require particular attention.

The first involves the amount of opposition that claimsmakers encounter in their attempts to convince the public and policy-makers that a particular type of remedy is necessary. In other words, some kinds of claimsmaking are more adversarial than other kinds. Issues that do not have this adversarial quality are sometimes referred to as *valence issues*. Child abuse, crimes against the elderly, and computer crime are valence issues in that most people would readily agree that they are problems requiring public intervention. By contrast, efforts by claimsmakers to organize public support for interventions directed against abortion or pornography are frequently met by resistance or by counter definitions of what the problem really is (Ross and Staines, 1972).

A second factor affecting the fate of claimsmaking is the wider social context in which this process unfolds. Prevailing social values and beliefs may at any time facilitate or hinder claimsmaking. Based on an analysis of a large number of case studies of criminalization, Hagan (1980) argues that successful claimsmakers are usually able to make effective appeals to dominant cultural values. For example, it has been argued that the social problem of crime against the elderly emerged in the 1970s because there existed a "ripe issue climate" in which rising crime, the needs of crime victims, and needs of the elderly were already seen as important problems.

While criminalization is clearly a form of claimsmaking, the passage of a law is not always enough to satisfy the claimsmakers. Much contemporary claimsmaking about crime is directed toward efforts to change the ways in which behaviour that has already been criminalized is treated within the criminal justice system. The recognition, in recent years, of crimes against women, victims' rights, impaired driving, and crimes against the elderly as problems requiring more vigorous enforcement or innovative approaches attests to the validity of this observation.

In general, an understanding of responses to crime as the product of claimsmaking, conflict, and power (rather than of social consensus) alerts us to the biases of these responses. Such arguments cast serious doubt on the value of approaches that characterize the law as a neutral arbiter that can be understood without reference to the societies that produced it.

What this means for our analysis of criminal events is that the law and its agents are active members of the transaction, which does not end with the action that we call an offence but goes on to encompass how this offence is defined by its participants and then by the police and the courts. The discretionary aspects of policing strongly affect which events will be targeted and acted upon. No group is more influential than the police in designating crime events.

THE POLICE AND CRIME

When an event comes to their attention, the police may invoke a wide array of discretionary powers (e.g., collecting evidence, investigating the claims of the victim[s], and arresting the offender or offenders). In short, the police have the power to "certify" an event as a crime by assessing the match between the event as they understand it and their working knowledge of what the law disallows.

How do the police encounter situations that they might designate as crimes? Attempts to answer this question have tended to emphasize the distinction between *proactive* and *reactive* policing services. Black (1970) notes that, in the case of proactive policing, the police become involved in incidents when their own investigative or patrol activities bring to their attention events that may be designated as crimes. Only about 10 percent of the cases in which the police are involved are the result of proactive policing. By contrast, in the case of reactive policing, the police become involved in criminal events when asked to do so by a member of the general public. Thus, it is important to understand the circumstances under which citizens request police intervention.

WHAT DOES IT MEAN?

Proactive vs. Reactive Policing

In proactive policing, the police become involved in incidents as a result of their own investigative or patrol activities which bring events that may be designated as crimes to their attention. In reactive policing, the police become involved in criminal events when requested to do so by a member of the general public.

Surveys of crime victims have proven to be a valuable source of information in this regard. The data from the Canadian General Social Survey reveals that in 1987 only 40 percent of the incidents described to survey interviewers by victims were brought to the attention of the police. The police were most likely to be informed of crimes of break and enter (70 percent) and motor vehicle theft (57 percent), and were least likely to be told about assaults (30 percent) and robberies (32 percent) (Sacco and Johnson, 1990: 105). Other surveys done in Canada, as well as in other countries, report a similar pattern (Gottfredson and Gottfredson, 1988; Solicitor General, 1984a; Skogan, 1984).

The Canadian survey also revealed that about three-quarters of the incidents or victimizations reported by the survey respondents had been brought to the attention of the police through the initiative of the victims (Sacco and Johnson, 1990). What motivates those who believe that they have been victimized to report the incident to the police? When asked about their willingness or unwillingness to call the police in the aftermath of a victimization experience, respondents in many different victim surveys have provided relatively consistent answers. Seventy percent of the nonreporting victims identified in the Canadian study indicated that they did not report the incident because they felt it was too minor to warrant such action (Sacco and Johnson, 1990). Survey respondents also typically indicate that they do not report incidents because there is nothing the police can do about them (Sacco and Johnson, 1990; Solicitor General, 1984a). This response is somewhat ambiguous. On the one hand, it may imply a realistic questioning of the constructiveness of any action taken after the fact; alternatively, it could suggest a lack of confidence in the competence of the police.

Other reasons given by surveyed victims suggest that nonreporting may also be related to the belief that the incident is a "personal matter" that need not concern the police, or to the perception that crime reporting is simply too inconvenient (Sacco and Johnson, 1990; Solicitor General, 1984a). Contrary to popular belief, victim surveys reveal that a fear of retaliation by the offender plays a relatively minor role in reporting decisions. Data from the Canadian General Social Survey indicate that only 10 percent of nonreporting victims gave this reason (Sacco and Johnson, 1990). However, the data also indicate that the fear of revenge was cited as a reason for nonreporting by 17 percent of women (compared to 4 percent of men) and by 38 percent of the female victims of violence.

There are, of course, other reasons why victims do not call the police. Victims may themselves be involved in some form of criminal activity at the time of the incident and may therefore be reluctant to invite a police investigation (Block, 1974). In some instances, victims do not report crimes because they have at their disposal other means of dealing with the situation (Kennedy, 1988). For example, a teenage boy who has been assaulted by a peer may be more likely to seek retaliation through personal action than through reporting the incident to the police.

Members of some social groups are somewhat more likely than members of other groups to report crime to the police, although differences in this regard are not particularly strong (Gottfredson and Gottfredson, 1988). Crimes involving female or elderly victims, for instance, have higher levels of reportability. This is perhaps because many women and many elderly have at their disposal fewer alternative resources for dealing with victimization and its consequences (Fattah and Sacco, 1989; Skogan, 1976). While it might be expected that people who view the criminal justice system negatively are less likely to contact the police, the influence of such attitudes appears to be slight (Block, 1974; Gottfredson and Gottfredson, 1988).

In contrast, available data indicate that reporting decisions are strongly influenced by the characteristics of the criminal events themselves. The more serious the event, the greater the probability that it will be reported to the police. Thus, incidents that involve physical injury, significant property loss, or the use of a weapon, or that occur in or near the victim's residence, are more likely than incidents without these characteristics to be brought to the attention of the police (Block, 1974; Gottfredson and Gottfredson, 1988; Skogan, 1977; Solicitor General, 1984a).

These findings are consistent with the view that people report crimes to the police when there is good reason to do so, and that they do not report crimes when the reporting involves costs that outweigh any potential benefits. For victims of sexual assault or wife abuse, fear of retaliation or concerns about stigmatization or mistreatment by the police negate the advantages associated with reporting. In general, reporting crime is best viewed as part of a rational decision-making process that takes account of the crime, the offender, the victim's resources, and the perceived limitations of police responsiveness (Gottfredson and Gottfredson, 1988).

How Much Crime?

Now that we have some sense of what constitutes crime and some factors that may affect its reporting, what does this mean for the overall volume of crime that comes to the attention of the police? As shown in Figure 1.1, there has been a fourfold increase in the amount of crime in Canada since 1962, the year in which the federal government started to code crime in *Uniform Crime Reports*. The largest amount of crime is property based, with the greatest amount in this category constituting theft (approximately 60 percent) and break and enter (about 25 percent) (Canadian Centre for Justice Statistics, 1992: 5). Property offences in the 30-year time frame have decreased from 68 percent to under 60 percent of the total. The greatest increase overall has been in the category of other Criminal Code offences, including mischief and disturbing the peace.

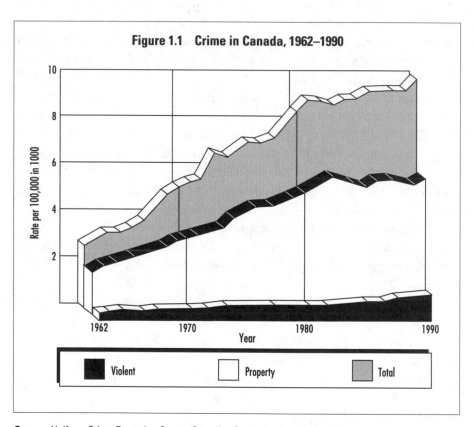

Figure 1.1 Crime in Canada, 1962–1990

Source: *Uniform Crime Reporting Survey,* Canadian Centre for Justice Statistics.

Table 1.1   Crime in Canada, 1990 [1]

Offence type	Number	Rate per 1,000 population	% of total
Violent crimes	269,440	10.1	9
Homicide	656	0.0	
Nonsexual assault	207,289	7.8	
Sexual assault	27,822	1.0	
Robbery	28,111	1.1	
Property crimes	1,554,588	58.4	49
Break and enter	379,512	14.3	
Theft	900,773	33.9	
Fraud	130,749	4.9	
Other Criminal Code	804,705	30.2	25
Total Criminal Code	2,628,733	98.8	
Drug-related crimes	60,039	2.3	2
Other federal statutes	31,900	1.2	1
Provincial statutes	349,416	13.1	11
Municipal bylaws	101,327	3.8	3
Total crime	3,171,415	119.2	100

[1] Excludes traffic offences

Source: *Uniform Crime Reporting Survey*, Canadian Centre for Justice Statistics.

Violent crime makes up approximately 10 percent of all crime. Representing the crime breakdown in Canada for 1990, Table 1.1 shows that violent crime constitutes only 9 percent of all crime events reported to the police. Nonsexual assault accounts for over three-quarters of all violent offences. Property crime makes up half of all reported crime, while other Criminal Code offences constitute 25 percent of the total (Canadian Centre for Justice Statistics, 1992: 8)

Crime tends to exhibit a pattern of increase as one moves from east to west in Canada, with the highest levels exhibited in British Columbia and lowest incidence in the Maritimes (see Figure 1.2). However, over the last ten years the rates of increase in assault and robbery have been higher in the east than in the west. Patterns and trends of crime are heavily influenced by

HOW MUCH?

Violent Crime

Violent crime, which attracts the greatest amount of attention in the media and in public discussion of crime, makes up approximately 10 percent of all crime.

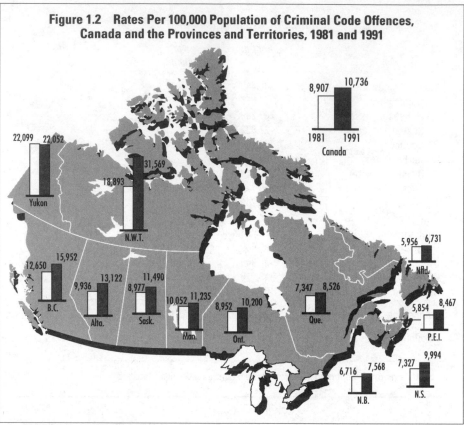

Figure 1.2 Rates Per 100,000 Population of Criminal Code Offences, Canada and the Provinces and Territories, 1981 and 1991

Source: Statistics Canada.

changes in the population and by the socioeconomic forces that impinge on daily life. We will examine these factors in greater detail in later chapters.

THE PUBLIC INTEREST IN CRIMINAL EVENTS

The fact that violent crime still constitutes a small proportion of all crime events is at odds with public views about the extent and pervasiveness of this type of crime. Public attitudes toward crime are strongly influenced by the extensive treatment of this subject in the media. The three crime stories that we introduced at the beginning of this chapter were given detailed treatment in a single issue of *The Globe and Mail*. Of course, such stories are high-lighted in the media because there is a widespread public fascination with the topic of crime. Lawbreaking figures prominently in what we see and hear in the mass media and in the conversations that we have with one another. What are these popular images of crime? Where do they come from? What implications do they have for the ways we think about and respond to crime?

CRIME NEWS

While there are differences across types of media and across communities with respect to the amount of coverage that crime receives (Liska and Baccaglini, 1990), generally speaking crime is widely reported by all popular news media (Dominick, 1978; Erikson, Baranek, and Chan, 1991). Why is this? The simple answer may be that media audiences are interested in such stories and therefore journalists rely on crime news because it "sells" (Gordon and Heath, 1981). Some audience members may view crime news as an important source of information about the "facts" of crime, while others may be caught up in the dramatic and sometimes lurid nature of crime news.

BOX 1.2   CRIME TOURS

The public ambivalence about crime manifests itself in various ways. Much of the popular culture that we find in television, books, and movies focuses on the sensational character of crime in society. While most members of the general public express concern about the problem of crime, it is an endless source of fascination.

This fascination has extended in recent years to the tourist experience. In many large American cities, visitors may take guided tours of famous local crime scenes (*Crimebeat,* 1992). In Chicago, Untouchable Tours provides customers with a scenic view of the city's most famous gangland locations, including the Biograph Theater (where the FBI shot and killed bank robber John Dillenger) and the former headquarters of gangster Al Capone. A tour company in New York City offers the Sidewalks of New York tour, which allows paying guests to visit famous Manhattan murder scenes. Visitors to Hollywood can ride in a Cadillac hearse as they visit local sites, including the places where Janis Joplin and John Belushi overdosed on drugs and the home where mobster Bugsy Siegal was murdered.

Vacation planning is made easy by travel guides such as *Unauthorized America* ("a travel guide to the places the Chamber of Commerce won't tell you about") by Vince Staten, *New York Notorious* ("a borough-by-borough tour of the city's most famous crime scenes") by Paul Schwartzman and Rob Polner, and *Murder USA* ("a true-crime travel guide to the most notorious killing grounds in America") by Tom Philben.

Why would people be interested in using their vacation time in this way? Do you think that notorious murder scenes today will be the tourist attractions of tomorrow?

Reference: *"Crime Tours," Crimebeat,* 1992 (January), pp. 29–31.

Katz (1987) argues that audience fascination with crime news has little to do with a search for the truth about crime or with the dramatic qualities of crime reporting. Instead, he maintains, crime news allows audience members to work out their own positions on moral questions of a general yet also personal nature. For example, many crime stories deal with the competence or insensitivity of offenders. As Katz (1987) expresses it, we read accounts of "ingenious, vicious, and audacious crimes—of deceptions that trick the close scrutiny of diligent customs inspectors, of the most bloody murders, of big heists in broad daylight" (50). Such stories demonstrate to the audience the nature and the limits of human competence and human sensibility. They are of interest to the audience precisely because the dilemma of assessing personal competence and maintaining one's own moral sensibility is routinely encountered in day-to-day life. For Katz (1987), reading crime news is a "ritual moral exercise," and, as such, "appears to serve a purpose similar to the morning shower, routine physical exercise and shaving" (72).

THE CONTENT OF CRIME NEWS

Studies on the content of crime news have yielded informative findings. First, there appears to be little direct correspondence between the amount of crime news and the amount of crime (as measured, for instance, in official statistics). In other words, objectively measured trends in crime do not correspond closely with trends in the amount of crime news (Katz, 1987; Garofalo, 1981). Second, the degree of media attention to crime depends on the type of offence. Violent, relatively infrequent crimes like homicide are emphasized, while property crimes, white-collar offences, and other nonviolent, frequently occurring crimes are underreported (Graber, 1980; Humphries, 1981; Randall, Lee-Sammons, and Hagner, 1988; Skogan and Maxfield, 1981).

Third, when compared to official measures, crime news presents an exaggerated image of the proportion of offences that result in arrest (Sacco and Fair, 1988; Skogan and Maxfield, 1981). In other words, the media portray the police as far more effective than they really are. Fourth, media attention is focused on the early stages of criminal justice processing, (i.e., detection and arrest); the later stages of legal processing are largely ignored (Hans, 1990).

Analyses of crime news also indicate that media coverage is notable not only for what it includes but also for what it excludes. Crime reporting is often criticized for ignoring the relationship between crime and broad social conditions. Jon Katz (1993) reports that gun murders have now become so common in major cities in the United States that the major newspapers and networks tend to ignore them. He says that the readership of large dailies reside in suburbs outside of the areas in which the violence is the greatest. As a result, only the most sensational of the violent crimes are reported, leaving the inner-city residents with no mainstream media to report on their most urgent problems.

Humphries (1981) suggests that while news reports associate criminal violence with youth, maleness, and minority membership, they ignore the historical view of how labour markets and related institutions shape employment opportunities and the size and composition of the pool of people vulnerable to arrest. This tendency to portray crime as a product of the behaviour of pathological individuals rules out alternative explanations. A report about a single mother accused or convicted of child abuse may describe her as "disturbed" and ignore the following questions: "Was the mother receiving welfare or was she unemployed? Was the child attending a day-care program or receiving any other social services? Had the mother been a victim of child abuse?" (Gorelick, 1989: 423).

The biased nature of media crime reporting is clearly illustrated in Voumvakis and Ericson's (1984) study on newspaper accounts of attacks against women in Toronto. While the accounts covered in this study offer explanations for the "crime wave," they do so by emphasizing (1) the ways in which the victims' actions placed them in conditions of risk; (2) the need for a more coercive, and presumably more effective, response from the criminal justice system; and (3) offender pathology. Voumvakis and Ericson maintain that these terms of reference, although not necessarily unreasonable, are restrictive in that they rule out alternative interpretations, particularly those that link crimes against women to more general patterns of gender inequality. Reporting that emphasizes the need for more police, more punishment, and more vigilance on the part of women does not allow for discussion of broader programs of social reform that might correct these inequalities.

THE SOURCES OF CRIME NEWS

Studies of news production emphasize the ways in which judgments of "newsworthiness" come to be applied to categories of events (Chibnall, 1977; Fishman, 1978). Such judgments reflect how journalists view their society, the work in which they are engaged, and the audiences that they serve. Criminal events (especially violent ones) conform closely to the professional values of journalists for several reasons (Ericson, Baranek, and Chan, 1987).

First, such incidents have spatial and temporal characteristics that lend themselves easily to news-production routines. Murders, thefts, and sexual assaults are discrete events that occur in the periods between the publication of successive editions of a newspaper or in the periods between successive radio and television newscasts. Second, reports of criminal events are comprehensible to an audience and thus require little in the way of background information. In addition, because there is an almost limitless supply of crime news, the number of crime-related stories can be expanded or reduced depending on the needs of media decision-makers and on amount of space or time that must be filled on any given day (Warr, 1991). Finally, many crimes lend themselves to a dramatic narrative form that features the exploits of clearly defined "good guys" and "bad guys" (Ericson, 1991).

The reliance of news organizations on a continuous flow of crime news has led to the establishment of well-defined relationships between news organizations and those who are viewed as reliable and credible suppliers of such information (Gordon and Heath, 1981). The police are the principal source of crime news, and the "police wire," press release, news conference, or beat reporter provide the link between the world of crime and the news media (Ericson, Baranek, and Chan, 1989). Because the police are able to supply a steady stream of stories that are "entertaining, dramatic, amusing and titillating" (Ericson, 1991: 207), journalists implicitly adopt a police perspective on the problem of crime (Fishman, 1981).

The police–journalist relationship is mutually beneficial (Zatz, 1987). It allows journalists regular access to a valued news commodity, and, through reference to the police as the official spokespersons on crime, it lends credibility, authority, and objectivity to media reporting. Correspondingly, the relationship allows the police to present themselves as experts on crime and at the same time reaffirms police ownership of the problem of crime.

This exploration of the role that sources play in the production of crime news helps to explain why interpersonal violent crimes such as homicide or robbery receive greater coverage than crimes by or against businesses (Ericson, 1991). First, the established source–journalist relationships that exist with respect to so-called common crimes generally do not exist in the case of business crime. Second, stories about business crime may be judged as less newsworthy because they are generally more complex, less dramatic, and may be more difficult to personalize (Randall, Lee-Sammons, and Hagner, 1988).

CRIME DRAMA

Crime drama has been an important part of television since the medium's inception. From *Dragnet, The Untouchables, and Racket Squad* to *Twin Peaks, In the Heat of the Night, and Street Legal,* each decade has witnessed countless lawyers, police detectives, and private investigators engaged in the prime-time pursuit of law and order.

As in the case of crime news, television crime drama conforms closely to the stylistic and commercial requirements of the medium. These programs rely heavily on dramatic conventions that emphasize suspense and violent action. The storytelling formula of crime shows typically provides a format in which these conventions can be conveniently maximized (Ericson, 1991). As crimes are investigated, and as wrongdoers are pursued and ultimately brought to justice, opportunities abound for car chases, fistfights, and gunplay. It is rumoured that a television executive was once asked why so many of the programs on his network dealt with the police and private detectives. He responded, "I suppose we could do a one-hour dramatic show about mail carriers. But just exactly would we have them do every week?"

Because the essentially escapist nature of television crime drama is well recognized, no one really expects the world of crime portrayed in such programs to constitute a valid portrait of real-life crime and criminals. The images have more to do with the needs of the medium than with a desire to accurately map reality. Still, it is worth noting that crime in television drama, like crime in the news, tends to be disproportionately violent (Dominick, 1978). Additionally, television criminals are generally older than their real-life counterparts, their age grouping more closely approximating that of the audience (Pandiani, 1978). Whereas crime data suggest that offenders are typically poor, television criminals are more likely to be affluent. Any suggestion of an association between crime and minority group membership is typically downplayed in crime dramas in order to avoid alienating a significant segment of the viewing audience, which would clearly not be in the best interests of a commercial medium. As a result of these influences, television criminals are typically, "white materialists, motivated by greed and lasciviousness" (Newman, 1990: 263).

The distinction between television news and television drama is less clear than it once was (Hans, 1990; Newman, 1990). Programs such as *America's Most Wanted, Unsolved Mysteries, Top Cops,* and *A Current Affair* combine traditional news-documentary techniques with the familiar narrative style of dramatic television. These program formats (sometimes labelled "infotainment" or "reality television") have proliferated because, first, they have proven popular with audiences and, second, they are relatively inexpensive to produce. Crime, like other social problems, continues to be a source of both "fun and profit" in the mass media (Gusfield, 1989).

The ongoing debate about violence in the media and its effects on audiences has recently intensified. Discussion of the issue in the United States Senate (in hearings chaired by Senator Paul Simon) and by a Canadian Parliamentary Committee on Culture and Communication has convinced many in the media business that if they do not do something voluntarily about lessening the display of graphic violence in their shows, they are likely to face legislated standards. The effectiveness of the Simon hearings in particular was indicated by the fact that all four American networks sent their presidents to testify the steps that they had taken—including self-censorship—to address these problems.

TALKING ABOUT CRIME

People not only read crime news and watch crime shows on television, they also talk about crime. A major study of reactions to crime in three major American cities found that people cited their friends and neighbours, rather than the mass media, as their principal sources of information about local crime conditions (Skogan and Maxfield, 1981). Nonetheless, talk about crime is frequently focused on events that have achieved a high degree of media notoriety. Heavy media coverage of serial killings, child abductions, or crimes committed by or against celebrities is likely to generate considerable public discussion. Much talk also centres on crime in the local environment. People who live in high-crime neighbourhoods are more likely to talk about crime (Skogan and Maxfield, 1981). Residents in such neighbourhoods are more likely to be personally acquainted with crime victims and thus have more stories to tell about crime and its consequences.

In their study on fear of crime among the elderly, Kennedy and Silverman (1985) report the surprising finding that respondents who expressed high levels of fear also had higher levels of contact with family members than did other respondents. The continuous cautions that the elderly (particularly those who live on their own) receive from their families may have the paradoxical effect of exacerbating rather than calming their fears.

CRIME IN RUMOUR AND LEGEND

Sometimes talk about crime seems to bear only a very tenuous relationship to social reality. In 1956, news spread throughout Taipei that a number of children had been victims of slashings with what appeared to be razor blades or similar weapons (Jacobs, 1965). In 1944, many residents of Mattoon, Illinois, were reportedly the victims of a "phantom anaesthetist" who entered their homes and sprayed them with a paralyzing gas (Johnson, 1945). In 1969, stories spread through the city of Orléans, France, that Jewish dress-shop owners were kidnapping young women and selling them into "the white slave trade" (Morin, 1971). More recently, stories have spread in many communities in North America about the threats posed to children by Halloween sadists, who poison or otherwise contaminate the "treats" they dispense to unsuspecting children (Best, 1990).

There was no real evidence to corroborate any of the above stories. Their fanciful quality suggests close kinship with sociological definitions of "rumour" (Rosnow, 1988; Rosnow and Fine, 1976). Like all rumours, they represent forms of "improvised news" that express anxieties and uncertainties about some aspect of social life (Shibutani, 1966). For example, Best (1990) argues that the spread of stories about Halloween sadists during the 1970s was a response to three forms of social strain that characterized the period. The first was an increasing public awareness of, and concern over, the vulnerability of children to child abuse and a range of other victimizing experiences. A second source of strain was the general increase in fear of crime and the threats posed to personal safety by anonymous strangers, and the third source was an increasing mistrust of persons outside of one's group. Best (1990) characterizes the Halloween sadist as a symbolic expression of these three anxieties.

> The sadist, like other dangers, attacks children—society's most vulnerable members; the sadist, like the stereotypical criminal, is an anonymous, unprovoked assailant; and the sadist, like other strangers, should be met with suspicion rather than trust (143).

BOX 1.3   TERROR ON CAMPUS: AN URBAN LEGEND

Folklorist Jan Harold Brunvand (1993) describes an urban legend that circulated around university campuses in the American South and Midwest in 1988. According to rumours, a psychic had predicted on television talk show that a mass murderer was going to terrorize campus residents on Halloween night.

From place to place, the specific details of the rumour changed. The talk show in question was variously named as *Oprah*, *Donahue*, and *Geraldo*, among others. The universities in question were variously named as Florida State, Purdue, Ohio Northern, and Slippery Rock.

According to the version of the story that circulated in Florida, a psychic on the *Oprah Winfrey Show* had predicted that a knife-wielding maniac, dressed as Little Bo Peep, was going to slash his way through a dormitory or sorority house. The story persisted despite statements from the show's producers that no such guest had appeared and no such prediction had been made. An elaboration of the story described proposed action by university officials to evacuate residences on Halloween, although such action was never considered. At Purdue, it was said that the prediction involved the deaths of twelve students living in an "X-shaped" dormitory.

According to Brunvand, rumours of this type frequently circulate around university campuses in the fall. Usually, the stories describe killings that will occur at a school, the name of which begins with a particular letter or which is situated near a particular configuration of mountains or rivers. In general, the target building is usually described as being of a particular shape and size or as having a particular type of name. Such stories have been circulating since at least 1968.

Brunvand states that, even though these stories lack a factual basis, some students are likely to react as though the stories are true. They may, for instance, move out of residence on Halloween night or barricade their doors.

Real-life mass murders on campus (such as those at the University of Montreal and Concordia) may lend to such stories an air of credibility.

WHAT IS IT?

Urban Legend

A captivating and plausible but mainly fictional oral narrative that is widely regarded as true.

Folklorists use the term *urban legend* to characterize many of the crime stories that travel along interpersonal channels of communication (Brunvand, 1981, 1984, 1986, 1989). Brunvand (1984) describes these legends as "highly captivating and plausible, but mainly fictional oral narratives that are widely told as true stories" (ix). Urban legends are widely circulated and typically deal with attempted abductions in shopping malls or amusement parks, psychopaths who terrorize babysitters, the contamination of children's "lick-and-stick" tattoos with hallucinogenic drugs, and criminally insane killers who stalk couples on "lovers lane." While these stories vary in their details from place to place and over time, their moral substance has remarkable durability.

Wachs (1988) argues that urban folklore regarding crime has considerable entertainment value in that both the telling and the hearing of the stories may provide opportunities for dramatic and frequently humorous release. She further characterizes these stories as "cautionary tales" that advise listeners of the dangers of urban life and the need for constant vigilance.

Some kinds of urban legends are more newsworthy than others. Stories about bicycle thieves generally have less currency than stories about killers on the loose. Skogan and Maxfield (1981) found that neighbourhood talk about crime, in the cities that they studied, was largely dominated by stories about elderly or female victims.

While talk about corporate and white-collar criminals appears to be infrequent (Kapferer, 1989), it is not nonexistent (Kapferer, 1989). Stories have circulated in recent years that some major businesses are under the control of satanic cults (Brunvand, 1984) or are willfully contaminating food products (Kapferer, 1989).

Sometimes stories have very real consequences before it becomes evident that they are in fact hoaxes. In the summer of 1993, a media scare erupted over the "discovery" of hypodermic needles in Pepsi cans. All aspects of Pepsi's operations were scrutinized to determine how this could have happened. After much bad publicity, Pepsi was able to demonstrate that it is virtually impossible to insert a needle into a can during the high-speed canning processes employed in its plants. Subsequently, the story was exposed as a series of hoaxes, but not before serious damage had been done to the image of this company. Some media pundits have since raised concerns not only about the believability of hoaxes such as these but also about the media's role in spreading the hoax and perpetuating public doubts about a product (Corcoran, 1993: B2).

SUMMARY AND CONCLUSIONS
■ ■ ■

The study of crime is an interdisciplinary endeavour that draws on a variety of techniques in highlighting different aspects of the criminal event. While crime is, strictly speaking, the breaking of the law, we need to understand more than simply offender motivation in explaining how crime occurs. There are a number of factors that influence the definition of criminal behaviour, including variations in legal interpretations, changing social morality, police actions, and (for various reasons) nonreporting of crime. Thus we need to be sensitive to social as well as legal definitions of crime events.

In attempting to explain crime, criminologists generally adopt one of two perspectives. The first approach, classicism, focuses on the offender as a rational being who reduces or avoids punishment through adherence to the law. The second approach, positivism, looks instead at the offender's behaviour as something determined by his or her constitution and/or social and economic conditions. The emphasis in these approaches is on the motivation of offenders.

Crime statistics compiled by the police indicate that the volume of reported crime has increased fourfold in Canada over the last 30 years. Property crime represents about half of all reported crime, while violent crime makes up about 10 percent of the total.

Crime events as presented in the media and in public discussions frequently do not accurately represent the true nature of crime. Media treatment of crime often creates the impression that certain types of crime (e.g., homicide or armed robbery) are more prevalent than is actually the case. Both crime news and crime drama emphasize the more exotic and "exciting" types of crime; their depictions of criminal events are often more entertaining than informative.

PART II

THEORIES

SOCIAL CONDITIONS AND CRIMINAL MOTIVATIONS

WHAT ARE CRIMINOLOGICAL theories and why do we need them? In day-to-day conversation, we tend to use terms like "theory" or "theoretical" to describe something that may be interesting but is also irrelevant, unimportant, or impractical. We can dismiss what someone tells us with the retort, "While that may be true in theory, it doesn't have much to do with reality!" As students of criminology, however, we need to recognize that, far from being irrelevant, theories can be extremely useful and practical analytical tools.

We can understand criminological theories as generalized explanations of criminal phenomena. We look to our theories to provide us with answers to questions about why crimes occur, why some types of people are more likely than others to be involved in crimes (as offenders or as victims), why crimes are more likely to occur in certain places and at certain times, and why agencies of social control respond to crime as they do.

Of course, criminologists are not alone in seeking answers to these questions. Angry newspaper editorials may offer what appear to be reasonable accounts of why crime rates are rising. On any given Sunday morning, television preachers explain crime and associated problems in terms of evil forces at large in the world. The victim of an assault may ask what it is that he or she did that led to the victimization. While they are not always recognized as such, these accounts of why and how crimes occur represent a kind of theoretical thinking. However, we expect somewhat more from criminological theories than we expect from so many of the "folk theories" that are part of our conventional wisdom.

First, criminological theories (at least of the type discussed in this book) are intended as general rather than specific explanations. Stated differently, we are usually not interested in why one particular offender committed one particular crime. Instead, theories should explain the patterns that characterize criminal phenomena. We want our theories to tell us, for example, why males are more likely than females to commit a violent offence, why the chances of becoming a victim of crime are reduced as people grow older, why big cities have higher rates of some kinds of crime than do small towns, or why rates of crime shot up in the 1960s.

Second, we expect that our theories will be consistent with (and can therefore make sense out of) the *facts* of crime as revealed to us in the research process. The gross facts of crime, as we currently understand them, are consistent with a variety of different theoretical viewpoints. As a result, it sometimes appears that the evidence lends partial support to apparently competing views. Why, for instance, do we find higher rates of theft in bigger cities? Some sociologists have argued that large cities undermine the social controls that might discourage people from stealing (Wirth, 1938). Others have suggested that bigger cities are more likely to be home to the kinds of people (e.g., young, unmarried males) who tend to steal no matter where they live (Gans, 1962). Alternatively, we might argue that the city provides a setting that accommodates an elaborate network of thieves, targets, and fences and thereby turns theft into a profitable and enduring activity (Fischer, 1975).

On the surface, it would appear that each of the above theories of crime and urban life is equally valuable, since each is consistent with the general pattern of empirical data. This implies that, in order to assess the relative value of these theories, we would need more detailed empirical knowledge about the relationship between crime and urban settings. As empirical data accumulated, we would hope to discover that one of the theoretical positions better accounted for the patterns that we were observing.

This brings us to a third requirement of criminological theories. Like all forms of scientific theory, they should be falsifiable. It is imperative that our theories be stated in terms that allow them to be tested through research so that we can discover which theories provide false accounts of the phenomena being observed. A theory that cannot be rejected no matter what we discover is of little use to us.

It is important to emphasize that criminological theories are not merely intellectual abstractions with no real-life implications. On the contrary, theories may be highly practical, particularly when we use them as guides in our effort to deal with crime as a social problem. Quite obviously, how we understand the causes of a problem has important consequences for the actions we take to resolve it.

Throughout its history, criminology has witnessed no shortage of attempts to theorize about crime. To the uninitiated, the choice of explanations can be bewildering as theories appear to contradict or at least compete with one another. Our review focuses on two major types of theoretical questions. The first concerns the behaviour of offenders. Why are some people more inclined than others to behave in ways that violate the law? This question, which has attracted the greatest amount of criminological attention, provides the subject matter for this chapter and the one that follows.

In Chapter 4, we turn to another type of theoretical question. How do we understand the situations that allow offenders to act on their propensities? As we will see, an emphasis on situations and opportunities complements the more traditional motivational theories of crime. In Chapter 5, the complementary nature of approaches that emphasize motivation and that emphasize opportunity will be given more extensive attention.

EXPLAINING OFFENDER MOTIVATION

For many theorists, the explanation of crime boils down to one simple question that has spawned several complicated answers. Why do offenders do what they do? Criminologists have offered two general types of answers to this question. On the one hand, criminal behaviour can be understood as the product of unique factors that *motivate* lawbreaking. This approach derives from the positivist school of thought and seeks to discover the causes of criminal conduct. On the other hand, criminal behaviour can be understood as the product of behavioural choices that are freely and rationally made. This approach derives from the classical school of thought and sees as misguided the search for causes of criminal behaviour (causes referring to those external factors that constrain people to act in particular ways).

These perspectives differ in terms of the prominence they accord the role of *will* in human affairs. Theories that derive from classical thinking conceptualize criminal behaviour as willful and purposeful, while theories that derive from the positivist school view will as a less significant characteristic of criminal behaviour and seek instead to understand how social and other factors compel, or at least encourage, criminal conduct. This chapter deals with those theories that reflect the positivist tradition; theories that reflect the classical tradition are discussed in the next chapter.

Most criminologists locate the sources of criminal motivation in the social worlds in which offenders live their lives. In this respect, three broad subthemes may be identified. The first views criminal motivation as resulting from deficiencies in the offender's physiological or psychological makeup. The second subtheme views offenders as a product of troublesome social conditions that propel them toward crime. According to the third subtheme, motivation arises from the offender's commitment to cultural beliefs that condone criminal conduct.

SOCIOBIOLOGICAL EXPLANATIONS OF MOTIVATION

GENETICS

In recent years, there has been a renewed interest in the influence of genetics and physiology on the creation of criminal offenders. This school of thought argues that certain individuals are more likely to commit crime due to faulty programming of their genetic structure. Some researchers have used genetic explanations of behaviour (Mednick, Moffitt, and Stack, 1984), while others have focused on the sociobiology or constitutional aspects of individuals (Wilson and Herrnstein, 1985), in arguing that there is a predisposition toward criminality in certain individuals. This predisposition may occur through intergenerational genetic defects or through a constitutional deficiency deriving from short time horizons (absence of long-term goals) and inadequate socialization in early childhood.

The genetic approach has been used in the effort to determine the importance of family ties or blood relations in the control of individual deportment. Violent crime, in particular, can be explained in terms of its connection with genetics: individuals with intimate family ties are subject to the protection afforded by animals to their blood connections, whereas individuals with less intimate ties (for example, adopted children) are more likely to be subject to violence from step-parents (see Daly and Wilson, 1988).

In the research that has been done to date, the efficacy of using genotypes to identify likely candidates for criminal behaviour is not very well established. The most credible research is provided by adoption studies, but these have in fact reported fairly low concordance rates between the historical

offending patterns of identical twins who have been separated at birth and raised with different families (Mednick, Moffitt, and Stack, 1984). In evaluating the relative importance of genetic structure and environmental influences, adoption studies report little evidence that genetic differences explain differences in criminality.

Walters and White (1989) summarize the problems of genetic-based research as follows:

> *Genetic factors are undoubtedly correlated with various measures of criminality, but the large number of methodological flaws and limitations in the research should make one cautious in drawing any causal inferences at this point in time. Our review leads us to the inevitable conclusion that current genetic research on crime has been poorly designed, ambiguously reported, and exceedingly inadequate in addressing the relevant issues (478).*

Until these deficiencies are addressed, there is no real scientific basis for arguing for (or against) the existence of a "crime gene."

CONSTITUTION

The biological approaches have also focused on the constitutional structure (including the body types and psychological propensities) of offenders. Having reviewed research by Garafolo (1914) on Italian convicts and studies by Sheldon (1940) on incarcerated juveniles, Wilson and Herrnstein (1985) conclude that one can detect certain physiological similarities among offenders (see Box 2.1). For example, young males who are short and muscular are the types most likely to appear in prison populations. According to Wilson and Herrnstein (1985), "[t]he biological factors whose traces we see in faces, physiques, and correlation with behavior of parents and siblings are predispositions towards crime that are expressed as psychological traits and activated by circumstance" (103).

The difficulty with the constitutional approach is that knowing about body type doesn't tell us much about a person's propensity to act criminally; it tells us (and only if we believe the research) that inmates tend to be short and muscular. Moreover, body typing ignores the fact that one of the most popular locations in men's prisons is the weight room, where 90-pound weaklings have the opportunity to turn themselves into Charles Atlases. It also fails to consider the fact that, in a violent encounter, the less muscular combatant will tend to lose the contest and end up in hospital, while the more muscular participant will emerge as the victor and end up in prison. Further, this approach doesn't address other important factors related to crime, including the circumstances under which a motivated offender comes to participate in criminal activity.

In defending the constitutional approach to criminality, Wilson and Herrnstein (1985) borrow from classical criminology to argue that crime is rational act based on a calculation of gain and loss. It is through this process that individuals weigh the possibilities that they will succeed in their endeavours. It is likely, in this calculation, that individuals may discount the costs through a process whereby immediate gratification becomes the paramount concern. This choice is not really a free choice, however, as it is predetermined by poor socialization and constitutional deficiencies. The short time horizons possessed by

BOX 2.1   BODY TYPE AND CRIMINAL BEHAVIOUR

In a famous study, researcher William Sheldon (1949) attempted to determine the relationship between physique and the tendency to engage in criminal behaviour. Sheldon used a method called *somatotyping* in order to categorize three basic types of body build—endomorphic, ectomorphic, and mesomorphic—each of which he argued was associated with a particular type of temperament.

As pictured in Figure 2.1, the body types represent extreme forms. Most individuals are a combination of all three types. The numbers to the left of each figure indicate the relative presence of endomorphic, ectomorphic, and mesomorphic characteristics respectively. The individual who is exclusively endomorphic would thus receives the extreme score "7-1-1," indicating the absence of ectomorphic and mesomorphic characteristics.

In comparing a sample of known delinquents with a control group of students, Sheldon maintained that delinquents were more likely to have mesomorphic physiques and the accompanying temperament, which emphasized risktaking, adventure, and an interest in physical activity.

Aside from the argument that might link body type to temperament, can you offer any other interpretation of Sheldon's finding that mesomorphs are disproportionately represented among known delinquents?

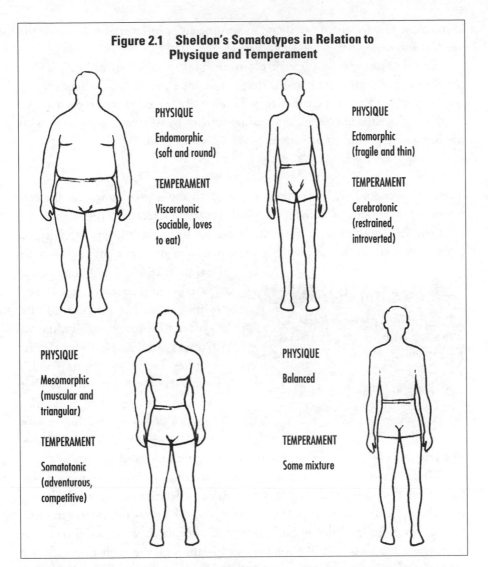

Figure 2.1 Sheldon's Somatotypes in Relation to Physique and Temperament

PHYSIQUE

Endomorphic
(soft and round)

TEMPERAMENT

Viscerotonic
(sociable, loves
to eat)

PHYSIQUE

Ectomorphic
(fragile and thin)

TEMPERAMENT

Cerebrotonic
(restrained,
introverted)

PHYSIQUE

Mesomorphic
(muscular and
triangular)

TEMPERAMENT

Somatotonic
(adventurous,
competitive)

PHYSIQUE

Balanced

TEMPERAMENT

Some mixture

Source: Curt R. Bartol, *Criminal Behaviour: A Psychosocial Approach.* Englewood Cliffs, N.J.: Prentice-Hall, 1980.

individuals with these deficiencies distort the way in which their decisions about the benefits and costs are made. Such individuals will tend to involve themselves in criminal activity for short-term gain. According to Wilson and Herrnstein, they represent criminal types who need to be isolated and subjected to high levels of deterrence, thereby restricting their behaviour and reducing the likelihood of criminality. It is the role of the state to set up contingencies that will reduce the benefits and increase the costs of misbehaviour.

The deterministic nature of constitutional theories firmly establishes them in a positivistic framework that maintains there is little offenders can do to change their propensities to act criminally. From this perspective, we need to reduce the likelihood of criminal activity by isolating individuals who are likely to be problem offenders.

DIET

Some researchers have expressed an interest in the degree to which diet can affect the behaviour of individuals. There is strong scientific evidence to support the idea that certain individuals are more prone to hyperactivity or aggressive behaviour following a sudden intake of sugar (hypoglycemia) (Dorfman, 1984). In a famous case, a San Francisco city supervisor claimed that his murder of the mayor and another individual in 1978 was attributable to his diet of Twinkies and other "junk food." His lawyers were able to use what has come to be known as the Twinkie Defence to convince a jury that their client suffered "diminished mental capacity" and was therefore not guilty of murder.

While the suggestion that such dietary factors are major causes of violence seems questionable, what has been acknowledged is the dramatic effect that changing dietary practices can have on the behaviour of inmates in institutions. In a study of detention homes in California, it was established that by revising the diets of 276 juveniles, mostly through the reduction of sugar intake via pop and junk food, antisocial behaviour declined by 48 percent, incidents of theft by 77 percent, incidents of assault by 82 percent, and refusal to obey orders by 55 percent (Kinderlehrer, 1983: 143). The same results occurred when supplies of orange juice were increased, a finding that has led some researchers to attribute the former negative behaviours not to excessive sugar content but rather to vitamin and nutrient deficiencies in the prisoners' diet (Dorfman, 1984).

The focus on nutrients has led to the research on the relationship between trace element patterns and a predisposition to violence. William Walsh conducted research on 24 pairs of violent and nonviolent brothers and a second study in which 96 violent males of mixed age and background were matched with 96 nonviolent males who were selected as a control group. Walsh found that the violent subjects fell into two groups: Type A's, who tested high in copper and low in sodium and potassium and who were episodically violent, and Type B's, who were the reverse and displayed consistently antisocial behaviour. As the Type A pattern tended to fade with age, hair analysis (a procedure for tracking trace elements) could be used by parole boards to predict, on the basis of the mineral content in the subject's body, when episodic violence would likely cease (Dorfman, 1984: 46).

The applicability of these findings to offenders outside of institutions is impossible to determine. They do provide some interesting suggestions about how our lifestyle, particularly what we eat, influences how we act. They do not tell us much about what situations elicit violence or about what social factors (e.g., early childhood socialization, peer pressure, or fear of stigmatization) may play a role in deterring it.

The ingestion of substances other than food has attracted a great deal of attention in criminological analyses. Drugs, including alcohol, are present in many criminal events. The criminality that surrounds the illicit sale and purchase of drugs makes their use of interest to us. As with dietary factors, what is unclear is how important drugs are in providing an explanation for criminality. Their presence in criminal situations may be related but not central to the explanation of criminality. Many people use (and abuse) alcohol without becoming violent and attacking other people. Yet, as evidenced by the many bar fights that occur, alcohol sometimes appears to serve as a fuel for violent attacks.

Explanations based on genetics, constitution, and diet can be summed up this way. If one accepts that crime is a cultural and social concept, defined through social custom and law, it seems unlikely that there is such a thing as a "criminal type" or a "crime gene" whereby behaviour is preprogrammed to deviate from this social construct, or, indeed, that certain people with particular body types or diet will generally offend. These explanations, while interesting, seem to be more useful for describing the conditions of incarcerated offenders and assisting in controlling their behaviour than in predicting the likelihood of criminality in the first place.

SOCIAL CONDITIONS AND CRIMINAL MOTIVATION

It has been argued that, in a variety of ways, the social conditions under which people live make it difficult for them to be law-abiding. From this perspective, criminal behaviour may be understood as the means by which people attempt to deal with the frustration or stigma that characterizes their lives and with the problems that confront them.

FRUSTRATED AMBITIONS

People who aspire to achieve goals that are not realistically available to them may feel pressure to behave in a criminal fashion. Such pressure is most likely to be felt by those who occupy disadvantaged positions in the social structure. Perhaps the best-known version of this argument was articulated in the late 1930s by the sociologist Robert Merton, whose interests lay in trying to understand how particular forms of social organization create the strains that lead to nonconformity.

Using American society as an example, Merton (1938) argued that if everyone in the society is encouraged to pursue the goal of material success, those who do not have access to the legitimate means by which success is to be achieved will be frustrated by their lack of opportunity. Those at the bottom of the social hierarchy—the poor, ethnic minorities, or recent immigrants—do not have easy access to quality education, inheritance, or other means by which the American Dream might be realized. Since success goals are still important to them, they must find ways of adjusting to the social strain that society imposes on them. The adjustments in many cases may involve criminal conduct.

Merton's anomie theory proposes that frustration and alienation develop when individuals who aspire to the economic goals of society (including upward social mobility) are not provided the means with which to achieve these goals. That is, a gap between expectations and real achievement appears. In responding to the anomie that develops as a result of this gap, certain adaptations develop (see Box 2.2). One such adaptation involves the use of criminal means to achieve conventional goals such as wealth. Blau and Blau (1982) argue that it is not absolute but relative inequality that results in frustration and a sense of personal injustice which in turn leads to criminal activity.

Consider the American gangster Al Capone. It can be argued that the goals to which he aspired did not differ significantly from the goals pursued by "legitimate" business leaders. Capone sought wealth, power, and celebrity. He differed from conventional entrepreneurs with respect to the means he employed to achieve these objectives but not with respect to the objectives themselves. Seen in this way, the behaviour of gangsters, thieves, and other

BOX 2.2 MERTON'S PARADIGM OF DEVIANT BEHAVIOUR

Robert Merton (1938) argued that nonconformist behaviour results when people find themselves in situations in which they are encouraged to pursue cultural goals that prevailing social arrangements do not allow them to achieve. While such individuals may have internalized these goals, they lack the legitimate means with which to achieve them. In such situations, individuals must adjust their behaviour to accommodate the gap between the goals and the means.

Merton identified five such adaptations in the goals-means relationship.

1. *Conformity*. Individuals who make this adaptation accept as legitimate both the goals and the means for achieving them. This is the adaptation that most people make.

2. *Innovation*. Innovation involves accepting the goals but rejecting the means of goal attainment. For example, the person who embezzles accepts material gain as a legitimate goal but rejects the culturally prescribed means for achieving it.

3. *Ritualism*. This adaptation involves accepting the means for achieving the goal but rejecting the goal itself. Individuals who engage in ritualism simply "go through the motions" without coming any closer to the goals they supposedly seek.

4. *Retreatism*. In the case of retreatism, there is a rejection of both the means and the goals. At least in terms of what the culture prescribes, those who opt for this adaptation may be described as dropouts.

5. *Rebellion*. Like retreatism, this form of adaptation involves rejecting both goals and means. Rebellion differs from retreatism in that it involves the substitution of other goals as well as other means by which they might be achieved.

Merton presented his five adaptations in schematic form as follows (where + means accept and − means reject).

	Goal	Means
Conformity	+	+
Innovation	+	−
Ritualism	−	+
Retreatism	−	−
Rebellion	−	−
	(+)	(+)

If high grades are a goal to be achieved and if study, essay writing, and exam taking are the means by which the goal is to be achieved, what specific forms of behaviour might each of Merton's adaptations represent?

goal-oriented criminals is best understood not as the product of a pathological personality but rather as a product of social arrangements that create a gulf between the things to which people aspire and what is actually available to them.

Frustrated ambition does not always manifest itself in individuals like Al Capone. It may come in more mundane forms. According to Messner (1989), criminality can be attributed to a number of factors, including race, income, and (particularly) unemployment. In contrast, Wilson (1983) has found that the research relating unemployment to crime is inconclusive. His explanations for criminality are consistent with the views of those who argue for frustrated ambition. His emphasis, though, is different. He says there can be many reasons why unemployed individuals commit crime and that it may not be the unemployment per se but rather the problems inherent in crime deterrence. He also says that crime may cause unemployment. What is not evident, he argues, is whether "some people turn to crime because they are poor, some people may be poor because they have turned to crime and are not very good at it, and still other persons may have been made poor and criminal because of some common underlying factor" (126). In Wilson's view, the lower classes are less likely to be socialized to the ways of society, and will thus have a greater tendency toward criminal behaviour. Support for targeting these groups for policing and for deterrence resides in the fact that their numbers are disproportionately represented in crime statistics (as perpetrators) and in prison populations.

It has been argued, however, that the lower classes are overrepresented in prisons because (1) the police tend to discriminate against them, (2) much of the lower-class behaviour is public and therefore more likely to be open to sanction, and (3) the crimes of the poor receive more attention than the white-collar crimes of the rich (Snider, 1992; Reiman, 1990). Property crimes like embezzlement can have a more detrimental effect on society than theft, or break and enter, and other crimes of the poor. Notwithstanding this view, Wilson (1983: 39) believes the rise in crime is not due to poverty or racism per se but rather a failure of individuals from the lower class to adopt behaviour that is more consistent with societal norms.

Several years after the publication of Merton's work, Albert Cohen followed a similar line in his investigation of gang delinquency among working-class juveniles. For Cohen (1955), the problem of much juvenile crime is rooted in the problems experienced by disadvantaged youth who aspire to middle-class status but who are judged inadequate by a school system that dispenses status rewards on the basis of middle-class criteria. In other words, children from a working-class background typically find that, because their socialization experiences have not prepared them to compete effectively for status within the classroom, they come up short when they are assessed by the school's "middle-class measuring rod." According to Cohen, working-class youth may experience feelings of frustration and inadequacy when they confront middle-class expectations regarding punctuality, neatness, and the need to postpone gratification.

One reaction on the part of youth may be to reject the source of their problem, namely, the middle-class value system of the school. Delinquency may signal such a rejection, partic-ularly if it celebrates standards that stand in direct opposition to those of the middle-class society. Delinquency that appears intended to offend members of conventional society rather than to achieve some specific goal may serve this pur-pose. For Cohen, much delinquen-cy has an "in your face" quality precisely because it is meant to signify a rejection of middle-class society and all that it represents.

The socially induced frustration that leads to crime may result not only when people aspire to goals they find unattainable, but also when they try to avoid negative situations and find their escape routes blocked. Agnew (1985a) argues that much juvenile crime may be motivated by thwarted attempts at avoiding pain. Youth who face abusive home situations, for instance, may react by running away, which may facilitate entry into a delin-quent lifestyle or which may in itself be considered a delinquent act in some jurisdictions. Alternatively, they may react to their frustration by "acting out" in violent ways toward those whom they define as vulnerable targets.

SOCIAL STIGMA

A school of thought known as labelling theory proposes a markedly different view of how the frustration created by particular forms of social arrange-ments may motivate criminal behaviour (Becker, 1963; Gibbs, 1966; Kitsuse, 1962; Rubington and Weinberg, 1987). Labelling theorists maintain that the social response to minor and sporadic criminal acts may create conditions that increase the likelihood of more serious patterns of criminality.

Labelling theorists place great emphasis on the ways in which the responses of the police and the criminal justice system to people identified as offenders create problems for those who must bear the label of "criminal." Such a label can be understood as a form of stigma that makes life difficult for those upon whom it has been imposed to lead normal lives. The person who is labelled a criminal, thief, delinquent, or troublemaker may find it difficult to obtain employment or to maintain friendships with others who tend to react to the powerful emotional content of the label. People who have been labelled may be frustrated by their personal circumstances, or they may view as hypocritical the response of those who condemn their conduct. Increasingly, legitimate associations may become less available and illegitimate associations more so.

Labelling theorists argue that the effects of societal reaction have important implications for the ways in which labelled people see themselves. Feedback that consistently provides the message that one is a disreputable person may eventually cause one to accept that definition. The effect of these labelling processes, then, may be to create a criminal self-identity, that is, secondary deviance (Lemert, 1951). The problems created by the labelling process increase the likelihood that engagement in criminal behaviour on the part of the labelled person will develop as a stable pattern. What labelling theory describes to us is a kind of self-fulfilling prophecy in that people who are treated as though they were beyond redemption will come to act as if they were. Thus, while the police and other criminal justice agencies intend to reduce involvement in crime, they very often have the opposite effect.

Criminologists have criticized the labelling approach for redirecting attention from the individual onto the agencies of social control, and for failing to develop a body of supporting empirical evidence (Wellford, 1975; Gove, 1975; Sagarin, 1975).

CULTURE AND CRIMINAL MOTIVATION

A third major approach locates the origins of criminal motivation in the cultural worlds to which offenders have exposure. The cultural milieu in which we are socialized provides us with our ideas about what is right and wrong, moral or immoral, appropriate or inappropriate. When our socialization is successful we come to see these views as our own, and we attempt to behave in ways that conform to the cultural standards that we have learned. It follows that, if we are exposed to beliefs and ideas that support behaviour that the law defines as criminal, we may be more likely to behave in criminal fashion.

Like theories that locate the sources of criminal motivation in the stress-inducing nature of social arrangements, cultural accounts present a "normalized" picture of the offender. In other words, it is not necessary to assume that there is anything pathological about offenders, only that they have learned a particular set of cultural lessons. Their behaviour is normal within a particular cultural context.

NORM VIOLATION

As we pointed out in Chapter 1, crime finds its origins in norm violation, norms being defined as a set of culturally defined acceptable behaviours. Are there societies in which it is possible to find complete compliance with all norms? Is it possible to have a society that is free of norm violation? Over the years, utopian communities have been depicted in literature as constituting the earthly expression of a spiritually inspired way of life. B.F. Skinner (1948), raises the possibility of developing and applying social intervention programs, such as those based on social learning theories, to design societies in which individuals will not feel the need or the inclination to deviate. In Skinner's utopian world, the motivations, needs, and aspirations of individuals conditioned through the use of reinforcement schedules designed to promote pro-social, nondeviant behaviour. Skinner argues that, in societies in which individual interests and abilities are properly assessed and managed, there will be no need for norm violation; in other words, the individual's socialization, intended to promote his or her self-interest, will have been programmed to coincide with the collective interests of the community.

The argument against the notion that we can be free of norm violation comes from the idea, promoted by Durkheim (1964), Becker (1963), and others, that societies are always subject to norm violation, due to their inevitable tendency to create outsiders and insiders. It is in the rejection of marginal individuals or outcasts that norms become defined in a way that justifies the exclusion of outsiders. Further, through this process, the legitimation of the norms for those who consider themselves insiders is reinforced by the application of sanctions against norm violators.

Now, is it true that as social morality declines, crime increases? The common view is that much of our social fabric has been heavily rent by the rapid changes that have occurred as a result of urbanization, modernization, and immigration. The breakdown of traditional communities and extended families has led to a crisis of confidence in our conventional institutions—the family, the schools, the church, and so forth. From this point of view, the reduction in the influence of these organizations and the increased individualization in society has diminished adherence to values that are pro-social. The increase in divorce, unemployment, transiency, and so on are accompanied by an increase in the levels of crime. The difficulty with the notion of a shared morality is that it centres on the adherence to traditional values. Rather than the loss of traditional values, or the transition to a new set of norms, it is the disorganization itself that contributes to criminality (Durkheim, 1964).

> ### IS THERE?
>
> **A Universal Form of Crime**
>
> Beyond expulsion from the group and shaming, there are myriad variations in the ways in which behaviour comes to be sanctioned. These variations reflect very different types of morality and lawmaking across societies.

Addressing this issue in a somewhat different way, we can ask, "Is there a universal form of crime?" Cross-cultural studies have shown that, while most societies condemn murder and incest, they do not always treat these behaviours as criminal (Douglas and Waskler, 1982; Schur, 1979). Sometimes an informal mechanism exists whereby such deviation comes to be sanctioned through civil action or through the social processes of expulsion from the group or shaming (Horowitz, 1990).

As far as other types of behaviour are concerned, the myriad variations in the ways in which they come to be sanctioned reflect very different types of morality and lawmaking across societies. Japan has been offered as a model of the kind of society that can attribute its low crime rate to certain cultural and social constraints that manage criminal behaviour. Yet one must approach this comparison with care, as a great deal of the behaviour in Japanese society that is dealt with informally would, in our society, probably end up being dealt with by the criminal courts. What we find across societies, then, is not always a difference in behaviour but rather a difference in the societal response to behaviour.

DIFFERENTIAL ASSOCIATION

Cultural approaches not only focus on norm violation as criminal behaviour but also on criminal behaviour that is normative. One of the early pioneers of this perspective was Edwin Sutherland, who in the 1930s proposed a cultural theory of crime that he called the theory of differential association. Contrary to the prevailing wisdom of his day, Sutherland (1939) maintained that crime is a learned behaviour. (See Box 2.3.) In the process of interacting

BOX 2.3 THE TENETS OF DIFFERENTIAL ASSOCIATION THEORY

Edwin Sutherland was one of the few criminologists to formulate a theory in terms of an interrelated set of propositions. The following statements, from Traub and Little (1980), refer to the process by which a particular person comes to engage in criminal behaviour:

1. *Criminal behaviour is learned.* Negatively, this means that criminal behaviour is not inherited, as such.

2. *Criminal behaviour is learned in interaction with other persons in a process of communication.* This communication is verbal in many respects but includes also "the communication of gestures."

3. *The principal part of the learning of criminal behaviour occurs within intimate personal groups.* Negatively, this means that the impersonal agencies of communication, such as movies and newspapers, play a relatively unimportant part in the genesis of criminal behaviour.

4. *When criminal behaviour is learned, the learning includes (a) techniques of committing the crime, which are sometimes very complicated, sometimes very simple; (b) the specific direction of motives, drives, rationalizations, and attitudes.*

5. *The specific direction of motives and drives is learned from definitions of the legal codes as favourable or unfavourable.* In some societies an individual is surrounded by persons who invariably define the legal codes as rules to be observed, while in others he is surrounded by persons whose definitions are favourable to the violation of the legal codes.

6. *A person becomes delinquent because of an excess of definitions favourable to violation of law over definitions unfavourable to violation of law.* This is the principle of differential association. It refers to both criminal and anticriminal associations and has to do with counteracting forces. When persons become criminal, they do so because of contact with criminal patterns and also because of isolation from anticriminal patterns.

7. *The process of learning criminal behaviour by association with criminal and anticriminal patterns involves all of the mechanisms that are involved in any other learning.* Negatively, this means that the learning of criminal behaviour is not restricted to the process of imitation.

A person who is seduced, for instance, learns criminal behaviour by association, but this process would not ordinarily be described as imitation.

8. *While criminal behaviour is an expression of general needs and values, it is not explained by those general needs and values, since noncriminal behaviour is an expression of the same needs and values.* Thieves generally steal in order to secure money, but likewise honest labourers work in order to secure money. The attempts by many scholars to explain criminal behaviour by general drives and values, such as the happiness principle, striving for social status, the money motive, or frustration, have been, and must continue to be, futile, since they explain lawful behaviour as completely as they explain criminal behaviour.

with others, whose own views support criminal conduct, one person can learn to be criminal just as another can learn to be a mechanic, a stamp collector, or a lover of classical music. According to Sutherland, the differential rate at which people associate with the carriers of criminal values determines the differential rate at which they engage in criminal conduct.

For Sutherland, differential association involves two important types of learning. First, one must learn actual techniques of crime commission. In some cases, these techniques are very simple and do not differ markedly from law-abiding behaviour. Stealing a car when the owner has left the keys inside is not so different from driving one's own car. In other cases, specialized skills are required (e.g., stealing a locked car when the keys have not been left inside).

Sutherland emphasized that knowledge or technical skills alone are insufficient to explain criminal behaviour. Everyone has some idea as to how to commit a wide variety of crimes. And yet while most of us could figure out how to murder or assault someone, we refrain from committing such acts. Sutherland (1939: 6) argued that, in addition to technical knowledge, one must have exposure to the "specific direction of motives, drives, rationalizations and attitudes." Stated differently, to behave criminally one must learn that crime is an acceptable type of behaviour. These types of learning imply the existence of cultural knowledge and cultural beliefs that promote criminality and to which only some of us have sustained exposure. Sutherland's approach has been particularly helpful in explaining why normally law-abiding individuals take up criminal activity in their work environments. According to Sutherland (1961), white-collar crime occurs because people have learned how to commit it and because they have learned from others that it is an acceptable form of behaviour.

SUBCULTURAL EXPLANATIONS OF CRIMINAL MOTIVATIONS

In complex, highly differentiated societies like our own, cultural pockets may be said to exist when many people are engaged in intensive interaction and when they confront common problems or share common interests. It is in this sense that we speak of subcultures of heavy-metal music fans, marathon runners, or the police. Because participants in these worlds are also participants in the larger culture shared by the rest of us, it is appropriate to think about subcultures as part of, but distinguishable from, the larger culture. It can be argued that subcultural involvement can promote criminal behaviour when the subcultural values in question are inconsistent with the conformist values enshrined in law.

Earlier in this century, Thorsten Sellin (1938) suggested that the high rates of crime among immigrant groups could be understood with reference to the culture conflict that ethnic subcultures encounter. His view acknowledged that when people migrate from one country to another they carry with them considerable cultural baggage. We recognize this fact when we visit a restaurant in Little Italy or attend a cultural festival in Chinatown. However, this cultural baggage may also include ways of acting that, although not considered criminal in the country of origin, are defined as such in the host country. By way of illustration, Sellin (1938) tells the story of a Sicilian father in New Jersey who "killed the sixteen-year-old seducer of his daughter, expressing surprise at his arrest since he had merely defended his family honour in a traditional way" (68).

Other theorists have used similar logic to explain patterns of homicide and assault. Noting that much interpersonal violence is concentrated socially (among young members of the urban underclass) or regionally (in, for instance, the American South), they argue that offenders (and frequently their victims) may behave as they do because they are immersed in a "subculture of violence" (Gastil, 1971; Wolfgang and Ferracuti, 1967). This subcultural orientation, it is argued, requires that some kinds of transgressions be resolved in a violent fashion. The longstanding feud between the Hatfields and McCoys is a stereotype of the violent subculture.

Much assaultive violence seems to originate from what many would consider to be minor or trivial altercations. An exchange that begins with a stare, a jostle, or an insult may end with one of the parties seriously injured or dead. Such patterns make sense, subcultural theorists maintain, only when we recognize the powerful cultural emphasis on social honour and the need to save face that lies behind them. Given this emphasis a derogatory remark made in a public setting may be enough to provoke physical retaliation.

To argue that violence in this sense is subcultural is to argue that it is normative. In other words, the physical defence of one's honour is not merely what one can do but what one *must* do if the respect of other cultural participants is to remain secure. Because the violence is normative, the person who behaves violently is unlikely to feel a sense of shame or embarrassment for doing so.

It is important to add that, within the context of the subculture of violence, it is the particular cultural interpretation given to an affront to character, not the affront per se, that is the source of the violence. Precisely because the cultural environments differ, a sneer is less likely to provoke trouble in a university faculty club than it is in a lower-class bar.

A weakness of the subcultural approach is that it tends to infer, rather than identify independently, subcultural values from subcultural behaviours. Hagan (1985) suggests further that there is little empirical evidence to suggest that groups adhere to deviant subcultures in which violence is considered an integral part of the group's functioning. Instead, it appears more likely that the violence is a consequence of situational factors such as opportunity and circumstance rather than a specific goal of the group.

IS MAINSTREAM CULTURE CRIMINOGENIC?

Subcultural arguments generally proceed from the assumption that it is useful to make a distinction between a subculture that somehow promotes criminality and a conformist mainstream culture that is reflected in criminal law. Yet not all theorists who have examined the relationship between crime and culture share this assumption. Some have attempted to argue that the so-called conformist culture may itself promote criminal behaviour.

For instance, an argument can be made that violence against women finds considerable support in broad patterns of cultural belief. For many feminist writers, sexual assault and wife abuse have less to do with the subcultural beliefs of a deviant minority than with pervasive cultural representations of women in mass media entertainment or advertising. When "slasher" movies, television programs, and sexually explicit, over-the-counter magazines and videos portray women as willing or deserving victims of violence, it is not surprising that the message will be picked up and acted on by some in the society.

In a similar vein, Coleman (1987) argues that the behaviour of white-collar and corporate criminals is to an important degree promoted by a "culture of competition" that defines wealth and success as the central goals of human action. He argues that criminal action in the support of either profit margins and bottom lines or personal success clearly reflects the influence of pervasive cultural beliefs. According to Coleman (1987), the "fear of failure is the inevitable correlate of the demand for success, and together they provide a set of powerful symbolic structures that are central to the motivation of economic behaviour" (417).

One of the most influential statements concerning the relationship between criminal behaviour and mainstream culture was provided by Gresham Sykes and David Matza (1961). Their analysis of juvenile delinquency led them to conclude that much youthful crime is better said to reflect *subterranean* values rather than subcultural values. Subterranean values are not, as subcultural values are, part of the belief system of some identifiable criminal minority. Instead, they are values that are held by many in society, although they may be in conflict with other cherished values.

Sykes and Matza suggest that, while many researchers have identified such values as "disdain for work" and "search for kicks and thrills" as subcultural values of delinquency, there is considerable evidence to indicate that these value orientations are much more widely held. Middle-class conformists and juvenile delinquents may express their disdain for work or search for kicks in very different ways, but the value orientations held by both groups appear to have much in common. Anyone who has seen *Terminator, Die Hard,* or similar financial-blockbuster movies would be hard pressed to make the case that violence does not have a wide cultural appeal.

According to Sykes and Matza (1957), the rules of conventional society are rarely as inflexible as subcultural theories make them out to be. In fact, those who learn the lessons of mainstream culture learn that, while criminal behaviour is usually wrong, there are times when it is not. Conventional morality prohibits acting criminally, but it also provides us with reasons why it is sometimes all right to do so. Sykes and Matza term these culturally derived justifications of criminal conduct "techniques of neutralization" and argue that, in a very real way, they make offending possible.

Sykes and Matza identify five such neutralization techniques that are used by juvenile offenders. First, by "denying responsibility" offenders express their belief that their crimes result not from ill will but from circumstances and conditions beyond their control. A second technique, "the denial of injury," is used to claim that the crime does not in fact harm others. Third, by "denying the victim" offenders accept responsibility for their actions and acknowledge the harmful consequences, but suggest that victims are to blame for what happens to them. Fourth, offenders may counteract the negative evaluations that others make of them by "condemning the condemners" (i.e., rejecting those who reject them). Finally, by "appealing to higher loyalties" offenders maintain that the actions in which they engage are necessary if obligations to family and peers are to be met.

The central point of the neutralization argument is that knowledge of techniques of neutralization precedes and makes possible involvement in criminal activity. From this perspective, people are able to break the law because they define the law as irrelevant to their own behaviour. Techniques of neutralization are acquired as one gains knowledge of the cultural environment to which one is exposed. Through this process of redefinition, individuals come to view criminal acts as acceptable and this gives them the freedom to commit such acts. The redefinition of vandalism as a "harmless prank," of assault as "getting even," or of theft as "borrowing" removes the moral inhibitions that might normally prohibit these behaviours.

Subsequent research has been unable to unequivocally support Sykes and Matza's claim that neutralization precedes rather than follows involvement in crime (Agnew and Peters, 1986; Hamlin, 1988). Recent work has attempted to account for the complexities involved in neutralization processes by arguing that neutralization is a "hardening process" (Minor, 1981). In other words, over time, criminal behaviour and techniques of neutralization become mutually reinforcing, such that attempts at neutralization may both precede and follow criminal involvement. As a result, over time, a commitment to the behaviour—and to the cultural definition of the behaviour as acceptable— intensifies. Thus, the employee who steals at work may define the pilfering as a legitimate substitute for unpaid overtime or, alternatively, as a harmless activity (given that the costs are covered by insurance). The behaviour that these definitions reinforce may also be self-reinforcing over time as the commitment to the art of stealing and the morality of stealing develop in a mutually supportive fashion.

SUMMARY AND CONCLUSIONS
■ ■ ■

"What causes some people to behave in criminal fashion?" is a question that reflects the influence of the positivist school of criminology theory, which views criminal behaviour as the product of causal forces working within or upon the offender. Sociobiologists have argued that the constitution of some individuals, programmed through their genetic structure, makes them more likely to commit crime. Wilson and Herrnstein claim that one can detect certain physiological similarities among offenders. In their view, offenders' constitutional deficiencies lead them to discount the costs of crime through a process whereby immediate gratification becomes a paramount concern. Such discounting can also be the consequence of physiological episodes brought about by problems of diet, drugs, alcohol, and so on.

There has been a strong sociological tradition criminology that emphasizes social conditions as a major influence on motivations to offend. This perspective views criminal behavior as the means by which people attempt to deal with the frustrations they face in day-to-day life. The frustrated ambitions of individuals who aspire to success goals but lack the means to achieve them result in the anomie that leads to criminal innovation. According to Robert Merton, criminogenic conditions reside in the gap between ambition and legitimate means.

This gap can widen as a result of the economic failure that comes from unemployment, particularly that which affects young people. Most crime is committed by individuals in the lower socioeconomic groups, and prisons are most likely to be filled with individuals from these communities. Some researchers have argued, though, that this is the case not necessarily because these groups are more delinquent but rather because they are easy targets for the police, who expend more effort attacking street crime than white-collar crime.

The focus on frustration led criminologists to turn attention toward gang delinquency among working-class juveniles. For Albert Cohen, much juvenile crime is rooted in the difficulties experienced by disadvantaged youth who aspire to middle-class status but are judged inadequate by a school system that assigns status rewards on the basis of middle-class criteria. Rejection of this value system, in Cohen's terms, may signal delinquency.

Labelling theorists argue that the frustration experienced by lower-class boys is not only turned into delinquency but is also amplified by the label that is applied to the offenders. The social response to minor and sporadic criminal acts may create conditions that increase the likelihood of more serious patterns of criminality. The label of criminal becomes a stigma that makes it difficult for those upon whom it has been imposed to lead normal lives. Such individuals may begin to perceive themselves as unable to lead normal lives and, as a result, fall even further into crime.

According to cultural theorists, the criminogenic conditions that influence individual behaviour emerge from the milieu in which offenders operate. It is not necessary to assume that there is anything pathological about offenders, only that they have learned a particular set of cultural lessons that, in their case, teaches them how to act criminally. Their behaviour, then, is normal within a particular cultural context and explicable given that they have been thrust outside of the normal operations of society. The same process that ostracizes offenders also serves to strengthen the bonds between insiders, as sanctions are applied against norm violators.

It is possible, then, to look at criminals as outsiders who are punished for failing to conform to the explicit norms of the dominant culture. It is also possible to look upon certain criminal behaviour as normative. Sutherland's differential association theory proposes that crime is learned behavior. For Sutherland, the differential rate at which criminals associate with the carriers of criminal values determines the differential rate at which they engage in criminal conduct. This perspective allows us to deal with the fact that certain cultural insiders, while adhering to the law in their personal lives, commit crimes in the context of their working lives.

The idea that there may be more than one set of values in society raises the possibility that mainstream culture is itself criminogenic. Sykes and Matza argue that those who learn the lessons of mainstream culture learn that, while criminal behaviour is usually wrong, there are times when it is not. Some acts can be rationalized or neutralized with explanations that find their basis in the tenets of mainstream society.

3
OFFENDING, SOCIAL CONTROL, AND THE LAW

THE THEORIES DISCUSSED IN the previous chapter would seem to suggest that since criminal behaviour has unique characteristics, it requires unique motivations. However, by putting so much energy into trying to determine what unique types of social arrangements or cultural exposure drive crime, motivational theories risk losing sight of a basic question, namely, is motivation sufficient or necessary to explain offending? Just because individuals are moved or inclined to behave in a particular way, does this mean that they will? Motivational theories assume that it is the propensity, desire, or willingness to offend that separates offenders from nonoffenders.

But many theorists do not agree with this position. They argue that motivation to behave criminally is probably much more widespread than actual criminal behaviour. We can all think of occasions when lying, cheating, or stealing may have been the most effective way of achieving the goals we were interested in pursuing. According to critics of motivational theories, what separates the offender from the nonoffender has less to do with the presence of motivation and more to do with the ability to act on this motivation. This position acknowledges that we are not always free to act in ways consistent with our motivations.

In this chapter, we examine approaches that focus on the ways in which informal and formal social controls influence criminal offending. The overall message to be learned from these perspectives is that criminal behaviour may not require a distinct or unique criminal motivation. Instead, people may offend when the social pressures that might prevent them from doing so are weak or absent. Thus, criminal behaviour is not so much the product of criminogenic forces as it is a rational choice made by individuals who feel no constraints about engaging in it. The emphasis on rationality, choice, and control reflects the legacy of the classical school of thought.

We begin by addressing the role played by informal social controls in suppressing criminal behaviour, and then move to a discussion of the law and its capacity to deter.

SOCIAL TIES TO CONFORMIST OTHERS

It has been argued that the social relationships that people share with others who support and promote the values of conformity are an important source of social control. Many theorists have argued, for instance, that the strength and quality of social ties that link juveniles to their (conformist) teachers, parents, and peers discourage involvement in delinquency.

WHAT DOES IT INCLUDE?

Theory of the Bond

The first strand, *attachment*, refers to the degree to which children are sensitive to the expectations of parents or teachers. *Commitment* refers to the size of the investment of time and energy that a youth has made to a conventional activity such as getting good grades. The third strand is *involvement*. Involvement in the world of conformity leaves little time for involvement in delinquency. The fourth strand, *belief*, refers to the degree to which youth believe that the conformist values of parents and teachers are worthy of respect.

Strong ties to parents, for instance, make possible effective adult monitoring and supervision of juvenile leisure activity (Gottfredson and Hirschi, 1990; Wells and Rankin, 1988, 1991). Parent–child relationships that are characterized by caring, trust, and intimate communication offer support to adolescents who may be contemplating delinquent reactions to the problems that face them (Patterson and Dishion, 1985).

The most influential statement of the relationship between social ties and social control is Travis Hirschi's theory of the bond. Hirschi (1969) argues that the causes of juvenile delinquency are not to be located in some type of unique delinquent motivation but rather in the weakness of the social bond that links delinquent adults to the world of conformist others. Weak bonds allow individuals to formulate behavioural intentions that reflect narrow self-interest. Lying, cheating, and stealing are frequently the outcome.

For Hirschi, the bond to conformist society is composed of four distinct strands. The first strand, *attachment*, refers to the degree to which children are sensitive to the expectations of parents or teachers. Sensitivity to expectations means that the potential reactions of conformist others must be taken into account when delinquency is contemplated. If a youth cares about the views of parents or teachers, delinquency is defined as a less attractive option.

The second strand, *commitment,* refers to the amount of time and energy that a youth has invested in a conventional activity such as obtaining good grades. According to Hirschi, the greater the investment, the less likely juveniles are to engage in behaviour that jeopardizes it.

The third strand is *involvement*. Hirschi points out that the world of conformity is a world of jobs to be done, projects to be undertaken, goals to be achieved, and deadlines to be met. In short, involvement in the world of conformity leaves little time for involvement in delinquency. Hirschi reminds us of the old adage that "idle hands are the devil's workshop."

The fourth element of the bond is *belief*. In Hirschi's view, one need not argue, as subcultural theorists do, that delinquents are committed to a set of distinctly delinquent values. Instead, one need argue only that juveniles differ in the extent to which they believe that the conformist values of parents, teachers, or others are worthy of respect.

Strong social bonds—defined by Hirschi as high levels of attachment, commitment, involvement, and belief—insulate youth against delinquent involvement. In order to explain the reasons why some youth are delinquent while others are not, we need to focus on the weakness of delinquents' bonds rather than on the factors that motivate them to behave in criminal fashion.

Power-control theory, which was developed by John Hagan, Ron Gillis, and John Simpson (Hagan, 1989; Hagan, Simpson, and Gillis, 1979, 1987, 1988) at the University of Toronto, provides another example of the ways in which family relationships permit or discourage delinquency. Of central interest to these writers is the fact that males are much more delinquent than females. Hagan, Gillis, and Simpson attempt to explain this fact in terms of the differential ability of the family to control male and female children.

Power-control theory argues that social control is stratified within the family setting. In traditional patriarchal families, which accept a cultural claim to male dominance, girls are subject to greater control than boys. In addition, mothers are assigned a greater responsibility for the control of dependent children. Two important implications follow from this position. First, the informal social control processes in which family members are involved affect female more than male family members. Mothers are more likely to be the subjects and daughters are more likely to be the objects of this control. Second, as a result of these differences, male children are considerably freer than female children to engage in a wide range of risktaking behaviour, some of which involves delinquency.

Terrence Thornberry (1987; Thornberry et al., 1991) and his colleagues refine arguments that link the quality and character of social relationships to controls over criminal conduct by proposing an *interactional theory of delinquency*. The central point of this theory is that, while weak social bonds to parents or teachers may make delinquency possible, delinquency that has already occurred may further affect these relationships. Consider the example of a youth whose weak bond to parents contributes to his or her engagement in delinquent activities. When the parents learn about the delinquency, they may react by rejecting the youth or by subjecting him or her to severe punishment. Such reactions may further undermine the relationship between child and parents, thus making delinquency an even greater probability. In terms of illuminating the criminal event, the real strength of Thornberry's argument is that it attempts to come to terms with the dynamic and fluid character of criminality.

INFORMAL SOCIAL CONTROLS IN THE COMMUNITY

Other theorists have speculated about the roles played by informal social control at the level of the local community or the neighbourhood. According to Wirth (1938), the larger, the more densely populated, and the more heterogeneous a community, the more accentuated are the characteristics associated with urbanism, including loneliness and social breakdown. Urbanism brings together individuals who have no sentimental or emotional ties to one another. From this emerges a spirit of competition, aggrandizement, and exploitation. To counteract this spirit, society reverts to formal controls.

People who are in frequent social contact with strangers and acquaintances also develop a reserve toward one another. The strong family and friendship ties that are necessary for intimate communities disappear in cities, and the result is higher levels of alienation, anomie, and delinquency. To prove the point, Wirth points out that crime rates in urban areas are higher than those in rural areas, where the informal social controls between intimates still operate.

If some urban neighbourhoods more effectively constrain the delinquent inclination of resident youth, then we might be able to explain why some parts of the city have higher rates of delinquency than do other parts of the city. Theoretical arguments of this type were originally proposed by Clifford Shaw and Henry McKay, two sociologists associated with the University of Chicago. Shaw and McKay (1942) were interested in trying to understand why some parts of the city of Chicago had consistently high rates of crime, delinquency, and other social problems. What intrigued them was the fact that rates of delinquency remained high even when the resident population, identified at any given point in time, moved out or died and were then replaced by new groups of urban residents. In other words, regardless of changes in the ethnic mix of the population residing within an area, rates of delinquency were relatively constant. For Shaw and McKay, urban variations in rates of crime are associated with the social context of urban areas rather than with the specific characteristics of the populations who live there.

According to Shaw and McKay, high-crime areas are characterized by a high degree of *social disorganization,* which may be defined as an inability on the part of area residents to achieve their common values or solve their common problems (Kornhauser, 1978). Shaw and McKay argue that areas characterized by a high level of social disorganization tend to be economically disadvantaged, to have a high level of population turnover, and to be home to diverse groups of racial and ethnic residents. In such areas, the informal social controls that might be expected to constrain delinquency are ineffective. As predicted by Wirth, local friendship networks are less likely to develop and the level of participation in formal or voluntary organizations is low. As a result, adults in these communities may be ineffective in their attempts to supervise or control teenage peer groups that are likely to become involved in delinquency (Sampson and Groves, 1989).

We see the logic of the social disorganization argument manifested in many forms of crime prevention that attempt to recreate a sense of community in high-crime neighbourhoods. Neighbourhood Watch and similar programs aim to increase the level of interaction among residents and at the same time to encourage them to develop a sense of responsibility for their neighbours.

Fischer (1976) argues that the city is not as disorienting—and its inhabitants not as vulnerable to social breakdown—as Wirth maintains. He points out that urban environments actually provide more opportunities for social support than do rural areas, and that the ties extend beyond the boundaries of neighborhoods to stretch across the city. In a direct test of Fischer's thesis, Tittle (1989) finds little support for the idea that large cities contain greater opportunities for deviance. The relatively minor effect of size of place on subcultures may be a function, Tittle speculates, of the access to information that is facilitated by modern technology, diminishing the need for a "critical mass" that would support deviant cultures. City size does, however, tend to increase noncriminal conflict among already existing subcultures.

According to Krohn, Lanza-Kaduce, and Akers (1984), Wirth's view of cities reflects the argument that deviant behaviour is a result of the weakening or severing of one or more of the social bonds (Hirschi, 1969). This perspective is consistent with the arguments put forward by control theories. Fischer's portrayal of an integrated but highly diverse urban setting offers a different view, one that emphasizes that learning deviant behaviour results from (differential) association with people who provide models, definitions, and reinforcements for such behaviour (Krohn, Lanza-Kaduce, and Akers, 1984: 355).

Krohn, Lanza-Kaduce, and Akers speculate that the differences in explanation provided by Wirth and Fischer revolve around the quality of the primary relationships across communities. Wellman and Leighton (1979) argue that modern cities have replaced intimate, spatially bounded communities with "liberated" communities (i.e., a network of friends and acquaintances who live outside of the individual's neighbourhood). Despite the view that the neighbourhood is not essential to social support, neighbourhoods that have a high degree of interaction are more likely to control crime informally through the residents' collective ability to respond to violations of the law and/or norms of their neighbourhood (Unger and Wandersman, 1985: 143). This informal control depends, however, on the neighbourhood having a consensus on values or norms, the ability to monitor behaviour, and a willingness to intervene when necessary. These characteristics are generally absent in urban neighbourhoods where crime is high.

While interpersonal conflict is a pervasive and inevitable feature of social life (Kennedy, 1990), most conflicts are resolved in a peaceful fashion. We might avoid the conflicting parties, give in to the demands that they make, report them to the police, or sue them. Horowitz (1990) points out that the law does not respond to all grievances in the same way. A teenager who complains that his elderly neighbours have been playing their Zamfir records too loudly will probably receive a cooler reception from the police than the elderly neighbour who complains about the volume of the teenager's Megadeth music. However, it has been argued by social conflict theorists that poor and racial communities are less effectively policed than more middle-class neighbourhoods, and that behaviour that would not be tolerated in higher-status areas is considered "normal" in areas characterized by greater social or economic disadvantage. These observations imply that teenagers or those who are socially disadvantaged may be more likely to engage in violent or other criminal forms of conflict expression in large part because the law is less available as a means for resolving conflicts. In some cases, these formal responses suggest an "overreach" of the law, the implication being that there is a low tolerance exhibited for certain behaviour that could be handled more effectively through informal sanction (Morris and Hawkins, 1970).

The incidence of crime may also depend on interethnic and interracial relationships that develop in areas where groups of different backgrounds come together. The confusion and misunderstandings that arise from differences in family practice and cultural values can lead to tensions and conflicts, which can develop into criminal behaviour along the lines proposed by Sellin (1938). Research by Smith (1982) suggests that many people use ethnic stereotyping as a pragmatic means of managing the dangers of urban life. These informal strategies usually entail setting up social and physical distances in order to avoid potentially harmful encounters. The avoidance of certain areas is a common strategy for coping with crime in urban centres.

In addition, Suttles (1972) found that, particularly in ethnic communities, boundaries are set by public displays of territorial marking (e.g., threatened gang fights). These boundaries indicate, through spatial mechanisms, "with whom it is safe to associate" (Suttles, 1972: 161). The marking of territory plays a role in reducing neighbourhood conflict by excluding those who are considered to be different or undesirable. Conflict with people outside of the neighbourhood takes on a symbolic character of threat and protectiveness to turf. A person's adaptation to a city full of anonymous strangers is facilitated by the use of neighbourhood structures that bring him or her into contact with trustworthy individuals.

In disorganized areas, people are less likely to know their neighbours or to be interested in their welfare. The high degree of cultural distance between different groups inhabiting the area and the rapid turnover of population mitigates against the development of a strong sense of community spirit. It is more difficult to monitor the behaviour of others in the neighbourhood when we do not recognize them and thus do not know whether or not they have a right to be there (Stark, 1987). Under such circumstances, we are not only less likely to fail to recognize people, we are also less likely to recognize their property; thus, stolen property that is carried around the neighbourhood by a stranger, or by someone we know, is unlikely to be identified (Felson, 1986). By contrast, in small, tightly knit communities in which the residents know one another both culturally and personally, we expect that informal community control will operate more effectively.

Many of the social institutions that might be expected to control the behaviour of youthful offenders are also less effective in socially disorganized areas. Churches and schools, for instance, may not enjoy a high level of community support and, as a result, their social control functions may be undermined (Stark, 1987). In well-integrated areas, we might expect that community organizations will form in response to the problem of local crime or delinquency. However, when the level of social disorganization is high, voluntary groups organized around the solution of community problems are less likely to develop.

RATIONAL OFFENDERS AND THE LAW

We need now to consider the process through which individuals arrive at a decision to break the law. The rational model proposed by the classical perspective suggests that individuals weigh the costs involved in pursuing deviant behavior and judge the likelihood of punishment in the event of detection. There are those, however, who argue that the rational model is restrictive in terms of how the law is created and administered. These critics of classical theory recommend that deterrence strategies, which emphasize punishment, be replaced by methods that encourage negotiation and mediation.

A weakness in the positivist explanations of crime is that they do not consider how deterrence works to reduce crime. While punishment strategies are not completely ignored in the positivist literature, since incarceration is one way to discourage motivated offenders from committing more crime, they are not considered in terms of their importance in stopping offenders from an *initial involvement* in crime events. To understand how the classicists have presented deterrence as a key element in reducing criminality, we provide a review of the deterrence doctrine below.

THE POWER OF LAW: THE DETERRENCE DOCTRINE

Laws threaten penalties for their violation and deterrence theories are concerned with the ways in which these threats are communicated to potential offenders. More specifically, deterrence theories attempt to determine how the reaction to the threat of penalties decreases the likelihood of offending. *Specific* or *special deterrence* refers to the ways in which individuals are deterred, through punishment, from offending or re-offending. For example, suppose you break into a house. You are apprehended for this crime and then sentenced to prison for a period of time. The prison term is considered to be a punishment that

WHAT DOES IT MEAN?

Specific vs. General Deterrence

Specific deterrence refers to the ways in which individuals are deterred from offending or re-offending by receiving punishment. *General* deterrence argues that individuals who see offenders who are like them receiving punishment will be deterred from breaking the law themselves.

is sufficient to deter you from repeating the crime. According to the principle of *general deterrence*, individuals are deterred from breaking the law when they see others who have done so receive punishment. Thus, in our examples, friends who witness the punishment that you receive for having broken the law will desist from breaking and entering.

BOX 3.1   THE PERCEPTION OF LEGAL AND OTHER THREATS

Arguments in support of deterrence assume that people will be discouraged from engaging in crime if they perceive as salient the threats of the criminal law. How do people perceive these threats? And how, in relative terms, do the risks of legal punishment compare with the risks of other misfortunes associated with illegal conduct?

A national study on drinking and driving provides some data that address these questions. The survey, which was sponsored by Health and Welfare Canada (1989), collected information about the beliefs, perceptions, and behaviour of approximately 10,000 Canadians in the ten provinces.

The survey revealed that more than one-third of Canadians aged 16 to 69 acted, the previous year, in at least one of several specific ways to avoid drinking and driving. Approximately one-half of these people said that they feared having an accident, while just over one-third said that they were afraid of getting caught by the police. Another 18 percent were afraid that they might lose their driver's licence or be jailed.

Respondents' reactions to the following hypothetical scenario further illustrate the nature of their perceptions:

A person goes to a bar after work to have a drink with friends, drinks enough to be impaired, and then drives five miles home.

In these circumstances, only a small proportion of Canadians (10 percent) think the chances are high that the police will stop the driver on the way home. However, more than a third (34 percent) believe the driver is highly likely to have an accident. The same people who think the impaired driver will *not* be stopped by police on the way home are the ones who are most likely to say they themselves have driven after drinking. However, those who think the chances are high that the impaired driver will have an accident are less likely to report drinking and driving themselves.

Having stopped the impaired driver, will the police lay a charge? Over half (54 percent) of Canadians feel this is highly probable. Not unexpectedly, a higher proportion of those who think the driver is unlikely to be charged also say they have driven after drinking. However, this group is also more likely to think that if the driver is charged, a drinking-and-driving conviction will follow.

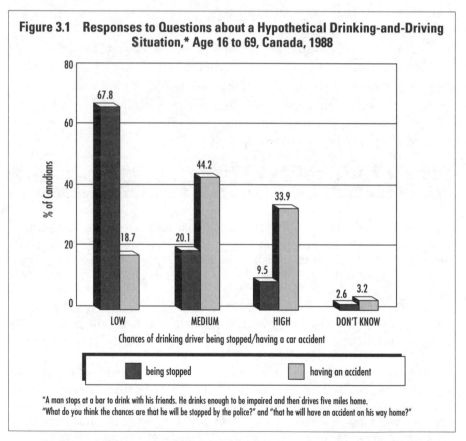

Figure 3.1   Responses to Questions about a Hypothetical Drinking-and-Driving Situation,* Age 16 to 69, Canada, 1988

% of Canadians

Chances of drinking driver being stopped/having a car accident

■ being stopped   ▨ having an accident

*A man stops at a bar to drink with his friends. He drinks enough to be impaired and then drives five miles home.
"What do you think the chances are that he will be stopped by the police?" and "that he will have an accident on his way home?"

Source: Health and Welfare Canada, *National Survey on Driving and Drinking, 1988: Overview Report.* Reproduced with permission of the Minister of Supply and Services Canada, 1993.

The success of specific and general deterrence is based on three properties of legal threats. The first such property is the *severity* of the penalty. Does the law threaten prison or a fine? Are offenders likely to be sentenced if they are caught, or are they likely to be released with a warning? The criminal law clearly states the punishment attached to each crime, and sentencing guidelines are set for judges to apply in the cases that come before them.

It is assumed that all individuals in society are aware of the law's prescriptions about punishment and are deterred in direct proportion to the escalating threat of this punishment. So, it should be widely understood that homicide is the most serious of all crimes and receives the greatest penalty. For first-degree murder (i.e., murder in which the killing is premeditated) Canadian criminal law states that the offender will receive a mandatory life sentence with a prison term of 25 years. Thefts and other property crimes are punished less severely. For these crimes, specific dollar limits (currently under $1,000 and over $1,000) are used to prescribe different levels of punishment. An ongoing review of the Criminal Code and its sentencing guidelines influences the ways in which punishments are meted out in society. The increased interest in such crimes as assaults within the family has resulted in the creation of new categories of offences, which may, in turn, affect the placement of already established crimes in the hierarchy of punishments.

The second property of legal threats is the *certainty* of punishment. Regardless of what the law threatens, how likely is it that an offender will be apprehended? A large number of research studies have argued that, with respect to possible deterrent effects, certainty is a more important characteristic of legal penalties than is severity. In other words, a high likelihood of being punished is more important than a lower likelihood of being punished in a specified manner.

Certainty of apprehension is clearly influenced by factors that relate to the reporting of crime. As we saw in Chapter 1, the majority of the crimes that are known to the police were brought to their attention by the public. For various reasons, however, many crimes go unreported. Furthermore, many crimes that *are* reported remain unsolved. In both cases, the offender "gets away" with the crime. The rational offender calculates the certainty of risk and then acts on this calculation: when risk is high, the crime is less likely to occur.

The third characteristic of legal threats is the *celerity* (swiftness) of punishment (Clark, 1988). When justice is delayed, there may be a perception that the punishment is either unfair or that it will have a diminished impact on the offender. Concern has also been raised that delayed justice may unfairly stigmatize an individual who is in fact innocent. Recently, in Ontario, the court backlog was such that the delay to hear cases would have run longer than a year. In the interest of fairness, many cases were simply dismissed without trial (i.e., without the determination of guilt or innocence). The message conveyed by these dismissals was that the criminal justice system is unable to handle cases swiftly and that this circumstance casts doubt on the likelihood of its handling them at all.

It has been argued that, in emphasizing the importance of penalty characteristics, deterrence theories have adopted too narrow a view of how legal threats discourage crime. Williams and Hawkins (1986) argue that the deterrent effects of legal sanctions may be supplemented by at least three types of sanctions: commitment costs, attachment costs, and the stigma the of arrest.

Commitment costs refer to the possibility that arrest may cause people to jeopardize the investments that they have made in some legitimate form of activity. The greater a person's investment in some conformist line of activity, the more he or she will be discouraged from offending by a belief that arrest might threaten that investment. Commitment costs may include concerns about future employment or educational prospects. *Attachment costs* refer to the costs associated with the loss of valued relationships with friends or family members. The belief that arrest will weaken these ties may make arrest a fearsome prospect.

Finally, the *stigma of arrest* relates to the belief that apprehension by the police may do harm to one's reputation. It is important to distinguish this fear that others will learn about one's arrest from the fear that they will learn that one has done the act. Williams and Hawkins point out that there is generally a lower stigma associated with driving while impaired than there is with being arrested for this action. In the case of homicide, however, the stigma associated with arrest for the act may not be much greater than the stigma associated with the commission of the act. In general, Williams and Hawkins argue that because attachment costs, commitment costs, and the stigma of arrest are forms of informal social control that are activated by formal controls, they should be viewed as part of the deterrence process.

An illustration of how this mix of legal and informal sanctions can work is provided by recent research on the contribution of arrest to the reduction of repeat wife assault. Dutton et al. (1992) examined data from Vancouver and Alberta. They compared results from a general population sample taken in Alberta with those from a group of arrested and convicted wife assaulters who were undergoing treatment, in Vancouver, in a court-mandated program for assaultive husbands. Respondents were asked to express their views of the likelihood (certainty) of specific legal and social sanctions, assuming they were to assault their wives. They were also asked to judge the severity of the punishment that would follow such an assault. Police arrest was among the legal sanctions offered. The social sanctions included police being called, partner leaving the relationship, disapproval of friends and family, and loss of self-respect.

The arrested assaulters reported a greater degree of confidence than those in the general sample that an arrest would occur if an assault took place. Interestingly, the general and treatment samples had similar responses to the question relating to the loss of self-respect. In terms of severity, the two samples were high with respect to all factors. Thus, deterrence appears to be not only a function of the arrest but also the social consequence of the arrest.

To test this theory further, responses made by assaulters before they entered the treatment program were compared with those made at the end of the treatment about a year later. Not only was there an increase in the perceived severity of arrest and conviction, but it was accompanied by a substantial increase in the judgment of the perceived severity of losing one's partner or facing social disapproval. According to Dutton et al. (1992), disclosure of these events, which are often kept private, can "be a first step toward generating informal sanctions from friends and family toward the assaultive male and an empowering support network for the victim. Because arrest makes disclosure more likely, that informal side effect of arrest could serve to reduce recidivism" (124). Here we have a case of legal sanction (arrest) and informal sanction (social disapproval) working together to increase deterrence.

Arguments about the deterrent properties of legal sanctions do not assume that potential offenders are accurately informed about the risks they face. How accurate their perceptions are is itself an empirical question of considerable scope (Henshel and Silverman, 1975). It can be suggested, however, that in terms of whether or not an individual will offend, what the law actually threatens is less significant than what people *believe* the law threatens.

AMBIVALENCE ABOUT CRIME AND DETERRENCE STRATEGIES

It is clear that deterrence arguments figure quite prominently in many public policy debates. Despite the perception that there is widespread consensus on the need to crack down on crime, public attitudes toward crime and its prevention suggest a strong degree of ambivalence, an ambivalence that has many sources. First, the public is concerned that the law is not adequately enforced (Currie, 1985). Research in this country suggests that Canadians feel that the law generally reflects their values (Moore, 1985: 48) and that they obey the law because they believe it to be right. At the same time, however, they are critical of the way in which justice is currently being dispensed. Many believe that the law favours the rich and the powerful, and that the legal process is too slow. The system as a whole is seen as ineffective in deterring serious crime, particularly in terms of the punishment that is administered (Brillon, 1985).

There is no consensus in the research literature, however, concerning the effectiveness of punishment in reducing criminal behaviour. Cook (1977) concludes from his review of the research on deterrent effects (including the impact of capital punishment on the eradication of violent crime) that little persuasive evidence has been produced concerning the size, or even the existence, of the deterrence mechanism. The lack of strong support in the research literature makes questionable proposals for strict punishment regimes, especially if they are contrary to our views of what is humane and just.

Second, as Braithwaite (1989) points out, confusion develops over what is perceived as a conflict between crime control and respect for civil liberties. There is a concern among some that too much informal social control impedes one's freedom. Neighbours spying on neighbours can be a real threat to personal privacy. However, punishment delivered by formal agents without the shaming that comes from informal social sanctions is ineffective. If the risk of arrest is perceived as low and the severity of punishment minimal, individuals may still be prevented from committing a crime by the stigmatizing reactions of others for being involved in crime itself, a point made above.

A third problem that contributes to ambivalence about crime is the indecision about the viability of expensive and seemingly ineffective incarceration (Miller and Anderson, 1986). As much as we would like to believe that there is value in decarceration, our society has formalized not only punishment but reintegration as well. Few communities are ready to receive criminals as they begin their transition to "normal" life. What this means is that just as informal sanctions are needed to deter crime, they are also needed when it comes to reintegrating offenders into society and keeping them from re-offending.

A fourth and final factor contributing to the ambivalence about crime is the general awe with which we regard it. While the reality of violent criminality is usually horrific, its depiction in the media is tempting, thrilling, and addictive. Promoting pro-social behaviour in a society in which criminals are often depicted as folk heroes is no easy task (Phelps, 1983). While Skipper (1985) suggests that the folk hero syndrome is on the decline, there still exists in our society a residual belief that the criminal should be admired for expressing some degree of resistance to convention.

North American ambivalence about the application of deterrence strategies is in sharp contrast to the Chinese government's actions subsequent to the army's move to destroy the "democracy movement" through the Tiananmen Square massacre in June of 1989. The show trials and rapidly ensuing executions provided a display of the ferociousness of Chinese justice, and yet they conformed very neatly to the principles outlined in the deterrence doctrine: that there be quick, certain, and severe punishment that incapacitates the offender and discourages others from following the same route.

What is interesting about the Chinese experience is that the democracy movement flourished at all, given the knowledge that draconian steps almost certainly would be used to effect its downfall. This fact underlines the role of the offender's perception about the nature of the crime being committed, the chances of getting away with it, and the likelihood of punishment if apprehended. In the Chinese case, there appeared to be a widespread belief that the democracy movement derived its moral strength from the widespread public support and contributed to some new form of ambivalence about punishment *(New York Times Magazine, 1989)*. The movement was further justified by its exposure of abuses of power on the part of those in government. The failure of the democracy movement may be summed up with the truism that, without the instruments of power, it is difficult to effect change. The power to sanction remained in the hands of government officials, who used this power to provoke and then criminalize their critics. Time will tell how effective the punishment has been in deterring further dissent. In the short term at least, it has been very effective in purging "criminal" elements from China's political scene.

REACTIONS TO CRIME

Why are some kinds of criminal events aggressively pursued by the criminal justice system while others do not seem to arouse much indignation? How do some types of "crime problems" become the central concern of policy-makers who talk about "the war on drugs" or the need for "zero tolerance" of family violence? Where do the laws that deem some types of events as criminal come from in the first place? Such questions require a systematic understanding of the social processes that shape and constrain organized reaction to criminal events. Theoretical approaches to these issues help us to recognize that these reactions should be understood not only as the decisions of police officers, policy-makers, or politicians but also as part of larger social processes that affect behaviour at the individual level.

BOX 3.2   CAN CRIME CAUSE CRIME?

Some researchers have argued that public reactions to rising crime rates can amplify subsequent crime-rate increases. The central mechanism in this process is the breakdown of informal social control at the community level. Lynne Goodstein and Lance Shotland (1982) have described the processes by which crime rates spiral upward as follows.

The cycle begins with actual increases in the crime rate or with the occurrence of one or several crimes that are particularly noteworthy. Such crimes might include an unsolved murder or a series of sexual assaults for which an offender has not been apprehended.

In the next stage, information about these crimes and the threats that they pose to other members of the community is disseminated widely. People learn via the mass media or rumour networks that crimes are increasing and/or that people like them are at risk.

As the information circulates, people begin to fear for their safety. This fear causes them to withdraw from the life of the community. They stay home at night rather than go out, and report that their enjoyment of the community has declined.

As people withdraw from the community, the delicate web of social relations begins to break down, as do the various informal social controls that regulate conduct. Thus, as the streets become less populated, they are subject to less control because citizen surveillance of them is reduced.

As the levels of community control decline, the levels of crime may be expected to rise; and as the levels of crime continue to rise, the cycle begins to repeat itself.

Goodstein and Shotland's argument is consistent with the theoretical view that crime is made more likely by the absence of controls that check it. As the authors note, there is empirical evidence to support each of the individual linkages described above. What is less clear, however, is the validity of the overall model, which has not been rigorously tested in its entirety.

Two theoretical explanations have been advanced to account for reactions to crime. One argues that these reactions emerge out of and reflect a social consensus about morality and about the need to respond to particular types of events in particular ways. The other view suggests that it is more appropriate to think about reactions to crime as having more to do with power, conflict, and inequality than with social consensus.

At a very broad level, these approaches may be distinguished with respect to the ways in which they conceptualize the role of social interests (Bockman, 1991). From the point of view of consensus theories, the members of a society have many interests in common and their reactions to crime may be said to serve these collective interests. Laws are written and enforced to meet the needs of the majority. Deviation from these laws is generally accepted as reason for punishment. Conflict theorists, on the other hand, argue that in a complex society social groups may pursue different interests and that the degree of success with which they do so depends on how powerful they are. In this framework, reactions to crime can be understood as reflecting particular class, cultural, or other social interests rather than more broadly defined collective interests.

THE CONSENSUS VIEW

In the study of reactions to crime, the concept of social consensus is meant to alert us to the apparently broad-based agreement in society about what kinds of acts are serious crimes and deserving of direct and immediate intervention and what types are not. This argument, which relates to our discussion of crime as an attack on social morality, is associated with a number of important scholars (Durkheim, 1964; Parsons, 1951; Pound, 1943). It suggests that, even in a complex, highly differentiated society like our own, people who differ from one another in terms of gender, age, ethnicity, and social class are likely to be in agreement about certain basic moral questions.

> **WHAT DOES IT MEAN?**
>
> *Consensus vs. Conflict*
>
> Social consensus is meant to alert us to the apparent broad-based agreement in society about what kinds of acts are serious crimes deserving of direct and immediate intervention and what types are not. Conflict approaches argue that responses to crime must be seen as part of a larger struggle between groups that attempt to use the law, or legal control, in the pursuit of their interests.

As we have said, deterrence is directed toward a commonly agreed-upon set of behaviours that offend social mores. We punish murderers more severely than we punish other criminals because there is a general agreement in society that murder is among the most serious infractions that a person can commit. We "criminalize," through the passage of law, behaviours that are widely understood as threatening to our shared values, and we attach the most severe penalties to those crimes that offend our sense of collective morality most deeply.

The consensus view has gone so far as to say that crime is functional, an idea that originated in the work of Emile Durkheim. According to the functional approach, without the contrast to "normal" behaviour that is provided by crime, we would have difficulty establishing acceptable and tolerable limits to human actions. Criminal definitions provide us with the boundaries of behaviour beyond which we should not, and dare not, go. As Kennedy (1990) notes, these boundaries create the illusion that crime is an isolated phenomenon, unrelated to other types of social activity. Theories of crime are based on classifications of the social forms and factors that are associated with criminal behaviour (Cain and Kulscar, 1981–82: 386). The preclusive view of delinquent behaviour that results from placing artificial borders around crime discourages criminologists from addressing conflict that occurs beyond these borders, conflict that may motivate crime in the first place. Using a functionalist perspective, there is no necessity to address the idea that the boundaries around crime may change as a result of change in individual and criminal justice system responses to criminal behaviour.

From the functionalist point of view, reactions to crime, as expressed in criminalization or punishment, may be understood as one of the most basic ways in which our sense of collective morality is communicated. The moral indignation expressed by the passage of a law, the policy decision to increase the penalties associated with a given type of crime, and the punishment of an offender are all reminders of what it is that binds us together as members of society. Consistent with this view, a large body of public opinion research indicates that, by and large, our legal responses to crime reflect widespread social sentiments (Cullen, Link, and Polanzi, 1982; Goff and Nason-Clark, 1989; Hansel, 1987; Miethe, 1982; Rossi et al., 1974; Sigler and Johnson, 1986; Warr, 1989).

The consensus position and the research it has spawned have attracted much criticism. Most generally, it has been argued that the consensus view oversimplifies the complex relationships between groups that pursue different interests with varying levels of resources. To measure consensus in a public opinion survey begs the question of where the consensus comes from in the first place. It is one thing to argue that a consensus spontaneously emerges from the collective will of the population and quite another to suggest that it results from the fact that some individuals have a vested interest in reacting to criminal events in a particular way and are able to convince the rest of us that their view of the world is the right one. In either case, we might find that public opinion data reveal widespread agreement about the relative seriousness of different crimes.

BOX 3.3   DON'T SOME LAWS REFLECT CONSENSUS?

The view that the law emerges out of and reflects special interests seems to be contradicted by the common-sense observation that some laws at least seem to reflect the interests of everyone in society. Laws against murder, robbery, or sexual assault would seem to be in everyone's interest rather than in the interests of only those who have the most power.

However, the late British sociologist Steven Box (1981) argued that it is not really correct to say that the law prohibits murder, sexual assault, or robbery. Rather, it prohibits certain types of such behaviours and at the same time does not prohibit other behaviours, which, while very similar, are likely to be committed by more powerful people.

With respect to murder, for instance, Box wrote that

the criminal code defines only some types of killing as murder; it excludes, for example, deaths which result from negligence such as employers' failure to maintain safe working conditions in factories or mines ... or deaths which result from government agencies' giving environmental health risks a low priority ... or death resulting from drug manufacturers' failure to conduct adequate research on new chemical compounds before conducting aggressive marketing campaigns (48).

Box concluded that

criminal laws against murder, rape, robbery and assault do protect us all, but they do not protect the less powerful from being killed, sexually exploited, deprived of their property, or physically or psychologically damaged through the greed, apathy, negligence and the unaccountability of the relatively more powerful (49).

Further, by assuming that crime is functional, we justify actions that are taken by the state to repress certain groups. The actions of the police and the judiciary become focused on the disadvantaged, on visible minorities, and on other groups that lack the resources to escape this kind of attention. Such criminalization is dysfunctional in that it exacts a human cost and at the same time devalues initiatives that attempt to deal with the problems faced by these groups in ways other than through law enforcement.

Sellin (1938) cautions that using an unqualified set of *legal* definitions as the basic units or elements of criminological inquiry violates a fundamental criterion of science. The scientist must be free to define his or her own terms in attempting to understand the crime event. Accepting without qualification the definitions of crime and criminals as laid down in law renders criminological research theoretically invalid from the point of view of science (Sellin, 1938: 24). What is necessary, from Sellin's point of view, is an approach to crime in which the definitions of criminal behaviour can change and evolve depending on the nature of the interactions among individuals and between them and the agencies that administer control over social behaviour. The way in which we articulate the problem of crime can help us focus on its root causes. Closing our minds to the flexibility that may characterize definitions of the criminal event will probably lead us to deal only with the symptoms of crime and not with the reasons for its development. However, we must know not just *what* these definitions entail but also *how* they are developed (Kennedy, 1990). Further, the negotiation of justice may be a reflection not only of what the agents of social control *can* do but also what they are *prepared* to do in attacking crime.

The definitions of crime through law, then, may be seen as unchangeable, determined by the rules of evidence in establishing guilt or innocence. Alternatively, law can be seen as defining the boundaries of behaviours that are unacceptable depending on circumstance, public tolerance, and judicial discretion. Agents of social control use the law not only to deter crime and punish criminals but also to reduce social conflict. Some behaviour that is *not* dealt with through the formal application of law may be disorderly, threatening, or dangerous. Any study of crime needs to account for behaviour that has these characteristics but is not yet unlawful. Criminologists must also consider alternative responses, such as community-based mediation, which have developed in society as a means of dealing with this kind of behaviour. Even though they do not elicit any specific legal sanction, alternative, or informal, responses establish the outside limits of criminality by redefining criminal justice responses to misbehaviour.

CONFLICT, POWER, AND THE RESPONSE TO CRIME

In contrast to the older consensus view, conflict theorists argue that, even if a consensus exists on what constitutes a serious crime and what does not, it is important to understand the source of the consensus. Moreover, they argue that it is incorrect to maintain that this consensus is a spontaneous product of group life. As one critic of the consensus position has recently written,

> Laws do not simply appear miraculously on our law books and do not reflect "society's" values. Instead, the acts and people we call "criminal" and our concern with crime at any given time reflect the activity of groups in this society seeking legal support for economic, ideological and status interest (Sheley, 1991: 39).

From this standpoint, responses to crime must be seen as part of a larger struggle between groups that attempt to use the law, or legal control, in the pursuit of their interests.

There is little agreement among scholars as to what competing groups in society look like. Marxian scholars, for instance, locate attempts to control the mechanisms for reacting to crime in the conflicts between social classes (MacLean, 1986; Reiman, 1990; Chambliss, 1986; Hepburn, 1977). For these writers, such conflicts are a central feature of capitalist societies. The powerful economic classes, which own property and industries, seek to expand and consolidate their control of the less powerful classes, which must sell their labour to the capitalist class in order to survive. The legal machinery provides one important means by which this may be accomplished (Schissel, 1992).

At the same time, Marxian scholars encourage us to recognize that industries that pollute the environment and victimize consumers are generally treated less harshly than the street criminal who robs a convenience store (Michalowski and Bohlander, 1976). This is because the criminalization or aggressive prosecution of these industry actions would not be consistent with capitalist interests. For the Marxian theorist, the fact that the average person might agree that the cold-blooded killer of a convenience-store night clerk should be treated more harshly than the CEO of a corporation that sells defective products does not demonstrate evidence of a spontaneous consensus about what types of crimes are more serious. It merely demonstrates the power of capitalist interests to manipulate the consciousness of the members of a capitalist society.

Other proponents of the conflict position favour a model of group relations that is more diffuse than the one embraced by the Marxians. Laws and other aspects of the legal machinery do not merely reflect class conflict but may involve a variety of other interests as well (Bernard, 1981; Gusfield, 1963; Turk, 1976; Jenkins, 1992). Conflicts arise between cultural, lifestyle, or ethnic groups, and the factors that propel groups to use the legal machinery in the service of their interests may be diverse. The conflicts in which social groups are involved are not necessarily fought on a level playing field. Groups differ in the degree to which they have access to resources that allow them to influence the outcome of the conflict. From this perspective, the machinery of legal control can be thought of as one such resource. Groups may wish to see laws passed in order to have their values officially recognized by society; or they may wish to see the law used to control a group they believe threatens their values or social position.

PEACEMAKING

In a recent interpretation of conflict theory, Quinney and Wildeman (1991) offer a perspective that emphasizes peace and social justice. They argue that many of the dilemmas and contradictions in mainstream ("bourgeois") criminology in the United States at the end of the 20th century are the result of a theoretical chaos that marks the field. As Quinney and Wildeman see it, this chaos stems from the persistence of certain myths that dominate the thinking about crime. These myths, as originally outlined by Pepinsky and Jesilow (1984), include the following:

- crime is increasing;
- most crime is committed by the poor;
- some groups are more law-abiding than others;
- white-collar crime is nonviolent;
- regulatory agencies prevent white-collar crime;
- rich and poor are equal before the law;
- drug addiction causes crime; and
- law makes people behave themselves.

In Quinney and Wildeman's view, the above myths fail to address the fundamental inequality in a society in which the power to control punishment, which lies in the hands of the state, dictates that certain groups will be unfairly treated by the criminal justice system. In this respect, criminalization is a means of imposing violence on the underclass.

Quinney and Wildeman encourage us to consider alternative ways of responding to social ills, and to consider the broader issues that generate criminality, including social and economic disadvantage. Their solution is to offer a criminology of peacemaking, which involves reducing punishment/imprisonment and enhancing programs that encourage treatment, rehabilitation, alternatives to prisons, mediation, and the realization of social justice. Peacemaking's nonviolent approach to crime reduction includes strategies of problem-oriented policing in which the emphasis is on *preventing* crime rather than reacting to crime in a punitive way (Quinney and Wildeman, 1991: 107).

FEMINIST CRIMINOLOGY

The ideas of peacemaking have found their way into feminist approaches to criminology (Simpson, 1989). In the feminist view, felicity and harmony are regarded as the highest values, and much emphasis is placed on the themes of caring, sharing, nurturing, and loving. According to Harris (1991),

> [t]his contrasts sharply [with] the orientation that values power and control above all else. Where the central goal is power, power conceived as "power over" or control, people and things are not viewed as ends in themselves but as instruments for the furtherance of power. Hierarchical institutions and structures are established both to clarify power rankings and to maintain them. The resulting stratifications create levels of superiority and inferiority, which carry differential status, legitimacy, and access to resources and other benefits. Such divisions and exclusions engender resentment and revolt in various forms, which then are used to justify greater control (88).

A major part of feminist effort, Harris suggests, involves attempts to identify and confront characteristics and values that are not conducive to the full realization of human potential. In addition, feminists reject negative values that are used to justify stereotyping and that work to support the groups in power. Consistent with the ideas offered in the criminology of peacemaking, the feminist view proposes that the emphasis on control (which is epitomized in incarceration) be replaced by an emphasis on strategies that address the serious disharmony in society. Undermining social inequalities and enhancing social interaction are ways in which the potential for violence and crime can be reduced.

In addition to seeking to understand the overall causes of crime, feminists explore the basic issues related to female criminality, starting with why female crime is so much lower than male crime. Naffine (1987) examines the different theoretical approaches that have dominated criminological thinking and finds them wanting in their explanation of female involvement (or non-involvement) in crime. Early strain theory, most particularly the version proposed by Albert Cohen, attributes male delinquency to unrealized expectations on the part of young males. In Naffine's view, the strain theorists have treated young females as marginal players in delinquent society; their lack of involvement in crime is seen to derive from their lack of motivation and lower expectations.

Naffine argues that differential association theory similarly views men as individualistic and women as dependent. Learning crime from others is an activity that is not very "feminine" and is therefore strongly discouraged. This view extends to social control theory, which examines the importance of family training in extending role expectations. Naffine criticizes the control theorist argument that women take on a passive, compliant, and conforming role by suggesting that it removes any sense of responsibility from the female who chooses not to offend.

Theories that Naffine characterizes as masculinity theories, as exemplified by Silverman and Dinitz (1974), have argued that men and women differ in terms of the traits that create a propensity toward criminal behaviour. According to Naffine, this perspective gives rise to a basic but serious empirical problem. "Those who theorize the significance of masculinity for criminality (and femininity for conformity) have never managed to specify exactly what it is about masculinity and femininity which triggers this behavior, let alone define these concepts in a consistent and convincing manner" (Naffine, 1987: 60).

Feminist criminologists argue that the reasons that we continue to see a limited growth in female crime is not that women are more passive and conforming but rather that they are more interested than men are in seeking alternatives to confrontation and aggressive action. Female crime occurs not because women become more like men but rather because the structural supports that women require to maintain relationships or to achieve their goals either are not available or are being used against them. Feminists have called for a new view of social control, one that moves away from the notion of the "reasonable man," with its emphasis on decision-making that is based on the male experience, to a perspective that encompasses the experiences of all individuals (Naffine, 1987: 1).

The feminist reinterpretation of social control is consistent with the fact that appearing in the legal landscape are an increasing number of claimsmakers who are not only representing certain groups as victims but are also negotiating to have offenders considered in a different light. A similar trend can be seen with respect to the cases of women who kill their husbands after a long experience with physical abuse at their hands. What has confounded the courts in dealing with these cases is that often there is no evidence of self-defence at the time of the murder and that in many instances the crime actually appears to have been premeditated. However, advocates argue that women charged with such crimes should not be judged by the rules that base evidence on the conditions that apply at the time of the act. Rather, adjudication of the act should include consideration of the serious problems of abuse that preceded it.

Increasingly, courts have come to accept the view that there may be an acceptable defence that the ongoing violence directed against women creates a "battered woman syndrome." This syndrome is characterized by a sense of helplessness through which women come to believe that they can neither leave the abusive relationship nor effectively act to reduce the violence, hence violence is their only recourse. Circumstances may result in the violence occurring when the abuser is asleep or otherwise vulnerable, which makes the act appear premeditated. In the case of *Lavallee v. R.*, the battered woman syndrome was accepted as a defence against the charge of murder. In this case, the accused had shot her common-law husband after he had hit her, taunted her, and then turned his back on her (Silverman and Kennedy, 1993: 150–155).

The Supreme Court of Canada has since expanded its concept of self-defence in murder cases to encompass situations in which a woman has reason to fear that, based on the past behaviour of the homicide victim, her life is at risk, if not immediately then in the near future. By acknowledging the battered woman syndrome as a valid defence, the Supreme Court has introduced a new conception of criminality, one that includes the recognition that power relationships may play an important role in influencing criminal acts. Clearly, the "rational man" position (i.e., "How would a rational man respond to this situation?") has little relevance to the battered woman syndrome.

> **WHAT DOES IT MEAN?**
>
> **Battered Woman Syndrome**
> This syndrome is characterized by the sense of helplessness felt by women who come to believe that they can neither leave an abusive relationship nor effectively act to reduce the violence.

SUMMARY AND CONCLUSIONS
■ ■ ■

Critics of motivation theories argue that many people feel like breaking the law but do not. Formal and informal social controls prevent them from acting in (sometimes) rational but criminal ways. Hirschi argues that delinquency emerges when controls diminish through the weakening of the social bonds that link adolescents to conformist others. Strong social bonds, which are based on high levels of attachment, commitment, involvement, and belief and which are built into the socialization that individuals experience at home and at school, insulate youth from delinquent involvement. These bonds are subject to pressure from changes in the ways in which families function. They are also influenced by the degree of social disorganization experienced in communities, disorganization that can lead to weakening social ties and increased levels of criminality.

Crime may emerge in the routine conflicts that occur between individuals in these groups. The escalation to violence may occur because there are no clear means by which individuals can de-escalate their dispute. This problem of conflict emerges in different spheres of life and the deterrence of harmful outcomes often depends on the skills that individuals learn to deal with one another in nonviolent ways. It may also be the case, though, that there is an overreaction to this conflict by authorities who do not understand its origins and fear that the problems will race out of control if not stamped out quickly. This has led to real conflicts between certain communities and the police based on misunderstandings regarding the harmful outcomes of certain behaviour.

The purpose of deterrence strategies is to communicate to individuals the threat that punishment will follow delinquent acts. If the law is not imposed in a quick, certain, and severe way, deterrence does not ensue. But deterrence depends on many things, including the fear that the individual has of punishment, his or her perception of risk, and so on. It has been suggested that what the law actually threatens is less relevant to the decision to offend than what people *believe* it threatens. Perceptions of deterrence are also affected by the widespread public ambivalence concerning the likelihood and efficacy of punishment.

Two different perspectives have developed to help explain how reactions to crime come to be organized. The consensus view argues that our reactions to crime emerge out of, and reflect, a social consensus about morality and about the need to respond to particular types of events in a particular way. On the other hand, the conflict perspective suggests that it is more appropriate to think about our reactions to crime as having more to do with power, conflict, and inequality than with social consensus.

It is useful to look at the process by which laws are passed and legal reforms are initiated as a claimsmaking process. Assertions are made about a problem that needs to be solved. This is followed by a concerted effort to generate public support for these claims and for the solutions that are offered. There often occurs during the claimsmaking process a struggle between the various interest groups and state agencies that have been empowered to define and administer the law. The result of this struggle may be a redefinition of harms done and legal responses to be made.

By forcing the law to be malleable and incorporate many different points of view in its evolution, claimsmaking provides a basis for peacemaking and feminist perspectives. Advocates of these approaches believe that the law must be a dynamic element in our understanding of criminality, not something that is set and immutable. From their perspective, the lines that are drawn around crime are actually artificial constructions of the legal process. Crimes will be poorly understood if they are studied only as legal events and not as social ones that occur in a dynamic and changeable social environment. It is this view of the criminal event that will allow us to present a more complete picture of the origins of crime and its impact on society.

4

OPPORTUNITIES, LIFESTYLES, AND SITUATIONS

T HE FACT THAT OFFENDERS are ready and willing to engage in criminal conduct, either because of their personalities, backgrounds, or views of the law, does not in and of itself explain the occurrence of criminal events. It is also necessary that potential offenders encounter opportunities that allow these criminal inclinations to be given expression. This is no less true of crime than of anything else. An inclination to learn the saxophone, go to graduate school, or become a skydiver does not ensure that these things will happen. In such cases, as in the case of criminal events, it is useful to consider how opportunities allow individuals to act on their inclinations.

DELINQUENT OPPORTUNITIES AND COMMUNITY STRUCTURE

Several decades ago, Richard Cloward (1959) and Lloyd Ohlin provided one of the earliest and most systematic treatments of urban juvenile crime. Their analysis (Cloward and Ohlin, 1960), which borrowed heavily from the writings of Robert Merton and Edwin Sutherland, attempted to demonstrate that a comprehensive theory of delinquency must explain not only why juveniles engage in delinquency, but also why they engage in one type of delinquency and not another.

Like Merton, Cloward and Ohlin argued that the motivation to delinquent conduct could be located in the discrepancy between the goals to which lower-class youth aspire and what is actually available to them. Cloward and Ohlin were also influenced by Merton's view that the legitimate means to goal attainment are socially structured such that not everyone in society finds the legitimate means to conventional goals equally available. For some people, the legitimate means of obtaining success goals, such as education or a good job, are out of reach, and it is precisely this lack of legitimate opportunity that creates the pressure to deviate in the first place. Cloward and Ohlin extended Merton's theory by arguing that it is important to recognize that illegitimate means are also structured. The opportunities to be criminal are no more evenly dispersed in society than are the legitimate means to achieve success goals. Building on this logic, Cloward and Ohlin theorized that the kind of delinquent one becomes depends on the kinds of opportunities one has to be delinquent.

Cloward and Ohlin used the term "illegitimate means" to encompass two major aspects of the delinquent opportunity structure. The first is the opportunity to learn a delinquent role. As Sutherland (1947) argued, learning how to be delinquent and why it is acceptable to be delinquent are necessary precursors to being delinquent. Second, the concept of illegitimate means implies the opportunity to actually play a delinquent role. An individual can become a member of a drug network or stolen-car ring only if such organizations exist in his or her social environment. For Cloward and Ohlin, then, a central theoretical problem was to understand how particular types of community organization make particular types of delinquent opportunity structures possible. Their analysis identified three forms of delinquent opportunity structure, each of which was associated with particular types of social conditions.

The first form, named the *criminal pattern*, is characterized by a rational delinquency that is oriented toward the pursuit of monetary objectives and is exemplified by organized theft or the sale of drugs or other illicit goods or services. Delinquency of this type is most likely to emerge in lower-class neighbourhoods in which there is a stable adult criminal world and in which the criminal and conformist sectors of the community are highly integrated. When such integration exists, the "cop on the beat" is willing to look the other way and the "honest" storekeeper is occasionally willing to fence stolen goods. The presence of a stable adult criminal world provides a structure for recruitment and upward mobility for juveniles who view criminality in career terms.

While neighbourhoods that give rise to the criminal pattern may be described as socially organized, we expect a different pattern to emerge from neighbourhoods that are characterized by a high degree of social disorganization. Socially disorganized slums lack a stable adult criminal world and thus an established criminal structure. This situation may be doubly frustrating for neighbourhood youths who have already experienced the disparity between legitimate goals and legitimate opportunities. Moreover, as Shaw and McKay (1942) point out, these areas lack the social controls that work to contain the behavioural manifestations of this frustration. For these reasons, Cloward and Ohlin discerned in socially disorganized areas a *conflict pattern* of delinquency. The conflict pattern is characterized by gangs who express their frustration fighting over contested neighbourhood turf.

Finally, Cloward and Ohlin maintained, it is unwise to assume that everyone who engages in criminal or conflict opportunities will be successful. We are not all cut out to be drug dealers or gang warriors. Cloward and Ohlin use the term "double-failures" to describe people who are unable to succeed through either legitimate or illegitimate means. Double failures tend to become involved in a *retreatist pattern* in which delinquency is organized around the consumption of drugs.

Cloward and Ohlin's analysis importantly extends the range of relevant theoretical questions beyond the search for motivational factors. It alerts us to the fact that it is not enough to explain why people might be motivated to break the law, since answers to this question generally do not explain why some laws rather than others end up being broken. It is also necessary to understand how criminal inclinations are channelled by the opportunities to be criminal to which people have access.

OPPORTUNITY THEORIES AND VICTIMIZATION

LIFESTYLE AND ROUTINE ACTIVITIES

Since the late 1970s, the study of criminal opportunities has been dominated by researchers interested in the study of victimization events. Known as "lifestyle-exposure" or "routine activities theories," these explanations focus

WHAT DOES IT INCLUDE?

Routine Activities Theory

First, there must be a motivated offender. A suitable target against which the criminal motivation may be directed must also be available. Third, there must be an absence of capable guardianship.

on how variations in levels of crime from place to place or over time are related to variations in the opportunities to commit crime rather than to variations in the numbers of people who are motivated to commit crimes.

The lifestyle-exposure theory of criminal victimization was formally developed by Michael Hindelang, Michael Gottfredson, and James Garofalo in their 1978 book, *Victims of Personal Crime*. Their theory, which was grounded in the data of victimization surveys, was intended to explain what is it about being male, young, single, or poor that increases the chances of being victimized.

BOX 4.1 MULTIPLE VICTIMIZATION

Studies of crime victims not only tell us that some people are more likely than others to be victimized; they also tell us that those who have been victimized once are more likely to be victimized again. In other words, for crime victims, the chances of being victimized by the same or another type of crime are higher than they are for those who have not been victimized. This is illustrated by data collected in the 1982 *Canadian Urban Victimization Survey*. The survey investigated 60,000 Canadians' experiences with crime in 1981.

The first set of data below relates to "repeat victimization"—that is, the risk that a person who has been victimized by a particular type of crime will be victimized by that crime one or more additional times. For each of the personal crimes (as well as for the household crimes), the chances of becoming a victim again are greater than those of becoming a victim in the first place. Thus, the chances that victims of personal theft will be victimized again are almost twice as high as the risk of initially becoming a victim of personal theft (115 per 1,000 vs. 63 per 1,000). The risks of repeat victimization are even more dramatic for the other offences.

The second set of data relates to the probabilities of being victimized again, but by a different type of crime. While approximately 6 percent of all of the respondents were victims of personal theft (i.e., 63 per 1,000), about 17 percent of assault victims, 19 percent of robbery victims, and 23 percent of sexual assault victims were victims of personal theft.

Such data seem to suggest that some people may engage in lifestyles or patterns of routine activities that make them *particularly* prone to crime. It appears from research done elsewhere that factors that seem to be linked to single victimization (e.g., evening activities outside of the home or alcohol consumption) are also closely related to multiple victimization (Lasley and Rosenbaum, 1988).

Table 4.1 Likelihood of Repeat Victimization of Personal Offences

Seven Cities

Type of Personal Incident	Victimization Rate per 1,000 Persons 16 and Older	Rate per 1,000 Persons Victimized More Than Once by This Offence
Theft of Personal Property	63	115
Assault	53	212
Robbery	10	90
Sexual Assault	3	105*

* The actual count was low (11 to 20), therefore caution should be exercised when interpreting this rate.

Likelihood of Cross-Crime Victimization of Personal Offences

Rates per 1,000 Population 16 and Older

Type of Personal Incident	All Persons 16 and Older	Persons Also Victimized by:			
		Theft of Personal Property	Assault	Robbery	Sexual Assault
Theft of Personal Property	63	—	167	194	231
Assault	53	140	—	307	234
Robbery	10	31	58	—	77*
Sexual Assault	3	13	15	30*	—

* The actual count was low (11 to 20), therefore caution should be exercised when interpreting this rate.

Source: Solicitor General of Canada, *Canadian Urban Victimization Survey Bulletin 10: Multiple Victimization.* Ottawa: Ministry Secretariat, 1988. Reproduced with permission of the Minister of Supply and Services Canada, 1993.

The linchpin of their argument is the concept of lifestyle. In general terms, lifestyle refers to the patterned ways in which people distribute their time and energies across a range of activities. We have no trouble recognizing that the lifestyle of a teenage male differs quite markedly from the lifestyle of an elderly female. Such differences relate to how time is spent, where time is spent, with whom one associates, and what type of leisure pursuits one enjoys. These lifestyle differences are not merely matters of personal choice; they also reflect the social roles one is required to play and the various types of social restraints to which one is subject.

BOX 4.2 EVENING ACTIVITIES AND RISK

Where and how people spend their time is related to their victimization risks. While the number of evening activities in which people engage outside the home in-creases the chances of becoming a crime victim, research suggests that some kinds of activities are more risky than others. This is illustrated below (Sacco and Johnson, 1990b) with data drawn from the 1988 *Canadian General Social Survey.*

Rates of Total Personal Victimization Per 1,000 Persons by Specific Activity Type, General Social Survey, 1988

Activity Type	Total	Activity Type	Total
Work, school, meetings		*Shopping*	
0	99	0	99
1–9	114	1–9	162
10–19	204	10–19	233
20+	226	20+	254
Restaurants, bars		*Visiting friends, etc.*	
0	67	0	88
1–9	146	1–9	119
10–19	334	10–19	269
20+	333	20+	387
Movies, plays, bingo			
0	90		
1–9	186		
10–19	357		
20+	—		
Sports, recreation			
0	92		
1–9	142		
10–19	190		
20+	333		

— Rate cannot be estimated reliably.

Hindelang, Gottfredson, and Garofalo (1978: 251–264) offer the following eight propositions about victimization that summarize the link between lifestyle and key demographic variables such as age, sex, marital status, family income, and race.

1. The more time individuals spend in public places (especially at night), the more likely it is that they will be victimized.

2. Following certain lifestyles makes an individual more likely to frequent public places.

3. The interactions that individuals maintain tend to be with persons who share their lifestyles.

4. The probability that an individual will be a victim increases with the extent to which victims and offenders belong to the same demographic categories.

5. The proportion of time one spends in places where there are a large number of nonfamily members varies according to lifestyle.

6. The chance that an individual will be a victim of crime (particularly theft) increases in conjunction with the amount of time he or she spends among nonfamily members.

7. Differences in lifestyle relate to individuals' ability to isolate themselves from those with offender characteristics.

8. Variations in lifestyle influence the convenience, desirability, and ease of victimizing an individual.

Rates of personal victimization are relatively high for young minority males because these individuals tend to associate with people who are likely to offend (i.e., other young minority males) and because they tend to frequent places (e.g., bars) where offending often occurs. An elderly female, by contrast, is likely to associate with other elderly females (whose level of offending is very low) and to avoid high-risk settings. Lifestyle in a sense structures victimization opportunities. In explaining empirical variations in levels of personal crime, Hindelang and his colleagues advance these opportunity structures, not offender motivation, as a central theoretical problem.

Cohen and Felson (1979) note that traditional motivational theories in criminology are unable to explain the dramatic increase in many forms of crime that occurred in Western nations in the post–World War II period. Many of the explanatory factors to which rising crime pointed (e.g., poverty, unemployment, size of inner-city population) indicated trends that suggested that crimes rates should have been falling during this period rather than

---

BOX 4.3   WARNING: SMOKING MAY BE HAZARDOUS TO YOUR HEALTH

Opportunity theories of victimization attempt to understand how particular elements of lifestyle increase exposure to the risk of criminal victimization. Several studies have shown that as alcohol consumption or the frequency of visiting bars increases, so does the risk of becoming a victim. Perhaps somewhat less obviously, University of California researcher Ichiro Tanioka (1986) has published evidence suggesting that victimization rates are higher for smokers.

The data for Tanioka's study came from the 1978 and 1983 General Social Surveys. Among the questions asked of respondents were had they ever been "punched or beaten by another person" and did they smoke. Because the tendency to become a crime victim and the tendency to smoke are related to other social characteristics, Tanioka included in the analysis measures of age, sex, marital status, urban residence, employment status, and frequency of bar attendance.

The analysis revealed that, independent of the effects of the other variables included in the study, smoking had a significant effect on the risk of assault. Overall, 32.3 percent of smokers had experienced an assault, compared to 17 percent of nonsmokers. However, the relationship is even stronger for single females aged 18–49, among whom 43.5 percent were victimized, compared to 20.0 percent of nonsmokers.

This is not to suggest that smoking is a *cause* of victimization in any simple sense. What is more likely is that a measure of smoking indexes certain other lifestyle preferences (unmeasured in the survey) that are more directly related to victimization risk.

---

climbing. How then could the problem of rising crime rates be reconceptualized?

According to Cohen and Felson, the presence of a motivated offender is only one component necessary to the completion of assaults, sexual assaults, homicides, break and enters, or other "direct-contact predatory violations." For such crimes to occur, two other conditions must be met. First, there must be a "suitable target" against which the criminal motivation can be directed (e.g., homes to break into, people to assault, and goods to steal). Second, there must be an "absence of capable guardianship," meaning that the motivated offender must meet the suitable target in the absence of anything (or anyone) that might prevent the crime from occurring.

Cohen and Felson suggest that variations in levels of crime are determined not only by the number of people willing to commit crimes but also by the numbers of suitable targets and by the levels of guardianship that are routinely exercised over these targets. Even if the numbers of suitable targets and the levels of guardianship remain unchanged, higher crime rates can be expected if the tempos and rhythms of social life affect the rate at which motivated offenders encounter suitable targets in the absence of capable guardianship. For Cohen and Felson, illegal activities must be understood as behaviours that depend upon, and feed off, the "routine activities" of the population. "Although the fox finds each hare one by one, the fox population varies with the hare population upon which it feeds" (Felson, 1987: 914). As the structure of the routine activities changes, so does the frequency at which crimes occur.

How do these insights inform our theoretical understanding of why crime rates changed as they did after World War II? Cohen and Felson argue that changes in patterns of routine activities substantially altered levels of target suitability and guardianship and the rates at which these elements and motivated offenders came together in time and space. This period witnessed a broad shift in the locus of routine activities. In increasingly large numbers, women whose lives had revolved around the household entered or returned to the paid labour force or school. In addition, vacation periods became longer and travel became cheaper, so that holidays were more likely to be spent away from home. Even the frequency with which people ate out at restaurants increased and gave rise to a booming fast-food industry. At the same time, divorce rates increased and people who were single were waiting longer before getting married. Both changes pointed to a significant rise in the number of smaller, single-person households and further contributed to the likelihood that leisure interests previously pursued at home would now be pursued elsewhere, among nonfamily members.

Not coincidentally, this period also witnessed "a revolution in small durable product design" (Cohen and Felson, 1979: 500). A general increase in the standard of living combined with technological advancement to produce a wide range of lightweight, durable consumer goods. Demand for tape recorders, television sets, and stereo equipment increased, as it later did for products like home computers, compact disc players, and VCRs.

These changes, according to Cohen and Felson, exerted a profound impact on the rates of direct-contact predatory crimes. Through their effects on target suitability and guardianship levels, they provided greater criminal opportunities and pushed crime rates upward. The shift in routine activities away from the home exposed increasingly large numbers of people to criminal dangers from which they previously had been insulated. Moreover, in

BOX 4.4 OPPORTUNITIES FOR CREDIT-CARD FRAUD

Fraud may be defined as the attempt to use deceit or falsehoold in order to gain goods, services, or financial gain without legitimate rights. Like other types of crime, levels of fraud depend on the availability of criminal opportunities. The table below shows that, while overall rates of fraud increased by 22 percent from 1980 to 1990, credit-card frauds increased 115 percent.

According to a study done by the Canadian Centre for Justice Statistics (Leroux and Morrison, 1992), this increase reflects the increasingly large increases in credit-card transactions. The study reports that the number of credit cards in circulation in Canada increases by two to three million each year. As a result, for many people, credit cards have become a preferred method for both spending and obtaining cash. The study cites the Canadian Chapter of the International Association of Credit Card Investigators as reporting that 12,000 banking machines exist in Canada and that, in 1990, these machines processed over 600 million banking transactions.

Trends in Fraud in Canada, 1980–1990

Year	Cheque Fraud		Credit Card Fraud		Other Fraud[1]		Total Fraud	
1980	67,025	(+8)	8,310	(+27)	26,920	(+17)	102,255	(+12)
1981	70,707	(+5)	10,840	(+30)	30,780	(+14)	112,327	(+10)
1982	72,027	(+2)	14,540	(+34)	31,830	(+3)	118,397	(+5)
1983	70,047	(-3)	16,258	(+12)	32,065	(+1)	118,370	(+0)
1984	74,541	(+6)	16,268	(+0)	31,966	(+0)	122,775	(+4)
1985	74,472	(+0)	15,430	(-5)	33,238	(+4)	123,140	(+0)
1986	78,957	(+6)	15,243	(-1)	36,359	(+9)	130,359	(+6)
1987	74,095	(-6)	14,702	(-4)	37,345	(+3)	126,142	(-3)
1988	72,967	(-2)	13,286	(-10)	38,519	(+3)	124,772	(-1)
1989	72,670	(+0)	13,457	(+1)	36,491	(-5)	122,670	(-2)
1990	74,069	(+2)	17,885	(+33)	38,795	(+6)	130,749	(+7)
% change 1980–1990	...	+11	...	+115	...	+44	...	+22

Numbers in parentheses show the change in percent over the previous year.

[1] Includes other categories of fraud such as criminal breach of trust, false pretenses, forgery, destroying or falsifying books and documents, trademark forgery, unauthorized use of computers, mail fraud, insurance fraud, fraudulent manipulation of stock exchange, etc.

Source: Table 1 (page 4) in J. Leroux and P. Morrison, "Fraud in Canada," *Juristat Service Bulletin* 12(5). Ottawa: Canadian Centre for Justice Statistics, 1992.

greater numbers, they left their homes unoccupied for increasing periods of time and thus deprived of capable guardianship. At the same time that guardianship was being lowered, homes were being stocked with larger numbers of highly desirable durable consumer goods that were easy to steal, easy to carry, and easy to sell or use. As guardianship declined, target suitability increased. One need not agonize over the question of criminal motivation, Cohen and Felson conclude, in order to understand an increase in crime over the period.

Newman (1972) borrows from the ideas of opportunity theory in arguing that the most effective way to reduce crime is to redesign public and private spaces in such a way that opportunities for crime are removed. The "defensible space" concept proposes that one can "harden" targets by installing locks or by improving surveillance, such that the criminal is deterred from committing the crime, either for fear of detection or simply because the target has been made inaccessible. The operators of 7-Eleven convenience stores redesigned their premises under the direction of Ray D. Johnson, who had served 25 years for robbery and burglary in the California state penitentiary system. The insights provided by a former perpetrator led to a design that removed the chance of concealment.

> To allow clear sightlines from the street into the store, they moved cash registers up front and removed all advertising from the front windows. They also put bright floodlights outside the entrance, forcing potential robbers to perform where any passerby could look in and see.
>
> They also installed special cash drawers that make it impossible to get at more than $10 every two minutes. This gives the would-be robber the choice of getting away with very little cash, waiting "onstage" to make the payoff worthwhile or simply going elsewhere (Krupat and Kubzansky, 1987: 60).

The incidence of robberies in the redesigned 7-Eleven stores was 30 percent lower than that in the stores that had not been redesigned.

In a similar vein, Sherman, Gartin, and Buerger (1989) identify high-crime areas known as "hot spots." These places may be public (taverns) or private (households that are frequently reported for family disturbances). The authors' prescription is to minimize or eliminate the crime at these hot spots by increasing police surveillance or by removing them altogether. The idea that crime will be deterred through defensible space or through targeting hot spots supports the idea that offenders are motivated by opportunity. However, removing these opportunities will not necessarily reduce desire to commit a crime—it may simply displace it to some other location. Police spend a great deal of time moving street prostitutes from certain areas only to have them reappear in other parts of town.

Over the last several years, a large body of research has grown up around the questions raised by opportunity theories of victimization (Maxfield, 1987b; Miethe, Stafford, and Long, 1987; Cohen, Kluegel, and Land, 1981; Skogan and Maxfield, 1981; Kennedy and Forde, 1990). In a very basic way, the ideas generated by this research have re-oriented criminologists' thinking about the causes of crime. Opportunity theories have provided an additional piece to the puzzle as to why and where criminal events occur. A major limitation of these theories is that they pay little attention to the nature of the offender's motivation or to the relationship between the offender and the victim. Opportunity theories assume that probabilities of offending can be worked out on the basis of a set of conditions relating to opportunities. We believe that to the notion of opportunity must be added questions about the characteristics of offender motivation.

CRIMES AS INTERACTIONS

An important theoretical question in the study of criminal situations relates to the manner in which these events unfold over time. They are set in motion by offenders who are inclined to make use of available criminal opportunities. In order to explain why they follow a particular course of action, it is necessary to raise questions about the specific behavioural choices that offenders, victims, and others make in the situational contexts in which they find themselves. In particular, it is important to understand how the choices that each participant makes influence the choices made by others. Victims and offenders act and react. In so doing, they exert mutual influence. Stated differently, crimes have an interactional character. What any one participant does depends on what others do. Although interactional dynamics have not attracted as much attention as issues like offender motivation, a general appreciation of how criminologists attempt to understand these interactions is necessary.

One of the concepts most frequently employed in the study of crime dynamics is that of victim precipitation, according to which the opportunity for crime is created by some action of the victim. In an early and influential study of 588 criminal homicides in the city of Philadelphia, the sociologist Marvin Wolfgang (1958) reported that in about one-quarter of these cases the victims could be said to have precipitated their own murder. In such cases Wolfgang noted, it was the eventual victim who, frequently under the influence of alcohol, was the first to brandish a weapon or to threaten deadly force. The eventual offender, fearing for his or her own safety, either intentionally or unintentionally reacted to the threat in a way that proved fatal for the victim. In a stereotypical case an altercation between two individuals at a bar escalates to the point at which one of the parties produces a knife or a broken bottle and says to the other party, "I'm going to kill you." The other party responds with haste and force and the person who uttered the threat is dead on the barroom floor.

> **WHAT DOES IT MEAN?**
>
> *Victim Precipitation*
> This occurs when the opportunity for crime is created by some action of the victim.

The concept of victim precipitation encourages us to understand how the outcome can be understood as the joint product of the behaviours of the offender and the victim rather than as the mere outcome of an offender's motivation to kill the victim. The killing can be said to result not from the killer's actions but from the killer–killed interaction. It is important to point out that what people might *intend* their words or their actions to mean in cases of this type are much less important than *how they are interpreted* by others engaged in the interaction. The person who brandishes a broken beer bottle and threatens death to a disputant may be expressing mere bravado rather than a serious intention to threaten the well-being of the other party. But to the disputant, whose judgment is clouded by alcohol and who believes the threat to be real, other interpretations of the situation are well out of reach. With respect to such cases, we might have little trouble understanding the potential explanatory value of the concept of victim precipitation. The homicide would probably not have occurred, we can conclude, if the victim had not initially behaved in an aggressive fashion; thus, the victim was an active contributor to his or her own violent demise.

Problematic from a theoretical standpoint is the degree to which the explanatory logic of victim precipitation is generalizable to other types of events. Is it reasonable, for instance, to argue that crimes such as robbery, theft, or sexual assault can also be victim precipitated? In these types of events, does it make sense to argue that victims actively contribute to their own victimization?

Amir (1971) concluded from a study of over 600 rape cases in the city of Philadelphia that about one case in five was victim precipitated. Amir classified rapes as victim precipitated if the victim "actually, or so it was deemed, agreed to sexual relations but retracted before the actual act or did not react strongly enough when the suggestion was made to the offender" (266).

While we might be inclined to agree that victims who initially threaten their offenders in some sense precipitate a homicide, we would not agree that victims who initially agree to sexual relations precipitate rape if they subsequently change their minds. For one thing, the assumption in the latter case seems to be that the female rather than the male is responsible for the level of male sexual arousal, and if that arousal is not satisfied the female must bear the violent consequences. In addition, it seems to imply that a subsequent decision not to engage in sex, when there has been some initial agreement to do so, is appropriately understood as precipitous of violence. Finally, homicide and sexual assault differ in a fundamental way that is obscured by the haphazard application of the concept of victim precipitation. The types of homicides described by Wolfgang involve events in which victims threaten their offenders with deadly force and are repaid in kind. In the cases of rape described by Amir, the victim is not behaving in a threatening or aggressive fashion, and the violence exhibited by the offender cannot be understood as "payment in kind."

Amir's study illustrates a serious concern that many people have with the concept of victim precipitation—that it is difficult to separate the moral dimensions of the concept from its explanatory dimensions. The claim that victims precipitate victimization seems uncomfortably close to the suggestion that victims should be *blamed* for their victimization. For many criminologists, victim blaming should be avoided at all costs (Timmer and Norman, 1984). At the same time, most people can express some degree of empathy for the abused wife, who, after years of being subjected to violence, kills her abusive husband. To call a killing of this type victim precipitated does not usually elicit a charge of victim blaming.

For some criminologists, the solution is to recognize that crude attempts to sort crimes into precipitated and unprecipitated are doomed to failure.

There are a variety of ways in which victims and offenders may contribute to the unfolding of a criminal event, and thus a broader taxonomy of victim and offender roles is necessary (Fattah, 1991; Karmen, 1990). Another solution involves recognizing that, in many cases, it is not appropriate to speak of victim or offender roles, since to do so minimizes our understanding of the ways in which the circumstances of events themselves determine who shall bear what label. In other words, there is a need to move beyond the study of victim precipitation to "the full round of interaction," which involves not only the eventual victims and offenders but also other event participants (Luckenbill, 1984).

THE SITUATED TRANSACTION

Goffman (1963) defines a "situated transaction" as a process of interaction that involves two or more individuals. If we are to understand criminal events as situated transactions, we need to emphasize the study of what goes on between the participants rather than what any one of them does. According to Goffman (1959), human behaviour is acted out as though part of a theatrical performance. It is the impression that the actor gives to others that is important in the interaction. Based on this impression, which generally involves the playing out of a partic-

> ### WHAT DOES IT MEAN?
>
> #### Situated Transaction
> A process of interaction involving two or more individuals that lasts as long as they find themselves in one another's presence. If we are to understand criminal events as situated transactions, we need to emphasize the study of what goes on between the participants rather than what any one of them does.

ular role in specific situations, individuals extract information about others in the interaction. When enough information is obtained for each individual to define the situation to his or her satisfaction, the roles can be properly acted out (Martin, Mutchnik, and Austin, 1990: 332). With these definitions in hand, individuals are able to sustain and complete a number of transactions throughout their daily lives. These transactions do not always have positive outcomes, however.

Luckenbill (1977) utilized an approach that drew upon symbolic interactionism in organizing an analysis of 70 homicides that occurred in California. Like other researchers, Luckenbill reported that these murders tended to occur in informal settings and generally involved people who were known to each other. What distinguishes his approach, however, is his view of homicide as a product of the situated transaction rather than as a product of the behaviour of individual participants. For Luckenbill, situated transactions should be viewed as "character contests" in which efforts on the part of the disputants to "save face" result in deadly combat.

Luckenbill discerns six distinct stages in the transactions that result in homicide. Stage 1, the opening move in the transaction, involves a threat by the (eventual) victim to the "face" of the (eventual) offender. In other words, the victim directs an insult or accusation at the offender. In Stage 2, the offender interprets the insult or accusation as personally offensive. In Stage 3, the offender engages in a retaliatory gesture intended to save face. If the offender has been threatened, he or she may threaten in return. If he is insulted, he may be insulting; if she is shoved, she may shove back.

In Stage 4, the victim is in the complicated position of preparing for fight or flight. Rather than demonstrate weakness of character, both victim and offender enter into a "working agreement" that the situation is one that must be resolved by violent means. In Stage 5, with the characters of both parties on the line, a brief battle ensues and the victim falls. In Stage 6, the aftermath of the battle, the offender chooses either to surrender to authorities or to flee.

Luckenbill's analysis characterizes homicide as a transactional product. A victim ends up dead because of what goes on between the parties involved. This perspective on criminal events is not meant to imply that situated transactions are restricted to one type. The kinds of transactions that result in acquaintance rapes differ from those that result in homicides. Even in the case of homicides, important differences characterize the nature of the situated transaction (Williams and Flewelling, 1988). For example, it is incorrect to argue that the murders committed by mass murderers or serial killers result from the fact that victims and offenders are combatants who are committed to battle. (This is not to deny, however, that these crimes too have situational dynamics.)

In many cases, the complexities of transactions blur in our minds whatever a priori distinctions we might wish to make between victims and offenders. How useful is it for us to say that individuals are of a certain "criminal type" when we know that their behaviour can be affected to such a large extent by the situations they face and by the roles they believe they must play in completing the transaction? It is the course of action that to a large degree determines the identity of the eventual victim and offender. We do not (as we do in cases of victim precipitation) look to the victim for the causes of the violence, but rather to the victim–offender exchange. With respect to the homicides described by Luckenbill, it should be clear that, up until the moment of battle, either party might have pulled out of the exchange or responded differently, resulting in quite different consequences. Questions about who should have done what (and when) to prevent the violence are likely to elicit more than one answer from interested observers.

According to Sampson and Lauritsen (1990), the difficulties that we have in identifying the offender and victim in many criminal events derive from the "principle of homogamy." This principle states that likelihood of victimization increases with the frequency of one's contact or association with members of demographic groups that contain a disproportionate share of offenders. In this matrix, the dynamics of the situation, as described above using Luckenbill's approach, make it likely that victims and offenders will be drawn from the same group, a view consistent with Hindelang, Gottfredson, and Garofalo's (1978) proposal that those with common lifestyles are more likely to be victimized by one another.

THE SIGNIFICANCE OF INTERACTIONAL ISSUES

The study of victim–offender interactions challenges many of the stereotypes that are inherent in other theoretical approaches. With respect to motivational theories, for instance, we are sometimes led to argue that crimes occur only because criminals are determined to commit them. Theories that focus only on opportunity, if not carefully interpreted, seem to suggest that crimes occur only because motivated offenders find the opportunities to translate their inclinations into action.

By contrast, interactional theories suggest that more than motivation and opportunity are needed to understand why and how crime occurs. Crimes are the outcome of social exchanges between people who find themselves in specific circumstances and must make quick decisions about how they should respond to each other's behaviour. A robbery does not occur merely because an offender with an inclination to rob encounters an opportunity conducive to robbery. The potential victim may resist in ways that turn a potential robbery into an attempted murder. The potential victim of an attempted break and enter may "overreact" by killing the offender. Victims of property crimes contribute to the interaction through the steps they take (or don't take) to protect their property; their actions, or lack thereof, send a message to the potential offender about the risks of trying to steal the property. Victims are not, therefore, merely passive objects of an offender's predatory desires; nor are they necessarily active contributors to their own victimization. They are, however, key event participants whose actions shape and constrain event outcomes.

Similar comments apply to other participants. The study of homicide by Luckenbill, for instance, revealed that the role of bystanders in situated transactions should not be minimized. He found that the presence of bystanders and the actions they took shaped the course of the transaction. In the early stages, they sometimes increased the likelihood of mortal battle by encouraging the offender to interpret an offensive remark as requiring a firm response, while in the later stages they sometimes supplied a weapon or blocked the exit of the potential victim. Of course, just as bystanders may facilitate the occurrence of a crime, they may also prevent crimes or transform one type of crime into another. A bystander who has the presence of mind to call "911" upon witnessing an assault, or who is familiar with cardiopulmonary resuscitation (CPR), may prevent an assault from becoming a murder.

SUMMARY AND CONCLUSIONS
■ ■ ■

The pressure to behave in a criminal fashion is not sufficient to explain why people commit one type of crime and not another. Cloward and Ohlin attribute differences in the types of crime that offenders commit to differences in the illegitimate opportunities that are available to them. Illegitimate opportunities are structured in the environment and generate systematic violations of the law. These opportunities are especially evident in neighbourhoods that are characterized by a high degree of social disorganization. Socially disorganized urban slums, for example, lack the social controls necessary to contain outbreaks of delinquency. This is manifested most often in conflict patterns characterized by gangs who battle over neighbourhood turf.

The idea of criminal opportunities has been extended by those who work in a routine activities tradition. According to those theorists, variations in levels of crime across places and over time are related less to variations in the numbers of individuals motivated to commit crime than to variations in the opportunities to commit crime. The concept of opportunities revolves around the notion that some individuals have certain lifestyles, or follow certain routines, that make them vulnerable to criminal victimization. This lifestyle exposure, coupled with the presence of motivated offenders and the absence of capable guardians, makes becoming a victim of crime more likely. Changing routines, hardening targets through architectural change, and attacking hot spots (places where crime is most prevalent) all entail removing the opportunity to commit crime.

When crimes do occur, they take on a dynamic character that involves choices by offenders, victims, and others, all of which affect the outcome. Crimes can thus be said to have an interactional character; what any one participant does depends on what others do. An important consideration in this equation is the role played by the victim, who, together with the offender and other main players, comes to be involved in what is called a situated transaction. In such transactions, the characteristics of the individuals involved in an interaction come to define the direction that a crime will take. In the early stages of these interactions, it is often difficult to predict the eventual victim and offender. It is the actions that occur that more clearly define these roles. Depending on the actions of third parties, harm and guilt are clearly worked out only after the fact.

Interactional approaches suggest, then, that crimes are the outcome of social exchanges between people who find themselves in specific circumstances and who must make quick decisions about how they should respond to one another's behaviour. Their responses determine the outcomes. These outcomes are not always predictable in that they can be affected by many factors in the situation. Interactional approaches help us to determine the effectiveness of various strategies that are used by victims or by the police in deterring or preventing crime.

The last three chapters have reviewed a number of key theoretical questions. We have asked about the motivations of offenders, about the factors that constrain criminal conduct, about why we react to crime as we do, about the ways in which environments provide opportunities for crime, and about how the interactions between offenders and victims shape the course of criminal transactions.

Two observations emerge from this discussion. The first is that each of these questions is important and interesting to the student of crime. The second is that no single contemporary theory seems capable of bringing into focus all that we wish to examine. What we need is a framework that allows us to reconcile the insights offered by various theoretical viewpoints. In this next chapter, we provide such a framework by focusing attention on the study of criminal events.

PART III

THE CRIMINAL EVENT

THE CRIMINAL EVENT

In this chapter, we will outline a framework for organizing our integrated approach to the analysis of crime and crime control. This framework emphasizes the study of crime as *criminal events* (Gould, 1989). We have already pointed out that, throughout most of the history of criminology, researchers have attempted to understand crime in society largely in terms of the actions of criminal offenders (Cohen and Felson, 1979). The simple implication of this approach is that crimes represent little more than the enactment of the will of people who are motivated to behave criminally. If this view is valid, the task of the criminologist is to try to explain why some people behave criminally, while the task of the police and other criminal justice agencies is to prevent offenders from behaving criminally or to capture and reform them after they have done so.

While it is, of course, impossible to try to understand crime in society without reference to the lawbreaker, it is also true, as we have already pointed out, that there is much more to crime than the offender. Crimes also involve, in many cases, victims who resist their victimization and in so doing affect the course of action (Kleck and Sayles, 1990; Webb and Marshall, 1989; Ziegenhagen and Brosnan, 1985). They may also involve bystanders and witnesses whose presence may either deter an offender or facilitate the commission of the crime

(Shotland and Goodstein, 1984). Bystanders or victims may also summon the police, whose appearance at the scene may affect the response of offenders.

The criminal event cannot be separated from the physical and social settings in which it occurs. Many forms of crime are intricately linked to the routine activities in which both victims and offenders engage, and to the places in which these activities occur (Sherman, Gartin, and Buerger, 1989). More generally, criminal events involve the members of the public whose response to perceived increases in crime levels results in pressure on the police to pursue more aggressively some categories of offenders. On an even broader scale, crimes involve the actions of lawmakers and the social groups to whom they are responsive. The concept of the criminal event encourages us to conceptualize crime in terms that encompass but also extend beyond the study of offenders. In other words, rather than "individual" events, crimes are "social events" (Gould, 1989).

CRIMES AS SOCIAL EVENTS

What is meant by a conceptualization of crimes as social events? To characterize crimes as *events* is to recognize that as incidents that occur at particular times in particular places. Like any other type of social event—a dinner

BOX 5.1   THE DIVERSE CHARACTER OF CRIMINAL EVENTS

CASE ONE

I'm on the seventh floor of a seven-story building, and there are steps to go to the roof, and there's nothing on the roof except tarpaper. For some obscure reason, people manage to get into the building. There's no intercom system, and there's just a buzzer. One night, the door buzzed, and we buzzed back because we had expected company. We go to the door and looked through the peephole. We see this body come up the steps, come off the elevator, and start looking around. So Rob [Karen's husband] stuck his head out of the door and said, "Get the hell out of here!" And the guy said, "If you come after me, I'm gonna knife you to death!" Rob quickly beat a fast retreat and shut the door. So we went and called the cops. In the meantime, the guy comes up the steps to the roof, and we hear shuffling around on the roof [group laughter]. So we go to the door again, and we're looking around the door—shuffle— [laughter]—and the guy comes down again to the seventh floor, and a light goes on when you push the elevator button. He pushed the button at the *exact* second that the cops hit the button. So you couldn't tell if someone downstairs was coming up. But you never saw anybody get such a *surprise in their entire life* when he's standing there to open the elevator door and there's these cops: *"All right, get outta here!"* [group laughter] (cited in Wachs, 1988: 9–10).

CASE TWO

Buried in secret files of the Ford Motor Company lies evidence that big auto makers have put profits ahead of lives. Their lack of concern has caused thousands of people to die or be horribly disfigured in fiery car crashes. Undisclosed Ford tests have demonstrated that the big auto makers could have made safer automobiles by spending a few dollars more on each car (Anderson and Whitten, 1976: B7).

CASE THREE

Another form of gaining extra money is "double dipping" whereby a practitioner can essentially claim two fees for the provision of one service. This form of abuse is exemplified by the salaried surgeon at a large city hospital who was billing the government health system for private patients he consulted with and operated on while working for the hospital. In effect, this surgeon was collecting extra income for the treatment given, a practice that almost doubled his salary. Health investigators who initially questioned the surgeon by phone on his billing patterns were astonished when the doctor confessed to "double dipping." He claimed that he was required to commit fraud because his hospital salary would not sustain his accustomed affluent lifestyle. RCMP investigation into the case stalled, however, when the surgeon's supervisor stated that permission had been given for "loose working arrangements" for the salaried position, enabling the surgeon to work whatever hours he chose at the hospital in addition to performing fee-for-service treatment. Despite the investigators' convictions that the supervisor was "covering up" for the surgeon, it was not possible to prove the case and the investigation had to be discontinued (Wilson, Lincoln, and Chappell, 1986: 133).

CASE FOUR

I remember one particularly violent time. When we were first married. He was out drinking and he came home stinking drunk. I suppose I must have said something. Well, he took a fit. He started putting his fist through the walls. Finally, he just picked up the Christmas tree and threw it at me (Gelles and Straus, 1988: 95).

CASE FIVE

The accused had been attending a party on a cold winter night. During the evening he started the car to warm the engine so the car would start when he was ready to go home. He did not intend to drive home, however, and had aranged for someone else to drive since he knew he was impaired. The police found him behind the wheel with the motor running. The Supreme Court affirmed the decision of the Court of Appeal which held the intent to drive the vehicle is not necessary for the offence. The court stated: "Care or control may be exercised where the accused performs some acts or series of acts involving the use of the car, its fittings or equipment ... whereby the car may be unintentionally set in motion creating the danger that the section is designed to prevent." (Barnhorst, Barnhorst, and Clarke, 1992: 236).

party, a corporate board meeting, or a car accident—they are more likely to happen under particular circumstances and to involve particular types of people. This conceptualization of crime runs counter to our tendency to think about criminal events as the mere by-products of chance. We speak of the crime victim as having been "unlucky." We maintain that crimes occur because some people are in "the wrong place at the wrong time." But if such events are accidents, they are *systematic* accidents (Felson, 1987). Like many other surprises in life, they are made more or less likely by the choices people make about how and where they spend their time, energy, and money.

The term event also conveys an *episodic* quality. Criminal events, like all forms of social events, have a beginning and an end. This is not to deny the fact that the participants in the event may have had a prior association or—in the case of a homicide, for instance—that some form of conflict may have predated the event (Luckenbill, 1977). It is to suggest, however, that the criminal event has its own distinct dimensions that are related to, but may be understood as distinct from, what went on before it. In a similar way, it is also possible to speak of the aftermath of criminal events, in which other social processes are set in motion. Much of the daily business of the criminal justice system is relevant in this respect. Offenders are accused and tried, court dispositions are carried out, and victims must learn to cope with the "pains of victimization" (Lurigio and Resick, 1990). As well, members of the public who learn about criminal events through mass-media reports or through conversations with neighbours may become more concerned about their personal safety or about the crime problem and its effect on society.

The *social* character of criminal events derives from the fact that they involve interaction between human beings. If the event has several offenders, these offenders interact with one another as well as with victims or bystanders. The police interact with these and other event participants. Even an act of vandalism involving a lone youthful offender and an unoccupied school building has social dimensions. A sticker on the door advising that the property is patrolled by security may encourage the offender to weigh the risks associated with the offence. Conversely, a run-down building with broken windows may be read by the offender as announcing that no one cares about the appearance of the property (Wilson and Kelling, 1983). In either case, the offender reads and (using past experience as a guide) interprets the signs, and then acts accordingly. The vandalism itself may be intended as a message to other youth, or to unpopular teachers.

The behaviour of any one participant in the criminal event, then, intersects with and influences the behaviour of other participants. This interaction importantly shapes the course of the event, determining the stages through which it will proceed and the extent to which it will be judged a serious one. In order to fully appreciate the complexity of criminal events, we must understand their behavioural and situational elements. A consideration of the principal participants in these events provides a useful starting point.

OFFENDERS

OFFENDER CHARACTERISTICS

The accumulated body of criminological research indicates that particular social characteristics are associated with a higher likelihood of offender involvement in criminal events. For most categories of offences, offenders tend to be young, disadvantaged males. The relationship between age and offender status has been well documented through the use of a variety of data sources (Gottfredson and Hirschi, 1990; U.S. Department of Justice, 1988). Involvement in offending is highest among those in late adolescence and early adulthood. Property-crime offending peaks at a somewhat earlier age than does violent offending (Flowers, 1989). In the United States, property-crime arrests peak at age 16 and drop by one-half by age 20, while violent offending reaches a peak at age 18 (U.S. Department of Justice, 1988). Crimes such as embezzlement, fraud, and gambling do not conform to this general trend in that they are characterized by higher levels of involvement somewhat later in the life cycle (Steffensmeier and Allen, 1991).

Offender status is also strongly related to gender (Campbell, 1990). In the United States in 1987, eight out of every ten people arrested were males (Flowers, 1989). Similarly, in Canada, only about one out of eight of the adults charged under the Criminal Code were females; the figure dropped to one out of ten in the case of violent crime. As shown in Table 5.2, the rate of offence for women in 1989 was 1,092 per 100,000 men and women, while the male rate was 6,652 per 100,000. Noteworthy in this table is the fact that the rate of offence for women rose from 476 in 1962 to 1,092 in 1989. Most of this increase was due to growth in property offences (from 66 to 414 per 100,000 in that time period). While there has been evidence in recent years that the gender gap in offending has been closing, much of the rhetoric about the "new female criminal" has overstated the case. The narrowing of the gender gap has occurred primarily with respect to nonviolent property

Table 5.1 Profile of Incarcerated Offender Populations in Canada, 1991–1992

Male			Female		
Profile	Number of Offenders[a]	%	Profile	Number of Offenders[c]	%
Age 20–34 yrs	8,604	(59.9)	Age 20–34 yrs	159	(53.0)
Single[b]	8,608	(60.0)	Single[d]	205	(65.5)
Common law	3,932	(27.4)	Common law	60	(19.2)
Married	1,813	(12.6)	Married	48	(15.3)
Serving first penitentiary term	8,527	(56.3)	Serving first penitentiary term	257	(82.1)
Serving a sentence of less than six years	8,685	(60.5)	Serving a sentence of less than six years	188	(60.1)
Serving a sentence for:			Serving a sentence for:		
Homicide	1,698	(11.8)	Homicide	58	(18.5)
Attempted murder	264	(1.8)	Attempted murder	3	(1.0)
Manslaughter	607	(4.2)	Manslaughter	43	(13.7)
Sexual offences	1,894	(13.2)	Sexual offences	5	(1.6)
Other violent offences	884	(6.2)	Other violent offences	23	(7.3)
Robbery	3,366	(23.5)	Robbery	45	(14.4)
Other nonviolent offences	2,267	(15.8)	Other nonviolent offences	61	(19.5)
Break & enter	2,058	(14.3)	Break & enter	4	(1.3)
Drugs	1,315	(9.2)	Drugs	71	(22.7)

[a] The profile was based on an on-register male population of 14,353.

[b] Includes offenders who are separated, divorced, widowed, and not stated.

[c] The profile was based on an on-register male population of 313.

[d] Includes offenders who are separated, divorced, widowed, and not stated.

Race	Male	%	Female	%
Caucasian	11,664	(81.3)	204	(65.2)
Aboriginal	1,546	(10.8)	62	(19.8)
Black	649	(4.5)	25	(8.1)
Asiatic	126	(0.9)	10	(3.1)
Other	368	(2.5)	12	(3.8)
Total	14,353	(100)	313	(100)

Source: Correctional Services of Canada/National Parole Board, *Basic Facts About Corrections in Canada, 1992 Edition*. Ottawa: Minister of Supply and Services Canada, 1992. Reproduced with permission of the Minister of Supply and Services Canada, 1993.

Table 5.2 Rate of Females (F) and Males (M) Charged per 100,000 Women and Men, by Selected Offences

Year	All Offences		Violent Offences		Property Offences		Total Code Criminal		Other Federal	
	F	M	F	M	F	M	F	M	F	M
1962	476	5,692	15	308	66	884	159	1,900	34	361
1965	601	6,448	19	363	102	849	207	1,959	25	317
1970	636	6,658	27	463	186	1,215	304	2,524	36	432
1975	809	7,258	43	505	312	1,453	480	3,016	73	744
1980	1,070	8,359	55	551	428	1,802	625	3,675	91	784
1981	1,098	8,638	55	550	449	1,907	648	3,779	87	773
1982	1,064	7,803	56	540	457	1,929	638	3,632	71	578
1983	1,075	7,623	65	619	460	1,934	661	3,749	70	538
1984	1,021	7,138	68	671	453	1,828	653	3,636	56	474
1985	975	6,655	72	714	436	1,677	637	3,490	52	445
1986	1,035	6,839	79	778	427	1,622	674	3,587	54	438
1987	1,090	6,919	88	845	438	1,592	719	3,690	58	447
1988	1,094	6,756	92	890	435	1,553	727	3,697	58	449
1989	1,092	6,652	98	947	414	1,454	715	3,641	72	491

Note: Numbers don't add to totals, as the category "all offences" includes provincial statutes and municipal bylaws.

Source: *Uniform Crime Reporting Survey,* Canadian Centre for Justice Statistics.

crimes, for which the gender differential has always been less extreme than it has been in the case of violent crime (Flowers, 1989; Hartnagel, 1992). For most types of criminal events, offending is still very much a male activity.

For many so-called common varieties of crime, such as assault, break and enter, robbery and homicide, offending is associated with various measures of social and economic disadvantage (Silverman and Nielsen, 1992). These differences emerge most clearly when the most serious forms of crime are examined (Harris, 1991). Offenders who show up in arrest data tend to be unemployed, temporarily employed, or in part-time, unskilled, or semi-skilled jobs (Flowers, 1989). Offending is also associated with minority group membership. Such an association has been extensively documented with respect to African-Americans in the United States and Native people in Canada (Sampson, 1985; Silverman and Nielsen, 1992). Corporate crimes suggest a departure from this pattern in that offenders involved in such crimes tend to be "predominantly well-educated people with good jobs" (Snider, 1992: 320).

An emphasis on the social and demographic characteristics of individual offenders should not detract attention from the fact that, in the context of many criminal events, offending has collective dimensions. Most delinquency, for instance, is committed in groups rather than by individuals (Giordano, Cernkovich, and Pugh, 1986; Sampson and Lauritsen, 1990). Criminal events involving corporate offending or organized crime may involve several complex levels of organization (Snider, 1992). These differing levels of offender organization strongly affect the course of criminal events.

OFFENDER PERCEPTIONS

Those who are defined by others as offenders may not share this view of who they are or what their actions mean. Black (1983) argues that much of what is regarded as crime by the criminal justice system is seen as something quite the opposite by those whom the criminal justice system labels as offenders. From the point of view of the offender, crimes frequently have a moralistic basis. According to Black, offending can be a form of social control when people use it to define and respond to behaviour they regard as having violated expectations of appropriate conduct.

Seen in this way, those who commit acts of assaults, vandalism, or even murder may be understood as individuals engaged in a quest for justice (Agnew, 1990; Katz, 1988). This position recognizes that those who are judged to be offenders frequently feel victimized by those against whom they offend. Studies of homicide have shown that the eventual victim is often the first event participant to brandish a weapon or threaten deadly force (Luckenbill, 1977; Wolfgang, 1958). Similarly, in many cases of assault, offenders may feel that they are merely responding to verbal or physical transgressions on the part of others (Felson, Baccaglini, and Ribner, 1985; Luckenbill, 1984). The wife who shoots her husband after decades of abuse may question a justice system that categorizes her as the offender and her husband as the victim.

HOW DO THEY DIFFER?

Excuses vs. Justifications

An excuse admits that a given act is wrong but denies responsibility for the act. A justification, on the other hand, accepts responsibility for the act but denies the immorality of the act.

If asked to explain their actions, offenders typically offer two types of accounts: excuses and justifications (Scott and Lyman, 1968). An *excuse* admits that a given act is wrong but denies responsibility for the act. A *justification,* on the other hand, accepts responsibility for the act but denies the immorality of the act. Such accounts provide distinct interpretations of offenders, their victims, and their offences.

A study of convicted rapists found that, while offenders admitted their offences, they denied that they were to blame for what had happened (Scully and Marolla, 1984). By offering excuses relating to the use of drugs, alcohol, or the persistence of "emotional problems," they attempted to disown their blameworthiness. In a similar way, police use of force against suspects may be excused by defining it as a natural outcome of the strong emotions that arise in the course of police work (Hunt 1985). White-collar offenders might argue that their crimes are committed out of ignorance or an inattention to detail, and, further, that they must be considered in the context of an otherwise law-abiding life. Even contract killers may offer self-definitions that mitigate personal blame. Levi (1981) maintains that organized-crime hit men deny responsibility by emphasizing the need to avoid the potentially fatal penalties that could result from their failure to fulfil a contract.

Offenders may claim that their crime has had positive effects. White-collar criminals, for example, might argue that their actions saved a failing business and thereby preserved much-needed jobs. They may also favourably compare their offences with those of "real" criminals like robbers or rapists (Benson, 1985). People who are guilty of workplace theft or income-tax evasion might defend their actions by arguing that "everyone does it" and "the only real crime is getting caught."

Offender accounts may also make reference to the culpability of victims. The rapist may contend that the victim seduced him; or that she said no but really meant yes (Scully and Marolla, 1984). While these justifications do not deny the accusation, they do deny the moral and legal interpretations that others attach to the behaviour. In the case of police violence, some types of people are defined by the police as legitimate targets of physical force because they are known "cop haters" or troublemakers (Hunt, 1985).

However, offender accounts may be driven by more than personal motivations. Frequently they reflect pervasive cultural beliefs. The excuses and justifications articulated by the rapist, for instance, borrow from more general sexist imagery about the blameworthiness of sexual assault victims. In addition, the cultural environment and the historical period partly determine the degree to which an offender account is viewed as plausible. In the late 20th century, people tend to dismiss accounts that propose demonic possession as an excuse for crime, although such accounts would have been accepted in an earlier period. By contrast, in the present era, the "culture" of large bureaucracies allows white-collar offenders to deny personal responsibility for their actions (Benson, 1984), but does so in a period in which there is increasing public sentiment that these individuals need to be held accountable for their actions (Snider, 1992).

Offender accounts also alert us to the fact that we apply the label of offender only with relative certainty. Most of us are unequivocal in our judgment of the man who hides in the bushes and subsequently sexually assaults a woman who is a stranger to him. Until recently, however, our feelings about labelling offenders who are intimately involved with their victims have been more ambivalent. Many people might argue that a husband who assaults a wife has somehow committed a less serious act than has a stranger who assaults another stranger (Bograd, 1988).

Our judgments about the suitability of an offender label may also be complicated by the social context in which the offending occurs. A homicide that results from a heated argument between drunken patrons of a bar may not seem as clear-cut as one that occurs in a more sedate environment. When we draw attention to the relationship between offender labels and offender characteristics, to the victim–offender relationship, or to the social setting, we are suggesting that the study of the offender is inseparable from the study of other dimensions of the criminal event.

When considering the offender, we must also take into account those factors that will restrict or curtail criminal behaviour. The contemporary debate about deterrence strategies revolves around differing views about the effects of punishment. According to Williams and Hawkins (1986), individuals are less afraid of punishment per se than of being judged harshly by others for having received it. By contrast, Wilson and Herrnstein (1985) are among those who argue that individuals are deterred only through a punishment scheme that takes into account their innate propensity to offend. This perspective focuses on specific efforts to incarcerate and immobilize rather than the social stigma and the role of community forces in reducing criminality.

'VICTIMLESS' CRIMES

For many types of criminal events, it is useful to recognize a victim role. Victims include the people whose purses are stolen, whose homes are broken into, and who are murdered in the course of the event. For other event categories, such as drug use or gambling offences, victims cannot be said to exist in any direct and immediate way, although many would argue that it is incorrect to consider such offences "victimless crimes" (Nettler, 1984).

The degree to which the law should be applied to victimless crimes revolves around the question of harm. While there is widespread support for legalizing various forms of vice, there persists great concern about the potential negative effects of doing so. The law currently deals with prostitution by restricting it to certain public places (although certain jurisdictions discourage all forms of prostitution, including that which occurs via massage parlours). The prevailing view is that victimless crimes are not victimless, and need to be regulated through the criminal law.

Arguments for removing the restrictions that have been placed on victimless crimes come from the view that policing these acts represents an overreach of the law. Consenting adults should have the freedom to partake in certain activities. Further, criminalization tends to affect only the disadvantaged and others who cannot pursue these activities in private. Advocates of legalization argue that many of the problems associated with victimless crimes would be eliminated were these behaviours allowed to operate in regulated (but legal) environments. From their perspective, it is not the behaviour itself but rather that fact that it has been driven underground that gives rise to the criminal subcultures that surround it.

VICTIM CHARACTERISTICS

Surveys of direct victims of crime demonstrate that involvement in criminal events as a victim, like involvement as an offender, is not a random matter. In fact, many of the social characteristics associated with offending are also associated with victimization.

Like offenders, the victims of crime tend to be young. A national study of crime victims in Canada, the General Social Survey, found that the highest rates of four types of personal victimization (personal theft, sexual assault, robbery, assault) were experienced by people who were between the ages of 15 and 24 (see Table 5.3). This group had a rate of victimization that was almost seven times the rate experienced by those between the ages of 45 and 64 (Johnson and Sacco, 1991). This finding is consistent with that of similar surveys done in Canada, in the United States, and elsewhere (Fattah, 1991). Despite much talk about a crime wave against the elderly, people over the age of 65 are least likely to be victims of crime (Fattah and Sacco, 1989).

Surveys of crime victims also indicate that, for most types of crime, males have higher rates of victimization than females (Smith, 1987). The General Social Survey found that the male rate of violent victimization was 90 incidents per 1,000, while the female rate was 77 incidents per 1,000. A victim survey conducted in seven major Canadian cities found that males have a rate of violence approximately twice as high as the female rate (Solicitor General, 1985a). The major exception to this pattern, of course, is the crime of sexual assault, which disproportionately victimizes women (Laub, 1990). It might be added that several researchers question the extent to which surveys of this type accurately portray the level of women's victimization, an issue we will return to in Chapter 6.

The link between social disadvantage and victimization is less clear-cut than in the case of offending (Cohen, Kluegel, and Land, 1981; Fattah, 1991). To some extent, the nature of the relationship depends on the type of event. For serious crimes of violence, studies generally support the conclusion that the poor and members of visible minorities are most likely to become victims of crime (Sacco and Johnson, 1990; U.S. Department of Justice, 1988). In Canada, aboriginal people account for about 2 or 3 percent of the population but comprise about 15 percent of murder victims (Silverman and Kennedy, 1993). Our ability to more generally describe relationships involving crime and ethnicity is impaired by the fact that such data are not collected in Canada, except in the case of homicide. With respect to some forms of household theft, and personal theft that does not involve contact between the offender and the victim, the risks of victimization are greater for higher-income groups (Laub, 1990; Sacco and Johnson, 1990; Solicitor General, 1983).

VICTIM PERCEPTIONS

Like offenders, victims may be reluctant to define events in which they are involved as crimes. In some cases, even while the event is underway, it may involve ambiguous or unfamiliar elements that are not readily understood as

Table 5.3 Personal Victimization Rates by Selected Population Characteristics (per 1,000), General Social Survey, 1988

	Total Personal	Theft	Violence
Total	143	59	83
Gender			
Male	148	58	90
Female	138	61	77
Age			
15–24	311	123	188
25–44	158	65	92
45–64	46	22	23
65+	—	—	—
Income			
Less than 15,000	142	46	96
15,000–29,999	149	55	94
30,000–39,999	146	61	85
40,000–59,999	121	56	65
60,000+	158	78	80
Education			
Some secondary or less	138	55	83
Sec. grad., trade school dip., etc.	117	46	71
Some postsecondary	174	74	99
Postsecondary degree or diploma	153	64	88
Marital Status			
Married or common law	88	44	45
Single	274	107	168
Widow or widower	—	—	—
Separated/divorced	274	66	208
Residence			
Urban	158	70	88
Rural	114	46	68
Main Activity			
Working at job or business	145	62	83
Looking for work	156	—	—
Student	360	151	210
Keeping house	81	28	53
Retired	—	—	—
Evenings Out (per month)			
Less than 10	55	26	29
10–19	88	46	42
20–29	153	63	89
30 or more	284	105	179
Alcohol Consumption			
Non-drinker	90	42	48
Occasional	141	56	85
Total current	164	67	97
< 1 drink/week	156	58	98
1–6 drinks/week	154	69	85
7–13 drinks/week	175	88	87
14+ drinks/week	294	—	220

— Rate cannot be estimated reliably.

Source: H. Johnson and V.F. Sacco, "The Risk of Criminal Victimization: Data from a National Study," in Robert A. Silverman, James J. Teevan, Jr., and Vincent F. Sacco, *Crime in Canadian Society* (4th ed.). Toronto: Butterworths, 1991.

criminal victimization. A study of mugging victims reported that many of those victimized did not immediately define the event as a predatory crime; some even thought the mugger was a neighbour in search of assistance or someone playing a joke (Lejeune and Alex, 1973).

Willingness to label an event a crime generally depends on the degree of coherence between the victim's definition of a "typical crime" and the characteristics of the event in question (Ruback, Greenberg, and Wescott, 1984). However, some types of crimes are inherently more ambiguous than others. The meaning of many forms of sexual victimization may be highly problematic with respect to the labels that victims assign to them. A study of 94 American women who were sexually assaulted found that they did not define the act as rape unless sexual intercourse was involved (Scheppele and Bart, 1983). Crime definitions are generally not ambiguous when the events contain elements that imply a high degree of legal seriousness (Agnew, 1985a).

To some extent, the reluctance to view oneself as a victim results from the fact that the label of victim may carry substantial social costs. Despite the gains made in recent years by various victims' rights movements, victimization is often associated with a loss of self-esteem. With respect to sexual assault, for instance, the culturally pervasive sexism that allows offenders to excuse or justify their actions also blames women for their own victimization. Acknowledging victimization in such instances may be seen as an admission of complicity or recklessness (Miller and Porter, 1983). Victims of burglary or the scams of clever con artists may engage in self-blame. They may feel that they acted foolishly and that their victimization signals some weakness of character. To call oneself a crime victim may be to embrace a negative self-image (Taylor, Wood, and Lichtman, 1983).

In addition, viewing oneself as a victim may necessitate a revision of assumptions about personal invulnerability. Most of us derive a certain amount of psychological comfort from believing our daily world to be a place that does not threaten us (Janoff-Bulman and Frieze, 1983). It is easier to get through the day if we think that we are not at risk or, at least, that we can control the risks that do confront us. Victimization, however, may erode these beliefs and encourage us to view the world as a more threatening place.

One way of coping with the trauma of crime is to engage in a "cognitive re-evaluation" (Janoff-Bulman and Frieze, 1983; Ruback, Greenberg, and Wescott, 1984). An ambiguous event that might be seen as a crime need not be treated as such. Defining a given incident as a crime from a legal perspective does not guarantee that victims will employ legal criteria in their attempts to make sense of the event (Agnew, 1985a). As we have seen, the definitions of events—including consensus about the identities of the offenders and victims, or about the facts of the event—are not always easily reached. As Nettler (1984) points out, in judging the actions of others, we must consider the possibility of accident, mental disorder, confusion, or some other factor that mitigates against the identification of a clearly defined offender and victim. If the criminal character of an event is undeniable, victims may minimize its seriousness by comparing their experience with that of others for whom the consequences of victimization were more severe, or by defining the event as one that actually produced positive consequences (Taylor, Wood, and Lichtman, 1983). If an event can be successfully redefined so as to diminish its victimizing character, many of the more immediate costs associated with the status of victim may be avoided.

The issue of family violence provides a particularly vivid illustration of the importance of victim definition processes. The reluctance of women to label as criminal or abusive violence that is encountered in the context of intimate relationships has been well documented (Ferraro and Johnson, 1983; Sedlak, 1988). As in the case of sexual assault, there has been (until recently) a firmly entrenched cultural tendency to blame women for their victimization in domestic relationships. If women remain in abusive relationships, they may be labelled "sick" or "masochistic," or they may be accused of "bringing it on themselves." If they attempt to flee the abuse, they may find relatively few supports available. A woman may be required to confront her abuser or spend time in hiding.

Such action may increase rather than decrease the risk of future victimization. As parents, in-laws, and neighbours choose sides, many may blame the victim for breaking up the family and suggest that if she really loved her children she would have "made the best of it." These factors may discourage a woman from viewing herself as a victim, since acknowledging that one's mate is an abuser is the first step in re-evaluating and changing one's life circumstances, a process that might entail violent retaliation by the abusive partner. A denial of the violent character of the victimization and the victimizer may allow the abused partner to tolerate conditions an outsider would think intolerable (Ferraro and Johnson, 1983).

BYSTANDERS AND WITNESSES

In many cases, criminal events involve individuals other than those who can be described as offenders or victims. Bystanders in many events are more than passive spectators. They may by their very presence deter an offender from committing a crime or they may prevent an event from escalating. Conversely, they may facilitate the offender's actions. A young male who is insulted by someone in the presence of his peers may be naturally inclined to respond to the insult in an aggressive fashion or else encouraged to do so by the peer group. Bystanders may also call the police or offer to act as witnesses (Shotland and Goodstein, 1984).

What bystanders do, if anything, depends on several factors. Their actions may be influenced, for example, by their view of, or relationship to, the victim and/or offender (Steffensmeier and Steffensmeier, 1977); by how they define the personal costs associated with intervention; and by how much confidence they have in their ability to intervene (Shotland and Goodstein, 1984).

Bystanders are also affected by what they perceive to be transpiring between victim and offender. According to Shotland and Straw (1976), bystanders are less likely to intervene in a violent assault perpetrated by a man against a woman if they perceive them to be married rather than strangers (Shotland and Straw, 1976). Davis (1991) suggests that when people witness adults physically abusing children in public their concern about intervening in a "private matter" overrides their concern about the welfare of the child. In a highly publicized case that took place in New York City a number of years ago, a woman named Kitty Genovese was attacked by a man in the courtyard of a large apartment complex (Conklin, 1975). The attack continued for a long period of time, during which Genovese's screams for help went unanswered. She finally succumbed to the attack and died on the street. Although many people in the apartment block witnessed the attack, no one called the police, much less intervened. According to those who researched the event, the apartment dwellers had interpreted the attack as a quarrel between a married couple and, therefore, as a private affair.

Criminal events are frequently ambiguous from the standpoint of bystanders. We do not expect to witness a crime and may be so engrossed in our own activities that an event may be well underway before it comes to our attention (Hartman et al., 1972). By the time we make sense of the event and think of a response, it may be too late. The presence of several bystanders tends to reduce the likelihood that any one bystander will take action to assist a victim. This is particularly true if the bystanders are strangers to one another and do not share a common cultural frame of reference (Shotland, 1976). One bystander among many is required to accept only part of the responsibility for not acting; he or she may provide the rationalization that somebody else would take action were something seriously wrong.

Bystanders may be asked to perform as witnesses. How valuable are eye-witness accounts in providing accurate depictions of the activities that took place in a criminal event? The research suggests that these accounts are quite inaccurate, with bystanders failing to remember even key characteristics of the offender or the event (Loftus, 1979).

POLICE

POLICE PRACTICE

Police involvement in criminal events may result from either proactive or reactive mobilization. As the police engage in routine patrol work, they may come upon people or situations they define as criminal. Proactive policing is not in any sense a random or arbitrary process. Rather, it is importantly influenced by police priorities, prevailing community concerns, available police resources, and the styles and traditions that characterize police work in particular areas (Desroches, 1991). In a comprehensive study of policing in suburban Toronto, Ericson (1982) reports that police officers who are engaged in patrol activities use cues that structure their proactive work. For example, their attention may be attracted by individuals who appear in particular places at particular times of the day. Conversely, events that could be defined as crimes are not labelled as such, because the police choose not to stop and question a suspect.

In his study of the policing of a heroin-using community in a western Canadian city, Stoddart (1991) reports that heroin users who act as police informants are less likely to be pursued by the police than are heroin users who are perceived as interfering with police work. His research suggests that proactive police activity is influenced not only by what the police do but also by the visibility of the offender's behaviour. Stoddart argues that changes in the nature of the heroin-using community over time have increased the probability of arrest. Members of the heroin-using community today are more apathetic than their predecessors about the fate of their colleagues and less attentive to the risks associated with illegal drug use. Such factors increase the visibility of the behaviour, thereby facilitating police intervention.

It is worth noting that the line between reactive and proactive police mobilization is frequently unclear (Ericson, 1982). Citizens may decide to mobilize the police reactively as a result of police-sponsored crime-prevention campaigns that encourage them to do so. On the other hand, widespread public concern about specific crime problems may influence the administrative decisions that are made by police with respect to proactive mobilization. Desroches (1991) reports on a police investigation of impersonal homosexual behaviour in public washrooms, known as "tearooms." While the fact that evidence was gathered through police-surveillance techniques would appear to suggest a proactive police stance on the problem, Desroches indicates this police involvement was largely a response to requests from citizens or businesses that enforcement in this area become more aggressive.

POLICE INVOLVEMENT IN DEFINING CRIMINAL EVENTS

The type of mobilization, whether proactive or reactive, does not determine how the police will intervene in a particular event. The action taken by the police officer may depend on a variety of contingencies, including the characteristics of the incident, the behaviour of the participants, and the nature of the requests being made of the police (Smith, 1987; Gottfredson and Gottfredson, 1988; Bayley, 1986).

Police tend to respond most emphatically to (i.e., treat officially) events that they perceive as conforming to legal definitions of serious crimes (Black, 1970; Gottfredson and Gottfredson, 1988; Gove, Hughes, and Geerken, 1985). Also of importance in determining police response is the relationship between the victim and the offender. According to Black (1970), the more distant the relationship between a victim and an offender, the more likely the police are to regard the incident as criminal. This observation is consistent with the frequently cited tendency of police officers to process crimes "unofficially" when the disputants are family members (Bell, 1987).

The characteristics of victims and offenders have been shown to influence police decisions. In an American study of police responses to interpersonal violence, Smith (1987) found that police officers are less likely to employ legal solutions in situations that involve African-American or female victims. In contrast, Boritch (1992) reports findings from Ontario that show that the criminal justice system deals more harshly with women offenders than male offenders, particularly those who deviate from accepted standards of feminine behaviour. Violence between males is more likely to result in arrest than is violence between a male and a female, which tends to be resolved through less formal means, such as the physical separation of the disputing parties. Police decision-making may also be influenced by the demeanour and the preferences of those involved in the event (Smith, 1987). Thus, the police are more likely to label an event as a crime when the complainant is deferential to them or requests that they take official action (Black, 1970; Gove, Hughes, and Geerken, 1985).

Increasingly, however, police discretion in particularly sensitive areas, such as family violence, is being removed (Ursel and Farough, 1986). Police officers are now required to lay charges when they have physical evidence that an assault has taken place, even if the victim is reluctant to lay the charge. This practice was established in response to Sherman and Berk's (1984) findings that arrest is the most effective way of deterring violence among intimates, and that mediative techniques do not curtail repeat offences. Sherman (1992) reports that, in the late 1980s, more than half of the police forces across North America had in place a mandatory charge rule for the handling of domestic assault cases.

For some observers, removing police discretion means reducing the chances that police bias will enter into decisions that are made about the seriousness of certain violent acts. For others, it means depriving police of the opportunity to defuse situations before they become dangerous. Recent research indicates that arrest may actually heighten rather than lower the chance of violence in domestic situations (Sherman, 1992). It has also been argued that we are creating new problems by bringing individuals into an overburdened court system that is not equipped to handle their problems.

THE SETTING OF CRIMINAL EVENTS

Modernization of our society over the last century has shaped the nature of social disorder and crime in contemporary cities. Gurr (1980) has extensively studied the ways in which crime in Western societies has been shaped by four aspects of modernization: (1) industrialization, (2) the growth of cities, (3) the expression of the state's powers and resources, and (4) the humanization of interpersonal relations. These factors have combined to create the pressures in modern society that have led to an unprecedented rise in crime. Further, because many of these factors are difficult to change, the range of options open to us in dealing with the growth of crime has been reduced.

Accompanying the increase in personal wealth in the late 19th and early 20th centuries was a demand for the protection of private property. Moral crusades led to calls for the constraint of undesirable practices such as gambling and vagrancy. The response to demands for more social order included devising techniques of legal criminalization, uniformed policing, and incarceration (Gurr, 1980:36). The development of formal structures led to a transformation from the use of local action in controlling deviant behaviour to the formalization of response through legal codes.

Gurr suggests that this formalization was accompanied by an increase in humanitarianism, in which emphasis was shifted from punishment to rehabilitation back into the community. In recent years, victims rather than offenders have increasingly become the subjects of this humanitarianism, a situation that paradoxically has resulted in an increased demand for harsher penal response to actions (including family violence) that previously were not included in criminal categories.

According to Gurr, the fear of crime that stems from the disorder of fast-growing cities has resulted in increased calls for more police and for more efficient and effective courts. The view that we are moving away from the community as the major basis of social control in society is counterbalanced by evidence that the community still plays a crucial role in both generating and controlling deviance. On the one hand, then, it is argued that the community has become less important as a forum of social control because state powers have assumed responsibility for protecting the victim. On the other hand, it is argued that the diversity of communities makes the imposition of a unitary state power difficult. This is a lesson that the police are learning in their experiments with community policing (see Chapter 10).

To suggest that there is a relationship between criminal events and the places in which these events occur is to imply that location involves something more than just happenstance. In other words, place matters. There is something about particular types of locations that increases (or decreases) the likelihood that criminal events will unfold. Any attempt to investigate these issues must deal with the fact that particular types of places are intricately linked to particular types of activities. People who live in the centre of a major Canadian city may structure their activities differently from those who live in the suburban fringe (Solicitor General of Canada, 1988a). Those of us who do not live in the downtown core may occasionally journey there in search of "excitement," but for rest and relaxation we head for the countryside. We shop at malls, drink in taverns, perform occupational tasks at work, and read or study at the library. We might ask why some of these places host more criminal events than others. Is this because certain types of people tend to be attracted to these settings? Does the physical character of a place make criminal events more or less likely? Are the activities associated with a particular setting more or less likely to lead to criminal events? While these issues are discussed in greater detail in later chapters, it is useful at this point to review some of the empirical evidence about the locations of criminal events.

According to data collected by police and survey researchers, rates of many types of crimes tend to be higher in urban centres than in rural areas (Brantingham and Brantingham, 1984; Fischer, 1976). The relationship between crime and urbanism is generally stronger with respect to property crimes and "crimes of public order" (gambling, drug use) than it is with respect to crimes of violence.

Data from the 1988 General Social Survey reveal that, for the calendar year 1987, people who lived in urban areas were more likely to report being a victim of crime than were those who resided in rural areas. In many cases, the differences were slight. For example, the rate of assault among urban dwellers was 72 incidents per 1,000 people, compared to 56 incidents per 1,000 among rural residents (Sacco and Johnson, 1990). By contrast, the rate of break and enter in urban areas was twice that of rural areas (64 versus 32 incidents per 1,000 households).

In urban centres, the rates of crime vary across neighbourhoods (Roncek, 1981). A 1985 survey of crime victims in the city of Edmonton found that violent victimizations were twice as high for residents of downtown Edmonton than they were for residents of the suburbs (Solicitor General, 1987), although rates of property crimes were not markedly dissimilar in the two areas (Solicitor General of Canada, 1988a). While research into the factors that characterize high crime neighbourhoods sometimes produces conflicting evidence (Brantingham and Brantingham, 1984), much of the data supports the conclusion that these areas are likely to be poor and densely populated, and to have transient populations (Cater and Jones, 1989; Flowers, 1989; Roncek, 1981; Stark, 1987).

Even in cities or neighbourhoods that are characterized by high crime rates, most locations are crime-free. While we may think of subway stations as dangerous places, data collected by Normandeau (1987) in Montreal reveals that most have relatively low rates of crime and that only a few stations account for most of the crimes that occur in the subway system. This point is more generally illustrated in Sherman, Gartin, and Buerger's (1989) study of the location of requests for police assistance in the city of Minneapolis over a one-year period. This study revealed that relatively few "hot spots" accounted for the majority of service calls; specifically, only 3 percent of the locations in the city (addresses or street intersections) accounted for 50 percent of the 323,979 calls. With respect to predatory crimes, robberies occurred at 2.2 percent, rapes at 1.2 percent, and automobile thefts at 2.7 percent of these locations.

THE PHYSICAL SETTING

What are the characteristics of the locations that host criminal events? With respect to some types of crimes, part of the answer to this question may be found in the physical design of places or the creation of "defensible space" (Newman, 1972). In the case of a property crime, settings that offer concealment in the form of poor streetlighting, large bushes or shrubs, or hidden alleyways may make a target more attractive to an offender (Shotland and Goodstein, 1984). (See also Figure 5.1.) Similarly, a convenience store that is located near a vacant field may be more vulnerable to robbery than one that is located on a busy city street (Sherman, Gartin, and Buerger, 1989).

In a somewhat different way, patterns of family violence may be related to some elements of physical design. Violence between husbands and wives typically occurs in private settings. The growth of single-family homes not

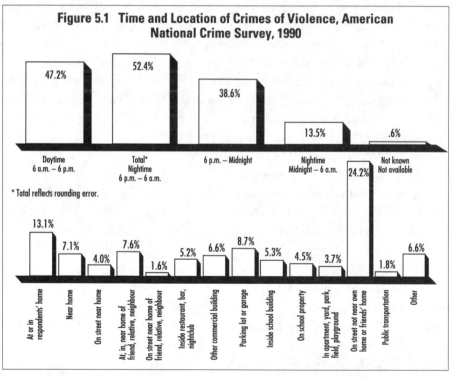

Figure 5.1 Time and Location of Crimes of Violence, American National Crime Survey, 1990

Daytime 6 a.m. – 6 p.m.	47.2%
Total* Nightime 6 p.m. – 6 a.m.	52.4%
6 p.m. – Midnight	38.6%
Nightime Midnight – 6 a.m.	13.5%
Not known Not available	.6%

* Total reflects rounding error.

At or in respondents' home	13.1%
Near home	7.1%
On street near home	4.0%
At, in, near home of friend, relative, neighbour	7.6%
On street near home of friend, relative, neighbour	1.6%
Inside restaurant, bar, nightclub	5.2%
Other commercial building	6.6%
Parking lot or garage	8.7%
Inside school building	5.3%
On school property	4.5%
In apartment, yard, park, field, playground	3.7%
On street not near own home or friends' home	24.2%
Public transportation	1.8%
Other	6.6%

Source: Bureau of Justice Statistics, *Criminal Victimization in the United States, 1990: A National Crime Victimization Survey Report.* Washington, D.C.: U.S. Department of Justice, pp. 73 and 75.

shared with boarders, lodgers, or servants—coupled with the widespread cultural understanding that the home is a private setting closed to neighbours, friends, or even other family members, except by invitation—helps ensure the concealment of such violence (Gelles and Straus, 1988). Within the home, not all locations are equally risky. According to Gelles and Straus (1988), violence most frequently occurs in the kitchen, followed by the living room and the bedroom (Gelles and Straus, 1988), although the latter place tends to be the setting for the most violent confrontations.

> *A fight that erupts in the bedroom, in the early morning, constrains both parties. It is too late to stalk out of the home to a bar and too late to run to a friend or a family member. The bed and the bedroom offer no protection and there are precious few places to flee or take cover (Gelles and Straus, 1988: 94).*

By contrast, the bathroom is relatively free of spousal violence in part because such rooms are small, have locks, and are understood to be places of individual privacy.

SOCIAL DOMAINS

Social domains may be thought of as major spheres of life, in which we invest most of our time and energy. In Chapters 7, 8, and 9, we focus on the three most important social domains—the family and household, leisure, and work. Each domain is distinguished by a particular location and pattern of activity (Lynch, 1987). People differ with respect to the amount of time that they spend in each of these domains. For the elderly retired person, the social domain of the household may be of greatest importance. Children spend much of their time at home but during the teenage years involvement in this social domain declines while involvement in the workplace and in leisure activities outside the home increases.

These social domains differ, as well, in terms of their private or public character (Fischer, 1981). The household is the most private of settings and the people we encounter there are generally better known to us than those we encounter at work or at leisure outside the home. While we tend to think of private domains as safer places than public domains, there is increasing concern about the prevalence of criminal actions that were previously seen as private acts. The definition of privacy is changing, as are the ways in which the law and the police treat privacy. The criminal event that may once have gone undetected or untreated in the "privacy" of the home is now more likely to attract public attention and strong police action.

The breakdown in the taboos about intervention in private lives reflects an increased concern about the harm done in violent events involving intimates. Private affairs in business are also attracting more attention, and there is an increased awareness of the need to prosecute white-collar criminals whose socioeconomic status once put them beyond the reach of the law. In addition, the private policing of private space has become more commonplace. Although the relationship between private and public policing is still an uneasy one, the surveillance that private police offer is an important component in the deterrence of property offences and is having an important impact on crime patterns, particularly in urban areas. Private police are not subject to the same legal controls under which public police operate. For example, private security guards may evict individuals from shopping malls without any recourse to due process.

The distinctions we make between social domains may not apply with equal force to all individuals. Some people work out of their homes, others restrict their leisure activities to the household. Still others may view the workplace as a leisure setting—a chance to gossip with co-workers. Despite these complications, the identification of distinct social domains helps us to clarify differences in patterns of criminal events.

The people we encounter in these social domains, the relationships we have with them, and the social activities that occur there strongly influence the kinds of criminal events that take place in a social domain, as well as the nature of the reactions to them. Victim surveys indicate that people who report that they frequently go out in the evening to bars also report higher rates of victimization (Sacco and Johnson, 1990). Moreover, observations of barroom behaviour (Stoddart, 1981) and police data suggest that taverns are the site of a disproportionate amount of crime (Roncek and Pravatiner, 1989).

More generally, many types of criminal events develop in leisure settings. Much juvenile crime (including drug use, vandalism, and fighting) resembles leisure pursuits (Agnew and Peterson, 1989) and is most likely to occur when youths are engaged in unsupervised peer activities such as "hanging out" (Riley, 1987; Kennedy and Baron, 1993). Many forms of sexual assault, especially "date rape," occur in leisure environments rather than in more structured environments (DeKeseredy, 1988; Thompson, 1986). Similarly, homicides are most likely to occur when the participants are engaged in recreational pursuits in informal settings (Luckenbill, 1977).

Other types of criminal events are more closely related to nonleisure activities. For the organized criminal, crime is a form of work. For the white-collar or corporate criminal, the offending behaviour may represent little more than a simple extension of his or her legitimate business practices. In other cases, a person's employment may be related to the risk of criminal victimization (Block, Felson, and Block, 1984; Linder and Koehler, 1992). People who handle money, who work in an environment that is open to the general public, or who travel from one work site to another, are especially vulnerable to many forms of victimization (Collins, Cox, and Langan, 1987; Mayhew, Elliot, and Dowds, 1989). It is partially because of these factors that taxi drivers, police officers, and nurses experience relatively high rates of violence (Block, Felson, and Block, 1984). In still other cases, it is an *absence* of activity that is related to the occurrence of criminal events. With respect to break and enter, for instance, households that are unoccupied for long periods of time are at greater risk of victimization than are households that have higher and more regular occupancy rates (Cohen and Cantor, 1981; Canadian Centre for Justice Statistics, 1988; Waller and Okihiro, 1978).

STUDYING THE CRIMINAL EVENT

We have argued that, in studying criminal events, it is important to develop explanations that move beyond the motivations of offenders or the responses of victims. A more comprehensive view must consider (1) the precursors of the event, including the locational and situational factors that bring people together in time and space; (2) how the interactions among participants define the outcomes of their actions; and (3) the aftermath of the event, including the reporting to the police, their response, the harm done and the redress required, and the long-term consequences of the event in terms of public reactions and the changing of laws.

HOW DO WE DEFINE?

The Criminal Event

The criminal event includes precursors, including the locational and situational factors that bring people together in time and space; the event itself, involving how the interactions among participants define the outcomes of their actions; and the aftermath of the event, including the reporting to the police, their response, the harm done and redress required, and the long-term consequences of the event in terms of public reactions and the changing of laws.

PRECURSORS

As criminologists, we are interested in more than just the motivation of the offender or the actions of the victims that led to the criminal act. These elements come together in a situated transaction that increases the likelihood that crime will take place. Understanding criminal events as deriving from predisposing conditions helps us to separate the social behaviour that is criminogenic from that which is not. Studying the precursors of criminal events also allows us to see that, depending on circumstance, behaviour that is defined or evolves into criminality in one situation may not have the same consequences in other situations. The relationship between participants, the interpretation of the harmfulness of the acts, the anticipated responses to certain behaviour, and the nature of the location may or may not combine to create a criminal outcome.

Of course, understanding preconditions will not necessarily allow us to predict criminal outcomes with greater accuracy. The difficulties of prediction are illustrated in the recent debate over the extent to which spousal homicide could have been anticipated on the basis of previous behaviour (Sherman et al., 1991). While the predictive capability of police is low with respect to spousal homicide, it is likely very high with respect to repeat interpersonal violence.

In determining the precursors of crime, we must reconstruct criminal events using information that may be distorted by faulty memories, rationalizations, and so on. But it is exactly this process that the courts use to establish guilt or innocence in the cases that are brought before them. In order to reflect legal as well as social reality, criminologists must incorporate a similar process in their approaches to crime.

THE EVENT

When we study the event itself, we move into an assessment of the incidents (under what circumstances?) and frequency (how often and how extensive?) of certain types of crimes. As we will see in Chapter 6, different types of data sources (e.g., Uniform Crime Reporting [UCR], victim surveys, self-report studies) tell us about different aspects of the event, or at least provide different perspectives on such events.

We are interested in the particular groups that are affected by different types of crime. It is in this context that we are able to examine the changes in offender behaviour and the extent of victimization. We are particularly interested in viewing the criminal event not in isolation but rather as it relates to social events as well to other criminal events. Discerning trends in these events helps us understand the extent to which we need to respond to them. We are also interested in understanding how trends in crime patterns coincide with trends in social conditions, economic changes, changes in resources for policing, and so on. The explanations that these types of analysis provide throw light on the vulnerability of certain groups to social change and the extent to which legal intervention can work to deter or alter criminal behaviour.

Earlier we discussed the problems associated with defining (or not defining) certains events as criminal. Victims may not immediately appreciate that they have been subject to crime, while offenders may rationalize their behaviour as something other than criminal. The strict definition of criminality comes with the actions of the police, who certify criminality through the enactment of legal process, either in naming an event as criminal or arresting an offender.

But what about the events that do not come to the attention of the police but that we could nevertheless define as being criminal? This hidden dimension of crime has important implications for how we define criminal events, as well as for the processes by which the police target certain victims or offenders. Criminal events, then, are dynamic not only in terms of their responsiveness to interactional factors in the environment but also in terms of the claims that are made about them by interested parties. These claims are continuously undergoing change in response to evolving political and cultural values.

THE AFTERMATH

The extent to which we can develop an integrated perspective is very much dependent on the types of information about criminal events to which we have access. We are concerned not only with the actual event but also with the reactions by the police, victims, and others. In considering the aftermath of an event, we are interested in the degree to which the victim has been harmed and in resources that are needed to aid in his or her recovery. We are also concerned with whether or not the offender feels that he or she can repeat the offence with impunity. With respect to punishment, has there been sufficient certainty, severity, or celerity to deter a repeat occurrence? These questions frame a great deal of the discussion about how we are managing our crime problems. Lending focus to this debate are the responses to different types of crime. We need to understand that the responses that we develop to criminality are a function of the perspectives that we use in interpreting the reasons for its occurrence; moreover, these reactions will influence the type of crime that we will experience in the future.

Summary and Conclusions
■ ■ ■

Crime is, strictly speaking, the breaking of the law. But the laws and their interpretation are an embodiment of social morality. As such, they are subject to change, as is our understanding of criminal events. Crime is a social construct that varies according to definition and response by legal authorities. It is the job of criminologists to assess how legal and moral definitions of crime coincide with the circumstances that people face and then evolve into events that demand enforcement and result in labelling individuals criminals.

The criminal event is a social event. Like all other social events, it has a beginning and an end. Criminal events are social in that they involve interaction between human beings. The nature and form of this interaction shapes the course of the event, determines the stages through which it proceeds, and defines how serious it is judged to be, in terms of harm done. Many different types of actors are involved in these events.

The most obvious participant is the offender. In the North American context, offenders tend to be young, disadvantaged males. At the same time, however, we are witnessing a growth in family violence; the major offenders in these crimes are frequently found among older and better-off males. Women are increasingly becoming involved in property crimes.

Much attention has been directed at trying to understand the motivations, as well as the group pressures, that influence the behaviour of criminals. The study of offender perceptions provides an important source of information about the pressures that direct individuals to behave in certain ways. Offenders may choose to deal with their blameworthiness by rationalizing their crimes.

While the victims of crime, like offenders, tend to be young and male, other groups are heavily victimized in particular types of crime. Sexual assault and family violence is disproportionately directed against women. The nature of victims and their relationship to offenders, then, is very much a function of the type of event that has occurred, and is governed by location and circumstance. Like offenders, victims may redefine the event as harmless or, at least, not criminal. Victim definitions can be very important in influencing the actions taken by criminal justice agencies in criminal events.

Bystanders and witnesses also have a role to play in defining and interpreting the social events that become crimes. They may defuse a violent situation or they may actually promote violence through their actions. While bystanders can be very helpful in clarifying what actually occurred during a criminal event, their accounts often prove to be inaccurate.

The police play a major role in criminal events. They have the power to certify an event as a crime by assessing the match between the event as they have come to understand it and their knowledge of what the law disallows. In reactive policing, the police respond to reports from citizens, who may be either victims or bystanders. In proactive policing, certain groups or communities are targeted for police attention as a way of preventing criminal events.

With respect to intervention, the police are heavily influenced by their perceptions of what they can do to reduce crime. Police use a great deal of discretion in their work. Used negatively, this discretion may be applied by police to discriminate against certain groups. Police discretion in family violence cases is increasingly being removed.

The police operate through the administration of the law, and, although they use some discretion in applying it, the legal structure outlines clear expectations vis-à-vis personal behaviour and the legal response to the breaking of these expectations. Law is a form of social control that defines individual actions on the basis of socially acceptable standards. Criminal events are social events and, as such, are governed by societal as well as legal tenets. Forms of control may also be socially based. Gossip, ridicule, and ostracism may combine with legal threat to discourage individuals from acting in a criminal manner.

The final aspect of criminal events that is important to consider are the conditions under which they occur. The different dimensions of people's lives, ranging from family interaction and work to leisure-time activities, all invite different types of behaviour and offer circumstances that may or may not give rise to criminal events. A comprehensive view of the criminal event must consider three key components: precursors of the crime, the event itself, and the aftermath.

Criminal events, like all forms of social events, are complicated affairs. This chapter has discussed their basic dimensions and, in so doing, has raised questions about who participates in these events, when and where they occur, and why they elicit particular forms of societal reaction. In order to understand a criminal event, we need to understand how each of its elements combines and interacts. We cannot address the issue of sexual assault by reducing the problem to a single question—why do some men commit sexual assaults? Instead, we need to put this question in an appropriate context that also asks why some women are more likely than others to be victimized by sexual assault, when and where such assaults are most likely to occur, and why police, lawmakers, and members of the general public think about sexual assault as they do.

PART IV

RESEARCH METHODS

RESEARCHING CRIMINAL EVENTS

T HE PREVIOUS CHAPTERS HAVE detailed some of the major ways in which modern criminologists think about and attempt to explain criminal events. In so doing, they raise several significant questions about why particular types of events occur, when and where they occur, why they unfold as they do, and why some people are more likely than others to be involved in events, either as offender or victim. This chapter takes up a related issue—how are the questions raised by criminological theory to be answered?

In assessing the validity of dominant explanations of criminal events, criminologists do not rely on idle speculation. Rather, they seek to determine the extent to which these explanations are consistent with the empirical evidence that describes these events. In other words, they have more confidence in a given theory if it is able to organize and make sense of the "facts of crime" as revealed by research data. This means of course, that they need to concern themselves with the quality of crime data.

This chapter discusses the major types of

information about crime to which criminologists have access. Our discussion includes not only a description of these data sources but also a critical evaluation of their various advantages and disadvantages. We begin by addressing two very general types of crime information—observations and reports.

OBSERVING CRIME

DIRECT OBSERVATION IN NATURALISTIC SETTINGS

At first glance, it may appear that the study of criminal events is a relatively straightforward matter. If researchers wish to investigate criminal events, why do they not just position themselves in a way that enables them to observe these events directly?

This could be accomplished in several ways. The researcher might (1) covertly observe a setting in which criminal events are known to occur with some frequency; (2) attempt to gain access to police or private security surveillance videotapes in order to monitor the action in a setting where crime is thought to be a problem (Desroches, 1990; Surette, 1992); (3) associate with people who engage in offending behaviour in order to observe their actions and the actions of those with whom they interact; or (4) obtain permission from the local police to join patrol officers for tours of duty on city streets (Black and Reiss, 1967; Ericson, 1982; Ferraro, 1989).

Although such methods of learning about crime events would seem to have an obvious advantage in that they allow researchers direct access to the types of information in which they are interested, they are not without serious limitations. First, they may not be very efficient. This is because, statistically speaking, crimes are relatively rare events (O'Brien, 1986). Even if one conscientiously observes a high-crime setting, criminal events will only infrequently be observed. Similarly, even if one develops associations with chronic offenders, it will become obvious that much of their time is spent in crime-free activity. A considerable amount of research energy would have to be expended to yield a sufficient number of observations to allow something meaningful to be said about offenders or offending (Nettler, 1984).

A second problem concerns the fact that criminal behaviour is usually secretive behaviour. There is every reason to believe that those who are engaged in such conduct will do whatever they can to ensure that external observers (including criminologists) will not have as good a view as they might like.

A third problem relates to the ethics of this approach to data-gathering. We have reason to be concerned about the legal and moral obligations of the researcher who observes a crime in progress. We also need to think very critically about modes of data collection that involve the covert observation of people who are going about their business or that involve researchers misrepresenting their real purposes to people who take them into their confidence.

Finally, we can suggest that the data yielded by these methods of direct observation are limited with respect to the types of questions they can address. In general, while they may allow us to observe criminal events, they do not necessarily tell us much about why the events occur where they do or why some people are more likely than others to be event participants. Systematic observation of a high-crime subway platform may provide an opportunity to witness a number of minor thefts or assaults. But our observations do not tell us how this subway platform differs from others where the crime rate is much lower. Similarly, observations (by whatever means) of juvenile misconduct, tell us very little about why some juveniles engage in law-violating behaviour while others do not. And while police ride-alongs might increase the researcher's exposure to particular types of events, they do so in a way that is subject to numerous limitations. As we have mentioned in previous chapters, the police generally become involved in criminal events only after receiving requests from citizens for police assistance. Thus, while police ride-alongs may do much to increase our understanding of the role played by the police in criminal events, they do relatively little to facilitate our direct observations of what transpires before police assistance is sought.

Observation alone generally does not tell us much about how offenders, victims, or other event participants perceive their own actions or the actions of others. We cannot glean from observation why the offenders act as they do, how they perceive their victims, why they are willing to risk punishment, or what they believe the rewards of their actions to be. Answers to such questions can only be inferred from the event we witness.

EXPERIMENTAL OBSERVATION

A second observational approach involves the use of experimentation. Rather than waiting for things to happen, the researcher interested in exploring some aspects of criminal events arranges for them to happen. Experimentation allows for controlled observation of behaviour. Also, since experimental conditions can be varied, experimentation allows researchers to determine how different conditions affect event outcomes (Steffensmeier and Terry, 1973).

For example, Shotland and Straw (1976) designed an experiment intended to shed light on how bystanders respond when a man attacks a woman. Subjects in the experiment were told that they were taking part in an "attitude study." Each subject was directed to a separate room where a questionnaire was to be completed. Shortly after beginning work, the subject heard a loud verbal argument between a man and a woman in the hallway.

> *After approximately 15 seconds of heated discussion, the man physically attacked the woman, violently shaking her while she struggled resisting and screaming. The screams were loud piercing shrieks, interspersed with pleas to "get away from me" (Shotland and Straw, 1976: 991).*

What the experimental subjects did not know was that the assailant and the victim were drama students who were confederates of the researchers. Shotland and Straw's study revealed that subjects were more likely to intervene when they believed that the attack involved strangers rather than a married couple.

Tracy and Fox (1989) designed an experiment intended to give insight into automobile insurance fraud, a type of white-collar crime that does not frequently come to the attention of enforcement officials. The researchers were interested in discovering whether automobile repair shops tend to provide higher estimates for body work on insured vehicles. In order to investigate this issue, drivers who were confederates of the researchers presented assigned cars to randomly selected body shops across the state of Massachusetts. The analysis, which took the amount of damage and several other variables into account, revealed that, on average, estimates for insured vehicles were 32.5 percent higher than estimates for uninsured vehicles, a difference that the researchers concluded was irrespective of the extent of the damage, the sex of the driver, or the location of the body shop.

As the above examples illustrate, experiments may provide a valuable means for answering some types of questions about criminal events. Still, experiments present some formidable problems and their use by criminologists has been limited. Most of the experimental work has not focused on what many consider to be the vital roles in criminal events—offender and victim. Instead, as in the case of the Shotland and Straw study, experiments have been used to study the reactions of witnesses or bystanders to contrived situations (Borofsky, Stollack, and Messe, 1971; Frinell, Dahlstrom, and Johnson, 1980; Shotland and Goodstein, 1984).

Experiments that are intended to entice people into real criminal conduct, or that feign the victimization of unsuspecting experimental subjects, pose obvious ethical dilemmas. In some circumstances, there could be a risk of physical or emotional harm not only to the study subjects but also to the researchers or their confederates.

Field experiments can also be used to assess the impact that criminal justice programs have in reducing the incidence of crime. Two well-known studies are the Kansas City Patrol Study conducted by Kelling et al. (1974) and the Minneapolis Domestic Violence Experiment administered by Sherman and Berk (1984). Both studies involved predetermining the police intervention that would take place in different targeted areas of the city and then assessing its impact on crime.

Kelling divided Kansas City into sectors and, with the compliance of the Chief of Police, allocated different types of patrol strategies to each sector. An effort was made in the design of the study to ensure that similar types of neighbourhoods received different patrol tactics. The police then adopted three strategies: high-visibility patrol, low levels of patrol, and standard levels. In analyzing the results, Kelling and his associates discovered that police patrol strategies had little effect on crime rates or fear of crime in the targeted areas. The areas that received high levels of police patrol were perceived as no more safe than those receiving lower levels. There was also little difference in the measured levels of crime.

Sherman and Berk's study was also based on a field experiment design. Its purpose was to reveal whether differences in how the police treat wife assaulters are associated with differences in the likelihood that these assaulters will re-offend. The study was restricted to cases of "simple" assault (assaults without serious injury). Each time the officers involved in the experiment encountered such a case, they were to follow experimenters' instructions, which involved a "random" choice among three forms of case processing: arrest, advice (which could include informal mediation), and an order to the suspect to leave the premises for eight hours. The behaviour of the suspect was tracked for six months after the incident in order to determine if different forms of treatment resulted in different levels of re-offending. Based on the findings, the researchers concluded that arrested suspects are less likely to engage in subsequent violence against their partners.

It is worth noting that several replications of Sherman and Berk's study have been undertaken, with later researchers attempting to fine-tune the original methodology. Three of the subsequent studies found results opposite to those reported by Sherman and Berk. Sherman and Berk reported that arrest led to higher levels of violence among the unemployed than among the employed. Sherman (1992) attributes the discrepancy in findings to the increased precision of the testing that was used in the replications, and to the differences in the demographic characteristics of the cities that were studied. He argues that it is exactly this ability to replicate and refine findings that makes the experimental approach so valuable as a means of guiding policy decisions using social science research.

While field experiments have indeed influenced policing strategies and shaped our understanding of crime incidence, they require a great deal of cooperation from the police. Concerns have also been raised about the ethics of shifting police resources to experiments that may end up endangering people. The experimenter might attempt to deal with safety or ethical issues by developing experiments that do not involve engagement in real criminal events but that are thought to approximate processes that are common to these events. Such an approach characterizes much of the research into the effect of violence in the media on behaviour. Typically, the researcher exposes experimental subjects to a film or video presentation depicting violence and then observes whether they behave in an aggressive fashion afterward. In the case of children, the measure of aggression may involve aggressive play, while in the case of adults, it may involve the willingness of test subjects to behave punitively toward a confederate of the experimenter (Bandura, Ross, and Ross, 1963; Malamuth, 1983).

While it can reasonably be argued that field experiments pose no real danger to those who participate in them, critics charge that, because the experimental situations are artificial, they tell us very little about real-life criminal behaviour (Surette, 1992). The essence of this charge is that there is a huge difference between the willingness to behave "violently" in an experiment—when such violence is encouraged and results in no apparent harm to anyone—and the types of criminal violence that concern the criminal justice system and so many members of the general public.

REPORTING CRIME

THE CRIME FUNNEL

The data most frequently used by criminologists interested in the study of criminal events come not from direct observation but from the reports of those who have direct knowledge of the event, principally the police, victims, and offenders.

It seems reasonable to expect that criminal justice system agencies besides the police would be important sources of information about criminal events. After all, such agencies are in the crime business and keep records of crimes that occur, people who are arrested, cases that go to trial, and the number of Canadians incarcerated.

If our interest centres on the criminal event, the data made available by the various criminal agencies differ in terms of their value. In part, this is because different agencies have different needs and therefore do not all collect the same type of information. Of equal importance is the fact that criminal justice agencies are connected to each other in a "volume-reducing system" (Reiss, 1986a). In other words, there is a high level of attrition as cases travel through the various stages of the criminal justice system: not all criminal events that come to the attention of the police result in an arrest; not all arrests result in a trial; and not all trials result in a sentence. Some writers have described this attrition process as a "crime funnel" (Silverman, Teevan, and Sacco, 1991). According to a federal government estimate in the early 1980s:

- 60 percent of all break-and-enter incidents are reported to the police;
- one-tenth of all break-and-enter incidents eventually result in someone being charged with the crime (17 percent of those incidents reported to the police); and
- one-seventeenth of all break-and-enter incidents result in a conviction (60 percent of those incidents that resulted in a charge) (Canada 1982).

In a similar vein, Dutton (1987) argues that, as cases of wife assault move through the criminal justice system, a "winnowing process" occurs. The probability of wife assault being detected by the justice system is about 6.5 percent. Once detected, the probability of arrest is about 21.2 percent. Given these contingencies, offenders in cases of wife assault have only a 0.38 percent chance of being punished by the courts.

POLICE REPORTS

For the purpose of studying criminal events, the data contained in police records are quantitatively and qualitatively superior to those maintained by court or correctional agencies. In a quantitative sense, police data speak to a larger number of criminal events. In a qualitative sense, police data are not directly subject to the various sorting procedures that occur later and that might remove cases from the system in a nonrandom manner.

Police crime data are based on criminal events about which police have knowledge. It will be recalled that any measure of "crimes known to the police" cannot be expected to be synonymous with all crimes that occur. This is because many crimes are not reported to the police. The data discussed in Chapter 1 indicate that as much as 50 percent of the crime reported by victims to survey interviewers is not reported to the police. (Events that are characterized by greater levels of legal seriousness are more likely to be reported.) It will also be recalled that proactive policing results in the discovery of relatively few crimes. The types and numbers of crimes about which the police have knowledge are, in the first instance, determined by members of the general public who may or may not call the police.

Further, not all of the criminal events that come to the attention of the police become part of the official record. A call from a citizen who reports a crime to the police may not lead to a car being dispatched, the result of which is that no subsequent action is taken (Gilsinan, 1989). Even when the police do arrive at the scene, they may decide to treat the matter unofficially or as something other than a crime.

Some types of event characteristics increase the likelihood that a crime will be recorded (Gove, Hughes, and Geerken, 1985). Events with elements that suggest a high degree of legal seriousness are more likely to be recorded as crimes (Gottfredson and Gottfredson, 1988). In addition, when there is strong physical evidence or compelling testimony that indicates that a crime has occurred, there is a higher probability that the event will enter the official record. An event is also more likely to be treated as a crime when the person who makes the complaint to the police expresses a preference that official action be taken (Black, 1971).

The recording of crime relates not only to the characteristics of the event but also to the characteristics of the policing agency. Specifically, more professional police departments are more likely to officially record crimes (Gove, Hughes, and Geerken, 1985). This is in part because these departments tend to make greater use of crime data for the purpose of developing departmental priorities or deploying resources. Highly professional departments also rely to a greater extent on existing official records in the processing of citizen complaints, which means that there is a stronger incentive at all departmental levels to "write up" a larger number of police–citizen interactions (Skogan, 1977).

The descriptions of events, which are officially labelled as crimes by an investigating officer, may undergo significant changes as they move through the internal bureaucracy of the police department. As information travels from the line officer through the communications section to the records division, offences may be shifted from one category to another, downgraded, or ignored (Skogan, 1977). Thus, the amount of crime recorded by the police department is affected by the internal organization of the police department and by the bureaucratic procedures by which information is processed (McClearly, Nienstedt, and Erven, 1982).

A study undertaken by the Canadian Centre for Justice Statistics (1990a) attempted to determine the extent to which the difference between Edmonton and Calgary in terms of crime levels could be accounted for by differences in record-keeping practices. Although the city of Edmonton has traditionally had a significantly higher rate of crime than the city of Calgary, this difference had never been adequately explained with reference to those factors (e.g., high levels of unemployment amd migration) that are usually thought to account for high crime rates. The CCJS study focused on the internal processing of information as a possible explanation. It revealed that information loss in the stages between the original call to the policing agency and the records section was greater in Calgary than in Edmonton. About 80 percent of the cases in Calgary reached the records section, compared to about 94 percent of those in Edmonton. To some degree, then, the higher crime rate in Edmonton is attributable to differences in the manner in which agency data are collected.

THE UNIFORM CRIME REPORTING SYSTEM

In Canada, as in the United States, police crime data are collected and processed as part of what is known as the Uniform Crime Reporting (UCR) system. The Canadian UCR has been in existence since 1961 and was developed through the joint efforts of Statistics Canada and the Canadian Association of Chiefs of Police. The stated objective of the UCR is to provide police departments with a consistent set of procedures for the collection of information relevant to crimes that come to the attention of the police.

In essence, the UCR is a survey in which police departments across

> **WHAT IS IT?**
>
> **The Uniform Crime Reporting System**
> In Canada (as in the United States) police crime data are collected and processed as part of what is known as a Uniform Crime Reporting (UCR) system. The stated objective of the UCR is to provide police departments with a consistent set of procedures for collecting relevant information about crimes that come to the attention of the police.

the country report crime information, in a standardized way, to the federal statistical agency (Statistics Canada) that then collates the information and makes it available to interested data users, including government departments, criminologists, politicians, and the mass media. Since 1982, the Canadian Centre for Justice Statistics, a division of Statistics Canada, has been responsible for collecting information from police departments that regularly respond to the survey.

Since its inception, the UCR rules for collecting information about crime have been subjected to much criticism (Schneider and Wieresma, 1990; Silverman, Teevan, and Sacco, 1991). Prior to recent changes in the UCR system, these critical charges included the following:

1. The UCR counting rules required that, except in the case of homicide, completed offences and attempted offences be included in the same category. In terms of the amount of harm done, there is usually a substantial difference between crimes completed and crimes attempted. But as aggregate counts, such measures obscured these differences.

2. When more than one legal violation occurred in the context of a single event, the UCR rules required that only the most serious act (according to legal definitions) be counted; thus, a number of crimes go uncounted.

3. The UCR system required that different counting rules be applied to personal crimes and property crimes. For personal crimes, the rules necessitated counting one crime for each victim. For property crime, the rules required that one crime be counted for each "separate and distinct incident." Thus, "in an incident where several privately owned vehicles parked in one block are all spray-painted with what appears to be the same spray can, it is concluded that one incident occurred and therefore one offence (of wilful damage) is recorded" (Statistics Canada, 1985: 17).

More basic problems related to the *types* of information that were collected and the *form* in which the data were presented. Until recently, the data collected in conjunction with the UCR survey were restricted to a few items, including the type of offence (as defined by the Criminal Code), the number of offences reported, and the number of offences that were "unfounded." Offences are unfounded when, on the basis of a preliminary investigation, a judgment is made that the crime that was reported to occur did not occur. The number of unfounded crimes is subtracted from the number of crimes reported to yield a count of "actual offences."

The UCR survey also reported some limited information about the persons charged with the offence (male or female, adult or young offender) and the "clearance status" of the incident. Clearance status refers to a judgment made by the police as to whether or not they can identify at least one of the offenders involved in the offence. If such a person is formally charged with the crime, then the offence is "cleared by charge." If, however, circumstances do not allow a charge to be made, the police can count the incident as "cleared otherwise." This might happen if, for instance, a victim refuses to sign a complaint or if the offender dies before he or she can be charged.

Table 6.1 presents representative crime data for the calendar year 1990. The table suggests that offences differ quite markedly in their clearance rates. Of the crimes described, the gambling offence (betting house) has the highest rate. This is because typically such crimes are proactively policed and enter the official record only because police are able to identify suspects in the first place. First-degree murder also has a high clearance rate, in part because homicides frequently involve offenders and victims who know each other. It is also clear from the table that, in the case of break and enter and vandalism, fewer offenders are identified and thus crimes are cleared with greater difficulty.

Table 6.1   Selected Uniform Crime Report Data, Canada, 1990

	Reported	Unfounded		Actual	Cleared		%
		#	%		By charge	Other-wise	
First-degree murder	393	47	11.95	346	225	41	67.7
Break and enter (residence)	227,359	11,998	5.27	215,361	17,668	6,155	10.47
Betting house	385	—	—	385	378	2	98.70
Mischief (property) $1,000 and under	371,900	9,670	2.60	362,230	26,619	27,120	14.44

Source: Canadian Centre for Justice Statistics, *Canadian Crime Statistics*. Ottawa: Statistics Canada, 1991 (Table 2).

Problems with the *form* of data collection and presentation related to the fact that, prior to the recent revisions, the UCR system required that the monthly reports by police departments to the Canadian Centre for Justice include the "aggregate totals" for each offence category. Aggregate totals represent summaries of police activity for each UCR category in the month for which the report is made. For example, in a given month, a police department might report that 100 assaults occurred and that 90 assaults had been cleared by charge. However, because these numbers represent summaries of police activity for the month, they do not necessarily have anything to do with each other. Many of the assaults that were cleared by charge may have been committed during the previous month. Similarly, some portion of the males or females who were reported to have been charged during the month may have actually committed their crimes during previous months.

That problems of this type have undermined the quality and limited the usefulness of UCR data has been long recognized. It is largely for this reason that, in 1988, the Canadian Centre for Justice Statistics and the police community began to phase in a revised UCR survey (Canadian Centre for Justice Statistics, 1990b). For each incident, the revised survey collects previously unavailable information relating to the location of the incident, the use of weapons, and the value of stolen property. The new UCR also collects more detailed information about the characteristics of accused persons; and, unlike the previous UCR, it gathers data about the victims of violent crime. Included in this information are not only the basic social characteristics of offenders and victims but also the relationship between them and their use of alcohol or drugs (Morrison, 1991a).

Equally important, the new UCR has changed from an aggregate to an "incident-based" reporting system, which means that data relating to offenders, victims, and criminal events are compiled on an incident-by-incident basis rather than as summaries, as was previously the case. As a result, the various kinds of information collected by the police are not collated as monthly totals but can be linked together in the context of particular incidents or criminal events (Canadian Centre for Justice Statistics, 1990b).

The above changes will make UCR data much more informative and should minimize many of the problems that plagued the system in the past. Most importantly, because the kinds of information collected by the survey have been expanded, and because the system is incident-based, it will be possible to use UCR data to address a wide variety of questions that could not be addressed previously, including questions about the characteristics of victims of crime, the location of criminal events, the differences between stranger and intimate violence, and the relationship between weapon use and level of injury. However, while these revisions to the UCR will greatly enhance the quality of police data about criminal events, they leave unaddressed those crimes that never come to the attention of the police in the first place.

VICTIM REPORTS

Reports from victims of crimes are a second major source of information about criminal events. Victims may be asked to describe what transpired during the event, how they reacted, whether the police were summoned, and what physical or psychological costs they may have sustained as a result of the incident. Data from victims of crime are usually collected via victimization surveys, large-scale studies that ask randomly sampled members of major urban centres about their experiences with crime. To date, two major victimization surveys have been undertaken in Canada. The first, known as the Canadian Urban Victimization Survey (CUVS), was undertaken in 1982 in seven major Canadian urban areas (Solicitor General, 1983). The second major study, the General Social Survey (GSS), was a national survey conducted in 1988 (Sacco and Johnson, 1990). It is intended that the GSS victimization survey will be regularly undertaken at five-year intervals.

Because criminal victimization is a statistically rare event, victimization surveys require that a very large number of people be interviewed in order to yield a sufficient number of cases for analysis (O'Brien, 1985). The CUVS gathered data from approximately 60,000 urban Canadians, while the GSS employed a sample of about 10,000. Due to their large sample sizes, victimization surveys are very expensive research projects. In order to increase the efficiency of the undertaking, it is common in victimization research to conduct the interviews over the telephone. (See Appendix 6.1 for an example of this kind of survey.) In such cases, researchers may use sampling procedures that generate a sample of telephone numbers to be called, rather than addresses to be visited, for the purpose of conducting the interviews.

WHAT ARE THEY?
Victimization Surveys
These are large-scale studies that ask randomly sampled members of some larger population about their experiences with crime.

Victimization interviews, in the CUVS and the GSS, as well as in most surveys conducted in the United States, Great Britain, and elsewhere consist of two parts. First, all respondents (whether they have been victims of crime or not) are asked questions from a "screening questionnaire." In addition to supplying social and demographic information about themselves, respondents are questioned about their fear of crime and attitudes toward the criminal justice system. More importantly, the screening questionnaire is used to identify those respondents who experienced one or more of the types of victimization that are of interest.

A detailed series of questions about the victimization incident comprises the second major part of the interview. Victims may be asked about the location and circumstances of the crime or about their relationship to the

BOX 6.1   EXCERPT FROM VICTIMIZATION SURVEY

SECTION D

D1   The next few questions ask about some things which may have happened to you during 1987.

	Yes	How many in 1987?	No
D2 From January 1st to December 31st 1987:			
a) Did anyone take or try to take something from you by force or threat of force?	Yes ⁰¹ ○ ⟶	⬚⬚	No ⁰² ○
b) (Other than the incidents already mentioned), did anyone illegally break into or attempt to break into your residence or any other building on your property?	Yes ⁰³ ○ ⟶	⬚⬚	No ⁰⁴ ○
D3 Now I'm going to ask you a question about being attacked. An attack can be anything from being hit, slapped, pushed or grabbed, to being shot, raped or beaten.			
a) (Excluding incidents already mentioned,) were you attacked by anyone at all, including members of your own household?	Yes ⁰⁵ ○ ⟶	⬚⬚	No ⁰⁶ ○
b) (Other than the incidents already mentioned,) did anyone, including members of your own household, threaten to hit or attack you, or threaten you with a weapon?	Yes ⁰⁷ ○ ⟶	⬚⬚	No ⁰⁸ ○
D4 During 1987, did you or anyone in your household own a motor vehicle such as a car, truck, motorcycle, etc.?			
Yes ¹ ○ No ² ○ ⟶ Go to D6			
D5 (Other than the incidents already mentioned:)			
a) Did anyone steal or try to steal one of these vehicles or a part of one of them, such as a battery, hubcap or radio?	Yes ⁰⁹ ○ ⟶	⬚⬚	No ¹⁰ ○
b) (Other than the incidents already mentioned,) did anyone deliberately damage one of these vehicles, such as slashing tires?	Yes ¹¹ ○ ⟶	⬚⬚	No ¹² ○
D6 (Excluding the incidents already mentioned,) was anything of yours stolen during 1987:			
a) From the things usually kept outside your home, such as yard furniture?	Yes ¹³ ○ ⟶	⬚⬚	No ¹⁴ ○
b) From your place of work, from school or from a public place, such as a restaurant?	Yes ¹⁵ ○ ⟶	⬚⬚	No ¹⁶ ○
c) From a hotel, vacation home, cottage, car, truck or while traveling?	Yes ¹⁷ ○ ⟶	⬚⬚	No ¹⁸ ○
D7 (Excluding the incidents already mentioned,) during 1987, did anyone steal or try to steal anything else that belonged to you?	Yes ¹⁹ ○ ⟶	⬚⬚	No ²⁰ ○
D8 (Other than the incidents already mentioned,) did anyone deliberately damage or destroy any property belonging to you or anyone in your household, such as a window or a fence?	Yes ²¹ ○ ⟶	⬚⬚	No ²² ○
D9 Were there any other crimes which happened to you during 1987, which may or may not have been reported to the police?	Yes ²³ ○ ⟶	⬚⬚	No ²⁴ ○

D10 INTERVIEWER: *Total the number of incidents reported in D2 to D9 and enter* ⟶ TOTAL	⬚⬚⬚

D11   In order to determine your longer term exposure to crime, the next question concerns incidents which happened to you in the last three years. In total, how many crimes happened to you since January 1st 1985?

⬚⬚⬚ or None ⁰⁰ ○

D12   INTERVIEWER: *COMPLETE THE NUMBER OF ACCIDENT AND CRIME INCIDENT REPORTS AS GIVEN BY TOTAL BOXES ON PAGES 6 AND 7*

Source: Vincent F. Sacco and Holly Johnson, *Patterns of Criminal Victimization in Canada: General Social Survey Analysis Series (no. 2).* Ottawa: Statistics Canada, 1990.

offender. They may also be questioned about any financial loss or physical injury they might have sustained. Information may also be gathered about whether or not the victim reported the crime to the police or took any other action in the aftermath of the victimization episode.

Claims about the value of victim reports of crime derive from several assumed advantages of the research approach. First, it is frequently argued that because victimization surveys collect information directly from victims of crime, they can tell us about crimes that have not been reported to the police (Fattah, 1991). In so doing, victim surveys provide a more valid estimate of the actual crime rate.

BOX 6.2   VICTIMIZATION IN PRISON

Sometimes victimization surveys are carried out with special populations. Victim surveys that focus on family violence or crime in schools are examples of such studies, as is sociologist Dennis Cooley's study of criminal victimization among prison inmates.

In Cooley's study (1992), interviews were conducted with 117 inmates in five prisons, spanning three security levels in one region. The survey was designed to determine whether respondents had been involved in any of several types of victimization incidents while housed in a federal prison during a twelve-month period.

Incidents and Victims by Victimization Type

Type of Victimization	Number of Incidents	Rate per 1,000 Inmates	Number of Victims	Rate per 1,000 Inmates
Robbery*	4	34.2	3	25.6
Sexual Assault	6	51.3	1	8.6
Assualt**	30	256.4	22	188.0
Threats**	23	196.6	21	179.5
Extortion	2	17.1	2	17.1
Theft	42	358.9	23	196.6
Vandalism	0	–	0	–
Personal Victimizations	65	555.6	49	418.8
Property Victimizations	42	359.0	23	196.6

  * Includes attempted robbery
** With/without weapons

Second, because victimization surveys use samples drawn from the general population, data are collected from both victims and nonvictims over a given period. This allows researchers to compare the two groups and to analyze which social and demographic groups face the greatest risks of victimization as well as how these risks are affected by particular kinds of lifestyle behaviours such as drinking alcohol or living alone. These data can inform the development of theoretical models that link victim involvement in criminal events to factors of this type (Hindelang, Gottfredson, and Garofalo, 1978; Laub, 1987).

Finally, victim survey approaches permit an investigation of the consequences of victimization and how victims cope with these consequences. As suggested earlier, they may be asked how their victimization experience has affected their attitudes about crime and the criminal justice system.

OFFENDER REPORTS

Interviews with offenders can give us important insights into their behaviour, attitudes, and motivations. We might learn why they commit the type of offences that they commit, how they feel about their victims, and how they assess their risk of being apprehended by the criminal justice system (Bennett and Wright, 1984).

REPORTS FROM KNOWN OFFENDERS

Perhaps the most obvious form of offender report makes use of data gathered from a sample of known offenders such as prison inmates or those who have been convicted of an offence and are awaiting sentence (Baunach, 1990). Surveys of this type can shed light on a range of subjects, including the use of weapons by offenders (Wright and Rossi, 1986) and the characteristics of offenders' victims (Innes and Greenfeld, 1990). Understanding such subjects gives us useful insights into how offenders regard their own actions as well as those of other event participants.

One major concern with surveys of known offenders relates to the generalizability of the findings (Flowers, 1989). Given that many offenders are not captured and that many of those who are captured are not convicted or sentenced, what we learn in interviews with convicted offenders may not be representative of what we would learn in interviews with offenders who have eluded conviction.

Early studies on criminals focused on their physiological characteristics. Research conducted by Cesare Lombroso in the 19th century included measures of cranial structure. From his research on criminals, Lombroso developed profiles for identifying "criminal types" in the general population. Despite the dangers inherent in using a "captive" population to study crime, this is a popular form of research, primarily because it is relatively inexpensive and offers an accessible study population. Research on body type that was conducted on inmate populations by William Sheldon in the early 1900s has been revived by authors such as Wilson and Herrnstein (1985) as a way of explaining criminality.

PARTICIPANT-OBSERVATION

Participant-observation provides another means by which information may be gathered from known offenders. As a research strategy, participant-observation moves beyond the use of a structured interview as the researcher attempts to develop more intimate associations with the people being studied (Wright and Bennett, 1990). The researcher gathers offender accounts by informally participating in and observing the social world of the offender.

This approach rests on the assumption that research methods that employ formal interviews with offenders are very limited in what they can achieve. It may be very difficult to gain access to members of "outlaw" motorcycle gangs, organized crime groups, and pro-

> **HOW DO YOU?**
>
> *Conduct Participant-Observation Studies*
> Participant-observation requires the researcher to gather offender accounts by informally participating in and observing the social world of the offender.

fessional thieves through conventional means (Ianni and Reuss-Ianni, 1972; Wolf, 1991). However, if researchers are able to cultivate informal relationships with offenders, they may be able to penetrate their social world and thereby learn much that would be invisible to an outside researcher. Studies of street gangs, such as those done by Stephen Baron on punk groups in Victoria, provide insights into life on the street that could not be gleaned in police statistics or victim surveys (see Baron, 1989; Kennedy and Baron, 1992). Chambliss (1975), a proponent of this method of urban ethnography argues that

> [t]he data on organized crime and professional theft as well as other presumably difficult-to-study events are much more available than we usually think. All we really have to do is get out of our offices and onto the streets. The data are there; the problem is that too often the sociologist is not (39).

WHAT IS IT?

Self-Report Study

Instead of being asked about their involvement in criminal events as victims, respondents are asked about their involvement as offenders. Like the victimization survey, the self-report study is intended to uncover crimes that have not been reported to the police (as well as those that have).

SELF-REPORT STUDIES

Self-report studies predate victimization surveys, having become popular during the 1950s and 1960s. Like victimization surveys, these studies gather data from the members of some large population. However, instead of being asked about their involvement as victims in criminal events, respondents are asked about their involvement as offenders. Like the victimization survey, the self-report study is intended to uncover crimes that have not been reported to the police (as well as to elucidate those that have). Also like victimization surveys, self-report studies allow the sample to be broken up into respondents who have and who have not been involved in criminal events over a specified period. This allows the researcher to compare offenders and nonoffenders in terms of social and lifestyle characteristics that might be useful in testing explanations of criminality.

Self-report research has most frequently been used in the study of juvenile crime, although there is nothing in the approach that prevents it from being applied to the study of adults (Laub, 1987). The emphasis on juveniles has largely been a matter of convenience in that juveniles, in the context of the school classroom, represent a captive audience for the researcher (Chilton, 1991).

Once a sample of respondents has been selected, the data about self-reported delinquency are collected in one of two ways (O'Brien, 1985). Some researchers use a questionnaire that includes a checklist of delinquent acts. Subjects are asked to indicate whether they have committed each of the acts and, if so, how frequently over a given period. Alternatively, researchers may ask respondents about their delinquent conduct in face-to-face interviews. Each approach has its advantages. The questionnaire makes it easier to assure the respondents of anonymity. The interview, however, allows for more detailed questioning about the circumstances surrounding the delinquent conduct (Gold, 1970).

THE LIMITATIONS OF CRIME REPORTS

Much of what we know about criminal events is based on the reports provided by offenders, victims, and the police. In addressing the limitations of these data, two issues require consideration: the type of event that is captured by each method of data collection, and the perspective brought to bear on those events that are captured.

Each of the methods that we have discussed in this section is somewhat restricted in terms of the kinds of events it illuminates.

Victim surveys usually ask respondents only about those events that have a direct and immediate victim (Reiss, 1986b). Because they are household surveys, they tend to exclude crimes that victimize businesses or the wider

---

BOX 6.3   MEASURING SELF-REPORTED COMPUTER CRIME

How adequate are the data of official agencies, victim surveys, or self-report offender surveys in revealing the causes of computer crime? In theory, at least, each approach should be as applicable to the study of computer crime as it is to any other type of crime. However, our experience with these data sources is not so extensive as to allow definitive judgments to be made about their relative value.

Official data relating to computer crime seem to share many of the same problems with data relating to more traditional offending (Taber, 1980). The more routine problems of victim nonreporting and selective enforcement, however, are complicated by uncertainties about how computer crime should be defined (Bequai, 1987). The literature also indicates that researchers who attempt to survey organizations that are victimized by computer crime face serious difficulties with respect to sampling and data access.

While researchers have made only very limited use of self-report offending surveys, Sacco and Zureik (1990) provide some indication of how such a survey might proceed. These researchers undertook a survey of anonymous student respondents who were enrolled in computing courses at a medium-sized Canadian university. Respondents were asked to complete a 22-page questionnaire that dealt with a variety of computing behaviours, attitudes, and perceptions. A total of 202 questionnaires were distributed in class to students who were enrolled in courses required for a Major in computing science and other applied science disciplines. The sample spanned the usual four years of undergraduate instruction. Slightly more than 50 percent (105) of the participating students completed and returned the questionnaire.

In one section of the questionnaire, respondents were asked to indicate whether, during the previous year, they had engaged in any of five specific types of computer misbehaviour. The most frequently reported behaviour was the unauthorized copying of copyrighted material for personal use (62 percent). The least frequently reported behaviour was the unauthorized use of a program that was the property of a time-share system (5 percent). Equal portions (15 percent) reported that they had rummaged through discarded printout "for interesting program listings" or had used an unauthorized password. Twenty-nine percent indicated that they had used a program in such a way that they avoided being charged for its use.

community (e.g., vandalism of public property). Victim surveys also exclude victims to whom access is limited, including children, the homeless, and residents of psychiatric or other institutions (Weis, 1989).

Self-report studies have been used primarily to obtain information about the "common delinquencies" of youth. They have been criticized for excluding the more serious, but less frequently occurring, types of delinquency (such as extreme forms of violence) while emphasizing nonserious forms of behaviour (such as "cutting classes" or "disobeying parents") (Braithwaite, 1981; Elliott and Ageton, 1980; Gove, Hughes, and Geerken, 1985; Hindelang, Hirschi, and Weis, 1981). When students in criminology classes are asked to demonstrate with a show of hands whether or not they have committed any of the "crimes" listed in the questionnaires used in self-report studies, a large number always respond in the affirmative. Even U.S. presidential candidates and Canadian federal leaders have admitted to experimenting with marijuana as youths. A loose interpretation of these data, then, can make everyone a criminal (Figlio, 1990).

The police reports that form the basis of the UCR are in some ways the most comprehensive data source. They include information on over 100 types of criminal events that correspond to all major Criminal Code as well as other legal designations. Unlike the victim survey, the UCR includes crimes without direct victims. It also includes crimes committed against businesses, the community, and those individuals who are unlikely to appear in surveys (Reiss, 1986b). A limitation of the UCR system is that the data it collects are based only on those crimes that the police know about.

WHOSE PERSPECTIVE?

The issue of perspective is central to any attempt to make proper use of crime report data. Each method offers a limited perspective since it elicits information from only some types of event participants. As we saw in Chapter 2, event participants may differ quite markedly in how they understand criminal events. We expect, therefore, that their reports will reflect these differences.

Victimization data rely on victims' perceptions of criminal events. As such, their quality is subject to whatever intentional or unintentional distortions characterize these perceptions. The accuracy of respondents' reports are subject to numerous compromises. For example, respondents may fail to disclose experiences in which the researcher is interested (Skogan, 1986). If someone is victimized during the course of an illegal activity, he or she may not want to tell the researcher about it. If the event is of minor significance, it may be forgotten by the time of the interview; this may be a particular problem when the reference period about which the respondent is asked is very long. The opposite problem involves what is called *telescoping* (Skogan, 1986). In this case, crimes the victim regards as significant life events may be reported as having occurred during the reference period when, in fact, they actually occurred at an earlier time. Telescoping is most likely to be a problem in the study of serious violent crimes.

WHAT DOES IT MEAN?

Telescoping

Crimes that the victim regards as significant life events may be brought forward in time, such that the respondent reports them as having occurred during the reference period when they actually occurred at an earlier time. This problem is most likely to arise in the study of serious violent crimes.

In many cases of serious victimization, the victim may be discouraged from reporting the event to a researcher. This may be true, for instance, in cases of family violence when the victim feels shame or embarrassment or believes that reporting the event may put him or her at risk. According to a study by Catlin and Murray (1984), sexual assaults and victimizations involving nonstrangers are less likely to be reported to survey interviewers than to the police.

There are other ways in which the perspectives of victims are limited. If respondents cannot or do not define an event as a crime, they are unlikely to tell a researcher about it (Block and Block, 1984). In some cases, people may be victimized but not realize it. Many forms of fraud are intended to accomplish precisely this outcome. Similarly, if a purse is stolen but the victim believes that she has lost it, she will not report it to a researcher who asks her a question about theft. Much of the criminal harm that is perpetrated by corporations and governments is not readily apparent, even to those who are directly affected; as a result, victims may have no idea that they have been victimized (Walklate, 1989).

Respondents are also likely to differ in their views as to what level of violation constitutes a crime (Gove, Hughes, and Geerken, 1985). Some studies show, for instance, that the reporting of assault victimization is more likely among highly educated people. Such a finding is most reasonably interpreted in terms of class differences in the definition of injury or in the willingness to tolerate violence rather than in terms of the greater threats of criminal violence faced by more highly educated respondents (Skogan, 1990a).

Self-report studies allow us to understand criminal events from the perspective of the offender. Yet it is possible that offenders who have the most to hide may be least willing to participate in the research (O'Brien, 1985). Moreover, some offenders may exaggerate their wrongdoing (perhaps as a show of bravado), while others may be reluctant to admit to involvement in criminal activity (Wright and Bennett, 1990). When the latter do report, they may be more willing to admit to trivial rather than serious offences (Jupp, 1989).

In the case of the UCR system, it is the organizational perspective of policing agencies that determines the rules for data collection. Administrative or political pressure may dictate that the policing of certain kinds of criminal events (e.g., impaired driving) be emphasized over others (e.g., soft drug use) (Jackson, 1990; O'Brien, 1985; Schneider and Wieresma, 1990). Police practices, public tolerance for particular kinds of behaviour, and the needs of the agency for particular kinds of data all influence the ways in which data are collected (Savitz, 1978).

Reiss (1986a) argues that the perspective implicit in police data offers a distinct advantage over self-report and victimization data. Whereas the latter two data sources reflect the view of highly self-interested parties, police data allow for a more balanced picture. Police reports of criminal events are based on a wider variety of information sources, including the victim, the offender, bystanders, and witnesses. In addition, police data are normally collected closer in time to the actual event than are victim or offender surveys. As a result, police data are less likely to be influenced by the selective effects of memory.

In a similar vein, Gove, Hughes, and Geerken (1985) suggest that, in comparison with other data sources, official statistics provide more rigorous criteria for the definition of criminal events. They argue that victim surveys give us only the victim's perspective, which is insufficient in determining whether or not a crime has in fact occurred. In order to make this judgment, we also need to know the offender's intention, the circumstances surrounding the event, and the condition of the victim (Mayhew, Elliot, and Dowds, 1989).

Criminal events that are recorded in official statistics have passed through two filters. First, they have been judged sufficiently serious to be worth reporting to the police. Second, they have been certified by the police as serious events deserving of criminal justice intervention. According to Gove, Hughes, and Geerken (1985), the reports contained in the UCR provide a good indicator of "the extent to which citizens feel injured, frightened, and financially hurt by a criminal act" (489).

These different perspectives have very important implications for how criminal events are understood. If, for example, an individual gets into a fistfight with a drinking companion, the event might be understood differently within the context of different data collection systems. If the individual is asked in a victim survey if anyone has hit him or threatened to hit him, and he responds honestly, the event will likely be counted as a victimization incident. If he is asked in a self-report survey about whether *he* has hit anyone, and he answers honestly, he is likely to be counted as an offender. If the police are called by a witness to the fight, they may, because of the circumstances and the relationship between the parties, screen the event out so that it never enters the official record.

We do not necessarily expect reports from different event participants to tell us the same things. Victim surveys and UCR data may disagree because they employ different criteria in determining the types of events that are to be included (Booth, Johnson, and Choldin, 1977; Block and Block, 1984; Blumstein, Cohen, and Rosenfeld, 1992; Gove, Hughes, and Geerken, 1985; O'Brien, 1983, 1985, 1986, 1991; Menard and Covey, 1988). Thus, if researchers undertook a victimization survey in a given community, and then compared the survey rates to the UCR rates for that same community, several sources of variation would be apparent. While the UCR measures would encompass crime committed against businesses, those living in institutions, and individuals who do not have a permanent residence, the victim survey would probably omit such crimes. The UCR rates would include crimes committed within the policing jurisdiction, irrespective of the place of residence of the victim. Thus, the UCR might include crimes committed against tourists who were visiting the community as well as crimes against commuters who work in the community but live elsewhere. By contrast, the victimization study, because it usually involves a household survey, would restrict attention to crimes committed against community residents, regardless of whether the crime occurred in the local community or elsewhere.

Similarly, the descriptions of offenders that emerge from police reports of crimes serious enough to have passed through citizen and police filters cannot be expected to concur with offender profiles that emerge from self-report studies that utilize nonserious measures of delinquency (Hindelang, Hirschi, and Weis, 1981; West and Farrington, 1977).

Although for decades criminologists have engaged in an intense debate about the relative value of specific crime measures, it seems clear that no single data source is by itself sufficient to answer all of the questions that we might have about criminal events (Jackson, 1990; Menard and Covey, 1988). Because our data sources tell us different things, it does not really make sense to think about one data source as *better* than another. While subsequent chapters will make extensive use of data derived from these sources, it is important that these data always be approached cautiously and critically. The need for such caution is well illustrated in the following section.

MEASURING WOMEN'S VICTIMIZATION

One of the most consistent findings to emerge from the UCR and victimization surveys is that men are more likely than women to experience certain kinds of victimization (Sacco, 1990; Wilson, 1985). By most accounts, men are more likely than women to be the victims of homicide, serious assault, and robbery; and although women are more likely to be victims of sexual assault, the data also indicate that sexual assaults occur less frequently than do other offences that are routinely investigated by victimization researchers. A recent analysis of revised UCR data from fifteen Canadian police departments revealed that overall, for the year 1991, women were as likely as men to be victims of violence (Trevethan and Tajeshwer, 1992). However, men were more likely to be victims of aggravated assault, assault with a weapon, "other assaults," and robbery, while women were eight times as likely as men to be victims of sexual assault and more likely than men to be victims of assaults without weapons or serious injury.

These findings have implications that extend well beyond a narrow concern with crime measurement on the part of academic researchers. They strongly influence the ways in which the public agenda is formulated, and they tend to legitimize the activities of some, but not other, social problems claimsmakers. Feminist social critics who attempt to raise public awareness of the problem of crime against women are frequently opposed by those who claim that the fear of victimization expressed by women is not rooted in reality, but rather suggests a nonrational reaction to a world that threatens men more than it does women (Sacco, 1990). In responding to their opponents, some feminist researchers have generated research findings that provide estimates of female victimization that are wildly at odds with the data yielded by more traditional measures (Gilbert, 1991).

These observations point to a need to understand the patterns of female victimization revealed by the UCR and the victimization survey. The logical starting point in such an exercise is to determine areas of agreement across methodological approaches to women's victimization. Two such patterns are consistently reported by the advocates of both traditional and more critical research approaches (DeKeseredy and Hinch, 1991; Riger, 1981; Solicitor

General of Canada, 1985a; Stanko, 1985; 1990; Timrots and Rand, 1987; Wilson, 1985). The first pattern concerns the fact that women are more likely than men to be victimized by people they know or with whom they have some ongoing relationship. The second, related pattern suggests that women have a greater tendency than men to be victimized in private (most notably the home) rather than public settings.

These patterns are clearly exemplified by gender differences in homicide victimization. Women are more likely than men to be killed in their own homes, and they are more likely to die at the hands of someone who is related to them. In 1986, 61 percent of female homicide victims were killed in their homes, compared to 40 percent of male victims. Moreover, 62 percent of female victims (vs. 27 percent of male victims) were murdered by someone who was related to them through kinship, marriage, or common-law union. Seventy-nine percent of the victims of spousal homicide were women (Johnson, 1990).

The two types of assault that we most closely associate with the victimization of women—domestic assault and sexual assault—also illustrate the private and intimate character of female victimization. In order to understand why official data and victimization surveys portray female victimization as they do, we need to assess how adequately these measures investigate crimes that are committed in private places and that involve offenders and victims who are in intimate relationships.

As we have discussed, many woman who are abused in the context of marital relationships do not define what is happening to them as criminal (Kantor and Straus, 1987). Several cultural factors encourage these women to view such incidents as normal and to blame themselves for the violence (Ferraro and Johnson, 1983). Even the fact that a woman phones the police to report an attack by a spouse does not necessarily mean that she defines the event in criminal terms; her action may have less to do with "reporting a crime" than with trying to obtain immediate assistance in order to prevent injury (Johnson and Chisholm, 1990). Even if women do define such events as crimes, they may not phone the police for a variety of reasons (Kantor and Straus, 1987). They may perceive that taking such action places them at greater risk, or they may be concerned that the police or other criminal justice agents will not take the crimes seriously (Canadian Centre for Justice Statistics, 1990c).

As we have seen, the appearance of the police at the scene of a domestic violence incident does not always mean that the event will be counted as a crime. If there is no clear evidence of physical harm, the police may engage in mediation by attempting to attempt to cool the parties down, listening to their respective accounts, or issuing stern warnings (Bell, 1987; Kantor and Straus, 1987). The victim may be given information or advice or referrals rather than treated like a complainant in a criminal matter (Johnson, 1990).

In many domestic disputes, the law may be viewed by the police as a means for dealing with the disorderly situation that confronts them rather than as a means for addressing the problem of wife assault (Gondolf and McFerron, 1989). The consequence of this is that, in many cases, no legal action is taken because the situation is not seen to demand a legal response. Even those cases that do involve a legal resolution do not necessarily require that official note be taken of the fact that a woman has been victimized. In conducting research in Newfoundland, O'Grady (1989) discovered that many instances of domestic violence were legally recorded not as assaults but as "weapons" or "drunk and disorderly in the home" offences.

As we pointed out in Chapter 5, some jurisdictions have attempted to reduce the use of police discretion in the handling of domestic assaults by passing laws that make arrest mandatory in these cases. However, such laws do not completely remove the discretionary decision-making in which police engage. In one jurisdiction, police arrested an abuser in only 18 percent of the cases in which arrest was possible, despite the existence of a presumptive arrest law (Ferraro, 1989).

Victims of sexual assault, like victims of domestic violence, may be reluctant to apply a criminal label if the offender is an acquaintance. Using U.S. national victimization data, Lizotte (1985) reports that factors that make a strong case for prosecution are closely related to women's reporting decisions regarding rape. Thus, women are less likely to report an incident to the police when they are unmarried, when the offender is not a stranger, and when the offender has a right to be in the location in which the offence occurs. As a result, the UCR measures sexual assaults for which the legal evidence is relatively clear, but which are not necessarily typical of women's sexual victimization.

While it is often claimed that victimization surveys broaden the search for incidents of women's victimization, it is also evident that this technique excludes many types of events. Most notably, these studies undercount crimes that involve intimates—precisely the types of crimes that disproportionately victimize women. Moreover, victimization surveys usually ignore victimization in the form of obscene phone calls, exhibitionism, and sexual harassment in the workplace (Gillespie and Leffler, 1987; Hanmer and Saunders, 1984; Junger, 1987; Stanko, 1985).

Several recent research innovations reflect attempts to provide a more valid assessment of women's victimization. Much research in the area of family violence, for instance, has made use of measures based on something other than traditional legal categories. The most frequently used measure, developed by Murray Straus and Richard Gelles, is known as the Conflict Tactics Scale (CTS). As shown in Box 6.4, CTS items are ranked in order of increasing seriousness. Items A–J describe nonviolent means of conflict resolution (e.g., use of verbal skills), while items K–S describe the kinds of violent tactics that constitute wife abuse. In order to investigate such abuse, husbands or wives may be asked how frequently they or their partners utilize each of these strategies in conflict situations. In one sense, the CTS may be understood as an approach that combines victimization and self-report measures.

BOX 6.4   THE CONFLICT TACTICS SCALE

Q35. No matter how well a couple get along, there are times when they disagree, get annoyed with the other person, or just have spats or fights because they're in a bad mood or tired or for some other reason. They also use many different ways of trying to settle their differences. I'm going to read some things that you and your (spouse/partner) might do when you have an argument. I would like you to tell me how many times (Once, Twice, 3–5 times, 6–10 times, 11–20 times, or more than 20 times) in the past 12 months you (READ ITEM).

Q36. Thinking back over the last 12 months you've been together, was there ever an occasion when (your spouse/partner) (READ ITEM)? Tell me how often (he/she) ...

Q37. (IF EITHER "NEVER" OR "DON'T KNOW" ON ITEM FOR BOTH Q35 *AND* Q36, ASK Q37 FOR THAT ITEM) Has it *ever* happened?

Q35. Respondent In Past Year	Q36. Spouse In		Q37.
	1—Once 2—Twice 3—3–5 Times 4—6–10 Times 5—11–20 Times 6—More than 20 0—Never (don't read)	1—Once 2—Twice 3—3–5 Times 4—6–10 Times 5—11–20 Times 6—More than 20 0—Never (don't read)	1—Yes 0—No
A. Discussed an issue calmly	1 2 3 4 5 6 0	1 2 3 4 5 6 0	1 0
B. Got information to back up your/ his/her/ side of things	1 2 3 4 5 6 0	1 2 3 4 5 6 0	1 0
C. Brought in, or tried to bring in, someone to help settle things	1 2 3 4 5 6 0	1 2 3 4 5 6 0	1 0

D. Insulted or swore at him/her/you	1 2 3 4 5 6 0	1 2 3 4 5 6 0	1 0
E. Sulked or refused to talk about an issue	1 2 3 4 5 6 0	1 2 3 4 5 6 0	1 0
F. Stomped out of the room or house or yard	1 2 3 4 5 6 0	1 2 3 4 5 6 0	1 0
G. Cried	1 2 3 4 5 6 0	1 2 3 4 5 6 0	1 0
H. Did or said something to spite him/her/you	1 2 3 4 5 6 0	1 2 3 4 5 6 0	1 0
I. Threatened to hit or throw something at him/her/you	1 2 3 4 5 6 0	1 2 3 4 5 6 0	1 0
J. Threw or smashed or hit or kicked something	1 2 3 4 5 6 0	1 2 3 4 5 6 0	1 0
K. Threw something at him/her/you	1 2 3 4 5 6 0	1 2 3 4 5 6 0	1 0
L. Pushed, grabbed, or shoved him/her/you	1 2 3 4 5 6 0	1 2 3 4 5 6 0	1 0
M. Slapped him/her/you	1 2 3 4 5 6 0	1 2 3 4 5 6 0	1 0
N. Kicked, bit, or hit him/her/you with a fist	1 2 3 4 5 6 0	1 2 3 4 5 6 0	1 0
O. Hit or tried to hit him/her/you with something	1 2 3 4 5 6 0	1 2 3 4 5 6 0	1 0
P. Beat him/her/you up	1 2 3 4 5 6 0	1 2 3 4 5 6 0	1 0
Q. Choked him/her/you	1 2 3 4 5 6 0	1 2 3 4 5 6 0	1 0
R. Threatened him/her/you with a knife or gun	1 2 3 4 5 6 0	1 2 3 4 5 6 0	1 0
S. Used a knife or fired a gun	1 2 3 4 5 6 0	1 2 3 4 5 6 0	1 0

Source: Murray A. Straus and Richard J. Gelles, *Physical Violence in American Families: Risk Factors and Adaptations to Violence in 8,145 Families.* New Brunswick, N.J.: Transaction, 1990.

Although the CTS has been widely used in both Canada and the United States, it has been criticized for ignoring both the consequences and the context of violent behaviour (DeKerseredy and Hinch, 1991). The scale is unable to distinguish between a situation in which a husband offensively strikes his wife, causing serious physical injury, and a situation in which a wife defensively strikes her husband and causes no injury.

It should be evident that claims that are made regarding the low rates of crime experienced by women must be assessed with extreme caution. This is not because the research is done in a careless or unsophisticated fashion but because all research approaches are subject to inherent limitations.

CRIME RATES

The form in which we most frequently encounter reports of criminal events is the crime rate, a measure that is widely used in criminology. Although journalists and politicians, among others, frequently issue declarations about rates of crime, we are seldom encouraged to think critically about what crime-rate measures really are.

THE NATURE OF CRIME RATES

What are crime rates? As defined by Nettler (1984),

> [a] rate compares events during a specified time against some base of other events, conditions or people. It takes the form (m/P)k, where m is a measure of some occurrence, P is a population count (or tally of some other condition of interest), and k is a constant (47).

The above definition suggests that computing crime rates is a fairly straightforward matter. First, one develops some estimate of the numerator (m). This would be some count of criminal events. We have already discussed the major forms of such counts—crimes recorded by the police or reported in victimization surveys or self-report studies. Second, we need to have a measure of the denominator (P). This is generally thought of as a measure of the population that is exposed to the events, or is at risk of being involved in the events, as offenders or victims (Reiss, 1986a). Finally, the expression that divides the number of criminal events by the measure of risk is multiplied by some constant (k). This is so the rate can be expressed per k units of exposure. The selection of the constant is largely an arbitrary matter, but rates are traditionally expressed per 1,000 or per 100,000 units of exposure. An example of crime-rate construction is provided in Box 6.5.

SOME USES OF CRIME RATES

In subsequent chapters, we will make extensive use of crime rates in our investigation of criminal event patterns. The analysis of these rates allows us to assess the value of particular theoretical arguments about how and why these events occur. Crime rates are also used by noncriminologists for a variety of other purposes. One of the most popular uses of the crime rate is as a "social barometer" that indexes the quality of life (Bottomley and Pease,

BOX 6.5 CALCULATING CRIME RATES

In order to calculate a crime rate, three quantities are required. The first is a count of the number of crimes. In the expression (m/P)k, this is the quantity m. Based on the data gathered in the 1988 General Social Survey, it was estimated that, in 1987, 1,685,000 incidents of violence involving victims over the age of 15 occurred in Canada.

Next, we need a measure of the population that could have been involved in these crimes as victims or offenders. In the expression (m/P)k, the measure of the at-risk population is P. Based on census data, we estimate the 1987 population of Canadians over the age of 15 to be 20,194,000.

Finally, in the expression (m/P)k, we need a constant, k, which will allow us to express the number of crimes that occur per k members of the population.

Putting all of the above together, we can calculate the rate of violent incidents per 1,000 Canadians over the age of 15 as follows:

$$\frac{1,685,000}{20,194,000} \times 1,000 = 83$$

1986). Thus, just as the gross national product is employed as an indicator of our collective economic well-being, crime rates are frequently read as indicators of our social well-being (Waller, 1982).

At a personal level, we may factor information about crime rates into our decisions about whether we will buy a home in a particular neighbourhood, spend out vacation in a particular city, or allow our children to attend a particular school. At a national level, for many Canadians, the lower rate of violence in Canada relative to that in the United States serves as a source of national pride.

Crime rates are also used to assess the effectiveness of community-based crime-prevention programs such as Neighbourhood Watch or Operation Identification and a large number of other criminal justice interventions (Gabor, 1990b; Rosenbaum, 1988). As we have discussed, changes in crime rates are frequently used to evaluate the quality of police services.

Claimsmaking activities often include organized efforts to produce and publicize crime-rate data that are said to document the issues to which the claimsmakers wish to draw attention (Best, 1988; Bottomley and Coleman, 1981). According to Gilbert (1991), such efforts "embody less an effort at scientific understanding than an attempt to persuade the public that a problem is vastly larger than is commonly recognized" (63). Best (1988) and Hotaling and Finkelhor (1990) have written about how "advocacy numbers" have been used in defining the problem of missing children. They suggest that "guesstimates" of the number of children abducted by strangers have greatly overestimated the prevalence of the problem. Best maintains that the use of crime data for political purposes generally proceeds from three basic working assumptions: (1) big numbers are better than small numbers, (2) official numbers are better than unofficial numbers, and (3) big official numbers are best of all. As a result, data collection agencies, official or otherwise, may experience more pressure to keep numbers high than to keep them accurate (Reuter, 1984a).

Crime rates provide an important standard by which we are able to compare the relative extent of crime incidence across jurisdictions and across groups. In this context, they have been offered as a way of measuring the exposure that individuals have to crime or risk.

CRIME RATES AS MEASURES OF RISK

In most of the cases described above, we are interested in crime-rate measures because we understand them as measures of risk. When we are told that the homicide rate per 100,000 people is four times higher in the United States than in Canada, we are led to understand that when the differences in the size of the population are taken into account, the risk of homicide is much greater south of the border than north of it. Similarly, when we are told that the neighbourhood to which we are thinking of moving has a much higher crime rate than the neighbourhood in which we currently live, we may want to reconsider our decision.

How adequate are crime rates as measures of risk? Our answer to this question depends on how much confidence we have in the numbers that are used in the calculation of the crime rate. We have already discussed the many problems that confound our tallies of criminal events (i.e., the numerator of the crime rate). However, there is also reason to be concerned about crime-rate denominators.

In selecting a crime-rate denominator, the usual practice is to use the total population residing within the jurisdiction in which the count of events has taken place. Such measures are usually referred to as "crude" crime rates because they provide only a very general assessment of the level of risk (Silverman, Teevan, and Sacco, 1991). They do not take account of the demographic characteristics of the population or the empirical fact that different segments of the population are involved in criminal events with different levels of frequency. This problem is sometimes countered through the use

Crude vs. Age-Specific Crime Rates
In selecting a crime-rate denominator, the usual practice is to use the total population residing within the jurisdiction in which the count of events has taken place. Such measures are usually referred to as "crude crime rates." Age-specific crime rates make use of a denominator that better reflects the population at risk. For example, the base number for calculating the rate might include only those individuals aged 18 to 24.

of a denominator that better reflects the population at risk. In age-specific crime rates, the base number for calculating the rate might include only those individuals aged 18 to 24. However, the difficulties inherent in determining a number that accurately reflects particular subpopulations sometimes leaves such rates open to charges of inaccuracy.

Nonetheless, it is reasonable to argue that a more refined measure would take account of the differential risks faced by distinct segments of the population. Thus, since most of the crimes counted in crime and victimization rates involve young males, it may make more sense to standardize the level of risk in terms of the proportion of young males in the population rather than in terms of the total population (Johnson and Lazarus, 1989). This is because a shift in the size of this segment of the population will exert a more significant effect on the overall rate than will shifts in other segments of the population, for instance, elderly women.

Not only the demographic composition but also the location of communities may be relevant to an understanding of crime rates (Gibbs and Erikson, 1976; Stafford and Gibbs, 1980). The concept of *ecological position* refers to geographic and economic relationships that link the community for which the rate is being calculated to other communities that are in close proximity. While the police have always been interested in ecological factors, given their responsibility to patrol specific neighbourhoods, until recently they have not had the ability to do a quick and detailed analysis that considers not only changes in crime rates across neighbourhoods but also other factors that may change, such as age composition. With the appearance of patrol cars equipped with terminals, the development of high-powered computers, and large-scale data-processing packages that offer analysis on a geographic basis, the police now have the resources to do ecological analyses quickly, thereby enhancing their ability to respond to changes in neighbourhoods.

Ecological analyses are relevant in explaining why two communities may have populations of similar size and demographic composition but differing crime rates. Community A, for example, may be a considerable distance from neighbouring communities such that the residents of these other communities do not commute to Community A, either to work or for recreational purposes. In other words, the members of the neighbouring communities are not regularly available as offenders or victims in Community A. When the official crime rate of Community A is calculated in terms of the population residing within Community A, most of the at-risk population will be taken into account.

By contrast, Community B may be a "central city" within a larger metropolitan area. Members of neighbouring communities may travel to and spend most of their working days in Community B. In addition, residents of these satellite communities may regularly attend cultural events or shop in the central city. If the residents of the satellite communities commit crimes or are victimized as they visit Community B, their crimes may be counted in the official crime rate of the central city. However, because these individuals are not residents of Community B, they are not counted in the denominator. If we fail to take account of the differences in the ecological positions of Community A and Community B, we may be at a loss to explain why the latter community has a generally higher crime rate.

A study by the Canadian Centre for Justice Statistics (1990a), which was mentioned earlier in this chapter, suggests that some of the variation in the crime rates of Edmonton and Calgary may be attributable to differences in ecological position. While the city of Calgary has no significant suburban population, approximately 100,000 people reside in suburbs surrounding the city of Edmonton. When the rates for the two communities were recalculated on the basis of metropolitan area rather than city populations, the total Criminal Code crime rate for Edmonton decreased by 8.2 percent while the corresponding decrease in Calgary was only 0.43 percent.

At a more basic level, it is reasonable to ask whether population measures are adequate as indicators of risk in the calculation of crime rates. Population measures provide us with some indication of the numbers of people who expose themselves to risks (of offending or victimization), but they do not provide us with any direct indication of the frequency with which this exposure takes place. Populations may differ not only with respect to demographic structure but also with respect to the degree to which the members of the population engage in behaviour that involves risks of crime. For example, a community in which people regularly spend a great deal of time engaged in evening activities outside the home may have a very different rate for some types of crimes than a community in which most people stay at home most of the time. The risky lifestyles that characterize the former community make its members more vulnerable to victimization (Kennedy and Forde, 1990).

For these reasons, many sociologists have argued in recent years that we need to measure risk more directly (Balkin, 1979; Fattah and Sacco, 1989; Lindquist and Duke, 1982; Stafford and Galle, 1984). For instance, it has been suggested that the elderly may have lower rates of victimization because their level of exposure to victimization risk is lower; if their victimization rates were to be adjusted for differential exposure, they might more closely approximate those of younger people (Lindquist and Duke, 1982). Efforts to examine such hypotheses have met with only limited success (Clarke et al., 1985; Fattah and Sacco, 1989). Any comprehensive investigation of these issues must await some considerable refinement in terms of how the concept of "exposure" is defined for research purposes.

Finally, in a very different way, Hackler and Don (1990) argue that police crime rates might be made more useful measures if explicit account is taken of the fact that the recording of some crimes (e.g., assault) involves considerably more discretion (screening) than does the recording of other crimes (e.g., robberies). They argue that more useful information about provincial differences in rates of violence might be obtained by dividing the official assault rate by the official robbery rate in order to produce a "recording index." This index takes account of the police practices that record crime selectively, and in so doing "provides a better indicator of actual criminal behaviour" (Hackler and Don, 1990: 262).

SUMMARY AND CONCLUSIONS
■ ■ ■

Research data are indispensable to the understanding of criminal events. They allow for the testing of theoretical ideas, they help us chart the dimensions of criminal events for policy purposes, and they provide us with indicators of the quality of life. While data about criminal events may derive from many different sources, they tend to be generated by one of two basic investigative strategies: observations and reports.

Criminal events may be directly observed either in naturalistic settings or in the context of field or laboratory experimentation. While there is much to be learned about criminal events by waiting for things to happen (as in the former case) or by making them happen (as in the latter one), most contemporary research depends on information revealed by reports about crime.

The most widely used of such reports come from those who are most active in criminal events: the police, the victims, and the offenders. The data collected by the police through the Uniform Crime Reporting system describe a wide range of crimes and provide a continuous national time series. Recent revisions to the UCR survey are likely to increase the value of these data for both academic and policy purposes. The major limitation of these data relates to the fact any police-based information system can tell us only about crimes that come to the attention of the police in the first place. A significant number of crimes that the police do not learn about are not included in the information system.

Surveys of victims and offenders are intended to illuminate those crimes that are not recorded by the police. Despite the valuable information they provide, these surveys are subject to all of the problems that characterize any type of survey. Victims and offenders are not always as accessible as we would like them to be, and we cannot always be sure that they will not, intentionally or unintentionally, distort the truth in response to our questions about their involvement in criminal events.

The problems associated with these major sources of crime data—police, victim, and offender reports—do not suggest a lack of knowledge or awareness on the part of those who collect the data. Rather, they alert us to the fact that any attempt to investigate complex social phenomena is fraught with inherent difficulties. Our discussion of the ways in which crime data construct our statistical images of crimes against women illustrates this fact.

We have also seen that no single data source is likely to answer all of the questions that we have about criminal events. Our major data sources tell us quite different things. This is because they are likely to capture different types of events and to bring different perspectives to bear on these events. For this reason, it is unproductive to engage in endless debates about the superiority of one data source over another. To a considerable extent, the usefulness of any data source depends on how well it helps us to address particular questions.

It is important that we not dismiss crime data just because our data sources are flawed and less comprehensive than we would like. A great deal can be learned from a judicious use of crime data. Although we know that our data are problematic, in many cases we also know *how* they are problematic. Frequently, the errors that characterize our efforts at data collection are not random, but systematic; knowing the sources and consequences of these systematic errors makes data more valuable than they might otherwise be.

I am an interviewer of the survey company [company name]. We are holding a survey at the request of [sponser's name] about the views of the public about crime and crime control. This survey is part of an international project which is being done in all major European countries, the USA, Canada and Australia. May I please ask you some questions about this? This interview won't take much of your time. Your answers will, of course, be treated confidentially and anonymously.

If respondent is suspicious or doubtful: If you want to check whether this survey is done for the [sponsor's name] I can give you the phone number of someone at [sponsor's name] who can give you more information.

If respondent insists to know: Our contact at [sponsor's name] is [contact name]. His/her phone number is [contact number]. May I call you back in 30 minutes?

1.   Has anyone in your household had for private use any of the following types of vehicles over the last year?
     Interviewer: count total number of vehicles at the <u>same</u> time.

     a. a car, van or truck
         If yes: how many most of the time   Y/N
            Coding: (1, 2, 3, 4, 5 and more)
     b. a moped, scooter, motorcycle (or mofa)*
         (*) only if relevant in country   Y/N
         If yes: how many most of the time
            Coding: (1, 2, 3, 4, 5 and more)
     c. a bicycle *(Interviewer: include children's bicycles)*   Y/N
         If yes: how many most of the time
            Coding: (1, 2, 3, 4, 5 and more)

     If no car/van, continue with question 5
     If no car/moped etc., continue with question 6
     If no car/moped or bicycle, continue with question 7

     I now want to ask you about crimes you or your household may have experienced during the past five years. It is sometimes difficult to remember such incidents so I will read these questions slowly and I would like you to think carefully about them.

2.   *If cars/vans/trucks (yes at question 1a),* in the past five years have you or other members of your household had any of their cars/vans/trucks stolen? Please take your time to think about this.
     ○ yes
     ○ no
     ○ don't know

     (to car/van/truck owners only)
3.   Apart from this, over the past five years have you or have members of your household been the victim of a theft of a car radio, or something else which was left in your car, or theft of a part of the car, such as a car mirror or wheel? *(Interviewer: vandalism must not be reported here, but under next question; if the car itself was stolen as well, other thefts must not be reported here.)*
     ○ yes
     ○ no
     ○ don't know

4.   *If cars/vans/trucks,* apart from thefts, have parts of any of the cars/vans/trucks belonging to your household been deliberately damaged (vandalized) over the past five years?
     (Interviewer: if person thinks it is deliberate, it will count. Traffic accidents should <u>not</u> be reported.)
     ○ yes
     ○ no
     ○ don't know

     If no moped etc., continue with question 6.
5.   Over the past five years have you or other members of your household had any of their mopeds/scooters/motorcycles/(mofa's)* stolen?
     (*) If relevant in country.
     ○ yes
     ○ no
     ○ don't know

6.   Over the past five years have you or other members of your household had any of their bicycles stolen?
     (Interviewer: include children's bicycles)
     ○ yes
     ○ no
     ○ don't know

7. Disregarding thefts from garages, sheds or lock-ups, over the past five years, did anyone actually get into your house or flat without permission, and steal or try to steal something?
    (Interviewer: do not count burglaries in second houses.)
    ○ yes
    ○ no
    ○ don't know

8. Apart from this, over the past five years, do you have any evidence that someone tried to get into your house or flat unsuccessfully. For example, damage to locks, doors or windows or scratches around the lock?
    ○ yes
    ○ no
    ○ don't know

    Next I want to ask you some questions about what may have happened to you <u>personally</u>. Things that you have mentioned already or which happened <u>to other members of your household</u> must <u>not</u> be mentioned now.

9. Over the past five years, has anyone taken something from you by using force or threatening you or did anyone try to do so?
    (Interviewer: pickpocketing must be reported under 10)
    ○ yes
    ○ no
    ○ don't know

    (interviewer: read slowly)
10. Besides robberies there are many other types of theft of personal property, such as pickpocketing or the theft of a purse, wallet, clothing, jewellery, sports equipment at one's work, at school or pub or in the street. Over the past five years, have you personally been the victim of any of these thefts?
    ○ yes
    ○ no
    ○ don't know

11. I would now like to ask you some questions about crimes of violence of which you personally may have been the victim.
    (Women only)
    Firstly, a rather personal question. People sometimes grab or touch others for sexual reasons in a really offensive way. This can happen either inside one's house or elsewhere, for instance in a pub, the street, at school or at one's workplace. Over the past five years has anyone done this to you? Please take your time to think about it.
    ○ yes
    ○ no
    ○ don't know

12. Apart from the incidents just covered, have you over the past five years been personally attacked or threatened by someone in a way that really frightened you, either at home or elsewhere, such as in a pub, in the street, at school or at your workplace?
    (Interviewer: include here sexual violence against men, if mentioned by respondent.)
    ○ yes
    ○ no
    ○ don't know

    Could I now go back to ask you about the crimes you said that happened to you.

13a. First of all, you have said you had been the victim of a theft of a car *(yes at question 2)*.
    When did this happen? Was it last year, that is in 1988?
    If no, was it before 1988 or was it in 1989?
    (Interviewer: if respondent has been a victim more than once, ask if this happened at least one time in 1988.)
    ○ yes, in 1988 (at least one time)
    ○ no, only before 1988
    ○ no, only in 1989
    ○ don't know

Source: *Experiences of Crime Across the World: Key Findings of the 1989 International Crime Survey.* Deventer, Neth.: Kluwer Law and Taxation Publishers, 1990.

PART V

DOMAINS OF CRIME

THE FAMILY AND THE HOUSEHOLD

In PART 1, WE presented the different theoretical perspectives that criminologists have used to explain criminal behaviour and the evolution of criminal events. Part 5 focuses attention on the ways in which criminal events cluster in particular social domains. Chapters 8 and 9 are concerned with the leisure and work domains. In the present chapter, we analyze the domain of the family and the household.

In these chapters, we present crime events in an integrated fashion, reviewing what we know from current research about who offends, who is affected, the circumstances under which these events occcur, and so on. Throughout our discussion, we will alert you to the relevant theories that best explain the aspect of the event that we are examining. Some theories, particularly those that focus on motivation, work better in providing a framework for precursors. The event itself is generally best understood using the situated transaction and opportunity perspectives, while the aftermath can be analyzed using insights drawn from deterrence theories.

Throughout these chapters, we encourage you to think about the research findings being discussed using the theories that we have reviewed. The theories provide us with the road map through the detail of research findings, helping us to identify commonalities in social behaviour and to provide an understanding of the complexities of social interaction.

Our interest in criminal events in the family and household domain centres on two substantive issues. The first issue is family violence. How do we make sense of the ways in which family members victimize each other? The second issue is crime against the household. Many types of property crime can be understood as crimes in which the household unit is the victim. How do we make sense of these types of events? We begin with a description of the family and household domain.

THE FAMILY AND THE HOUSEHOLD

The concept of family has several different meanings in the literature of social science. A narrow definition might view the family as "husband and wife, with or without never-married children of any age, living at home, or a lone parent with or without one or more never married children at home" (Deveraux, 1990c: 33). Broader definitions, however, suggest that the concept of family includes any adult–child grouping (e.g., with lesbian or gay parents), and all intimate cohabiting or consciously committed support groups, including childless couples, communes, or networks of friends (Luxton, 1988).

In general, we understand the family as referring to any relatively enduring pattern of social relationships through which domestic life is organized (Miller, 1990). Customarily, the family is distinguished from other intimate groupings in that the relationships are based on kinship (Luxton, 1988). However, what we consider to be a family is as much a matter of cultural definition as social organization. It is, for instance, our cultural view of the family as a unit of procreation that leads many people to define a family in which the father is absent as a "broken" home (Wells and Rankin, 1986).

The household is generally understood as the social and physical setting within which family life is organized. Many surveys (such as those used in the census) lead us to equate families with households, but in doing so they may distort the empirical reality of family relations. Family relations in many cases extend beyond any particular household. Husbands and wives who are separated, for instance, usually maintain separate households, although (perhaps because of dependent children) family relations may be sustained.

It is clear from a wealth of demographic data that family relations have changed a great deal in recent years. For example:

- People are waiting longer to marry. The current average age of marriage is 28 for men and 26 for women. Thus, the average couple is married three years later than was the case in the early 1970s (Adams and Nagnur, 1990; Glick, 1990).

- Couples are living longer and enjoying a better standard of living, after their children leave, than ever before (Glick, 1990).

- Participation of women in the labour force has increased dramatically over the last several years. In 1979, 49 percent of women with children under the age of 16 were employed outside of the home compared with 69 percent in 1989 (Parliament, 1990a).

- The number of children per family has decreased over the last two decades (Deveraux, 1990a, 1990c).

- The proportion of people living in common-law relationships doubled during the 1980s (from 4 percent in 1980 to 8 percent in 1990) (Stout, 1991).

- Increasingly large numbers of elderly people are living alone.

- Between 1966 and 1986, the number of single-parent families increased 130 percent (Moore, 1990); over 80 percent of these families are headed by women (Oderkirk and Lochhead, 1992). In 1986, single-parent families represented 13 percent of all families (up from 8 percent in 1966, but below the level of 14 percent recorded in 1931).

- Between 1981 and 1986, divorced people constituted the fastest-growing marital category, followed by those who are separated (Deveraux, 1990b). Over this period, the currently divorced population increased from 500,000 to 690,000.

The social character of families, then, is changing. We are witnessing a move away from the conventional single-family unit to variations that include single parent, multiple singles, and lone individuals. These varying structures make social relations within families different from what we would have expected a number of years ago. In addition, as growing numbers of households come to be occupied by the elderly, the dependence that this group has on children who live outside of the household is increasing.

Reflecting the change in family social relations are the significant changes that the physical setting of households has undergone (Hasell and Peatross, 1990). In the typical suburban home, formal dining rooms have been replaced by family rooms or TV rooms. Master bedrooms have increased in size and have walk-in closets and en-suite bathrooms, both of which allow couples rather than individuals to get ready for work in the morning. In a similar way, kitchens have grown larger so that adults in a hurry can jointly engage in meal preparation. All such changes have important implications for the types of criminal events that occur in the family domain, as well as for the rate at which they occur.

FAMILY VIOLENCE

The popular cultural tendency to idealize the family as the most intimate and most nurturing of social groups has traditionally not encouraged an understanding of the extent to which violence is a part of family life (Miller, 1990). Consequently, the recognition of family violence as a social problem has occurred only very gradually, and in distinct stages, consistent with the evolution of claimsmaking, which we reviewed in Chapter 1. In the 1960s, the problem of child abuse emerged as a policy and research issue (Best, 1990; Nelson, 1984; Pfohl, 1977). A decade later, wife abuse moved onto the agendas of researchers and criminal justice professionals (Loseke, 1989; Tierney, 1982). In the 1980s, elder abuse came to be recognized as a form of family violence requiring attention (Leroux and Petrunik, 1990). More recently, criminologists have begun to research and theorize about other forms of family violence, including sibling violence (Pagelow, 1989) and adolescent violence toward parents (Agnew and Huguley, 1989).

Until recently, it was widely believed that there was little that the police could do to respond to the problem of violence within the family. However, revelations about the pervasiveness of family violence have focused attention on the structure and dynamics of family life, and have given rise to feelings that this problem should be a concern of criminal justice and other social agencies.

PRECURSORS

Any discussion of the preconditions of family violence must begin with a critical look at the social organization of family life, which may be said to contain within it the seeds out of which violent episodes grow. Interpersonal conflict theory has been used to shed light on how families run into the kinds of problems that lead to interpersonal violence. The following four proposals draw upon the insights provided by interactionist theories.

1. *Family life provides the social setting for omnipresent conflict* (Brinkerhoff and Lupri, 1988). Family members spend a great deal of time

with each other and their interactions cut across a wide number of dimensions, ranging from how money will be spent to who will spend it; from where vacations will be spent to who will take out the garbage; from who will prepare dinner to what that dinner will consist of. The frequency of those interactions, coupled with their often intense nature, sets the stage for conflict. In addition, because the family is a heterogeneous social grouping—including within it males and females, and people of different ages—it also provides the context for the playing out of gender or generational conflicts that find their origins in the wider society. Because family members usually know each other so well, they are aware of each other's weaknesses and vulnerabililties. Such intimate knowledge facilitates the escalation of conflicts into violent exchanges.

2. *Family life is private life.* What happens between family members frequently goes on behind closed doors. The private character of family life reflects a consensus view that families are different from other groupings in society. The privacy of the family has structured the ways in which the police and the courts have responded to family members who behave violently. Neighbours, friends, or co-workers may not know about violence that occurs between family members, since family privacy allows it to remain hidden. Even if they do know about it, they may regard it as none of their business. Moreover, the view that violence in the home is a family matter may be shared by the victims of violence. All such factors reinforce the low visibility of violent conflict in the home and suggest the extent to which it is immune to many of the informal social controls that operate to reduce the occurrence of such behaviour among nonintimates. Those who take a feminist perspective argue that concerns for the privacy of the home simply shield the abuser from the sanctions of the public justice system. Such concerns, they argue, reflect a bias toward maintaining in the family a power relationship that favours the men while ignoring the injustices perpetrated against women.

3. *Cultural attitudes toward family violence are highly ambivalent.* In the family, unlike in the workplace or other more formal settings, physical violence continues to be tolerated. This is most evident with respect to the spanking of children (Steinmetz, 1986). A majority of parents believe that there are conditions under which it is perfectly appropriate for one family member to use physical force against another family member. This is not to suggest that spanking is necessarily abusive (although it well may be), but rather that rules about violence in the home are different from rules about violence in other social domains. Nor does the tolerance of physical

violence extend to dependent children alone. In the recent past, violent behaviour by husbands against wives was regarded with the same degree of toleration as parental violence toward children is currently viewed. Most people still continue to regard violence among siblings as normal and natural and, despite obvious physical consequences, not really a form of violence at all.

4. *The family is a hierarchical institution.* This means that some family members have more power than others. Most obviously, parents are more powerful than children. As power-control theory would predict, in traditional patriarchal family structures that are characterized by the presence of an adult male authority figure, it is assumed that the husband has the right to make decisions that are binding on other family members (Kalmuss and Straus, 1990; Hagan, Gillis, and Simpson, 1985). Such authority relations, which are recognized by law and custom, create a situation that allows those with more power to behave with relative immunity toward those who have less power. In addition, the widespread support for existing authority relations allows those with power to believe that they have a right to expect compliance from those who are less powerful. Violence may be understood as one effective way in which such compliance is gained.

As we have said, consensus views of the family have been challenged by those who see that the inequality in family relations renders some people more vulnerable than others to violence in the family. Our tendency to categorize the major forms of family violence as "wife assault," "child abuse," and "elder abuse" explicitly recognizes this fact. The consequences of this hierarchy rest most heavily on the shoulders of women, who have historically been economically dependent on men (Davis, 1988). Not surprisingly, as both children and adults, females face greater risks of violence than do males. Victimization surveys typically show that women comprise between 80 percent and 90 percent of victims of spousal violence (Harlow, 1991; Klaus and Rand, 1984; Canadian Centre for Justice Statistics, 1990c). According to data from the seven-city Canadian Urban Victimization Survey, women were the victims in 77 percent of family-related assaults, 90 percent of assaults between spouses, 80 percent of assaults between ex-spouses, and 55 percent of assaults involving other relatives (Solicitor General of Canada, 1985a).

Studies that use the Conflict Tactics Scale, which we introduced in Chapter 6, have presented findings which suggest that, in the context of the family, women are as violent as men. This has led some observers to argue that it is necessary to focus attention on the "battered husband" as well as the battered wife (Steinmetz, 1977–78). However, the above-mentioned studies provide counts of violent acts that do not clarify the context, motives or consequences associated with the violence (DeKeseredy and Hinch, 1991). As Saunders (1989), notes by most measures of victimization—who initiates the violence, who uses violence offensively rather than defensively, and who is injured most—there is little question that women are more frequently victimized.

In the case of children, patterns of violence also reflect patterns of inequality and dependency. An analysis of Canadian UCR data for seven cities for the years 1988 to 1990 revealed that 40 percent of those accused of committing violent crimes against children were parents or other relatives (Wright and Leroux, 1991). In the case of sexual assaults, 24 percent were committed by parents and 17 percent by other family members. Only 11 percent of child homicides between 1980 and 1989 were committed by strangers. Two-thirds of child victims were killed by their parents (one-third each by mothers and fathers), while a further 10 percent were killed by stepparents, foster parents, or other relatives. Another form of abuse that reflects hierarchy and dependency relationships is elder abuse, the victims of which may be infirm and reliant on a spousal or adult-child caregiver for the basic necessities of life (Pillemer and Finkelhor, 1988; Podnieks, 1990; Quinn and Tomita, 1986; but see Pillemer, 1985).

Conflict, privacy, ambivalent attitudes about violence, and inequality are not the only factors that contribute to the occurrence of violence in the family. When families are isolated from the wider community of kin, friends, and neighbours, the negative effects of privacy may be increased (Straus, 1990b). Under such conditions, those who behave violently may become increasingly insensitive to prevailing community standards regarding appropriate conduct. Further, they and their victims may lose or find less accessible the social supports that could be crucial in ending or preventing violence or in mediating the conflicts that lead to violence.

Conditions of economic stress may also contribute to violent conduct. As strain theories would predict, a husband or father who is out of work may use violence to compensate for the feelings of inadequacy that the perceived failure to play the breadwinner role may promote (Frieze and Browne, 1989). This interpretation is consistent with the widely reported finding that rates of family violence are generally higher among lower-income groups (DeKeseredy and Hinch, 1991; Klaus and Rand, 1984; Lenton, 1990; Schwartz, 1988; Steinmetz, 1986; Straus and Smith, 1990). A study of wife assault in Toronto found that, among women sampled in 1987, 27 percent of respondents from the lowest income group reported having been abused, compared to 8 percent from the highest income group (Smith, 1988). Strain may also arise from noneconomic sources such as illness or the death of a loved one. In the case of child abuse or elder abuse, strain may originate from the demands of the caregiving experience (Fattah and Sacco, 1989).

THE EVENT

How frequent are violent events within the family? As our discussion in earlier chapters would suggest, answers to the question of frequency depend very much on how the concept of violence is defined for research purposes. Despite differences in research approaches, the relevant body of literature suggests quite clearly that violent events within the family occur more frequently than many of us would like to believe. Silverman and Kennedy (1993) report that approximately 40 percent of all homicides that occurred in Canada over the past 30 years involved family members.

For reasons discussed in Chapter 6, victimization surveys typically provide low estimates of levels of family violence. The 1988 General Social Survey, for instance, estimated that 7 women per 1,000 in the Canadian population were assaulted one or more times by their spouses in 1987 (Canadian Centre for Criminal Justice Statistics, 1990c). Quite clearly, victimization studies like the GSS can tell us only about those violent events that women label as criminal and are willing to report to a survey interviewer.

Studies that have used the Conflict Tactics Scale provide estimates of wife assault which suggest that the problem is far from uncommon. A survey of Alberta couples by Kennedy and Dutton (1989) found that the rate of wife abuse was 11.2 percent overall, and that the rate of severe abuse was 2.3 percent. In the city of Calgary, Brinkerhoff and Lupri (1988) found the overall rate to be 25 percent and the rate of severe abuse to be 11 percent. Smith (1988) reports that, among married or cohabiting women in Toronto, the rate of overall abuse in 1987 was approximately 14 percent, while the rate of severe abuse was about 5 percent. These figures suggest levels of violence that are comparable to those revealed by American researchers. A national survey of U.S. couples found that, in 1985, one out of eight husbands carried out one or more violent acts against their partners and more than three out of every 100 women were severely assaulted by their partners (Straus and Gelles, 1990). Table 7.1 shows a comparison of Alberta and national American data on husband-to-wife violence as measured by the Conflict Tactics Scale.

Table 7.1 Husband-to-Wife Violence: Comparison of Specific Acts for U.S. (1985) and Alberta (1987) Surveys

	Rate per 100 couples	
Violent Act	U.S. (1985)	Alberta (1987)
A. "Minor"		
1. Threw something	2.8	4.2
2. Pushed/grabbed/shoved	9.3	9.2
3. Slapped	2.9	1.7
B. "Severe"		
4. Kicked/bit/hit with fist	1.5	0.9
5. Hit, tried to hit with something	1.7	1.6
6. Beat up	0.8	0.2
7. Threatened with gun/knife	0.4	0.1
8. Used gun or knife	0.2	0.0

Source: L.W. Kennedy and D.G. Dutton, "The Incidence of Wife Assault in Alberta," *Canadian Journal of Behavioural Science* 21(1): 49.

We know less about violence against children than about violence between spouses. While we know that the rate of child homicide is about 2 1/2 times lower than the rate for adults (Wright and Leroux, 1991), we lack information about other forms of violence toward children (Health and Welfare, n.d.). As discussed earlier in this chapter, part of the problem in generating such data concerns the widespread attitude that some types of violence against children, such as spanking, are permissible. Data collected by American researchers are instructive in this respect. Straus and Gelles (1990) report that, in surveys conducted in 1975 and 1985, over 90 percent of parents said that they had hit their children. Further, the rates are quite high with respect to severe violence, which includes hitting the child with an object; 11 out of every 100 parents reported hitting a child in a way that probably fits most people's definition of abuse. These results are consistent with those of a Toronto study by Lenton (1990). She states that relatively mild forms of violence are common and that "even the most severe actions are not infrequent" (Lenton, 1990: 169). During the survey year, 12 percent of mothers and 15 percent of fathers reported that they had beat their child.

Research on violent events involving elderly victims is still in the very early stages in this country. One survey, undertaken by Podnieks (1990), investigated the incidence of several types of abuse among a representative national sample of noninstitutionalized elderly Canadians. Podnieks found that the overall rate of abuse was 40 per 1,000 elderly people, a figure that translates into approximately 100,000 victims of elder abuse. However, most of the types of abuse revealed by the survey were nonviolent in nature. Using a modified form of the Conflict Tactics Scale, the study revealed the rate of violent victimization of elderly people by family members or other intimates to be 5 per 1,000.

The location and timing of violent events in general reflect the importance of the precursors discussed above. Most violent events that involve family members occur in the home. Data from the Canadian Urban Victimization Survey revealed that 88 percent of spousal assaults occurred in the home of the victim, while a further 7 percent occurred in the home of someone else (Solicitor General of Canada, 1988b). The reasons for these findings are obvious. The home is where family members are most likely to confront each other and where privacy allows these events to develop.

Family violence events are most likely to take place in the evening or late at night. Arguments that begin in the early evening may turn violent if they are unresolved as the night wears on (Gelles and Straus, 1988). The late-night and early-morning hours bring with them a reduction in the options available to the parties in the conflict through which the matter could be resolved without violence. It is too late to call a family member or to leave the house in order to visit a friend. Stressful events that fuel tensions or challenge parental or patriarchal authority increase the likelihood of a violent episode involving children. Despite the attention paid to the physical mistreatment of very young children by parents, it appears that much violence is directed against teenage children whose various forms of adolescent rebellion may be viewed as requiring strict physical discipline (Pagelow, 1989).

On some occasions, the factors that contribute to the likelihood of a violent event come into sharp relief. Gelles and Straus (1988) note that violent events occur with higher than usual frequency during the Christmas or Easter holidays. At these times, the sources of both economic and noneconomic stress may be especially pronounced. Family members spend more time than usual together and may entertain unrealistically positive expectations about how others will behave. In addition, family celebrations may involve drinking alcohol, which can facilitate the movement toward violence.

Perhaps the most distinctive characteristic of family violence events is their repetitive and cyclical character. In contrast to forms of victimization that result from a chance encounter between a victim and offender, the intimate relationships in which family members are involved increase the probability that violent events will reoccur or escalate. Minor acts of violence may be self-reinforcing when those who engage in them come to see violence as an effective means of achieving compliance when the use of violence carries few sanctions (Feld and Straus, 1990). While most victims try to resist the physical violence, their resistance is more likely to be passive (reasoning with the offender, trying to get help) than active (Klaus and Rand, 1984; Harlow, 1991). Silverman and Kennedy (1993) note that most spousal homicides are not the result of a sudden "blow up," but rather represent the culmination of serial violence, which is fuelled by the presence of drugs and alcohol, a lack of problem-solving skills and the effects of longstanding quarrels and antagonisms. Many cases of family violence escalate into more serious forms of victimization. At a minimum, the physical violence that does occur is probably part of a much larger pattern that involves a variety of forms of emotional and psychological mistreatment.

The violent events in a household may take on the character of routine activities (low-level conflict) that escalate to violence. The opportunities for this violence are facilitated by the privacy of the home, which protects the offenders from detection and provides them with objects with which to vent their anger. The violence is likely to be repeated (the opportunities for victimization rarely change), at least until the victim decides to flee or seek outside help.

THE AFTERMATH

Family violence may result in severe physical consequences, even death. There is evidence to suggest that violence in the home is more likely than other types of violent episodes to result in injury (Harlow, 1991; Klaus and Rand, 1984; Solicitor General of Canada, 1985a, 1988b). This finding may be explained by the repetitive character of family violence and by the relative inability of victims to escape violent encounters that occur in the context of the family.

The effects of violence are emotional and psychological as well as physical. Victims of violence in the home, like other victims of violence, experience many forms of fear, trauma, and stress (Wirtz and Harrell, 1987). Indeed, there is reason to argue that violence in the home is more likely than other forms of violence to produce these consequences (Gelles and Straus, 1990; Canadian Centre for Criminal Justice Statistics, 1990c). Violence may be more threatening if it occurs in environments that individuals have defined as "safe" (Burgess, Holmstrom, and McCausland, 1977). In addition, being victimized by an intimate may produce greater stress since one has to cope with the fact that the violence has been at the hands of a trusted individual (Sales, Baum, and Shore, 1984).

Despite the seriousness of their injuries, victims may decline to seek medical aid so as to avoid having to explain to others the sources of the injury (Canadian Centre for Criminal Justice Statistics, 1990c). The stigma of being a victim may also keep women from seeking help (Solicitor General of Canada, 1985a). Even when they do seek help, they may encouter emergency-room personnel who are less than sympathetic. According to Kurz (1987), some ER personnel describe abused wives as "AOBs" (alcohol on breath) and as troublesome people who deserve the trouble in which they find themselves.

Victims of family violence may, for similar reasons, decline to report the incident to the police (Klaus and Rand, 1984; Canadian Centre for Criminal Justice Statistics, 1990c). For many female victims of spousal abuse, calling the police is a last resort, even when the violence is severe (Kantor and Straus, 1987). Victimization surveys suggest that the victim's fear that the offender will retaliate through violence against the victim (and possibly against dependent children) figures largely in the decision not to report (Solicitor General of Canada, 1988b). The victim may also have concerns about how an arrest may lead to a loss of financial support (Steinman, 1992).

In the past, police have been reluctant to intervene in family situations or, when intervention did occur, to take the offender (most often the husband) out of the situation to "cool off." Increasingly, however, the police are taking steps to invoke the law as it applies to family violence. Williams and Hawkins (1986) argue that the sanction which results from such action may be a deterrent to future offending. As was pointed out in our review of deterrence theories in Chapter 3, research has shown that there is a considerable stigma associated with arrest (Dutton et al., 1992).

There is also a strong sentiment among victim groups that more has to be done to help victims of family violence. The number of safe houses is considered inadequate to meet the needs of women who feel at risk. It is also argued, at a more basic level, that it is unfair that women have to flee their homes for safety's sake. Browne and Williams (1989) attribute the 25 percent reduction in female-perpetrated spousal homicide in the United States, in the decade since 1980, to the fact that there has been increased public awareness of the difficulties women face when dealing with violent spouses. Accompanying this awareness has been an increase in the resources available to women victims—resources that have enabled them to escape their partner's violence rather than respond with violence themselves.

Providing resources such as shelters is helpful in managing the more serious forms of violence. But the day-to-day problems that people encounter most often do not come to the attention of the authorities. Many of these problems are, however, known to neighbours, friends, and others. We are becoming increasingly aware of situations of serial violence, eventually resulting in homicide, in which outsiders knew of the conflict over a long period but were either reluctant to intervene or were not taken seriously by authorities when they attempted to do so. Box 7.1 describes such a case, which attracted international attention.

BOX 7.1   FAMILY VIOLENCE

In recent years, several cases of family victimization have captured public attention. One of the most notorious involved the murder of 6-year-old Lisa Steinberg by her adoptive father, Joel Steinberg.

The homicide, which took place in New York City on November 2, 1987, represented the culmination of a pattern of escalating abuse. When paramedics arrived at the location of the fatal assault—the Steinberg apartment—they discovered a shocking scene: walls smeared with blood and urine; drug paraphernalia scattered everywhere; floors were covered with broken televisions, VCRs, and other electronic equipment; Lisa's 16-month-old adoptive brother tied to a urine-soaked crib; and Steinberg's common-law wife, Hedda Nussbaum, evidencing signs of severe physical and psychological abuse.

This case attracted attention for several reasons. One of the more obvious was the apparent respectability of the people involved. Steinberg presented himself as a lawyer (although it was subsequently discovered that he had obtained his licence to practise fraudulently), and Nussbaum was an editor of children's books. Their social status suggested the extent to which abuse cuts across class lines.

In addition, the subsequent investigation revealed that, although neighbours, teachers, and others had reported their suspicions about child abuse in the Steinberg home to child-welfare agencies, no action was taken. The case thus signalled to many the inadequacy of child-protective services.

These factors, combined with the history of wife and child abuse in the Steinberg household, galvanized public opinion about the case. Steinberg became for a brief time the most hated man in New York, if not in the United States. Edward Koch, the Mayor of New York, called him a "monster" and said that he should be "boiled in oil." Hundreds attended the funeral and visited the site of Lisa's victimization. At his trial, Steinberg was fined $5,000 and sentenced to the maximum prison term allowed by law.

The publicity that accompanied the Steinberg case significantly increased public awareness about the problem of child abuse in the late 1980s.

One very important issue that is being considered by researchers who are interested in the aftermath of family violence is the way in which violent behaviour by one family member promotes violent behaviour on the part of others. The fact that courts are becoming increasingly willing to accept the psychological consequences of violence as a defence for killing indicates that we cannot always rely on the notion of rational behaviour when judging why people act as they do. Arguments about acts performed in the "heat of passion" have always been recognized when one partner kills another in a jealous rage. But the idea that violence begets violence is only now being viewed as contributing to a condition that may constitute a justifiable defence.

In a related way, it has been argued that the use of physical violence against children may increase the risk that they will themselves behave in either violent or nonviolent criminal ways. While physical punishment may induce conformity in children in the short run, over the longer term it may create the very problems it is intended to prevent (Straus, 1991). While some delinquency researchers, including Wells and Rankin (1986, 1991), have emphasized the importance of the broken home as a cause of delinquency, this line of research reflects the view that it is the quality of family interaction rather than whether or not the home is legally broken that is the important issue in the study of delinquency.

How does physical violence against children increase the risks of delinquency? Several types of effects may derive from such violence. First, social control theorists have argued that the bonds between juveniles and their parents (and other conformist role models) provide a certain insulation against involvement in delinquency. A high degree of parental attachment means that the parent is better able to teach the positive social skills that facilitate an individual's success in the workplace or at school (Currie, 1985; Patterson and Dishion, 1985). Quite obviously, parental abuse may weaken this bond and lessen the degree of juvenile sensitivity to parental expectations of appropriate behaviour (Rankin and Wells, 1990).

Second, if parental behaviour is abusive, the child or adolescent may seek to avoid contact with his or her parents. To the extent that delinquency is prevented by the ability of the parent to monitor and supervise the behaviour of children, delinquency in such situations may be expected to increase, as predicted by control theory in general and by transactional theory in particular (Gottfredson, and Hirschi, 1990; Thornberry, 1987).

Third, violent delinquency may be a form of acting out on the part of the child (Agnew, 1985a). Children may run away from home or engage in other "escape crimes." Their resulting homelessness, combined with a lack of labour market skills, may increase the likelihood that they will make use of whatever delinquent or criminal opportunities present themselves (McCarthy and Hagan, 1991). In addition, they may behave violently toward classmates or other acquaintances as a way of expressing their frustration about the abusive home situation.

Fourth, growing up in a violent home may provide children with lessons in the use of violence as a means of achieving goals and controlling others (Peek, Fischer, and Kidwell, 1985). A child who witnesses spousal violence may come to see it as a legitimate way of resolving conflict (Fagan and Wexler, 1987; McCord, 1991). According to Hotaling, Straus, and Lincoln (1990) homes in which there is child assault or spousal assault have higher rates of sibling violence and higher rates of violence by the dependent children against children outside of the home.

CRIMES AGAINST THE HOUSEHOLD

INTRODUCTION

Crimes against the household are very common in Canada (Fedorowycz, 1992; Morrison, 1991a; Solicitor General of Canada, 1986). According to the 1987 General Social Survey, 40 percent of the 5.4 million victimization incidents uncovered by the survey were property crimes (Sacco and Johnson, 1990). Some data describing the national rates of property crimes are presented in Table 7.2. Overall, there were 216 incidents of household victimization for every 1,000 households. This number includes (for every 1,000 households) 54 incidents of break and enter (actual and attempted); 51 incidents of theft of motor vehicle or motor vehicle parts (actual and attempted); 48 incidents of theft of household property (actual and attempted); and 63 incidents of vandalism.

Table 7.2 Household Crimes in Canada, 1987

Crime	Rate Per 1,000 Households	Percent Reported to Police
Total household crime	216	54
Break and enter*	54	70
Motor-vehicle theft*	51	57
Theft of household property*	48	43
Vandalism	63	45

* Includes attempts

Source: V.F. Sacco and H. Johnson, *Patterns of Criminal Victimization in Canada.* Ottawa: Minister of Supply and Services, 1990.

The routine activities theory of predatory crime, which was described in Chapter 4, explains such crimes in terms of how offenders encounter opportunities for offending. With modern lifestyles forcing people to spend long periods outside of the house working or pursuing leisure-time activities, the household may remain unoccupied and unguarded, enhancing its appeal as a target for crime.

Not all households are equally likely to be victimized. The patterns of household victimization as revealed by victimization and UCR data suggest that opportunities for property crimes are structured. Location of households raises the likelihood of victimization. The more urbanized the household, the higher the rates of household crime (Cohen and Cantor, 1981; Maguire and Bennett, 1982). The 1988 General Social Survey revealed that rates for these crimes were about 70 percent higher in Canada's urban (as opposed to rural) regions (Sacco and Johnson, 1990). This discrepancy in rates might be explained by the fact that formal and informal social controls are less effective in urban centres. Alternatively, larger cities may provide a fertile breeding ground for criminal subcultures that provide an intricate network for the distribution of stolen goods (Fischer, 1976).

Not all urban neighbourhoods face the same risk of household crime. Residents of socially disadvantaged areas may face greater risks than do those who reside in more affluent areas (Evans, 1989; Maguire and Bennett, 1982). Poor areas may have many characteristics that increase the risks of household crime. Lower income may translate into fewer precautions taken to protect the household, particularly when such precautions involve the use of limited discretionary income. Such areas also contain a disproportionate number of single-parent households, leaving children with generally lower levels of adult supervision (Maxfield, 1987b; Smith and Jarjoura, 1989; Canadian Centre for Justice Statistics, 1988). Mixed land use in these areas may mean the presence of bars and stores that bring large numbers of strangers through the neighbourhood. Under such conditions, it may be more difficult to know who does and who does not belong in an area (Lynch and Cantor, 1992). Finally, the greater degrees of residential instability and social heterogeneity in poor areas may undermine the development of collective community sentiments and thereby diminish effective informal social control at the local level (Smith and Jarjoura, 1988, 1989). In other words, as people become less tied to one another, there is less reason to worry about what others think and to conform to their expectations.

The fact that poor *areas* have higher rates of household victimization than more affluent ones does not necessarily mean that poorer *households* have higher rates of victimization than their more affluent counterparts (Maguire and Bennett, 1982). In fact, several studies have shown that the risk of many forms of household victimization increases with household income (Cohen and Cantor, 1981; Cohen, Kluegel, and Land, 1981; Solicitor General of Canada, 1986; Sacco and Johnson, 1990). This may be because offenders choose the more affluent targets in less affluent areas or the wealthier homes located near such areas (Waller and Okihiro, 1978).

The findings of victimization research also suggest that some types of housing structures are more susceptible to various forms of household crime than are others (Massey, Krohn, and Bonati, 1989). Most susceptible are those dwellings that offer the thief or the burglar easy access or that provide cover during the commission of the crime. Thus, the risks of break and enter are higher when a housing structure offers multiple points of entry, when doors or windows are covered by trees or shrubs, when the house is located on a corner or near a major route that allows easy escape, or when neighbours' houses do not directly overlook the target (Bennett and Wright, 1984; Evans, 1989).

The 1988 General Social Survey found that residents of high-rise apartment buildings had the lowest rates for most of the types of household crime investigated in the survey (Sacco and Johnson, 1990). Access in and out of dwellings of this type is problematic for offenders. Further, it is difficult for them to determine whether or not anyone is home (Solicitor General of Canada, 1988a; Waller and Okihiro, 1978). In contrast, residents of doubles, duplexes, and townhouses reported the highest rates of household victimization, while residents of single-family houses reported rates in between the two extremes.

Crimes against the household are also made more or less likely by the levels and types of household activities. Most notably, when the home is left vacant for extended periods, the risks of household crime increase dramatically (Evans, 1989; Hough, 1987; Miethe, Stafford, and Long, 1987). Victimization survey estimates indicate that as many as nine out of ten break-and-enter incidents occur when the household is unoccupied (Solicitor General of Canada, 1986, 1988a).

The General Social Survey data from 1987 indicate that risks of all forms of household victimization increase along with the tendency of household residents to spend time away from home. For respondents who reported that they engaged in 30 or more evening activities outside the home per month, the rate of household victimization per 1,000 households was 319, while for those who reported ten or fewer such activities, the rate was 125 (Sacco and Johnson, 1990). On weekdays, when children are in school and adults are at work, households are more vulnerable (Maguire and Bennett, 1982). During the night, when cars are parked in driveways and potential guardians are asleep, the risks of automobile theft increase (Morrison, 1991b; Solicitor General of Canada, 1986).

The rhythms and tempos of family life affect the risk of household crime in other ways. A good deal of traffic in and out of the home is an expected characteristic of large families. Doors are more likely to be left open or unlocked, and property may not always be put away, which makes such homes an attractive proposition for thieves (Sacco and Johnson, 1990; Smith and Jarjoura, 1989). The summer months, which bring warm temperatures and open windows and vacations spent away from home, may also bring an increase in the opportunities for household crime (Sacco and Johnson, 1990; Waller and Okihiro, 1978).

THE EVENT

While we may think about opportunities for crime as an objective feature of the social environment (an open door invites theft), the situation is more complicated than this. Criminal opportunities also have a subjective quality. For criminal events to occur, it is necessary that a potential offender define the open door as an opportunity for theft. While one person might see the large shrubs that block the view from the street of a residential window as nothing more than interesting landscaping, another might see this shrubbery as providing cover during a robbery attempt. Stated differently, opportunities for crime only exist when potential offenders define them as such.

What are the characteristics of the property offender? Like many other types of predatory offenders, these individuals tend disproportionately to be young males, many of whom come from socially disadvantaged backgrounds (Maguire and Bennett, 1982; Canadian Centre for Criminal Justice Statistics, 1988; Waller and Okihiro, 1978). In the case of break and enter, according to the Canadian Centre for Justice Statistics, more than 80 percent of those charged are between 18 and 25 years of age and about one-third are between the ages of 12 to 17 (Fedorowycz, 1992). The overwhelming majority of those charged with the offence are male. Similarly, UCR data also indicate that one-half of those charged with motor-vehicle theft are between 18 and 25 while another one-third are young offenders. As in the case of break and enter and other household crimes, persons charged with motor-vehicle theft are usually male (Morrison, 1991b).

It is useful to distinguish between two broad types of property offenders (Evans, 1989). On the one hand, there is the professional offender, who is sometimes characterized as the "good burglar" (Shover, 1973, 1983). These offenders may be considered the "elite of the criminal world" (Cromwell, Olson, and Avary, 1991). They have a considerable degree of technical competence and are connected to a network of other thieves and tipsters, as well as fences to whom the stolen property is sold. Professional thieves think of themselves as "specialists" and understand their offending in occupational terms; they speak of pulling a "job" or "working" a particular area (Maguire and Bennett, 1982). The crimes in which they engage are generally said to reflect careful planning that involves a rational assessment of the risks and benefits associated with a particular offence.

The professional offender usually figures very prominently in media portrayals of household crime and police rhetoric about the typical offender. However, several researchers argue that popular images of the highly specialized and rational property offender may be exaggerated. According to Cromwell, Olson, and Avary (1991), much of what we know about such offenders comes from interviews with offenders or ex-offenders who may engage in "rational reconstruction." In other words, in recalling their crimes, they suggest that far more planning took place than was actually the case. While it is sometimes said that the professional seeks opportunities for crime, Cromwell and his colleagues maintain that these offenders do not so much seek opportunities as develop a special sensitivity to the opportunities they happen to encounter.

Hough (1987) suggests that, despite the activities of some unspecified number of professional household thieves, these individuals are probably responsible for only a minority of the crimes revealed in victimization surveys. This speculation is supported by the fact that such surveys generally uncover large numbers of crimes that point to amateurish offenders with little technical knowledge or experience (Waller and Okihiro, 1978). Many household crimes are committed by unsophisticated offenders, the majority of whom are probably juveniles. These "occasional offenders" commit crimes when opportunities or situational inducements present themselves (Evans, 1989). Property crimes such as theft and break and enter (irrespective of the level of professionalism of the offender) are motivated by instrumental needs (Bennett and Wright, 1984). These crimes do not reflect expressive needs like anger or revenge, but are prompted by a desire on the part of the offender to obtain the property of the victim.

Engagement in household theft, as well as movement out of this type of crime with advancing age, can be understood in terms of control theory.

Thefts from households are crimes that easily resist detection (Maguire and Bennett, 1982). Offenders learn from their own experience, and from the experiences of others, that the chances of getting caught in the commission of any particular crime are very slim (Bennett and Wright, 1984). They also recognize, however, that if they become known to the police as thieves, and if the method of crime commission remains the same, their chances of getting caught become greater over time, thus reducing the attractiveness of this form of crime (Cromwell, Olson, and Avary, 1991). While the professional thief may be said to have a lengthy criminal career, a substantial number of juvenile offenders commit crimes only rarely and do so with even less frequency as they get older (Shover, 1983). While the number of repeat offenders as measured by the recidivism rate for burglary is higher than that for many other crimes, there are many juvenile offenders who do not recidivate at all (Maguire and Bennett, 1982).

As events, crimes against the household can be relatively uncomplicated affairs. An opportunistic thief may pass a house and notice some item of value unguarded on the front lawn or in the driveway (Lynch and Cantor, 1992). Seeing no one about, the thief removes the item and continues on his or her way. Similarly, under cover of darkness in the early hours of the morning, the thief may happen upon an unlocked car and steal either its contents or that car itself.

Crimes of break and enter vary in terms of how much planning they require. In a large number of these events, young offenders target a house not far from their own residence (Brantingham and Brantingham, 1984; Cohen and Cantor, 1981; Hough, 1987). The proximity of the target may reflect two distinct considerations. The first is the relatively limited mobility of the offender, who is too young to drive. The second concerns the fact that offenders may have direct knowledge of both the contents and routine activities of the households they encounter in the course of their own routine activities. In such cases, entry may be "child's play" (Maguire and Bennett, 1982). The offender tests the door and, if it is open, enters the house. (According to Solicitor General of Canada [1988a], as many as one-third of break and enters uncovered in the Canadian Urban Victimization Survey did not involve the use of force.) The thief moves through the house quickly, more interested in getting in and out quickly with something of value than with the wanton destruction of property (Maguire and Bennett, 1982; Waller and Okihiro, 1978). The items stolen may include money, alcohol, and light electronic goods such as portable television sets or VCRs.

The more professional burglar may work harder at the selection of a target. The selection process may include several stages as the offender makes decisions about which neighbourhood, which block in the neighbourhood, and which house on the block will be victimized (Taylor and Gottfredson, 1986). Unlike the occasional thief, who stumbles across opportunities for theft, the more professional burglar seeks out these opportunities in a more concerted fashion. Relationships may be cultivated with "tipsters" who can provide information about vacant homes and potentially large "scores" (Shover, 1973). Some tipsters may be "fences" who are attempting to ensure their inventory, while others may be thieves who for some reason are unable to undertake the crime themselves. Additionally, thieves may, in the course of their regular travels through the neighbourhood, be attentive to homes that appear empty or that promise easy entry. Waiting at a traffic light may provide potential burglars with the opportunity to view potential targets without attracting attention (Cromwell, Olson, and Avary, 1991).

Irrespective of the level of professionalism, burglars who are intent on breaking and entering must consider three questions (1) can they get away with the crime (risk)?; (2) can they get anything out of it (reward)?; and (3) can they commit the crime without great difficulty (ease)? (Bennett, 1989). Of these three factors, the first (degree of risk) is probably the most serious (Bennett and Wright, 1984). Homes that provide cover from surveillance by other homes present the offender with fewer risks. The mere presence of passersby may not influence the decision to offend, since thieves are concerned not about being seen but about being seen *and* reported (Cromwell, Olson, and Avary, 1992).

The occupancy of the household may be the most important aspect of risk. The presence of a car in the driveway or signs of movement or activity in the house may encourage the potential offender to look elsewhere (Bennett, 1989). Some offenders may engage in more sophisticated "occupancy probes" in order to establish whether or not the household is vacant (see Box 7.2).

An occupied home is to be avoided not only because of the risk of detection but also because of a concern on the part of the offender that, if someone is home, the crime of break and enter could escalate into a more serious offence. Kennedy and Silverman (1993) in Canada and Maxfield (1990) in the United States have observed that, although a rare occurence, there is a higher than expected number of homicides involving elderly victims in their homes. This finding may result from the fact that the elderly occupy households in areas that appear uninhabited during the day. The burglar, surprised by an unexpected encounter, may strike out against the elderly person, with fatal consequences. The occurrence of such unpremeditated homicides, coupled with the occurrence of break and enters that are

BOX 7.2   OCCUPANCY PROBES

In their interviews with burglars, Cromwell, Olson, and Avary (1992) discovered that these offenders use several imaginative methods to determine whether anyone is home.

1. If working as part of a team, the most "presentable" burglar knocks on the door or rings the doorbell. If someone answers, the burglar asks for directions or for a nonexistent person.

2. The burglar rings the doorbell and, if someone answers, claims that his or her car broke down and that he or she needs to use the phone. If the resident refuses, the burglar may leave without attracting suspicion. If the resident consents, the burglar may have an opportunity to check out the merchandise in the home as well as whatever security measures may exist.

3. The burglar telephones the residence to be broken into from a nearby phone. The burglar then returns to the residence. If he or she can hear the telephone ringing, it is unlikely that anyone is at home.

4. The burglar targets a house next to a residence that has a "for sale" sign on the front lawn. Posing as a buyer, the burglar can examine the target household from the vantage of the sale property.

One informant in the Cromwell et al. study would dress in a tracksuit, jog to the front door of the target household, remove a piece of mail from the potential victim's mailbox, and ring the doorbell. If anyone answered, he would say that he found the letter and was returning it. The tracksuit explained why a stranger might be ringing a doorbell in the neighbourhood, while the apparently neighbourly gesture suggested that the burglar was a good citizen and therefore above suspicion.

not completed due to the presence of the householder, suggests that offenders may not be as quite adept at assessing occupancy as is sometimes thought (Hough, 1987).

The second factor (ease of entry) concerns the relative difficulty burglars encounter in attempting to enter the residence. In general, this factor cannot be assessed until the offence is underway (Bennett and Wright, 1984). In many cases, it is a simple matter to break a door or a window; even the presence of special locks and security hardware may not serve as a strong deterrent (Lynch and Cantor, 1992; Maguire and Bennett, 1982). However, while many professional burglars report that they can, if required, deal effectively with alarms or watchdogs, they also report that the large number of households that are unprotected by such measures makes attempts into protected homes unnecessary (Maguire and Bennett, 1982).

The final factor (potential reward) is probably the least important selection measure. It may be impossible for offenders who engage in break and enter to determine before the commission of the crime what of value is to be gained (Miethe and Meier, 1990; Lynch and Cantor, 1992). As stated, however, information from a tipster may decrease uncertainty and higher-status households may hold the promise of greater rewards. However, in most situations, it can probably be assumed with relative certainty that something of value may be collected in the course of the crime (Cromwell, Olson, and Avary, 1992).

THE AFTERMATH

Data from the 1988 General Social Survey indicate that, in 1987, Canadians incurred financial losses in 92 percent of household crimes; 15 percent of all household crime involved losses of $1,000 or more (see Figure 7.1) (Sacco and Johnson, 1990). The Canadian Urban Victimization Survey found that, while the greatest gross losses occurred in the case of motor-vehicle theft, the high rate of recovery for this crime resulted in a somewhat lower net loss. The highest net loss occurs for crimes of break and enter, since there is a

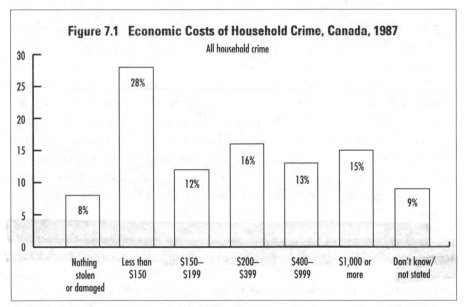

Figure 7.1 Economic Costs of Household Crime, Canada, 1987

All household crime

- Nothing stolen or damaged: 8%
- Less than $150: 28%
- $150–$199: 12%
- $200–$399: 16%
- $400–$999: 13%
- $1,000 or more: 15%
- Don't know/not stated: 9%

Source: V.F. Sacco and H. Johnson, *Patterns of Criminal Victimization in Canada*. Ottawa: Minister of Supply and Services, 1990.

relatively small chance that stolen property will be recovered (Solicitor General of Canada, 1985b). Lower-income groups, which are less likely to have insurance, generally experience the greatest net loss for household crimes.

Such figures provide only a partial picture of the impact of household crime. Incidents of illegal entry that escalate into assaults, robberies, sexual assaults, or homicides have very direct and immediate physical consequences (Warr, 1988). Because incidents of this type are relatively rare, and because household crimes generally involve small net losses, it is sometimes assumed that these crimes have little psychological impact on victims. Such is not the case, especially with respect to break and enter. Many victims—particularly women—may be badly shaken by the event (Maguire and Bennett, 1982; Waller and Okihiro, 1978). Victims may experience feelings of vulnerability, concern that the offender will return, and fear of being alone, even in situations that are not directly related to household crime (Sacco and Johnson, 1990; Solicitor General of Canada, 1985b, 1988a). They may also experience long-term sleeping disorders or require tranquillizers for an extended period. Maguire and Bennett (1982) report that, in a sample of British burglary victims, negative effects were reported by 65 percent of the victims four to six weeks after the crime.

As in the case of other criminal events, many crimes against the household are not reported to the police. The 1988 General Social Survey found that, overall, only 54 percent of respondents had reported these offences to the police (Sacco and Johnson, 1990). As Table 7.2 shows, 70 percent of the break and enters were reported, compared to 57 percent of thefts of motor vehicles and motor-vehicle parts and 43 percent of households thefts. The failure of victims to report was related to their perceptions that the crimes were too minor to warrant official intervention or that there was little that the police could do in any case. The sense of embarrassment some victims may feel about not having taken precautions to prevent the crime may further discourage reporting (Solicitor General of Canada, 1985b; Waller and Okihiro, 1978).

Crimes against the household also indicate that it is *what happens to the victim* rather than *who the victim is* that determines whether an event will be reported (Evans, 1989). In other words, the likelihood of reporting is not very strongly related to the social and demographic characteristics of victims. Instead, the crime is more likely to be reported when it has characteristics that might be interpreted as indicators of greater seriousness. Reporting of break and entry is more likely when there is evidence of forced entry or malicious destruction, and when the loss is relatively high (Solicitor General of Canada, 1985b; Waller and Okihiro, 1978). Thus, unreported household crimes, at least in the legal context, are generally less serious than those that come to the attention of the police (Maguire and Bennett, 1982).

Victims who do report household crime do so with the hope that the police will be able to apprehend the offender and recover the stolen property. At a minimum, victims expect that the police will undertake an investigation and treat them with some sympathy (Maguire and Bennett, 1982). In the aftermath of household crime, victims may seek the assistance of a friend, neighbour, or landlord in addition to, or instead of, the police (Waller and Okihiro, 1978). When losses are substantial, victims may seek compensation through private insurance.

Reported household crimes carry with them a low certainty of arrest. According to Fedorowycz, (1992), about three-quarters of break and enters are not "cleared"; among those that are cleared, only 18 percent are cleared by charge. The low clearance rates for such crimes results from the fact that, by the time they are reported to the police, they have been over for some time; as well, unlike in the typical crime of violence, there is no immediate suspect (Maguire and Bennett, 1982).

In the aftermath of the crime, offenders are probably less concerned with arrest than with the uses to which the stolen merchandise might be put. Cash or alcohol may be used for "partying." Although some stolen merchandise may be kept and used by the offender, there is a limit to how much loot one can put to personal use. Retaining too many stolen goods may also increase the risk of arrest.

Much of what is stolen may be converted into cash through the sale of merchandise. There is a substantial market for stolen goods, particularly lightweight electronic goods. Despite this fact, the offender recoups a relatively small amount from each item. Some stolen goods are sold directly to private buyers for their own use. Such people may see this exchange not as a criminal activity but as "good business." Their reasoning may be that "it was already stolen and if I don't buy it someone else will" (Cromwell, Olson, and Avary, 1991). Merchandise is also sold to "fences," who purchase the items for the purpose of resale. Some fences are businesspersons who do not have a criminal record, while others are ex-thieves (Maguire and Bennett, 1982).

One popular public response to the increase in property crime has been to make homes less vulnerable to attack. Target-hardening activities include installing deadbolt locks and bars on windows; purchasing alarms and watchdogs; and developing programs (e.g., Neighbourhood Watch) that will serve to increase the surveillance of property (Krahn and Kennedy, 1985). Such forms of protection are becoming a routine part of architectural design, with notions of "defensible space" governing how many residential areas are constructed (Newman, 1972).

Summary and Conclusions
■ ■ ■

Violent events within familes can be partially attributed to the values that our society places on family privacy. Feminist researchers see family violence as an acceptance of the differential power within families, where men use violence against women and children as a form of control over their actions (Simpson, 1989: 611).

For a more complete understanding of family violence, we must also consider the stresses placed on families; the reluctance of victims to report the violence; the modelling of parental behaviour in managing conflict and anger; the breakdown of social control mechanisms that restrain interpersonal violence; and the paucity of deterrence strategies. The discovery in recent years of the extent of family violence, coupled with changes in societal values, has been influential in defining violent events within families as criminal events. Changes in the laws and in the police enforcement of those laws have come increasingly to reinforce such a definition.

Property crime is a booming business. The target of most of this crime is the household, which is filled with portable appliances that can be easily transported and resold with little difficulty. Much property crime is opportunistic in nature, involving the presence of a thief at a place and time in which property is unguarded and easy to steal. A good deal of property crime committed by youthful offenders falls into this category. The more complicated crimes of break and enter often require considerable planning and technical expertise; such crimes tend to be committed by professional burglars who not only take the time to plan the event but also ensure that the merchandise can be disposed of after the fact. Sometimes, due to a miscalculation on the part of the offender, residents may be unexpectedly encountered in the course of a household burglery; the consequences—especially for elderly victims—can be fatal.

Many property crimes are not reported to the police. People who do not report may feel either that there is little that the police can do to solve the crime, or that the crime is not serious enough to warrant such action.

Increasingly, homeowners are engaging in target-hardening activities that are intended to discourage both opportunistic and professional burglars.

There has been increased interest in dealing with crimes that both occur in and are directed toward the household. Intrafamily violence is attracting a great deal of public concern, and there have been demands that more action (in the form of education and changes in the law) be taken to reduce the likelihood that such violence will occur. Attempts have been made to give victims of family violence greater protection under the law and provide them with safe havens, as well as to treat offenders. (We will examine these actions in greater detail in Chapter 10.) As our review of family violence has shown, it is important to consider different theoretical approaches to the problem. New perspectives that draw attention to such things as power differentials in the family have become increasingly effective in providing us with explanations of family violence and in suggesting ways in which we should respond to it.

There are many different views about why people are motivated to commit property crimes, as well. Obviously, not everyone who is given the opportunity to steal will do so. Depending on your view of human behaviour, you might assume that people will steal if they know they won't get caught (social control); if others are doing the same thing (cultural); or if they feel pressured by social circumstances (strain). All of these explanations of motivation rely on the idea that the offender has the opportunity (and some skills) to commit the crime and little fear of detection. Making opportunities less available should provide the most effective way of reducing this type of crime.

8
LEISURE

In THIS CHAPTER, WE discuss a second social domain that is significant to the study of criminal events—the leisure domain. As we will see, there are several interesting dimensions to the relationship between leisure and crime. People who are "at leisure" seem to be particularly susceptible to the risk of many different types of criminal victimization. As well, many types of offending—particularly juvenile offending—are themselves forms of leisure. Our language expresses this recognition when, for instance, we describe illegal drug use as "recreational drug use" or when we describe stealing a car to use for fun as "joyriding." The leisure preferences of young people may also be seen as a cause of crime. This is evident in periodic scares in our society about the criminogenic effects of violent television, popular music, fantasy role-playing games, and video games.

We will also see that leisure settings, such as taverns or sports complexes, are frequently scenes of crime and victimization. The street is also a likely location for such scenes, as we begin to adopt lifestyles that take us away from our homes and into public areas in search of leisure pursuits. We begin our review of the relationship between leisure activities and criminal activities with a discussion of the concept of leisure.

WHAT IS LEISURE?

Leisure may be defined in a variety of ways (Wilson, 1980). Frequently, we use the term in an objective way to describe the "spare time" or "free time" that is left over after paid work or other obligations (such as child care) have been taken care of (Iso-Ahola, 1980). However, leisure has a subjective as well as objective character. In other words, it is not just free time, but rather free time that is used in a particular way. Leisure usually denotes the use of time for play or recreation. Leisure activity may be regarded as intrinsically satisfying in that it contains its own rewards (Roberts, 1983). In addition, we usually assume that leisure activities are freely chosen and that leisure interaction occurs among peers. By contrast, family- or work-related activities tend to be less voluntaristic and to be characterized by authority relations that are enforced by law or custom.

Like other scarce resources, leisure time is unequally distributed (Wilson, 1980). Teenagers and the elderly tend to have more leisure time than young parents or middle-aged individuals (Jones, 1990). And because household tasks and child-care responsibilities reduce free time, men generally have more leisure time than women. People also differ with respect to their leisure preferences and the resources they have to pursue them. Those in higher-income groups are more likely to frequent restaurants (Robbins, 1990). Young people are more likely to go to bars, movies, or video arcades (Provenzo, 1991), while the elderly are less likely to go out in the evening for leisure of any kind (Golant, 1984). Elderly people who do engage in leisure outside the home, tend to visit friends or to go to the mall (Graham, Graham, and MacLean, 1991).

The amount of leisure time that people have available to them, and the uses to which they put it, are important elements of what we refer to as lifestyle, a concept we introduced in Chapter 4. Moreover, the leisure content of people's lifestyles has important implications for the kinds of criminal events in which they are involved, whether as offenders or victims. Opportunity theories are particularly attentive to the linkage between lifestyle and crime.

PRECURSORS

What does leisure have to do with the timing, location, and relative involvement of particular types of people in particular types of criminal events? There are two answers to this question. One stresses the ways in which specific types of leisure activities motivate offenders or free them from constraints against offending. The other argument suggests that leisure activities and settings facilitate encounters between offenders and offending situations. These perspectives are not contradictory, but they do differ in their fundamental emphases. While the former is offender-centred, the latter is opportunity-centred.

LEISURE AS A CORRUPTER

Arguments about the corrupting influences of leisure have typically been made with respect to the youthful offender. Throughout this century, every major form of youth leisure preference has been characterized by interest groups as a corrupter of young people. Feature films, rock and roll, rap and heavy metal music, video games, comic books, and Saturday morning television have all, at one time or another, been accused of weakening youthful inhibitions, providing negative role models, destroying childhood, and disrupting the bonds between adolescents and adult authority figures (Best, 1990; Gray, 1989; Tanner, 1992).

Literally hundreds of studies have been done on the negative effects of television violence, and the issue has been the focus of attention of parliamentary committees, royal commissions, and blue-ribbon presidential panels (see Box 8.1). The argument that television violence has some effect on violence in real life would seem to be supported by much anecdotal evidence (in the form of so-called copycat crimes, for example). In addition, this argument seems consistent with common sense. We know that television is a powerful persuader; otherwise advertisers would not spend so much money buying commercial time in which to convince consumers to purchase their products. We also know that television is a violent medium and that young people (who are most likely to behave violently) have high levels of exposure to such content.

Leisure

BOX 8.1 TELEVISION VIOLENCE

Public concern about television reached another high in the early 1990s. In 1992, a 14-year-old student from Quebec named Virginie Larivière launched a petition drive intended to affect public policy regarding the violent content of Canadian television. The teenager's action was prompted by the rape, robbery, and murder of her 11-year-old sister, actions she attributed to media violence. Her petitions, which were signed by 1.3 million Canadians, were presented to the communications minister and to the prime minister.

On November 18, 1992, the House of Commons referred the petition of Virginie Larivière to the consideration of the Standing Committee on Communications and Culture (1993). After conducting hearings on the subject of television violence, the committee issued its report, *Television Violence: Fraying Our Social Fabric.* Among the committee's findings were the following:

1. Canadians who watch a large number of American television programs are exposed to a high level of television violence.

2. Television violence is one of many factors that may contribute to real-life violence, although these effects are not clear and require further study.

3. The problem of violence should be addressed cooperatively by all the players—including the industry, parents, and government—and with minimal legislative intervention.

4. An amendment of the Criminal Code is needed to control extremely violent forms of entertainment, such as slasher/snuff films and videos.

However, despite the presence of anecdotal evidence and the common-sensical character of the arguments, the nature and the significance of the effects that televised violence has on crime are unclear. The effects of television violence on criminal motivation are likely limited by several factors. First, UCR data indicate that violent crimes comprise only about 10 percent of total Criminal Code violations. Therefore, unless we want to argue that violent portrayals affect nonviolent crime in some as yet undetermined fashion, the amount of crime that could be causally linked to violent content is going to be limited, even if the effects on violence are substantial. In fact, some researchers have suggested that the real effects of television may be on property rather than violent crimes (Hennigen et al., 1982). The basis for this argument is that the media emphasis on consumerism raises expectations

---

BOX 8.2   THE CONCERN ABOUT YOUTH CRIME

Much of the concern about leisure as the corrupter of youth is fuelled by perceptions of rising rates of youth violence. According to Statistics Canada (Frank, 1992), in 1991, 22 percent of the 679,000 federal statute charges were laid against youth (between ages 12 and 17). Of the youth charges, 13 percent involved violence. These 18,800 violent charges marked a 102 percent increase from 1986. During this period, the size of the youth population decreased by 1.8 percent. In 1991, there were 855 violent-offence charges for every 100,000 youth, compared to 415 violent-offence charges per 100,000 in 1986. As the graph shows, while the adult violent charge rate was about the same for youth and adults in 1986, the adult rate has risen more slowly.

When these trends are more closely examined, it appears that most of the increase in youth violence is caused by increases in less violent offences. Minor assaults represented about one-half of all violent charges in 1991. The rate of minor assault charges in 1991 was 406 per 100,000 youth, whereas the rates for more serious assaults and homicides (actual and attempted) per 100,000 youth were 226 and 5 respectively.

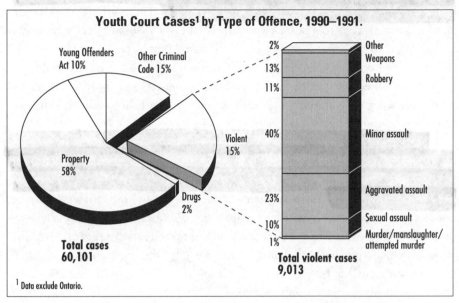

Youth Court Cases[1] by Type of Offence, 1990–1991.

Young Offenders Act 10%

Other Criminal Code 15%

Property 58%

Violent 15%

Drugs 2%

Total cases 60,101

[1] Data exclude Ontario.

2% Other Weapons
13% Robbery
11%
40% Minor assault
23% Aggravated assault
10% Sexual assault
1% Murder/manslaughter/ attempted murder

Total violent cases 9,013

Source: Statistics Canada, Canadian Centre for Justice Statistics, Youth Court Survey, 1990–91.

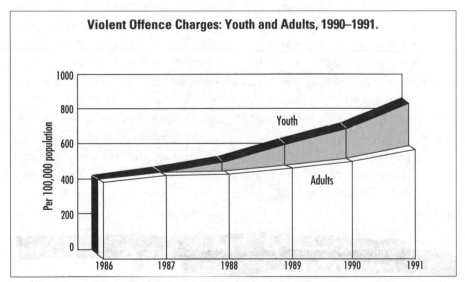

Violent Offence Charges: Youth and Adults, 1990–1991.

Per 100,000 population

Youth

Adults

1986 1987 1988 1989 1990 1991

Source: Statistics Canada, Canadian Centre for Justice Statistics, Uniform Crime Reporting Survey, 1986–91.

about the amounts of material goods to which people think they are entitled (Surette, 1992). The link between television and property crime has not, however, received sufficient research attention.

Second, given that criminal motivation is a complex issue, whatever effects media exposure produce must be understood in the context of many other factors that encourage or restrain offending. The amount of variation that is attributable to media exposure is likely to be smaller than many observers would argue. Some researchers claim that 5 to 10 percent of the difference between violent and nonviolent behaviour may be attributed to exposure to media violence (Surette, 1992). Whether this means that television violence is a relatively important or unimportant factor in real-life violence is a matter of debate among researchers.

Third, while many research experiments have been able to show that exposure to violent content in the laboratory setting affects violent arousal, it is not necessarily the case that the same effects are produced by media exposure in the real world. In experiments carried out in the lab, subjects may be encouraged to behave violently (or at least not discouraged from doing so); by contrast, violent behaviour in most social contexts is discouraged. Also, the ways in which violence is measured in the lab (e.g., the willingness of children to play with violent toys or of subjects to administer a harmless electrical shock to another person) may not have much to do with the willingness of people to assault, rob, or kill others. Studies that attempt to find effects of television violence on aggressive behaviour in real-life settings have frequently been less successful than those that try to find these effects in the laboratory.

The factors outlined above imply that the effects that television violence have on criminal violence are more complicated, and perhaps less substantial, than we sometimes think. Much of the research supports the view that television violence may influence the behaviour of a pool of at-risk individuals who may be particularly susceptible to its effects. In other words, television violence may be most likely to affect the behaviour of those who are already predisposed to behave in an aggressive way. Unfortunately, we lack detailed knowledge of the size of this at-risk pool or of the factors that put them at risk. The effect of media violence may be not to cause interpersonal aggression in any direct way, but rather to reinforce pre-existing tendencies or to shape them in particular ways. In the case of copycat crimes, for instance, media violence may not motivate someone to commit a crime, but it may affect *how* that person commits a crime.

In many cases, the effects of television (or movie) violence may be short term. Anyone who has ever left a movie theatre feeling excited or energized may intuitively understand the nature of this temporary arousal. We also know that such effects tend to dissipate rather quickly as we return to the household, work, or school responsibilities that structure our lives. Thus, whether people behave violently subsequent to such arousal may have as much to do with the situations and circumstances in which they find themselves as with their level of arousal. It is also important to note, though, that we know relatively less about the ways in which high levels of violent content in media affect cultural beliefs and social practices over the longer term.

The work of sociologist David Phillips (1983) illustrates how some of the media effects on crime might work. In a number of studies, Phillips has shown that media portrayals of homicide or suicide may exert temporary effects on the rates of such behaviour. In the case of homicide, for instance, Phillips studied what happened to homicide rates after highly publicized prize fights. These media events are particularly interesting since they involve violence that is both widely publicized and generally approved rather than condemned. In a very careful assessment of homicide trends, Phillips was able to show that, in the few days immediately following a highly publicized fight, homicide rates increased by about 12 percent and that such effects could not be attributed to seasonal, monthly, or other temporal patterns. Much of the rancorous public debate about television violence has recently begun to find a parallel expression in debates about video games. Not only is the content of these games typically violent but, because they are interactive, it is argued that they may be more likely than television viewing to produce delinquency. While we have not yet amassed a significant body of research on the subject of the criminogenic influences of video games, it so far appears that concerns about the effects of these games on serious criminal offending may be overstated (Ellis, 1984; Provenzo, 1991).

Debates about the corrupting influence of popular culture are not restricted to juveniles. Public alarm about the effects of pornography on sex crimes reflects concerns similar to those voiced by the critics of television violence. Yet, in a similar way, drawing direct causal links between violent pornography and sex crimes does not capture the complexity of the issue (Brannigan, 1987). A large body of experimental literature suggests that exposure to such pornography promotes negative attitudes toward women, a greater acceptance of rape myths (e.g., that rape victims are to blame for what happens to them), and a decreased sensitivity toward female victims of violence (Malamuth and Donnerstein, 1984; Malamuth, 1983). Yet, as in the case of television violence, it may be that the effects of violent pornography on crimes of sexual violence are most likely to be evident in the case of men who are already predisposed to behave violently toward women.

LEISURE AND FREEDOM FROM SOCIAL CONTROL

In the case of juveniles, it is sometimes argued that patterns of leisure activity increase the likelihood that crimes will occur by freeing youth from the social controls that might be expected to check or restrain delinquent conduct. This position builds on the arguments suggested in the theories presented in Chapter 3.

Juvenile leisure is most frequently pursued out of the sight of parents or teachers and in the presence of peers (Agnew and Peterson, 1989). The modern video arcade, like the pool hall of an earlier era, is off limits to adults. "Hanging out" at the video arcade or mall or on the street corner may provide the behavioural freedom that makes group delinquency possible (Lotz, Poole, and Regoli, 1985). A study by Riley (1987) of juvenile crime in England and Wales found that offenders and nonoffenders engaged in different types of leisure activities. Nonoffenders generally spent more time with parents and around the home, while offenders were more likely to spend their time in peer activities away from home. In addition, offenders were more often out in the evening, were expected home later, and were more likely to spend their money on youth-oriented amusements. Such leisure activities remove some of the obstacles that work against delinquency by lessening the chances of apprehension and by providing exposure to behavioural contexts that facilitate delinquent action.

By contrast, leisure activities organized by adults or leisure time spent with parents may be expected to decrease the possibilities of delinquency. Leisure activities of these types may strengthen social bonds and thereby render delinquency less attractive (Agnew, 1984; Messner and Blau, 1987). A study of American teenagers found that, while "hanging out" and social activities such as dating and partying were associated with higher levels of delinquent involvement, organized leisure was associated with lower levels of delinquent involvement (Agnew and Peterson, 1989). The researchers also reported, however, that it is not sufficient for youth to be engaged in "positive" leisure for a decrease in delinquency to occur. It is also necessary that they enjoy the activity. In other words, coercive leisure cannot be expected to bring about a decrease in offending behaviour.

The role of leisure in the development or the freeing of delinquent motivation may have more to do with the behaviour of males than that of females

(Riley, 1987). In part, as power-control theory has argued, this is because female adolescents have traditionally been subject to higher levels of control, which restrict their leisure options (Singer and Levine, 1988; Hagan, Gillis, and Simpson, 1985). These gender differences may be rooted in patterns of family socialization. As we saw in Chapter 3, while risktaking behaviour is encouraged in male children, female children are generally subjected to significantly greater degrees of parental control. Gender differences in delinquent leisure may reflect these patterned gender differences in risktaking and control.

LEISURE ACTIVITIES AND OPPORTUNITIES

Leisure activities provide important occasions for criminal events of various types. This is evidenced by the times and places at which crimes occur. A large number of personal victimizations occur during the evenings and on weekends when most people are "at rest," when they have dropped their more serious work roles, and when the formal social controls of the school and the workplace are not operative (Luckenbill, 1977).

Personal victimizations also occur disproportionately in leisure settings. These are informal contexts that host a wide range of activities such as drinking or gambling, dancing and playing games. In a study of high-school youth in Tucson, Arizona, Jensen and Brownfield (1986) found partying, cruising, and visiting bars—in general, the social pursuit of fun—to be significantly related to victimization risk.

Taverns are good examples of such "permissive environs." Not only are the taverns themselves the site of large numbers of criminal events, but so are the blocks on which they are located (Roncek and Maier, 1991; Roncek and Pravatiner, 1989). There are many reasons for this. Bars do most of their business in the evenings when people are freed from many of the social controls that structure their working days. It is also the case that bars deal in cash and liquor, which are easily stolen and easily used by the offender. Bars also tend to place no real restrictions on who can enter and they are particularly popular among young people. It is also true that, for many people, the consumption of alcohol increases the probability of interpersonal conflicts and impairs judgments about the scale of these conflicts.

More generally, activities that bring people out of their homes in the evening increase the likelihood of personal and household crime (Kennedy and Forde, 1990). Messner and Blau (1987) found that the volume of leisure activity in the home (indexed by levels of reported television viewing) is related to lower rates of victimization, while the volume of leisure activity outside of the home (indexed by the number of sports and theatrical facilities) is related to higher rates of victimization.

A similar pattern has repeatedly been revealed by victimization surveys. Violent and household victimization increase as evening activities outside of the home increase, and this relationship is independent of marital status, employment status, and age (Gottfredson, 1984; Solicitor General of Canada, 1987). Going out on weekends increases these risks more than going out during the week, while going out for leisure increases risk more than going out to work or to school (Gottfredson, 1984; Lasley and Rosenbaum, 1988; Smith, 1982). The American National Crime Survey data indicate that about 30 percent of violent or theft victimizations occur while people are taking part in a leisure activity away from home, compared to about 13 percent that occur when people are at work and about 3 percent while they are asleep (U.S. Department of Justice, 1992).

In general, leisure can be part of a risky lifestyle that has dangerous consequences (Kennedy and Forde, 1990). Some types of leisure are clearly riskier than others. Young single males are more likely than others to go to bars where, as we have seen, the risks are higher. By contrast, elderly people are less likely to leave their homes for leisure in the evening; when they do, they are less likely to come into contact with potential offenders.

Several studies suggest that forms of leisure that are themselves criminal may pose particularly high victimization risks (Gottfredson, 1984; Jensen and Brownfield, 1986; Lauritsen, Sampson, and Laub, 1991; Sampson and Lauritsen, 1990). This is partially because offenders make good victims. They may be unlikely to call the police and those who do have difficulty establishing their credibility.

THE EVENT

The content of criminal events varies across leisure settings and activities. Criminologists have focused particular attention on the street, bars, dating, and tourism; each of which is discussed below.

THE STREET

For many youth, the street is itself a leisure setting. For others, it is the route that they take from one setting to another or from these settings to their homes. Criminal events in the street seem to reflect the argument of opportunity theorists (most recently the routine activities theorists) that people are victims of routines that leave them vulnerable to offenders. In fact, research indicates that, despite the horror stories from inner-city areas where people of all ages are vulnerable to crime, the group that is most likely to be involved in these "risky" routines on the street are young males. Their behaviour tends to be more public than that of most other groups and they frequent the street to a greater degree than others.

As stated earlier, the group most vulnerable to assaults in public places are young, unmarried males who frequent bars, go to movies, go out to work, and spend time out of the house walking or driving around. This lifestyle creates exposure to risk. While violent crime may be spontaneous, its targets tend to be people who are in places that are conducive to violent conflict. This explanation does not account for the motivation behind violent crime, but it does explain the high levels of victimization among particular groups based on their exposure to crime. Kennedy and Forde (1990) report a similar pattern for robberies; young unmarried males who frequent bars and who are out walking or driving around are more likely to be victims of this crime.

The behaviour of young males who just hang around on the street is often seen as criminogenic. According to Skogan and Maxfield (1981), urban residents are most afraid of areas in which there is a great deal of urban decline and in which there are young teens hanging around on street corners. Even if the loitering is harmless and the individuals who engage in it never become involved in crime, the street is seen as a dangerous place.

If these young teens are loosely attached to one another, those whom they encounter in street situations are likely to be acquaintances and the chances of violence tend to be low. When individuals are more closely affiliated, as in a gang, the chance of violence increases, although, as Kennedy and Baron (1993) report, this may be unpredictable (i.e., not a routine outcome of activity by gangs on the street). Much of the crime engaged in by gangs actually occurs when they attempt to defind themselves against other gangs. Minor theft and robbery certainly occurs, but not to the extent that the public believes. In addition, the view that gangs pursue violence for violence's sake, as would be predicted by the subculture of violence theory, is not substantiated by the research.

The same individuals who are on the street representing the potential group of offenders can also be victims. Young men in risky areas can easily be targets of assaults and robberies. When alcohol or drugs are involved, violence may erupt. In this situation, spontaneous conflict arises between individuals who may be complete strangers to one another. Motivation in the violence that occurs between young males, whether in gangs or not, may simply be based on tests of character (Luckenbill, 1977).

Although women may be present in street environments, they are less likely to become involved in conflicts directly, even though they may act as third parties in increasing or reducing the conflict. Women out alone tend to avoid those areas they perceive as risky (particularly the street) or situations that may lead to violence or robbery. Of course, women can be targets of robbery just as easily as men—purse snatching is all too common. Nonetheless, street crime appears to be predominantly the domain of young men, both as offenders and victims.

The precursors of assaults or robberies may depend on conflict styles that vary with individual personality and the social situation that individuals confront (Hocker and Wilmot, 1985: 38). Hocker and Wilmot assume that people develop patterned responses to conflict. Decisions about style are made on the basis of past experience and learning. People learn conflict styles by observing others' behaviour and by trying out different responses.

Third parties are important, as well, in affecting the conflict escalation. Young boys often jokingly exhort their friends to physically restrain them when they are confronting a foe. The opponent is advised, "You're lucky he's holding me back, or you'd be sorry!" While this type of posturing, which is facilitated by third parties, may work to dissipate conflict, it may also have the opposite effect. The joking may become serious and the third parties may promote the conflict instead of acting to reduce its outbreak. However, even when one participant lands a blow that might be seen as criminal assault in legal terms, it is probably not viewed as such by the parties involved. There is likely too much confusion over the identities of the instigator and the victim. It is only when there is real harm that requires medical assistance that these situations lead to the involvement of a formal third party (i.e., the police).

Kennedy and Baron (1993) found that punks absorbed a great deal of verbal abuse and that individuals became involved in a fight only when they felt that they needed to protect themselves, not when they felt that backing down would make them look foolish. This finding suggests not that the punks were unprepared for the violence or that they would just walk away if attacked, but rather that the crime in which they engaged was more likely to be characterized by spontaneous outbursts of violence than by conscious, planned events (Gottfredson and Hirschi, 1990).

People's attitudes toward city streets may be affected not only by the presence of gangs but by the graffiti and other signs of vandalism and decay they witness there. People notice these signs, in addition to the patterns of movement around them, and their fearfulness may be awakened. While vandalism is not a criminal event in conventional terms (i.e., an event in which at least two parties are involved in a criminal action) we can in fact view it in event terms. Vandalism differs from other criminal events in that there is a time delay between the offence and the victimization.

Criminologists have focused greater attention on the consequences rather than causes of vandalism. Skogan (1990b) and Wilson and Kelling (1983) identify vandalism as a major contributor to the public's declining sense of security in their neighbourhoods. Wilson and Kelling argue that disorder and crime are inextricably linked in a kind of developmental sequence. Wilson (1985: 78) notes that social psychologists and police officers tend to agree that if a building window is broken and left unrepaired, the remaining windows will soon be damaged. Vandalism occurs more frequently in areas in which surveillance is low. In generating what Wilson calls "untended" behaviour, vandalism leads to a breakdown of community controls and the degeneration of the neighbourhood into one that may become criminogenic. The fear that accompanies this degradation may discourage people from routinely using the streets or providing informal surveillance as a way of constraining disorderly behaviour. As vandalism increases and the neighbourhood continues its decline, residents may move to safer, more congenial environments.

While abandoned buildings appear to be the most frequent targets of vandalism, we are witnessing the growth of public vandalism, which involves tagging (writing of graffiti) on walls, public vehicles, or whatever else is available. Graffiti-filled trains and stations have long been the scourge of New York public transit and have created the impression of a system that is dangerous, even though there are fewer incidents of crime on the subway than on the streets of New York. The New York City transportation department has taken extreme steps (discussed later in this chapter) to ban all graffiti on its subway trains. Similar strategies have been used in other cities, as well. In an effort to reduce the chance of further vandalism, Toronto's transit system has a policy of not sending out trains that have been subject to vandalism or graffiti.

While most tagging takes place at night, when there is little possibility of detection, graffiti writers are becoming bolder and are sometimes recognized for their skills at leaving their mark in daylight hours. This bravado may be the natural response of taggers who have come to see themselves as artists; to most people, however, graffiti is nothing more than simple vandalism.

What motivates most vandalism? Thrill-seeking and the fact that it doesn't appear to harm anyone are probably significant causative factors. And notwithstanding the efforts made to curtail it in many cities, vandalism is almost impossible to detect and deter.

BARS AND TAVERNS

Bars and lounges are places people go to relax, meet friends, listen to music, and drink. Although most bars escape the frenzied aggressiveness that may lead to crime, some attract it. In these locations, where alcohol and drugs mix with loud music and bravado, violence often occurs. Taverners are increasingly concerned about this violence but often are confused about what to do to reduce it. They hire private guardians (bouncers) to remove the most raucous of their clients, but sometimes the actions of bouncers incite more violence. When one asks college or university criminology students where they would go to find a fight on any given night, they can easily list two or three notorious bars in town in which violence occurs with regularity. It would appear that these taverns attract clientele who tend to be more aggressive than average, a conclusion that supports the views of those who propose a subculture of violence perspective.

Criminal events that occur in bars tend to be characterized by minor assaults, particularly between young males. These events may also involve vandalism (breaking windows, chairs, and tables). Events that involve interpersonal conflict may conclude without violence, with the protagonists walking away or being pulled away from one another. When there is escalation, violence may erupt. As a member of a band who has played for student gatherings told the authors, a crowd that is docile throughout an entire gig may become suddenly violent when the band stops playing at the end of the night. It is, he said, almost like they can now hear one another speak and don't like what is being said! The jostling and shoving that may occur in these situations may be seen by all parties as constituting no harm, but violence may ensue if the aggressiveness accelerates. While this description suggests that the event is spontaneous, the idea that certain bars attract this type of problem implies that some individuals go there in search of trouble. It is in these situations that Luckenbill's characterization of the character contest, discussed in Chapter 4, would seem to be appropriate. The jostling and shoving that precedes a fight might be combined with insults and threats. When the fight breaks out, those around the combatants may add fuel to it by offering encouragement or by joining in.

According to popular thinking, adolescent dating is a context for innocent exploration rather than violence. Violence is instead thought to be a feature of conflict-ridden and constricting marital relationships (Sugarman and Hotaling, 1989). However, in recent years, it has become clear that violence figures prominently in some unknown proportion of dating relationships. The efforts of researchers to estimate levels of dating violence are fraught with the same difficulties that characterize attempts to understand violence in families; as a result, estimates of the size of the problem are highly variable (see Box 8.3). While the terms "dating violence" or "courtship violence" have no precise meaning, they are generally used to refer to various forms of sexually and nonsexually assaultive behaviours (Thompson, 1986). In dating behaviour, as in marital relationships, it is typically women rather than men who are the victims of violence (DeKeseredy, 1988; DeKeseredy and Hinch, 1991).

Most of the contemporary discussion about dating violence has focused on the subject of "date rape." Because such rapes occur in a social context in which consensual sex is a possibility, there has been, until recently, a widespread tendency to view date rape as something other than "real rape" (Bechhofer and Parrot, 1991). This has led to a victim-blaming strategy, as well as to a popular willingness to dismiss the injury or trauma experienced by victims. A more realistic appraisal suggests that date rape is rooted in culturally supported dating rituals that reflect patriarchal assumptions about male power and privilege (Muehlenhard and Linton, 1987). Research suggests that male sexual aggression is more likely when males exert greater control over the dating process—that is, when they control the initiation of dating, assume responsibility for expenses and transportation, and choose the dating activity (Harney and Muehlenhard, 1991).

Male control may translate into sexual aggression in two distinct ways. First, many men may interpret a woman's willingness to allow the male to make decisions about where they will go on a date, what they will do, and who will pay for it as a sign of interest in sexual activity (Johnson, Palileo, and Gray, 1982). Such men might reason that if women don't object to coming back to their room, or accompanying them to a secluded spot, they must be interested in sex, even if they say otherwise. In particular, a woman's heavy use of alcohol may be interpreted by the male as a sign of sexual interest (Benson, Charlton, and Goodhart, 1992; Muehlenhard and Linton, 1987).

Second, to the extent that the male controls the circumstances of dating, he controls the opportunities for offending. When he controls transportation,

BOX 8.3   DATE VIOLENCE

In 1992, Walter DeKeseredy and Katharine Kelly, two sociologists at Carleton University, undertook a study of woman abuse in Canadian university/college dating relationships. The study (DeKeseredy and Kelly, 1993) was intended to provide information that would be representative of different types of post-secondary institutions, different regions of the country, and different programs and periods of study.

Two versions of a questionnaire were distributed to students in the classroom. Although both questionnaires included some similar questions, one was designed to elicit women's experiences while the other was designed to elicit the experiences of men. Students were assured that their participation in the survey was strictly voluntary and that all information would be kept confidential.

After the questionnaires were collected, the researchers provided a brief lecture on dating violence and all respondents were given a list of local support services that they could contact if they needed assistance.

The final sample consisted of 1,835 women and 1,307 men. Among the measures used by the researchers were those derived from the Conflict Tactics Scale. Male and female reports of female victimization tactics are outlined in the table below.

Physical Abuse Incidence Rates

Type of Abuse	Male Respondents (N = 1,307)		Female Respondents (N = 1,835)	
	%	N	%	N
Physical				
Threw something at her (you)	3.5	40	5.3	85
Pushed, grabbed or shoved her (you)	11.5	132	19.8	319
Slapped her (you)	2.6	30	5.3	85
Kicked, bit, or hit her (you) with your (his) fist	1.4	16	3.8	61
Hit or tried to hit her (you) with something	1.7	20	3.3	54
Beat her (you) up	0.6	7	1.3	21
Choked you (her)	0.9	10	2.1	32
Threatened her (you) with a knife or a gun	0.8	9	0.6	9
Used a knife or a gun on her (you)	0.7	8	0.1	2

for instance, he can effectively impede the ability of the female to escape a situation in which sexual assault is likely. The woman who is in a deserted spot with a sexually aggressive male may be reluctant to leave the car because she has been warned that even greater dangers confront women who are not protected by male companions. Not surprisingly, date rapes typically occur in the home of the offender, inside an automobile, or in some other isolated location (Harney and Muehlenhard, 1991). These two consequences of male control—misinterpretation of sexual interest and the creation of opportunity—frequently work in concert. For example, "parking" combines the privacy, which provides the opportunity for sexual aggression, with the likelihood that the male will overestimate the female's willingness to engage in sexual relations (Muehlenhard and Linton, 1987).

In courtship violence, like marital violence, violence is supported by the patriarchal belief that the use of force by men against women is legitimate (DeKeseredy, 1988; Lloyd, Koval, and Cale, 1989). Women who are assaulted by boyfriends frequently cite jealousy or attempts to terminate the relationship as the precipitating factors. Ironically, such dating violence may be viewed as a sign of love by either or both parties (Health and Welfare Canada, 1990). According to Sugarman and Hotaling (1989), assaultive violence in dating relationships is most likely to occur on weekends. It may occur in settings that are private (e.g., the residence of one of the partners) or relatively public (an automobile or out of doors).

TOURISM

It is impossible to ignore the growing importance of tourism in our society. Large amounts of money are spent on tourist areas and people are allocating increased amounts of their disposable income to travel. Increasingly, there is a growing awareness that tourists are not immune to crime. Despite this, it has only been recently that hotels and travel companies have begun to warn tourists about potentially dangerous areas. Tourists tend to be easy pickings for the pickpocket or the robber. And it is not just the property that tourists take with them that is at risk. One scam involves thieves reading the identification tags of departing travellers and then going to their homes to burglarize their now unoccupied homes!

These problems of travelling are certainly not new. In the Middle Ages, castles were built in the south of France to protect pilgrims who travelled through areas inhabited by thieves and robbers. And although modern tourism has left the impression that tourists are not likely to be victims, they *are* and they need to take precautions to protect themselves. As tourists become increasingly aware of their vulnerability, many once-popular tourist destinations are finding that the tourists stay away.

Major outbreaks of violence against tourists receive widespread media attention, which may also consist of advice to tourists about special precautions they can take to protect themselves (see Box 8.4). Attacks on foreign tourists in parts of East Africa and Egypt recently have led to a worldwide alert to avoid these areas. Canadians have recently received highly publicized warnings about travel in Florida—a very popular destination for families and the elderly. Also, travel agencies and tour groups now steer clients away from areas they consider dangerous. The governments of many countries issue warnings to their nationals to avoid certain areas, particularly those characterized by a pattern of violence and robbery against tourists or a great deal of political instability; in the latter situation travellers may become a target of local anger and frustration. Some countries are responding to crime against tourists by developing programs that enhance security in resort areas and by educating travellers about the hazards they may encounter in certain areas. Tourist-directed crime would seem to be best explained by opportunity theorists, who see tourists as vulnerable targets in areas where surveillance may be low and precautions more difficult to take.

BOX 8.4 RESPONSES TO TOURIST-DIRECTED CRIME

Crime is not a significant danger for North American visitors to most of the Caribbean and the Bahamas, according to officials in Ottawa and Washington, but travellers should note that safety varies by island. And normal precautions are recommended throughout the region.

On most islands, petty street crime is not uncommon.

"Normal precautions" for travellers generally include not walking alone on unfamiliar, deserted streets at night; being alert to potential pickpockets or purse snatchers, particularly in crowded places and on public transportation; not carrying large amounts of cash; keeping car doors locked; not leaving valuables unattended; and, in general, looking over your shoulder.

But on some islands, safety conditions are more severe. In Jamaica, although the government has recently taken steps, including increased police patrols and better training for hotel security personnel, to enhance tourist safety, officials concede that crime remains a problem, particularly in the Kingston area.

The U.S. State Department, for instance, warns that "persons out walking after dark or who take other than licensed taxicabs are at particular risk. There is sporadic gang violence in inner-city Kingston."

Some parts of the city "are also, on occasion, subject to a curfew."

Despite Kingston's problems, Jamaica is still considered generally safe—if you do not mind the hordes of street hawkers selling soft drugs. Among the safest lodgings, according to independent observers, are the self-contained resorts, which offer a high degree of security. Many provide escorted group tours of Jamaica's cities and countryside for visitors who enjoy venturing beyond their hotel.

Although Barbados is generally considered a safe destination, "street crime, sometimes involving assault," was mentioned in a recent U.S. State Department crime note. Barbados Tourism representatives acknowledged that violent incidents have occurred in "crowded inner-city parts of Bridgetown" (the capital) and in the city's outskirts to the south and east, where a lot of the country's nightspots are located; and where tourists who drink are easy targets.

As in other resort destinations, cruise ship passengers are viewed as easier targets than hotel guests since it assumed that their stay will be brief and they won't stick around to testify against thieves. Cruise passengers planning to explore the island (or other islands) independently might be wise to avoid "telltale" tourist clothes—T-shirts with the cruise line logo, fancy cruisewear—when disembarking.

Safety statistics have been improving in St. Martin, where a "serious crime problem" was reported in 1990. Tourism officials say that both sides of the island have since increased their police forces significantly, and new officers are being trained. Back roads that were totally dark have now been lighted; and lighting has been upgraded along the main connecting Lowlands Road. Petty crime last year was down 32 percent.

Far more severe is the security situation in Haiti, no longer popular among tourists due largely to the country's political instability and a current trade embargo.

"Foreigners are at risk from increased criminal attacks, particularly in the urban areas," according to the Bureau of Consular Affairs in Washington. What makes Canadians and Americans targets is "their relative affluence."

But no place is immune. Even among some of the safest islands, population destinations like Antigua and Barbuda, "petty street crime occurs, but is unusual" and "valuables left on the beach are subject to theft," the U.S. State Department says.

Source: Elizabeth Wissner-Gross, "Emphasize Safety in the Caribbean as Anywhere Else," *The Toronto Star*, January 30, 1993, p. F7.

The tourist is more likely to be a victim of theft or robbery than of personal attack. Most commonly, luggage is stolen or pockets picked. As thieves develop sophisticated techniques for breaking locks, cars are increasingly becoming the object of attack. One scam that car thieves use involves the following. The thief drives along a beach road that is not too crowded and checks out the cars that are there. If there are signs of an attractive target (e.g., a foreign license plate or a rental car), and if the owner(s) is nowhere to be seen (and thus presumably down at the beach), the thief parks behind the car and begins the crime. Up until this point, because of the flow of traffic, little suspicion is aroused.

The thief approaches the car and breaks through the lock. With special tools this can be accomplished fairly easily. Then, a quick search is done. People may leave backpacks behind in their cars (having a view of one's car from the beach may give one a false sense of security). They may hide them under the seat, which, of course, is the first place that a thief would look! Following the search, which may take only ten seconds, the thief exits the car with the loot. Slashing a tire prevents the victim from attempting pursuit.

Tourists may also run into problems when travelling simply because they do not understand the local customs or language. As a result of the case in which a 16-year-old Japanese exchange student was shot and killed in a Louisiana neighbourhood because he did not understand the warning "Freeze!" the Japanese government is publishing a guide of helpful phrases for U.S.-bound tourists. The youth in this case had been looking for a Halloween party and did not stop when he was accosted and told to freeze by a homeowner with a gun. The latter, Rodney Peairs, said that he had felt that his life had been threatened by the costumed youth. Peairs was acquitted under a Louisiana law that allows citizens to use deadly weapons to protect themselves. The forthcoming Japanese guide will include about 30 phrases that few Japanese learn in their language classes, among them "Get lost," "Watch out," and "I mean it" (Sanger, 1993: A9). Not only the translations but also the different cultural meanings of the 30 phrases will be imparted as a way of letting the tourists know that the person issuing the warning is being serious.

THE AFTERMATH

Victimizations that occur in leisure settings frequently go unreported. The victim who is a tourist, for instance, may not know the local language or how to find the police. If the loss or the injury is not great, the tourist-victim may decide that reporting to the police may not be worth the hassle and that little is to be gained. Victimizations may also go unreported when the leisure activity is itself regarded as a form of disreputable behaviour. Victims who have been drinking or who encounter offenders in a known "deviant context" may be reluctant to bring the incident to the attention of the police. Given the general negative attitude toward many forms of youthful leisure, it is not surprising that crimes that occur in these settings remain undiscovered or unrecorded by police.

Victims may respond to crimes committed against them in leisure settings in other ways. One response may be to avoid the types of encounters or circumstances in which the victimization occurred. Since leisure activity is, by definition, discretionary activity, it is easier to avoid than home- or work-related activities, which may also be associated with criminal events. Thus, the victim of courtship violence may refrain from dating, and the jogger who is mugged may stop jogging and take up "mall walking," which may be perceived as a safer environment than city streets.

In other instances, the victim of a "street fight" or "barroom brawl" may prefer to contemplate revenge rather than reporting the crime to police. The status of such victims may itself be questionable, as they themselves may have struck the initial blow or instigated the fight. As well, many criminal events involving young males may be of little interest to police. In recent times, police have been encouraged to manage their excessive workloads by assigning a higher priority to the victimization of women and children than to young males.

While the long-term consequences of leisure-related victimizations are not yet evident, it may be that, with the exception of the sexual assaults, the effects are short-lived. For example, the punks that Baron (1989) talked with simply shrugged off their own victimization, believing that it was just a routine hazard of life on the street. The degree to which individuals are deterred from becoming involved in leisure-related crimes may have more to do with the risk of being hurt than with the risk of being arrested. This is not to suggest that the police do not deter; their presence on the street or in bars plays an important role in keeping such potentially dangerous behaviour under control. The evidence would seem to indicate that the behaviour of young males on the street and in other settings can change from violent to passive fairly easily, particularly given the fact that victims and offenders are often hard to distinguish and that guardians are not always available to stop a brewing conflict from becoming serious.

The need for guardianship has long driven the policy whereby police attempt to maintain a high profile on the street. This has been achieved through the use of random patrol (i.e., cars cruising neighbourhoods looking for problems). As we discussed in Chapter 1, however, patrol tactics appear to have little influence on the amount of neighbourhood crime. As a result, the police are now turning to the idea that they can increase their effectiveness in neighbourhoods by working out of mini-stations. They are increasing foot patrols and neighbourhood consultations; tactics they believe can prevent and deter crime more effectively than can a highly visible police presence in the form of random patrol. Still, the most effective guardians against crime are not the police, but rather other people who frequent leisure settings and who call the police when needed.

Leisure settings are best described as settings in which crimes occur according to opportunity. As we will discuss in Chapter 10, attempts have been made to reduce opportunities for crime by making changes to the environment. Target hardening can include anything from increased and better-situated lighting to surveillance cameras (Newman, 1972). Following the murder of a young woman in the washroom of a Light Rapid Transit station in Edmonton, the city council spent over one million dollars on surveillance cameras for underground platforms and walk areas around the stations. These cameras were said to lend a sense of guardianship in the absence of police or others.

In a related example, a multimillion-dollar program has been initiated by the New York City Subway Authority to clean all trains of graffiti. After each journey, trains are checked and cleaned of debris. Subway police patrol stations make use of night-vision glasses and cameras to catch graffiti artists in the act. Scratch-proof glass on the trains is being developed, and there are plans for paint-resistant exteriors. There is even talk of banning spray cans and wide-tip marker pens in order to limit the resources available to graffiti artists. All of these measures are being taken to increase public confidence in the safety of the subway system.

The problem of escalating violence in some bars has led the police to begin a more active program of monitoring these places and encouraging owners to establish deterrence strategies of their own. Some bars in various Canadian cities have large signs that read "No Knives"—a reminder to clients to check their weapons at the door. The idea behind the signs is to acknowledge that conflicts are likely to occur in such places and to ensure that these conflicts do not become fatal.

There have also been attempts to influence the use of leisure as a crime-control mechanism. Particularly conspicuous have been efforts to develop "positive" leisure alternatives for young people who are actually or potentially delinquent (Agnew and Peterson, 1989). This approach reflects the maxim, made explicit in social control theory, that "idle hands are the devil's workshop." Youths get themselves into trouble (through various forms of "hanging out") because they lack positive options. The reasoning behind the positive-leisure approach is that summer camps, organized clubs, and other so-called forms of healthy recreation will expose youth to an environment that discourages involvement in crime and delinquency.

A parallel approach focuses on the need to control what are widely viewed in some quarters as negative and corrupting forms of youth leisure (Tanner, 1992). This approach seems to reflect the view that, if they are left to make their own leisure choices, youth will almost always make the wrong ones. The last several decades have witnessed numerous crusades intended to impose legal and social restrictions on the ability of young people to make these choices. These campaigns were directed against feature films in the 1930s; comic books and rock and roll in the 1950s; the presumed drug-influenced protest music of the 1960s; and rap and heavy metal music, fantasy role-playing games (e.g., Dungeons and Dragons), and video games in the 1980s and 1990s. Television violence has been the subject of recurrent crusades every five or ten years since the 1960s (Best, 1987; Gray, 1989).

However, there is an ironic character to such crusades. According to Tanner (1992), they reflect a

> *perennial tendency on the part of adults to rediscover, to stigmatize and to attempt to control the culture and behaviour of the generations that follow them. Thus, the Elvis Presley and Beatle fans. The Hippies and student radicals of earlier eras express bewilderment and concern about the corruptive nature of the cultural worlds in which they believe their own children to be immersed. Contemporary charges that modern heavy metal music inspires teen suicide and sexual promiscuity or that it promotes mysticism and devil worship tell us more about the ways in which anxieties about youth are reproduced across generations than about the uniquely deviant characteristics of contemporary youth (228).*

SUMMARY AND CONCLUSIONS
■ ■ ■

When people are "at leisure," they are also at risk of involvement in criminal events, as offenders or victims. The relationships that link leisure activity and criminal activity are highly varied. Some forms of leisure might be seen as causes of crime. The content of youth-oriented media, for instance, may be seen to provide the motives for crime. Alternatively, engagement in peer activities may suggest freedom from the social controls that might be expected to inhibit offending.

Much leisure activity takes place in public spaces. Street crime involves people who are passing through areas in transit from one place to another, or who are using the street as a location of leisure. In these contexts, crime may itself constitute leisure, as appears to be the case in the motivation behind vandalism and graffiti writing. In leisure settings such as the street and taverns, it is often difficult to distinguish the offenders from the victims when conflict turns into assault or other forms of violence. This form of opportunity crime tends to be based on the risky lifestyles of the individuals involved, and is more likely to be deterred by retribution than by reporting the crime to the police.

In date rape, the routine activity of courtship takes on a criminal character when aggressive behaviour translates into sexual assault, against an unwilling participant. Much of this behaviour also goes unreported. Tourism crime targets people who are at leisure in unfamiliar places where their poor understanding of what areas are safe or not may put them at risk. It is often difficult for tourists who have been victimized to find someone to whom to report the crime. They may decide that they simply do not want the hassle of getting involved with police in a foreign country. Travel agencies and governments are increasingly briefing tourists on how to travel safely and advising them of areas that should be avoided altogether. A tourist's most effective deterrent against crime is to not travel in unsafe areas at all, thereby removing the opportunity for crime.

Some types of leisure pursuits place people at particular risk of victimization. The risky lifestyles in which people engage may make the search for a "good time" result in a "bad time." It must be emphasized that, in the leisure domain, as in other domains, the processes that we are describing are not deterministic. In other words, exposure to criminogenic influences or to threats of victimization does not guarantee the development of a criminal event, but rather only increases its probability by bringing together opportunities for crime and motivations to offend.

9
CRIME
AND WORK

IN THIS CHAPTER, WE consider
the social domain of the workplace. As we will see,
among the characteristics in which jobs differ is the
accessibility to criminal opportunities they afford. Our
discussion is organized around two broad topics. The
first is the relationship between work in the legitimate
labour force and the occurrence of criminal events.
Two major issues concern us here. The first relates to
the ways in which patterns of victimization are associated with patterns of employment. How do the jobs we
have affect the victimization risks we face? The second
issue focuses on the ways in which seemingly honest
work makes available opportunities for criminal behaviour. These may involve opportunities for offending
against employers (or employees) or members of the
general public.

Crime as a type of occupational activity constitutes
the second major theme to be explored in this chapter. In
exploring this theme, we consider the concepts of the
"criminal career" and the "career criminal." We also
examine "enterprise crime," which involves the exploitation of opportunities for the development of criminal
business.

CRIME, EMPLOYMENT, AND UNEMPLOYMENT

The Canadian labour force has undergone several important changes in the last few decades. It is well know that the impact of recent recessionary trends has resulted in increases in levels of unemployment; although, during the 1980s, annual labour force increases averaged 1.9 percent (Parliament, 1990b). By 1989, the rate of unemployment had fallen to 7.8 percent—about the same level that it had been at the beginning of the 1980s. This rate was much lower than the 1983 rate of 11.8 percent (Parliament, 1990b). Unemployment has been particularly marked in the 16 to 24 age group—the group that, as we already know, is at highest risk of involvement in criminal events as offenders *and* victims (Gower, 1990). Female labour-force participation has increased dramatically in recent years. Labour market growth has largely been in the service sector rather than in the goods-producing sector of the economy. When compared to goods-producing jobs, service jobs tend to be lower paying and to more frequently involve part-time work. There has also been a marked increase in the rate of self-employment (Cohen, 1990).

Not only the size and nature of the work force, but also the nature of work itself has undergone important changes. Many of these changes are attributable to various types of technological innovations, particularly in computer technology. While these changes are intended to make the workplace more efficient (and, from the point of view of the employer, more profitable), they affect the pacing and timing of jobs. Employees may have in their homes computer hookups that allow them to reduce the amount of time required at their formal places of work. Fax machines quicken the pace at which information can be transmitted, and cellular telephones have worked to blur, for many executives, the distinction between private time and time at work.

How do patterns of employment or experiences in the labour force relate to patterns of involvement in criminal events? One approach to this question is to ask whether victimization risks differ between those who are employed and those who are not. This question is not as straightforward as it may at first appear. Part of the problem concerns how we choose to define the reference group against whom the employed should be compared. If we define this group broadly, including not only those who are unemployed but also those who are retired, institutionalized, sick, or who define their main activity in surveys as "homemakers," then the risks associated with being employed are generally higher for most types of victimization risks (Miethe, Stafford, and Long, 1987). This is because those who occupy these other status positions are likely to be people whose social and demographic characteristics are usually associated with lower victimization rates.

When we compare those who are employed with those who are unemployed, the disadvantages associated with employment diminish in many surveys. In other words, unemployment is associated with higher victimization risks (Cohen and Cantor, 1981). The size and significance of this relationship varies. Data from the American National Crime Survey (U.S. Department of Justice, 1988) indicate that those who are unemployed have rates of violent crime that are more than double the rate for those who are employed (76 versus 32 per 1,000 population) and rates of property crime that are marginally higher for this group (90 versus 81 per 1,000). Differences in the 1988 Canadian General Social Survey are smaller but in the same direction (Sacco and Johnson, 1990).

Much more frequently discussed than the relationship between unemployment and victimization is the relationship between unemployment and offending. Most of the theories of offending that we reviewed in Part II would lead us to expect that risks of offending are greater for unemployed people. Theories that emphasize the role of social inequality in the generation of crime quite naturally suggest that not having a job may encourage the development of criminal motivations. Moreover, this view is perfectly consistent with common sense.

There are many reasons why we would expect measures of unemployment to be related, in empirical studies, to measures of criminal offending. First, we would expect that some proportion of property crimes are committed out a sense of need or desire for things that people want but cannot buy. If people lack the means to a stable income, they may experience greater temptations to take what is not theirs. Second, it can be argued that occupational status is an important mechanism for integrating people into conventional society. Jobs provide a "stake in conformity" (Toby, 1974). Not having a job may weaken the hold that conformist institutions have over people. Third, being unemployed may result in the adoption of behaviours, such as drug use, that are themselves associated with criminal offending (Hartnagel and Krahn, 1989). Fourth, unemployment may be related to family instability and thus to the ability of parents to monitor the criminal behaviour of dependent children (Sampson, 1987). Fifth, since rates of unemployment are high among young people, who seem to be most "crime prone," we might expect the criminogenic effects of unemployment to be particularly strongly related to offending among this segment of the population.

Despite these obvious theoretical and common-sensical connections between unemployment and offending, for many criminologists, arguments about this relationship are quite controversial (Chiricos, 1987; Freeman,

1983; Gottfredson and Hirschi, 1990). While many criminologists would argue that unemployment is causally related to crime, they are unsure of the size and significance of the effect. Others dispute whether being unemployed has any independent causal influence on the propensity to behave criminally.

Sorting out the relationship between unemployment and offending is no simple task. First, just as efforts to measure crime are fraught with difficulties, it is also quite difficult to measure unemployment in a valid way (Gramling, Forsyth, and Fewell, 1988). Unemployment is usually measured in terms of the number of people who are not employed but who are actively looking for work. Such measures thus exclude those who have "dropped out" of the labour pool. This bias in our measures of unemployment may have the effect of including those who are most highly motivated to gain entry to the conventional world and excluding those who are least motivated. The overall effect may be to weaken the measured relationship between crime and unemployment.

Second, some researchers have argued that not only unemployment per se but also the quality of labour-force experiences is related to criminal offending (Allan and Steffensmeier, 1989; Currie, 1985; Hartnagel and Krahn, 1989). Precarious, low-paying jobs that offer few of the advantages generally associated with employment are counted as "employment" in a labour-force survey, despite the fact that such jobs might not provide a strong cushion against the various criminogenic influences to which the job-holder may be exposed. Third, many researchers attempt to study the relationship between unemployment and crime at the provincial or national level (e.g., by asking if the national rate of employment is related to the national crime rate) (Chiricos, 1987). But this may be too broad a level for the investigation of this issue, one that may obscure relationships that exist at the community or neighbourhood level.

Despite the popular view of the relationship between unemployment and crime, some studies support alternative interpretations. It has been suggested, for instance, that delinquent involvement is greater among employed teenagers than among unemployed ones (Tanner and Krahn, 1991). The former group, it is argued, may be less susceptible to parental controls and more susceptible to delinquent peer influences. Other researchers have suggested that crime causes unemployment (not the other way around) in that people who are criminally inclined are less interested in conforming to the routines demanded by legitimate labour-force participation (Wilson, 1983). Still others maintain that the relationship between crime and unemployment is "spurious" in the sense that no real relationship exists between them; the appearance of a relationship is created by the fact that being unemployed and behaving criminally are both related to a "common cause" such as a low degree of self-control (Gottfredson and Hirschi, 1990; Wilson and Herrnstein, 1985).

It may be that it is impossible to generalize about the relationship between unemployment and crime. The nature of the relationship may depend on the type of crime, the social characteristics of the labour-force group, and the social policies in place to assist those who are not employed (Allan and Steffensmeier, 1989; Currie, 1985). Cantor and Land (1985) have argued, moreover, that the rate of unemployment may have more than one type of effect on the overall rate of crime. Consistent with arguments made earlier in this chapter, they suggest that unemployment may encourage the development of criminal motivation among some people. This implies that unemployment will be positively related to the rate of crime such that the crime rate increases as the unemployment rate increases. But Cantor and Land also argue that the unemployment rate may have a negative effect on the rate of crime. This effect is related not to criminal motivation but to criminal opportunity. According to Cantor and Land, the unemployed are much less likely to engage in routine activities that take them away from the home for predictable and extended periods. In other words, unemployment may be related to increases in the level of guardianship exercised over persons and property. In addition, because the unemployment rate can be understood, at least in part, as a general indicator of the overall well-being of the economy, we can assume that when the unemployment rate is high, there will be in circulation fewer goods for thieves to steal. Cantor and Land's analyses of American Uniform Crime Report data for the period 1946 to 1982 support the argument that both types of effects may be possible.

We have reviewed the relationship between the general effects of employment and unemployment on the likelihood of committing crime. Now we can examine how particular forms of labour-force participation make crime possible. Two issues concern us here. The first is the relationship between the jobs people have and the victimization risks they face. The second is the ways in which the jobs that people have give them opportunities to behave criminally.

VICTIMIZATION AND WORK

Public awareness of "workplace stress" has been increasing in recent years. According to a government survey, 38 percent of people who had a job or were self-employed had encountered a work situation within the previous year (1991) that had caused them excess stress or worry (Geran, 1992). Stressors included job demands and hours of work, the threat of layoff, poor interpersonal relations, the risk of accident or injury, harassment, and discrimination.

BOX 9.1   MURDER IN THE WORKPLACE

From the office manager who just fired an employee to the emergency room nurse who fears the stabbing victim's shady companion is fingering a weapon, workers are increasingly worried about being murdered on the job.

By some estimates homicide may now be the third highest work-related cause of death in the United States, according to Joseph Kinney of the Chicago-based National Safe Workplace Institute.

Such crimes are sometimes page one news:

- In Tampa, Fla., a disgruntled former employee killed three men at lunch who were once his supervisors, wounded two others, then took his own life.

- Seven workers at a fried chicken restaurant in suburban Chicago were mowed down during a robbery after the store closed for the evening.

- In 1986 and 1991, two postal workers, one fired and the other threatened with dismissal, took out their rage on postal centres in Oklahoma and Michigan. Nineteen died in all.

But other cases rate only a line or two on the evening news—typically a rejected suitor or ex-spouse stalking his or her mate to a violent death in the office or shop.

"Violence in the workplace is escalating and I think there are two root causes," Kinney says.

"One is a feeling of increased vulnerability that workers and managers now feel. In fact, at least a million managers have lost their jobs because of corporate downsizing or mergers in the last 10 years.

"The other thing is just the increased willingness of people to use violence in our society—to deal with emotions and problems. Stress is rising all over the place."

He says he expects these kinds of violent reactions to escalate.

"Just a generation ago, workers and managers expected to have one employer for life. Now, not only can we expect to have multiple employers, but there is talk about having two or three career changes during a lifetime.

"But, we don't have in place yet the kind of social and educational institutions, public and private, that are responsive to this increased feeling of vulnerability and disloyalty.

Eric Hickey of California State University says mass murders in public places are running at the rate of two or three per month in the United States.

Usually the killer "is making a final statement to the world," he says. "The ultimate motivation is the same—having control over other people when you don't have control over your own life."

Paul Levy of the department of psychology at the University of Akron says he is not 100 percent sure that workplace violence has increased as dramatically as it seems.

"But there probably has been some increase," he says. "When our competence or our security at work is undermined, that causes a great deal of stress and frustration. In addition, the economic situation is so bad that people feel very insecure in their jobs."

Job loss, Levy says, is nearly as stressful as facing the death of a loved one.

Source: "Murder in the Workplace on the Increase in U.S.," *The Toronto Star*, February 9, 1993, p. F10. Reprinted by permission of Reuters America Inc.

Although it is not generally recognized as such, the threat of criminal victimization may be an important form of job stress for many people. Victimization surveys tell us that the chances of being a victim of crime are not randomly distributed across occupational groups. While work roles may have much in common, irrespective of the unique characteristics of particular jobs, there are dramatic differences in the nature of the work that people do, where they do it, and with whom it brings them into contact. As we will see, the characteristics of some jobs increase risk while the characteristics of other jobs decrease risk. Such differences may be obscured when the victimization experiences of the employed are compared with those of the unemployed.

Yet even when we compare the victimization risks associated with different occupations, it may be difficult to determine whether it is the job itself or the characteristics of people who hold such jobs that affect the risk of victimization. For instance, if we were to discover that part-time employees of fast-food restaurants faced particularly high risks of victimization, we would not necessarily be justified in concluding that there is something about cooking or serving hamburgers that makes one more vulnerable to criminal danger. Fast-food employees tend to be teenagers and, in view of the relationship between age and victimization, the higher risks may involve age-related rather than work-related factors. In fact, we might not even be surprised to discover that, while these employees report higher rates of crime, the experiences that they tell us about typically occur outside of work rather than on the job. Thus, a cursory review of victimization risks and occupation may be misleading. Also, many jobs, such as construction and mining, are inherently hazardous, and have high rates of mortality that occur through accidents. These events should be considered as occupational safety problems that are separate from the dangers of criminal victimization.

Information about how victimization risks vary across occupations is hard to come by. This is because the statistical rarity of victimization incidents does not, in many cases, allow survey researchers to compute separate victimization rates for a detailed inventory of occupations. Some research indicates that risks are higher for members of the military (Harlow, 1991), probation officers (Linder and Koehler, 1992), police officers, welfare workers, and those who work in bars (Mayhew, Elliott, and Dowds, 1989) and other occupations that involve regular and frequent contact with high-risk populations.

Perhaps the most comprehensive study of this type was undertaken by Block, Felson, and Block (1984), who calculated the victimization rates for 426 different occupations using data on 108,000 crime incidents reported to National Crime Survey interviewers between 1973 and 1981. For the five offences these researchers examined (robbery, assault, burglary, larceny, and automobile theft), victimization risk was inversely related to "occupational status," which they defined as the average income for each occupation. In other words, as the average income of an occupation increased, the risks of being victimized decreased. More specifically, the study revealed marked differences in levels of victimization risk. For instance, amusement and recreation workers and restaurant workers such as busboys, dishwashers, and servers were among the five highest-risk occupations for all offences. Sheriffs and police officers had the highest assault rates, while taxi drivers and newspaper vendors were among the most frequently robbed. The lowest rates of victimization were found among certain farm workers, as well as telephone and electrical workers, opticians, stenographers, and radio operators.

The authors readily acknowledge that data of this sort are difficult to interpret:

> On the one hand, better jobs tend to provide more good things in life, presumably including safety and security from crime. More income and credit allow people to purchase security devices, safer locations to live in, better parking spots and the like. Better jobs may also help people avoid public transit and unfavourable hours for trips to work and elsewhere. Better credit allows avoidance of cash. In general, more resources, including money, credit and control over time, should help people to obtain security from crime.
>
> On the other hand, better jobs may bring with them more luxury goods to attract offenders. Higher strata may also go out more at night, enjoying sport and cultural events or visiting restaurants or other night spots. Good jobs are often found within a metropolis rather than in rural areas with lower risk. One suspects that modern offenders have little trouble finding the higher occupational strata in order to victimize them, security efforts notwithstanding (Block, Felson, and Block, 1984: 442).

Thus, while analyses of the victimization rates of different occupational groups are interesting and informative, they do not necessarily tell us very much about crimes which occur in the workplace. This requires a more focused investigation of the crimes that happen while people are at work.

PRECURSORS

In very general terms, workplace settings have characteristics that both encourage and inhibit victimization. On the one hand, full-time employees spend many hours "at risk" to whatever threats the workplace presents. On the other hand, workplace settings tend to be much more highly structured than, for instance, leisure settings and thus more subject to a variety of social controls that tend to discourage victimization. Some degree of order and control is usually deemed necessary if the organizational goals of the workplace are to be achieved in an efficient fashion.

How much crime occurs in the workplace? Data from the 1990 American National Crime Survey provide a broad answer to this question (U.S. Department of Justice, 1992). According to this survey, about 13 percent of violent crimes occurred while the respondents were "working or on duty." This figure included 14 percent of assaults, 7 percent of robberies, and 3 percent of rapes. A further 6.4 percent of violent crimes occurred while respondents were on their way to or from work. With respect to crimes of theft, about 20 percent occurred while the respondents were at work. However, these data underestimate the relative proportion of workplace crime in that they represent proportions of the total number of incidents—that is, incidents involving those who are and who are not members of the paid labour force.

Data from the 1988 British Crime Survey allow us to separate out the proportion of workplace crimes reported by employed respondents (Mayhew et al., 1989). These findings reveal that 71 percent of the thefts, 22 percent of the assaults, 11 percent of the robberies, and 13 percent of the vehicle thefts occurred while respondents were at work. In all cases, the vast majority of the crimes occurred while the victims were inside the workplace rather than in some other work-related location, such as out of doors at work or on the street near the workplace.

One type of worksite for which detailed information regarding the nature of victimization risk is readily available is the school. In recent years, much attention has been focused on schools as settings that pose serious criminal dangers to both students and teachers (Auty, 1992; Toby, 1983;

U.S. Department of Justice, 1988). American National Crime Survey data (1985–1988) indicate that, with respect to teenage victims aged 12 to 15, 37 percent of the crimes of violence and 81 percent of the crimes of theft occurred while the victims were at school (Whitaker and Bastion, 1991). A special survey of school crime undertaken by the U.S. Department of Justice as a supplement to the 1989 American National Crime Survey found that an estimated 9 percent of students aged 12 to 19 were victims of crime in or around their schools over a six-month period; 2 percent reported experiencing one or more violent crimes; and 7 percent reported at least one property crime (Bastian and Taylor, 1991). Sixteen percent of the respondents claimed that a student had attacked or threatened a teacher at their school in the six months before the interview. The violent crimes typically involved "simple assaults" (e.g., schoolyard fights) which did not involve weapons and which resulted in relatively minor injuries. A survey of 881 Ontario schools suggests that much school crime involves not only students but also teachers and other school staff (see Box 9.2).

BOX 9.2 SURVEY OF ASSAULTS IN ONTARIO SCHOOLS

Physical and verbal assaults are rising at an alarming rate in Ontario elementary and secondary schools, according to a recent survey initiated by the Ontario Teachers' Federation (OTF, 1992). In response, school principals are urging formation of clearer policy on managing violent behaviours, professional development programs for teachers, stronger support from the courts, and a review of relevant legislation, particularly the *Young Offenders Act*.

The survey was conducted by the five affiliates of OTF. OTF coordinated the data collected and prepared a report. Each affiliate sent a survey form to its members who were school principals, requesting information on incidents of assault during the school years 1987–88 and 1988–89 and asking for their specific concerns and recommendations. Three affiliates were able to provide more up-to-date information, using the years 1988–89 and 1989–90.

Four of the five affiliates reported a sharp increase in the number of assaults over the period covered by the survey. This increase was evident in both major incidents, which involved physical assaults as defined in the Criminal Code, and minor incidents, which included verbal abuse and damage to property. The victims were most often students assaulted by other students, but teachers and other school staff were also targets. At the secondary level, the perpetrators were sometimes intruders on school property.

A total of 441 major incidents of assault were reported by the 881 schools responding to the survey (about one in five Ontario schools). These ranged from biting, kicking and punching to the use of knives, firearms and other instruments that could inflict serious injury. Minor incidents were much more common, numbering 6,342. The most frequent type was verbal assault and profanity directed at teachers. Other minor incidents included insubordination, threatening (sometimes by parents), crank or obscene telephone calls, and damage to teachers' cars or homes.

In calling for stronger policies and more support from school trustees, parents, social service agencies and the judicial system, school principals emphasized a number of concerns:

- the incidence of trespassing is rising and is difficult for school administrators to control;
- verbal assaults with extremely abusive language have increased, reflecting its increasing prevalence at home, on the street, and in certain of the media;
- excessive alcohol consumption is a problem in secondary schools, especially on field trips and at athletic events held outside the school, and along with drugs contributes to violent behaviour;
- weapons in the school are becoming a problem;
- teachers are often assaulted in trying to break up fights between students;
- the *Young Offenders Act*, the apparent lack of concern shown by the courts, and the attitudes of some of the media tend to encourage rather than discourage antisocial behaviour.

Although the survey did not distinguish between rural and urban areas, the responses from school boards suggested that the incidence of assault was similar across the province. Elementary and secondary schools reported comparable rates of assault; in elementary school, however, the responses indicated that students with behavioural problems due to learning disabilities or emotional problems caused a disproportionate number of teacher assaults. This observation was consistent with the findings of a recent study by the Toronto Board of Education, and underlines the need for early identification and remedial programs for these children.

How do workplace characteristics relate to variations in the levels of workplace danger? Do these risks, for instance, have something to do with the nature of the work or with the location of the workplace? Answers to such questions are still fragmentary. Respondents in the 1988 British Crime Survey blamed the nature of their jobs for nearly one-quarter of the violent and theft incidents they experienced. The "public" rather than fellow employees were blamed for nearly three-quarters of the violent incidents and one-half of the thefts.

Data from victimization surveys have been used to describe the types of workplace conditions that seem to facilitate employee victimization (Collins,

Cox, and Langan, 1987; Lynch, 1987). These studies suggest that the risks of becoming a crime victim on the job are greater

- when the job involves face-to-face contact with large numbers of people on a routine basis (if the workplace restricts access to authorized persons, the risks of crime are lower);
- when the job involves handling money;
- when the job involves overnight travel or travel between worksites; and
- when the job involves the delivery of passengers and goods.

The importance of these factors becomes apparent when they are assessed in reference to routine activities theory and associated concepts such as exposure and guardianship. People who work in settings that leave them unprotected and at the same time exposed to large numbers of people (some of whom may be "motivated offenders") are more likely to be victimized in the workplace.

Victimization studies also indicate that it is the nature of the work, rather than the characteristics of the victims (e.g., sex and age), that affects the likelihood of becoming a crime victim in the workplace. In the case of schools, the structure of the workplace population might lead us to expect more crime than we observe. Schools, after all, are settings that concentrate on a daily basis the age groups at greatest risk of offending and victimization. Toby (1983) argues that the risks associated with school populations are compounded by the requirement of compulsory attendance. Disruptive or troublesome students who do not wish to attend school are required to do so. It is for this reason, he suggests, that in the United States, junior high schools have more serious rates of victimization than do senior high schools.

In addition, schools have until recently been relatively open settings, easily accessible to potential offenders who do not attend them. These "intruders," as they are usually referred to by school officials, might include not only the stereotypical predator but also the angry parent or the student who is disgruntled at having been expelled. Although schools are capable of exercising some degree of guardianship against victimization, a school of above-average size that allows students considerable freedom of movement may provide many settings that facilitate criminal activity. Within school buildings, more victimizations typically take place in less supervised areas, such as hallways and restrooms, than in more controlled places such as classrooms and libraries (Garofalo, Siegel, and Laub, 1987).

THE EVENT

Much of the violent victimization that occurs in the workplace results from conflict between employees and customers or clients. These situations include the bartender who tells the inebriated customer that he is "cut off"; the teacher who tries to enforce classroom discipline; the police officer who tries to intervene in an argument; and the sales clerk who refuses to accept returned merchandise.

BOX 9.3 POLICE OFFICER INJURIES IN DOMESTIC DISTURBANCES

It is widely believed that domestic disturbances are the most dangerous occupational activities in which police officers become involved. Desmond Ellis, a sociologist at York University, and two other researchers attempted to discover whether there was empirical support for this claim. To this end, they analyzed the official statistics gathered by three Canadian police forces and collected survey information from almost 400 members of these forces.

Their analysis (Ellis, Choi, and Blaus, 1993) revealed that, overall, domestic disturbances accounted for 2.5 percent of the reported injuries. However, the researchers reasoned, it is necessary to take into account the relative frequency with which police officers attend domestic disturbances in order to understand the comparative dangerousness of domestic situations. They discovered that, although domestic disturbances accounted for 2.5 percent of injuries, these disturbances accounted for 0.8 percent of all calls for service. By contrast, robberies accounted for 0.1 percent of all calls but resulted in 2.8 percent of all injuries.

In order to standardize these differences, the researchers calculated a "danger rate" by dividing the number of injuries by the number of calls. This method revealed robberies to be the most dangerous type of encounter in which the police are likely to be involved, followed by the arrest or transportation of suspects or prisoners. Domestic disturbances ranked third (of six occurrence types) in terms of the degree of danger.

What types of factors increase the risks of injury for police who attend domestic disturbances? The survey data revealed several tentative answers. Injury is more likely when the suspect has allegedly assaulted the victim, when the principals in the incident exhibit hostile behaviour toward the officer, and when the incident takes place in a detached house (as opposed to an apartment). The characteristics of the police officer (e.g., age, sex, height, weight) had little to do with whether injury occurred.

This pattern of employee–customer conflict is reflected in British Crime Survey data (1988) that describe "verbal abuse" at work. Fourteen percent of respondents in a survey by Mayhew, Elliott, and Dowds (1989) said that they had been verbally abused by someone other than a co-worker during the 14-month period preceding the survey. Although not strictly criminal, verbal abuse can contain threatening statements and may precipitate conflict that escalates to violence. Although male and female workers were about equally likely to be abused in this way, younger women appeared to be particularly susceptible. While incidents involving abuse by an adult were more likely to involve a single offender, incidents involving adolescents were about as likely to involve a group as a single offender.

Intoxication was a factor in almost one-tenth of the incidents. In 80 percent of the incidents workers were sworn at, and insulting comments about job performance were made in 40 percent of the cases.

The nature of the situational context of much workplace victimization is revealed in an American study of assaults of flight attendants by Salinger et al. (1993). (An assault was defined as "a violent attack, either physical or verbal, or an expression of threat with the intent to inflict pain, injury, or punishment.") This study found that flight attendants have rates of assault as much as ten times higher than the average member of the population. Most assaults involved a conflict between the passenger and the attendant over some mandatory aspect of the flight, such as baggage arrangements or food or drink service. The researchers discovered that first-class passengers, who comprise only 10 percent of the travelling public, accounted for 20 percent of the assaults, a finding that may be explained by the higher expectations of service, passengers' perception of their status relative to that of the attendant, and the amount of alcohol that is typically consumed. The study also found that assaults are most likely to occur during takeoff or landing, the most distressing time for passengers who are afraid of flying. In addition, at takeoff, the authority role of the attendant may not yet be clearly understood.

Violent school crimes, except perhaps those involving intruders, are probably more likely than other workplace crimes to include as participants offenders and victims who are known to each other (Whitaker and Bastian, 1991). According to Garofalo, Siegel, and Laub (1987: 333) many of these events result from

> frictions from peers arising from normal daily activities. School grounds and trips to and from school provide ample opportunities for interactions that can escalate into relatively minor victimizations. "Weapons" often consist of available items grabbed on the spur of the moment. Items stolen from victims often seem to be the targets of malicious even mischievous motivations (333).

Victimizations that occur in the workplace do not seem to differ appreciably from other categories of crime in terms of their levels of loss and injury (Garofalo, Siegel, and Laub, 1987; Mayhew, Elliott, and Dowds, 1989; Whitaker and Bastian, 1991). One important factor that probably reduces the potential severity of workplace crime is the presence of other co-workers, who can either provide or summon assistance.

As in the case of other social domains, much of the crime that occurs in the workplace is not reported to the police (Mayhew, Elliott, and Dowds, 1989). There are at least two specific characteristics of the work domain that may discourage such reporting. First, many work environments may have alternative means for dealing with crime. The handling of an incident might proceed no further than bringing it to the attention of a supervisor or private security. Businesses, restaurants, or even schools may choose to avoid the publicity associated with the visit of a police patrol car by using informal processing or nonprocessing to deal with the majority of less serious incidents.

Second, employees who are victimized as a result of their dealings with the public may be persuaded by their employers that such incidents only occur when they are not doing their job properly. In other words, they may come to believe that among their job responsibilities is "cooling off" belligerent customers or clients. In even more severe cases, the victim may fear being blamed for having started the incident by behaving rudely toward the customer (Salinger et al., 1993).

Jobs can become hazardous when they expose employees to clients and situations that may provide an opportunity for crime. One step that can be taken to deter these crimes is to provide employees with the resources they need to deal with client-related problems. Workplaces must further resolve to react strongly to crimes that occur on their premises, thereby ensuring that their employees can do their job with a greater sense of security.

CRIME AND LEGITIMATE WORK

INTRODUCTION

We have seen that the relationship between crime and employment is less straightforward than is commonly supposed. Being employed is no guarantee of immunity from crime or victimization. In this section, we explore some of the ways in which work makes offending possible. Put simply, how do particular types of work routines and particular forms of the social organization of work relate to particular styles of offending?

The scope of work-related crime is potentially as broad as the types of jobs that exist within the economic system (Croall, 1987). Employees who have unsupervised access to the stock of their employers may find that their work role allows them a unique opportunity for theft. Physicians and lawyers may charge for services that are not performed (Arnold and Hagan, 1992; Reasons and Chappell, 1985; Wilson, Lincoln, and Chappell, 1986). Stores may use illegal sales practices to defraud the public. Large corporations may engage in the sale and manufacture of dangerous products, pollute the rivers, and maintain unsafe working conditions. Work-related crime ranges from pilfering by a disgruntled employee to the gargantuan thefts associated with the American savings and loan scandal.

Modern interest in the concept of work-related crime is usually traced back to the writings of the famous American criminologist, Edwin Sutherland (see Chapter 2). Sutherland (1940) used the term white-collar crime to refer to "a crime committed by a person of respectability and high status in the course of his [sic] occupation." Sutherland saw a need to correct the imbalance in criminological thinking that associated crime almost exclusively with the actions of the poor and the powerless. Through a study of major American corporations, he sought to establish the proposition that those who were fully and gainfully employed, and whose jobs accorded them considerable power and economic security, were frequently responsible for serious breeches of the law.

Since Sutherland's time, the concept of white-collar crime has undergone adjustments that reflect changes in the meaning of white-collar work. For Sutherland, the term white-collar crime denoted the criminal conspiracies of major corporations. Today, many forms of white-collar work (e.g., sales and computer programming) do not involve manual labour, but they cannot be considered positions in some sort of economic or corporate elite. Criminologists have attempted to capture important distinctions in the study of crime and legitimate work by introducing such terms as professional crime, elite deviance, corporate crime, organization crime, respectable crime, and business crime. Our interest in social domains as the context of criminal events requires us to focus attention not only on the crimes of powerful jobholders but also on the crimes of those whose jobs denote lower-ranked positions in the stratification order. Encompassing both types of crime is the term "occupational crime," which Akers (1985) defines as the "violation of legal norms governing lawful occupational endeavours" (228).

Occupational crimes may be distinguished in two important ways. First, they differ with respect to the nature of the offender–victim relationship. Some kinds of crimes are intended to provide only the job-holder with direct benefits. The person who pilfers from an employer does so for personal benefit, as does the bank teller who embezzles or the systems analyst who steals computer time. In such cases, the agency or organization is the victim and the employee is the offender.

In other cases, the organization may be understood not as the victim but as a weapon that is used against those outside of the organization or at the bottom of the organizational hierarchy. In the context of such criminal events, the crime may profit the job-holder indirectly in that direct benefits accrue to the organization itself. Included among the victims might be other business organizations (e.g., a corporation hires industrial saboteurs to steal competitors' secrets); clients or customers (the corporation may engage in deceptive advertising or the sale of untested pharmaceutical or food products); or low-level organizational members (employers may maintain unsafe working conditions or violate laws relating to labour relations). Finally, we can recognize more general patterns of victimization with respect to those crimes that inflict harm on very broad segments of society. Such crimes include political bribery, which undermines the political system; tax frauds, through which people indirectly distribute their losses to members of the tax-paying public; and industrial pollution, which threatens the air and water.

BOX 9.4 GETTING SHORTCHANGED

Thomas Gabor and his colleagues at the University of Ottawa conducted an experimental study to determine the circumstances under which convenience-store clerks are likely to shortchange their customers (Gabor et al., 1986).

A total of 125 stores were visited by three university students. In each case, the research confederate entered the store and bought a newspaper costing 30 cents. The "customer" paid for the paper with a single Canadian dollar bill. The researcher, pretending to be absentedminded, walked toward the door without waiting for the change. The pace at which the researcher walked allowed the clerk sufficient time to correct that mistake if she or he wished to do so. The researchers interpreted the clerk's actions (whether the clerk stopped the "customer" and attempted to return the change) as a measure of theft.

The researchers found that the change due was not returned by the clerks in 16 percent of the cases. Cashiers who were estimated to be under the age of 25 were twice as likely to fail to return the change than were those who were estimated to be over 25. There was no difference between male and female clerks in the behaviour of interest. In addition, male investigators were considerably more likely to be victimized than were female experimenters. Interestingly, however, the female investigator was more likely to be victimized by a clerk who was an older male than by clerks from any other demographic category.

A second way in which occupational crimes differ concerns the nature of the organizational settings in which they occur. Some types of occupational crime involve an offender who acts alone or only a small number of offenders. Medical frauds or dishonest household repair schemes might each involve the actions of a single offender who deals directly with victims and whose activities are not dependent upon institutional supports made available by co-workers (Wilson, Lincoln, and Chappell, 1986). At the other extreme, corporate crime might involve "large vertical slices" of complex organizations (Snider, 1993). In such cases, it may be difficult to say who did and who did not behave criminally, since each individual's actions contribute in small ways to the criminal event.

We next present a more elaborate discussion of the social organization of work routines in order to understand how and why occupational crimes occur.

PRECURSORS

The relationship between work routines and criminal offending may be understood with reference to the concepts of opportunity and motivation (Coleman, 1987, 1991). In other words, the social organization of work may give people the means with which to violate the law, while their understanding of their jobs or employers may supply them with the reasons for doing so.

In terms of opportunity, some work routines give employers or employees access to people and things to victimize. Doctors have access to patients, lawyers have access to clients, corporations have access to markets, and bank tellers have access to "other people's money" (Calavita and Pontell, 1991). While such access does not necessarily result in criminal action, it can be said to make such action possible.

According to Coleman (1987, 1991), the evaluation of opportunities for white-collar crime is determined by at least four factors. The first is the perception of how large a gain can be expected from the use of this opportunity. The second factor is the perception of potential risks associated with the opportunity. The exploration of criminal opportunities is made more likely by circumstances that prevent the effective control of the misuse of such access. Many professional groups, for example, claim to be self-regulating and discourage the efforts of state agencies to assume an investigative function, except in the most extreme cases. Many crimes that are associated with large corporations are of such complexity that they are policed only with great difficulty. It has been argued that the power of professional groups and large corporations discourages effective enforcement by state agencies (Hagan, 1992; Pearce, 1991). The third factor is the degree of compatibility between the use of the opportunity and the potential offender's beliefs, attitudes, and ethical view of the situation. Finally, the evaluation of the opportunity is based on the potential offender's perception of the potential of one opportunity relative to others to which he or she has access.

The motivations for occupational crime are a matter of considerable debate. Some observers argue that these motivations reside in the nature of work itself or in the wider socioeconomic setting of the workplace. Insofar as capitalism promotes a "culture of competition" that encourages the pursuit of economic profit, the profit motive may be said to be the criminal motive (Calavita and Pontell, 1991). However, the ways in which particular businesses and industries are organized may also serve as important motivating factors. Industries that experience severe competition, that are engaged in the sale or distribution of potentially dangerous—and therefore highly regulated—goods, or that operate in an uncertain economic environment may feel pressure to use crime as a means of achieving organizational goals (Coleman, 1991; Keane, 1991; Snider, 1993).

In very large corporations or businesses, the pressures to behave criminally may be accentuated by the pressure placed on underlings to achieve organizational goals. In what Simon and Eitzen (1993) describe as "corporate Frankensteins," senior management may establish goals or quotas that everyone knows cannot be achieved within the limits imposed by current regulations. At the same time, management may be able to insulate itself from any covert criminal action that results from the establishment of such corporate objectives (Hagan, 1992). Those who make decisions about criminal wrongdoing may be actively or passively discouraged from reporting their activities to senior management (Coleman, 1987; Hagan, 1985). If the acts are discovered by enforcement agencies or the public, management can disavow any knowledge of wrongdoing. If the acts are not discovered, management can claim credit for the high profit yields (Snider, 1993).

By way of illustration, Farberman (1975) argues that the North American automobile industry is characterized by a "criminogenic market structure." He maintains that the economic organization of the automobile industry almost necessitates criminal behaviour on the part of car dealers. Dealership franchises are required by the large automobile manufacturing companies to sell cars in large numbers, but at comparatively low prices. A small profit markup per unit on a large number of units benefits the car manufacturer, but not the dealer, who, as a result, feels compelled to compensate for financial losses by resorting to dishonest repair schemes and other forms of fraud.

The role of market forces in shaping criminal events in the automobile industry is even more clearly illustrated in the case of the Ford Pinto. This car was placed on the market in 1970, largely in response to feared competition from Japanese car manufacturers. Lee Iaococa, who was president of Ford at the time, told his engineers that they had to produce a car that weighed less than 2,000 pounds and that cost less than $2,000. While the Pinto met these specifications, it also contained serious design flaws. Most critical was the placement of the gas tank, which increased the likelihood that the car would explode in a rear-end collision. It was subsequently discovered that the corporate officers had known about this design flaw, and about the actions that could be taken to correct it. Rather than act on this knowledge, however, they calculated the cost of these modifications and compared them to the costs likely to be incurred in lawsuits resulting from the death and injury of Pinto drivers. Since the costs of the improvements were estimated to be greater than the costs associated with death and injury, Ford decided not to repair the defect.

Despite organizational and market pressures and a culture that seems to extol success at any cost, not everyone uses his or her occupational role to achieve criminal ends. Criminologists have stressed the significant role played by "definitions of the situation," which favour criminal offending (Benson, 1985). Coleman (1987) proposes the following six such definitions:

1. defining acts of theft as "borrowing";

2. denying that white-collar crimes result in any real harm;

3. claiming that the laws that prohibit the behaviour are unfair or unjust;

4. claiming that certain types of criminal behaviour are necessary if organizational goals are to be achieved;

5. claiming that the behaviour is normal and "everybody does it"; and

6. claiming that employee theft is not really stealing since the money was owed (e.g., for uncharged overtime).

Thus, acts that may be seen as criminal by others may be seen as excusable behaviours by the embezzler who defines theft as "borrowing" and by the corporate executive who defines the violation of fair labour laws as "just good business" (Snider, 1992).

Much of the debate about the motivational character of occupational crime has centred on questions about the distinctiveness of occupational offenders. It has long been argued by many criminologists that white-collar offenders differ from street criminals in important ways that influence the likelihood of law violation. Many white-collar offenders are neither poor nor powerless. Their crimes are not impulsive, irrational, or the product of inadequate planning. Thus, many factors that are usually associated with crime and criminals would seem to have little to do with the behaviour of those whose crimes involve occupational activity, particularly that which occurs at the top of corporate hierarchies. It has been argued that the causes of these types of crime must lie elsewhere.

By contrast, Gottfredson and Hirschi (1990) argue that the similarities between street criminals and occupational criminals are more important than the differences. For Gottfredson and Hirschi, the key explanatory mechanism is "self-control." This mechanism is equally applicable to understanding the behaviour of the occupational criminal as it is to understanding the behaviour of the street criminal. Special theories are no more necessary to explain the criminal in the legitimate business than they are to explain the criminal in the university, the military, or the church. People who have low self-control are likely to engage in a variety of types of crime and deviance, as the opportunities to do so present themselves.

Because occupations that present significant criminal opportunities tend to be occupations that require a considerable degree of self-control, Gottfredson and Hirschi argue that the rates of occupational crime are lower than is popularly believed. Moreover, they argue that data suggest that, when differences in opportunity are taken into account, demographic correlates of street and occupational crime are similar. They conclude that there is no need to pose special motivational circumstances in the case of the occupational offender, such as "the culture of competition" or other types of factors described above. Instead, they assert that "the distinction between crime in the street and crime in the suite is an *offence* rather than an *offender* distinction [and] that offenders in both cases are likely to share similar characteristics" (Gottfredson and Hirschi, 1990: 200).

In a recent study, Benson and Moore (1992) used data on the sentencing patterns of a large number of white-collar crimes (bank embezzlement, bribery, income-tax evasion, false claims, and mail fraud) and common crimes (narcotics offences, postal forgery, and bank robbery) to test some of the implications of Gottfredson and Hirschi's theory. Specifically, they attempted to determine whether white-collar offenders were as "criminally versatile" as common offenders, and whether they were as prone to as wide a range of deviant activities. They found that, while a minority of white-collar offenders behaved as the theory predicted, the majority did not.

According to Benson and Moore, low self-control is not the only path to occupational crime. Offenders with high self-control may employ it to pursue ego gratification in an aggressive and calculating manner. The culture of competition rewards such individuals by giving them positions of trust and opportunities for committing crimes that are serious but frequently undetected. In between those with high self-control and those with low self-control are individuals who may take advantage of occupational opportunities depending on their personal situations. For these individuals, fear of economic or occupational failure may create a circumstance in which a previously adequate level of self-control may become inadequate; as a result, the individual's ability to resist occupational opportunities for crime may be weakened.

THE EVENT

It is very difficult to determine the amount of crime that is committed in the course of legitimate work. There are many reasons for this. Most basically, the nature of much of this crime ensures that it will never be discovered. Corporate crimes that victimize consumers, clients, or members of the general public are very often "invisible" (Coleman, 1987). For example, people do not necessarily know that some of the illnesses they experience are the result of inadequately tested drugs. Workers who are injured by hazardous working conditions may be inclined to blame themselves rather than their employers for their injuries (Croall, 1987). Our terminology encourages this in that we routinely call such occurrences "accidents" rather than "assaults on the worker" (Reasons, Ross, and Peterson, 1981).

Unlike more garden variety forms of offending, occupational crimes are largely hidden from public view. The employee who has access to opportunities that allow offending may escape public scrutiny. The offender who uses the computer to embezzle may do so in such a way that the crime goes undetected by the employer, co-workers, or enforcement agencies. Corporate conspiracies are even less visible. Evidence about corporate decisions regarding offending are not accessible to those outside the corporation. Moreover, because a corporate crime may involve actions by members at all levels of the organization, many of those who participate in the event may not even be aware of the true character of their actions.

As is the case with other categories of crime, occupational crimes do not come to the attention of policing or regulatory agencies as a result of vigorous enforcement practices. At the same time, victims may be poorly positioned to know about—and respond to—the occupational crimes that victimize them. The regulatory agencies that are supposed to police and scrutinize corporate behaviour face many obstacles. According to Snider (1992), these obstacles include:

- the massive economic and political power of corporations that favour nonenforcement;
- being understaffed and often underfunded;
- frequent lack of support from the governments that appoint them;
- the high cost of investigating each complaint;
- support only from weak consumer or labour groups; and
- minimal accountability to public or media scrutiny.

A consequence of the above obstacles is that many kinds of occupational crimes that are discovered are not reported. A business that learns that its employees have been embezzling funds may not wish the matter to be widely known because it would in all likelihood reduce public trust in the company. Thus, the long-range negative consequences of reporting may be seen to outweigh the immediate benefits of doing so.

UCR data on occupational offences are of only limited use. Not only are such offences underreported, but in many cases (e.g., fraud) it is not possible to determine whether the crimes occurred in the context of work roles. This is due in part to the fact that occupational crime is a conceptual rather than a legal category. While victimization surveys may supplement official record-keeping systems (see Box 9.5), they too are limited, given the absence in many cases of a "direct victim" as well as the inability of the victim to recognize occupational and corporate offending.

BOX 9.5 PUBLIC PERCEPTIONS OF COMMERCIAL CRIME

Frank Pearce (1991) describes a British victimization survey (the Second Islington Crime Survey) that asked respondents not only about their experiences with "conventional" crime but also about their experiences with several forms of "commercial" crime. Of 889 community residents:

- 9 percent believed that they had been given misleading information about goods or services. As a result, 45 percent complained and 49 percent received some kind of compensation;

- 19 percent believed that they had been deliberately overcharged for goods or services. Of these 68 percent complained and in 67 percent of cases received some kind of compensation; and

- 25 percent believed that they had paid for goods or work that turned out to be defective. Of them, 74 percent complained and 72 percent received some kind of compensation.

THE AFTERMATH

Our best estimates suggest that the crimes committed by people in the course of legitimate occupational activities result in considerable levels of financial and physical harm and loss of life. Snider (1993) argues that "[c]orporate crime is a major killer, causing more deaths in a month than all the mass murderers combined do in a decade." According to one estimate, Canadians are ten times more likely to die in the workplace (frequently because of inadequate safety measures) than to be murdered (Reasons, Ross, and Patterson, 1981). The Westray mine disaster that we introduced at the beginning of this book illustrates how inattention to safety *may* be seen as constituting criminal action. In the United States, it is estimated that the savings and loan scandal alone will cost American taxpayers as much as 500 billion dollars by the year 2022 (Calavita and Pontell, 1991).

Controlling crimes that occur in the context of legitimate work roles is no easy task. It is sometimes assumed that members of the public are less concerned about occupational crimes than about more direct forms of predatory crime; this appears, however, not to be the case (Hans and Ermann, 1989). Nonetheless, the fact remains that the low level of visibility associated with occupational crimes makes effective deterrence difficult (Coleman, 1987). Some studies suggest that the threat of legal sanction has less impact on corporate crime than does the market environment in which companies operate (Keane, 1991; Simpson and Koper, 1992).

CRIME AND CRIMINAL CAREERS

The notion that crime may be thought of in occupational terms is one that is widely shared both inside and outside of criminological literature. The true-crime section of any bookstore usually carries several titles that detail the exploits of the "professional thief," "professional robber," or "contract killer." Such books promise a look into a world of crime that, on the surface at least, seems to be organized in ways that reflect the occupational structure of legitimate work. In some fundamental sense, professional offenders view crime as their job. They have acquired the technical skills they need to perform this job and they derive their livelihood principally from successful job performance. Just how superficial are comparisons between crime and legitimate work? Does it make sense to conceptualize criminal involvement in career terms?

A useful place to begin this discussion is with a brief consideration of the concept of "career" itself. In occupational terms, the concept of career denotes "the sequence of movements from one position to another in an occupational system made by any individual who works in that system" (Becker, 1963: 24). This definition of the term is consistent with popular usage. We think of a work career as beginning at some specific point in time, and thereafter continuing until death, retirement, or a voluntary or forced career change. Over the course of the career, we can identify movement through various stages (which, in the context of formal organizations, we call promotions). Each stage brings with it new responsibilities and additional rewards and provides the individual with the skills, knowledge, or experience he or she needs to advance to successive stages.

The relative success that characterizes career movement is dependent on several "career contingencies." The occupational system may, for instance, allow for little career advancement or the individual may lack the training that would allow movement beyond a certain occupational level. Contingencies include any factors upon which career success depends. Within the setting of a business or other organizational bureaucracy, the suggested metaphor is a high-rise building. Each floor represents a career stage and the career may be understood as the elevator that carries people upward or, in unfortunate cases, downward. Clearly, the career concept has more general applicability. Think of your college or university career as having begun when you started your postsecondary education. As your career takes you through several well-defined stages, your success will be judged in large

BOX 9.6   ROBBERS AND ROBBERY

Robbery is probably the type of violent crime that most people associate with the "career criminal." Thomas Gabor of the University of Ottawa and Andre Normandeau of the University of Montreal undertook a major study of robbery, mainly in the area of Montreal and Quebec City (Gabor and Normandeau, 1989).

Part of the study involved detailed interviews with 39 convicted robbers, all but one of whom were serving sentences in the Montreal area. The study revealed that

- the offenders were male, and that most were under 30 years of age, had no more than a secondary school education, and came from a blue-collar background;
- their self-reported criminality of the offenders was far in excess of that reported in the files;
- the offenders were motivated to rob by the fact that robbery is a fast and direct way to obtain money compared to the less lucrative and more complicated acts of break and enter and fraud;
- unemployment, the need for drugs, and criminal associates were among the precipitating factors;
- most of the subjects began their careers committing other crimes, such as auto theft or break and enter, before advancing to robbery;
- early success at armed robbery allows the offender to gain confidence and to develop and refine "professional skills"; and
- as they aged, several offenders experienced increasing fear of prison sentences—a change motivated in part by their negative experiences in previous periods of incarceration and by the knowledge that successive sentences were likely to be longer.

part by the grades you receive. However, your success will depend on career contingencies such as the types of examinations that are used to judge performance, the restrictions placed on program enrolment, and your abilities as a student.

How valuable is the career concept in the study of crime? Although there is a long history of research and theory that attempts to link the study of offending to the study of careers (Letkemann, 1973; Miller, 1978), there is no agreement among criminologists that this is a worthwhile exercise. Some criminologists maintain that the career concept is useful in understanding the relative degree of involvement of offenders in criminal activity. From this point of view, every offender may be said to have a criminal career. The use of the term career in this context does not necessarily mean that crime provides the person's major source of livelihood. The individual who commits only one crime early in adolescence may have a short career in contrast to the person who engages in serious crime throughout his or her life. By focusing on criminal careers, we are encouraged to ask why offenders' careers develop as they do. While the "criminal career" is not a theory in and of itself, it is seen as a useful way of organizing what we know about crime.

Moreover, it is argued, the career concept encourages us to ask questions we would not otherwise be prompted to ask (Blumstein, Cohen, and Farrington, 1988a, 1988b). The first question has to do with entry into a criminal career, which is sometimes called "onset." Here we might ask what sorts of factors encourage movement into a criminal career. Or we might try to discover the ages at which people typically begin criminal careers. The second question has to do with the degree of career productivity, which, in the context of legitimate work, might be called the level of success. During the duration of the career, how many crimes do offenders commit and what contingencies affect the relative success of criminal careers? Finally, we might ask about what is called "desistance." How and why do offenders end their criminal careers?

Advocates of the career concept argue that, for theoretical reasons, it is important to distinguish questions about onset from questions about frequency and desistance, since factors that affect one aspect of the career may be unrelated to another (Blumstein, Cohen, and Farrington, 1988a). For instance, some of the apparently confusing findings about the relationship between crime and unemployment might become more comprehensible if we recognize that unemployment may not be related to onset, productivity, and desistance in the same ways. For example, the level of unemployment might not be expected to affect the onset of criminal careers that people typically begin in their teenage years, before they are eligible to enter the legal labour force. Once a criminal career has begun, the availability of legitimate work may affect the timing of desistance. An individual may abandon a criminal career if offered more profitable legitimate work. Conversely, although most people end their criminal careers before middle age, desistance may be delayed if the rate of unemployment decreases the likelihood of securing a legitimate job. In general, the career concept suggests that it may be misguided to try to find simple and direct effects between familiar criminogenic concepts and rates of crime. Factors such as employment may affect different career aspects in different ways, and a factor that is important at one point of a career may have no causal significance at a later point.

Perhaps the most interesting findings to emerge from the research on criminal careers are those that relate to "career criminals," that is, offenders who commit crimes at a very high rate. The extreme differences in the rates at which individuals offend were first documented in a cohort study undertaken by Wolfgang, Figlio, and Sellin (1972). The researchers attempted to examine the offending patterns of all males born in Philadelphia in 1945 for the period up to their eighteenth birthdays in 1963. The study identified 627 career criminals who, while they constituted only 6 percent of the original cohort and 18 percent of the delinquents, were responsible for more than half of all the crime engaged in by cohort members. More importantly perhaps, these career criminals were responsible for 71 percent of the murders, 73 percent of the rapes, and 82 percent of the robberies.

Later studies support the view that small numbers of offenders account for large numbers of crime. A longitudinal study in England, known as the Cambridge Study of Delinquent Development, found that about 6 percent of a sample of 411 boys accounted for about 50 percent of all of the criminal convictions (Farrington, 1989). In a study by the Rand Corporation of offenders in California, Michigan, and Texas prisons, the most active 10 percent of all inmates who had committed robbery reported committing at least 58 robberies per year, while the most active 10 percent of burglars reported committing 187 or more burglaries per year (Chaiken and Chaiken, 1982).

However, contrary to what we might expect, this research also shows that offenders whose careers are characterized by high rates of offending seldom specialize in only one type of crime (U.S. Department of Justice, 1988; Visher, 1991); instead, they tend to commit a variety of violent and property crimes (but see Kempf, 1987). The research into criminal careers also shows that there is general stability in levels of offence seriousness over the course of a career. It does not appear, for instance, that the longer offenders offend, the more likely they are to move from one type of crime to another type that requires more technical skill or knowledge.

These findings regarding seriousness and the tendency of so-called career criminals not to specialize in particular types of crimes have led some criminologists to be very critical of the career approach to offending. Gottfredson and Hirschi (1986, 1988, 1990) question whether there is anything of value to be gained from examining criminal careers. The concept of a career, they argue, usually assumes some notion of specialization and career progress; and yet the available evidence undermines the validity of such assumptions.

Gottfredson and Hirschi also contend that it is fruitless to search for the unique factors that explain desistance from criminal careers since all offenders—irrespective of the types of offences in which they engage, or the rates at which they engage in them—become less productive as they age. To argue that different factors are required to explain different career elements is also misleading, according to Gottfredson and Hirschi, since most of the factors in which career researchers are interested (such as unemployment) are only weakly related to crime. For these authors, the tendency to engage in crime is highly stable for all offenders and is related to a low level of self-control.

In a somewhat different way, Luckenbill and Best (1981) also question the value of the career concept as a way of understanding crime and other types of nonconformity. They maintain that analogies between legitimate and the deviant careers are very limited, in large part because legitimate careers must be understood in the context of organizational settings while criminal careers emerge in much less structured settings. Criminal careers are not formed in response to institutional requirements that "spell out the career's positions, pathways for mobility, and rewards, while authorities enforce these rules and ensure the career's security" (Luckenbill and Best, 1981: 197). By contrast, those who are involved in deviant careers are not able to draw upon such institutional resources. Moreover, they risk the possibility of social control sanctions and exploitation by deviant associates and their rewards from deviance are uncertain. Luckenbill and Best (1981) express the differences between legitimate and deviant careers in the following terms:

> *Riding escalators between floors may be an effective metaphor for respectable organizational careers, but it fails to capture the character of deviant careers. A more appropriate image is a walk in the woods. Here some people take the pathways marked by their predecessors, while others strike out on their own. Some walk slowly, exploring before moving further, but others run, caught up in the action. Some have a destination in mind and proceed purposefully; others view the trip as an experience and enjoy it for its own sake. Even those intent on reaching a destination may stray from the path; they may try a shortcut or they may lose sight of a familiar landmark, get lost and find it necessary to backtrack. Without a rigid organizational structure, deviant careers can develop in many different ways (201).*

While the debate about the value of the career approach to understanding criminality is unresolved (Dechenes, 1990; Gibbons, 1988; Greenberg, 1992; Langan, 1983; Walker, 1989), comparisons between the legitimate and the illegitimate worlds of work are particularly illuminating with respect to particular types of crime. One such type is known as "enterprise crime."

ENTERPRISE CRIME

We can define enterprise crimes as the "sale of illegal goods and services to customers who know that the goods or services are illegal" (Haller, 1990: 207). The nature of such goods or services may be highly varied and ultimately dependent on what the law disallows. The sale of illegal drugs or pornography, the operation of illegal gambling houses, loan-sharking, and "contract killing" all represent examples of enterprise crime.

What we call enterprise crime is usually referred to by criminologists and noncriminologists alike as "organized crime." This concept conjures up a number of familiar images gleaned from popular movies like *The Godfather*, popular novels, and newspaper coverage of "mob trials" (exemplified by the trial of John Gotti). However, for reasons that will become clear, the concept of organized crime obscures rather than enhances our understanding of the types of events in which we are interested.

WHAT IS ORGANIZED CRIME?

As it is popularly used, the term organized crime refers to long-term, highly organized criminal syndicates that are involved in a number of criminal businesses (U.S. Department of Justice, 1988). It is usually claimed that these syndicates are organized along ethnic lines and that they function in much the same way that legitimate business corporations function (Cressey, 1969). In this sense, they have well-established patterns of recruitment and authority.

The most widely discussed group of organized criminals in the criminological and popular literature on the subject is the Mafia, also known as La Cosa Nostra. This particular form of criminal conspiracy is said to be the major such group operating in North America (Abadinsky, 1987). It is said by many observers to have its origins in the Sicilian Mafia and to have been imported to Canada and the United States along with the waves of European immigration in the latter days of the last century (Carrigan, 1991; Smith, 1975).

In North America, it is claimed that the modern Mafia finds its origins in the so-called "Black Hand" gangs that operated in the ethnic enclaves of major American and Canadian cities. These gangs were simply groups of extortionists who preyed upon their fellow immigres (Pitkin and Cordasco, 1977; Dubro, 1985). Their name derived from the fact that they would send their victims letters signed with a black hand print. These letters would threaten that harm would befall the victim, or members of his family, unless he paid the extortionists the amount of money being demanded. The American experiment with national prohibition in the 1920s is said to have given organized crime groups an opportunity to consolidate their economic power. Throughout the 1930s, it is argued, these gangs developed into a national federation that came to control the operation of illegal business in all regions of the continent.

The above view of organized crime has been legitimated in the stories told by former Mafiosi (Kirby and Renner, 1986; Maas, 1969); in the reports of undercover police work; in federal investigations of organized crime (Moore, 1974; Smith, 1975); and in the writings of academic criminologists (Galliher and Cain, 1974). The major academic architect was the American sociologist Donald Cressey (1969), who, as a consultant to the U.S. president's Commission on Law Enforcement and the Administration of Justice in the late 1960s, wrote a highly influential report on the nature and influence of organized-crime groups in the United States. In a revised version of that report, published in 1969, Cressey argued that any attempt to understand American organized crime required recognition of eight "facts":

1. A nationwide alliance of at least 24 tightly knit crime "families" exist in the United States.

2. The members of these "families" are all Italians and Sicilians, or of Italian and Sicilian descent, and those on the Eastern seaboard, especially, call the entire system "Cosa Nostra."

3. The names, criminal records, and principal criminal activities of about 5,000 of the participants have been assembled.

4. The persons occupying key positions in the skeletal structure of each "family" are well known to law-enforcement officials.

5. The "families" are linked to each other and to non-Cosa Nostra syndicates by understandings, agreements, and "treaties," as well as by mutual deference to the "Commission," which is made up of the leaders of the most powerful families.

6. The boss of each family directs the activities (especially the illegal ones) that are undertaken by the members of his "family."

7. The organization as a whole controls all but a tiny part of illegal gambling, loan-sharking, and narcotics importation.

8. Information about the Commission, the "families," and family activities has come from detailed reports made by a wide variety of police observers, informants, wiretaps, and electronic drugs.

In Canada, a similar image of organized crime has been constructed by the police, journalists, and some members of the academic community (Carrigan, 1991; Dubro, 1985; Kirby and Renner, 1986). It is generally acknowledged that La Cosa Nostra has never become as firmly entrenched in Canadian as in American society. Instead, it is argued that organized crime groups in Toronto, Hamilton, and Montreal have, like their legitimate counterparts, operated as branch plants of powerful American families located in New York City and Buffalo (Dubro, 1985). According to a recent law-enforcement report,

> [t]here are approximately 14 traditional organized crime groups in Ontario with an estimated membership of 280. These groups are branches of the American La Cosa Nostra. They are involved in legitimate businesses which enable them to launder the profits obtained from their illegal activities. Their illegal ventures include extortion, fraud, gambling, loansharking, counterfeiting, murder and trafficking in drugs (Canadian Association of Chiefs of Police, 1991: 40).

In Canada, increasing attention is being focused on the organized crime activities of Chinese or Vietnamese groups, as well as those of outlaw motorcycle gangs. In a similar way, American observers have expressed concern about the increasing involvement of Cuban, Afro-American, and Jamaican groups in such activities.

Despite the popularity of the above view of organized crime, many researchers have called into question both its accuracy and value. Several shortcomings have been noted. First, the view of organized crime as an "organized parasitic conspiracy" deflects our attention away from any critical assessment of the ways in which our own society makes such crime possible. Despite the obvious implications of this view, it has been shown that the types of activity associated with La Cosa Nostra have not developed in all societies that have large numbers of Italian immigrants.

Second, researchers over the last two decades have called into question every one of Cressey's eight "facts" as well as the orthodox history of

BOX 9.7 CRIMINAL ENTERPRISE ON WHEELS

According to law-enforcement authorities, "outlaw motorcycle gangs" have become a major force in enterprise crime. Police intelligence pictures the regional distribution of gang activity as follows:

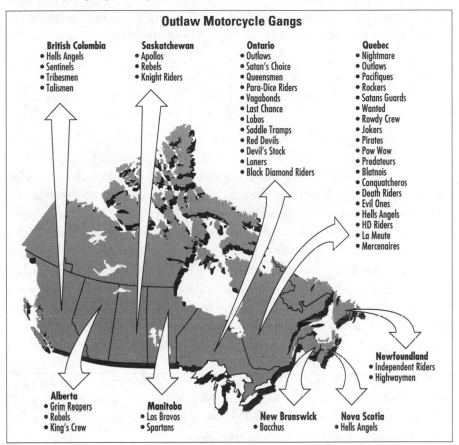

Outlaw Motorcycle Gangs

British Columbia
- Hells Angels
- Sentinels
- Tribesmen
- Talismen

Saskatchewan
- Apollos
- Rebels
- Knight Riders

Ontario
- Outlaws
- Satan's Choice
- Queensmen
- Para-Dice Riders
- Vagabonds
- Last Chance
- Lobos
- Saddle Tramps
- Red Devils
- Devil's Stock
- Loners
- Black Diamond Riders

Quebec
- Nightmare
- Outlaws
- Pacifiques
- Rockers
- Satans Guards
- Wanted
- Rowdy Crew
- Jokers
- Pirates
- Pow Wow
- Predateurs
- Blatnois
- Conquatcheros
- Death Riders
- Evil Ones
- Hells Angels
- HD Riders
- La Meute
- Mercenaires

Newfoundland
- Independent Riders
- Highwaymen

Alberta
- Grim Reapers
- Rebels
- King's Crew

Manitoba
- Los Brovos
- Spartans

New Brunswick
- Bacchus

Nova Scotia
- Hells Angels

Source: Canadian Association of Chiefs of Police, *Organized Crime Committee Report.* Ottawa: Criminal Intelligence Service Canada, 1993.

organized crime that is told and retold in the works of popular and academic writers. Critics of the orthodox view seriously question

1. whether something called the "Mafia" has ever existed *as a formal organization* in Sicily or anywhere else (Blok, 1975; Hess, 1973; Servadio, 1976);

2. whether a bureaucratically organized group known as La Cosa Nostra exists in North America (Albanese, 1989; Albini, 1971; Smith, 1975);

3. whether contemporary organized crime groups composed of Italian Canadians or Italian Americans find their origins in the black hand or Prohibition gangs of earlier eras (Hawkins, 1969; Jenkins and Potter, 1987; Smith, 1975);

4. whether police investigations or the investigations by government commissions or task forces have provided any independent evidence that such organizations exist (Albanese, 1989; Hawkins, 1969; Moore, 1974; Smith, 1975); and

5. whether the activities of organized-crime groups are overseen or coordinated by a national commission (Hawkins, 1969; Ianni and Reuss-Ianni, 1972).

Third, and most basically, the concept of organized crime is itself confusing and misleading (Smith, 1991). Logically, we might suggest that it refers to any type of activity that involves more than one offender acting in coordinated fashion. From this point of view, two juveniles who break into a house could be said to have engaged in organized crime. However, the term is almost never used this way. Instead, it is used to refer to large-scale criminal efforts that are diverse in nature and seem to have little in common beyond the fact that we associate them with particular stereotypical notions of who organized criminals are. Adding to the confusion, the term organized crime is sometimes used to refer to a particular type of activity (as in the statement, "gambling is a form of organized crime"), but other times used to refer to particular groups of criminals (as in the statement, "we must prosecute members of organized crime"). Such usage results in circular reasoning (Maltz, 1976). If we say, for example, "organized crime is involved in the drug trade," we have not really said anything. This is because, by definition, the drug trade is an organized crime and therefore any group involved in this activity must be involved in organized crime.

One way out of this impasse is to shift our attention away from the focus on alien, parasitic conspiracies and "organized crime" and toward the study of enterprise crime.

PRECURSORS

As previously defined, enterprise crime involves the sale and distribution of illegal goods and services. What kinds of social conditions make enterprise crime likely? The first such condition, of course, is the existence of laws that prohibit the goods and services in question. In other words, enterprise crime is made possible when the reach of law creates market opportunities. Prohibition, a law that was in force in the United States between 1920 and 1933 in a very real sense created the opportunity for financial gain that could be exploited by criminal entrepreneurs (Packer, 1969; Schelling, 1967). In a similar way, attempts to use the law to control the availability of illicit drugs—such as marijuana or cocaine, or to use of high rates of taxation to control the availability of legal drugs such as tobacco, make enterprise crime possible. The gap between what people want and what the law allows them to legitimately have suggests an important way in which our society provides

BOX 9.8 THE DRUG BUSINESS

The sale and distribution of drugs represents a major form of enterprise crime. In the 1980s, the concern about drugs dominated much of the discussion about crime and violence in North America.

The reporting of drug crimes differs from the reporting of crimes that involve a direct and immediate victim. Given that both sides are willing participants in a drug transaction, no one is likely to notify the police that a crime has been committed. Drug users, like other types of offenders, are interested in ensuring that their behaviour has low visibility. This means that official data on drug crimes are likely to reflect the vigour with which policing agencies pursue such crime.

According to the Canadian Centre for Justice Statistics (Wolff, 1991), supply offences (trafficking, importation, and cultivation) have increased as a proportion of total drug crimes since 1977. At the same time, recorded crimes of possession have fallen, although possession still represents the major type of drug offence.

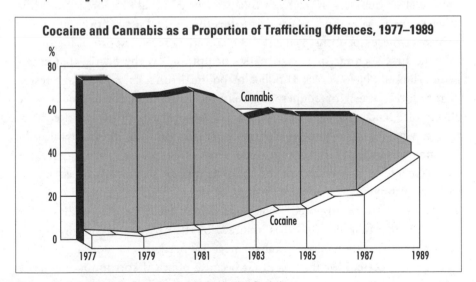

Cocaine and Cannabis as a Proportion of Trafficking Offences, 1977–1989

Source: Statistics Canada, Canadian Centre for Justice Statistics.

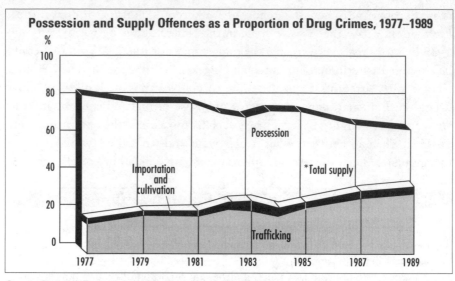

Possession and Supply Offences as a Proportion of Drug Crimes, 1977–1989

%

Importation and cultivation

Possession

*Total supply

Trafficking

Source: Statistics Canada, Canadian Centre for Justice Statistics.

the sources of enterprise crime. This point is obscured when we think of such crime as merely the product of an alien, parasitic conspiracy.

The existence of laws that create illegal opportunities for criminal enterprise help us understand why such crimes might occur, but not why they are organized as they are. Why, for instance, do some forms of illicit enterprise involve large numbers of relatively independent criminal entrepreneurs, while other forms involve more large-scale forms of criminal associations? In order to answer these questions, Haller (1990) considers three important factors.

The first such factor is systematic corruption. To the degree that enterprise criminals have access to police or political officials who are interested in the development of cooperative ventures with these entrepreneurs, the effects of agencies of legal control may be neutralized. Bribery and corruption may afford some enterprise criminals protection from the law while others may discover that they are the objects of much more aggressive enforcement. Just as occurs in the more legitimate sectors of the economy, the establishment of cozy relationships between those who do the policing and those who are supposed to be policed may facilitate the conditions by which greater market control is assured. In the absence of such mutually advantageous relationships, criminal enterprise markets are more unstable. It has been suggested, for instance, that because political corruption has never been as widespread in Canada as it has been in the United States, enterprise crime has never flourished to the same degree in this country (Murray, 1987; Sacco, 1980; Stamler; 1992).

A second precondition for the establishment of stable enterprise crime is the existence of partnership arrangements. Such arrangements have the same role in illegal businesses that they have in legal business ventures. They allow entrepreneurs to share risks (especially the risk of business failure), and they allow people with different types of resources to pool these resources. This means that individuals who have political influence, capital, or managerial skills can combine their talents in a way that increases the potential for profit.

This emphasis on partnerships suggests that, rather than being hierarchically or bureaucratically organized, enterprise crime is much more likely to involve informal styles of association (Albini, 1971; Ianni and Reuss-Ianni, 1972). Partnerships may arise when they are deemed necessary or desirable for business purposes, and they may be dissolved when they have served their purpose or when they cease to be profitable. Moreover, Haller (1990) notes, not everyone need be thought of as equal in these partnerships. Some entrepreneurs exercise much more power than others because they have the political or economic resources that allow them to participate in several enterprises simultaneously. In the book *Wiseguy*, by Nicholas Pileggi, ex-mobster Henry Hill describes the influence of mob boss Paul Vario in terms that clearly indicate the nature of these partnership arrangements:

> *There were hundreds of guys who depended on Paulie for their living, but he never paid out a dime. The guys who worked for Paulie had to make their own dollar. All they got from Paulie was protection from other guys looking to rip them off. That's what it's all about. That's what the FBI can never understand—that what Paulie and the organization offer is protection of the kinds of guys who can't go to the cops. They're like the police department for wiseguys (Pileggi, 1985: 56–57).*

More generally, Haller (1990) suggests that "[l]ike the Chamber of Commerce or Rotary Club for legal businessmen, the Cosa Nostra group would be seen, not as an organization that operates illegal (or legal businesses), but as an association that businessmen join partly to further their business careers "(227).

Finally, Haller notes, many types of economic factors shape the structure of illegal enterprises. Some of these factors work to bring about cooperation among groups while others work to reduce cooperation (Schelling,

1967). Enterprises that involve the importation of drugs may involve a high degree of cooperation among many groups located in both the exporting and receiving countries. Drug networks may also exist at the local level (see Figure 9.1). In addition, substantial drug transactions may require a large initial capital investment. Factors of this type may encourage the development of monopolistic tendencies, since relatively few groups are able to marshall the economic resources or possess the contacts needed to facilitate large-scale arrangements. By contrast, the illegal market for marijuana may be structured quite differently (Rogers, 1973). This illicit commodity does not have to be imported and can be distributed on a small-scale basis by independent entrepreneurs who cater to the needs of a small, local clientele. Markets of this type are much more resistant to monopoly.

THE EVENT

If we think about enterprise crime as a type of business, then the questions to which we seek answers are not unlike the questions we might ask about more legitimate businesses. What is the nature of the market? How are goods and services produced and distributed? What are the sources of capital that underwrite the costs of doing business? How do the various groups involved in these businesses cope with changing markets? Why are some types of people rather than others attracted to this particular line of work?

Criminologists are particularly concerned, however, with the fact that the business is illegal (Haller, 1990). As economist Thomas Schelling (1967) notes, when a business is made illegal, entry into the marketplace is restricted to those who are willing and able to behave criminally. In other words, the illegal nature of the business is perhaps most attractive to those who have no strong reservations about involvement in behaviours that are prohibited by law.

As we pointed out earlier in this chapter, much has been made of the ethnic character of organized crime. Apart from La Cosa Nostra, commonly cited groups include Chinese Triads, Jamaican Posses, and associations loosely referred to in the popular press as the Columbian, Irish, or Vietnamese mafias. This emphasis on ethnicity has frequently served to reinforce the popular view that criminal enterprise is an alien problem because it is associated with alien groups.

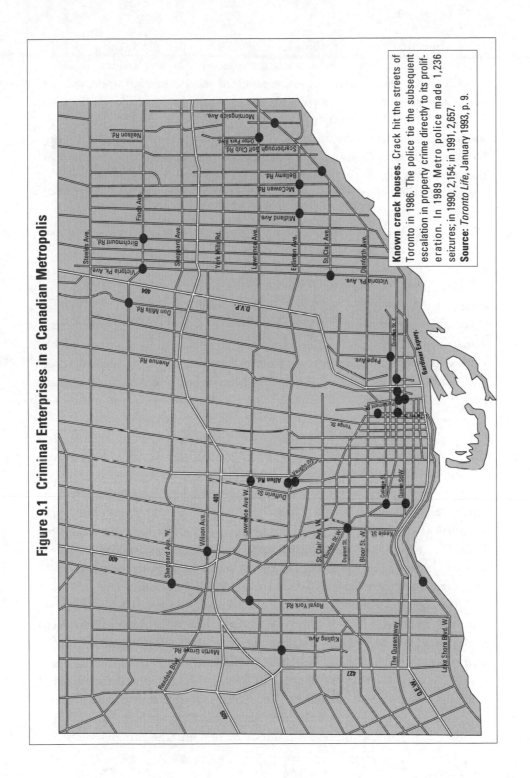

Figure 9.1 Criminal Enterprises in a Canadian Metropolis

Known crack houses. Crack hit the streets of Toronto in 1986. The police tie the subsequent escalation in property crime directly to its proliferation. In 1989 Metro police made 1,236 seizures; in 1990, 2,154; in 1991, 2,657. **Source:** *Toronto Life*, January 1993, p. 9.

In rejecting this view, the sociologist Daniel Bell (1953) argued four decades ago that organized crime functions as a "queer ladder of social mobility" in societies that emphasize material success but fail to provide all racial and economic groups with equal opportunities for achieving it. Like Robert Merton, Bell maintained that, as a result of the pressure to achieve social goals, groups that find the legitimate channels of upward mobility blocked, may turn to illegal alternatives. The very important implication of this argument is that enterprise crime, seen as a form of economic activity, is most attractive to those located at, or near the bottom of, the social hierarchy.

Ianni (1974), like Bell before him, argues that involvement in enterprise crime is characterized by an ethnic succession rather than by an enduring criminal conspiracy. Particular ethnic groups may dominate organized crime until legitimate channels of upward mobility become generally accessible. At this point, the influence of any particular group may decline as other groups move in to fill the void created by the outward movement. Thus, in the United States, the Italian presence in organized crime, which peaked in the period immediately before Prohibition, was preceded by an Irish and Jewish presence and succeeded by a Cuban and African-American presence (Ianni, 1974). The emergence in Canada of Vietnamese and Chinese gangs may illustrate a similar process of ethnic succession.

This is not to say that the domination of enterprise crime by any particular group is irrelevant to the ways in which markets are structured or exploited (Light, 1977). Members of ethnic groups may be able to draw on their cultural capital in ways that enable them to be especially effective in particular types of enterprise crime. They may also share particular forms of cultural traditions that facilitate criminal organization. According to Ianni (1971), the significance of the family as a central organizing theme in Italian culture has contributed to the creation of criminal enterprises— structured along kinship lines—that are remarkably durable.

A second important implication that flows from the illegal nature of criminal enterprises relates to the role of regulation. It is obvious that when a market is declared illegal, it cannot be controlled by the legitimate state agencies responsible for the mediation of disputes or the resolution of conflicts (Reuter, 1984b). As Henry Hill's earlier remarks make clear, the criminal entrepreneur is unable to seek recourse for harm done against him by going to the police or initiating lawsuits. One mobster cannot sue another because a promised shipment of heroin was not delivered or because a promise to influence the vote of a labour union was not kept. It is for such reasons that violence, or the threat of violence, looms so large in the business affairs of criminal entrepreneurs. Violence represents one of the few means by which contracts can be enforced and compliance with agreements can be assured (Black, 1983; Reuter, 1984b).

The types of criminal events that are central to enterprise crime—the acquisition and distribution of illegal goods and services—are complicated affairs. But much popular thinking on the subject glosses over these complexities. We are used to thinking about enterprise crime as nothing more than the acts of vicious gangsters whose ways of thinking and acting are foreign to the societies in which we find them. While this makes for good pulp fiction, it is not very illuminating. Enterprise-crime events are shaped by the societal context and are in no fundamental way alien to it. The gap between popular demand and efforts to legally control supply makes illegal markets possible in the first place. By declaring these markets off-limits to legal regulation, society helps to create circumstances in which the potential for violence is considerable. The stratified nature of society and the restrictions it imposes on upward mobility causes some who are adversely affected to see enterprise crime as a viable means of achieving the goals toward which their societies encourage them to aspire.

THE AFTERMATH

Public reactions to enterprise crime often fail to take account of the wider context, which, we have argued, is necessary if we hope to achieve an appropriate understanding of this type of crime (Morash, 1984). When we read about the gangland killing in an urban ethnic restaurant, or about a police seizure of drug assets, we rarely consider the social character of these crimes. We are encouraged to think about organized crime as a force at war with decent society, as it preys upon citizens, and threatens to corrupt our public officials and undermine our basic social institutions (Sacco, 1980). Rarely are we encouraged to think about criminal enterprise as a logical product of particular social conditions that prevail in North America. As McIntosh (1975) argues, criminal entrepreneurs are part of a larger configuration that includes not only the criminal but also victims, the police, politicians, customers, and others. The activities of the criminal entrepreneur cannot be understood by focusing on the entrepreneur alone. As these larger configurations change, so do the types of events in which criminal entrepreneurs are likely to be involved. In the absence of this more complex and detailed understanding, enterprise crime will be seen as alien and parasitic.

One important implication of traditional views of enterprise crime relates to the means by which such crime is to be controlled. The image of enterprise crime as an alien, parasitic conspiracy, rather than as a social product, supports the position that this type of crime is a law-enforcement problem. From this perspective, enterprise crime is best controlled through the aggressive prosecution of criminal entrepreneurs. And yet, when we conceptualize the problem in terms of criminal enterprise rather than in terms of organized crime, we recognize that this "gangbuster mentality" has serious limitations. If enterprise crime really does function like other economic markets, then the removal of criminal entrepreneurs (through arrest and imprisonment) will not significantly affect market operation, since such actions have no effect on the demand for illegal goods. We recognize this fact quite explicitly in the case of legal markets. When an entrepreneur who sells legal goods—for instance, shoes—is removed from the market as a result of death, illness, or retirement, shoes remain available (Van den Haag, 1975). This is because the demand for shoes will prompt others to enter the market to fill the void. In fact, it might even be argued that because an aggressive policy of prosecution increases the risks of doing business, the going rate for goods and services will increase and the profits to be gained may increase accordingly.

SUMMARY AND CONCLUSIONS
■ ■ ■

We have seen in this chapter that the roles we play in the workplace domain structure the kinds of involvement we are likely to have in various types of criminal events. Some jobs increase employees' risks of criminal victimization, while others provide them with opportunities to victimize others, be they subordinates, co-workers, clients, customers, or the society at large. Alternatively, illegal though they may be, various types of enterprise crime nevertheless constitute a form of work.

Throughout much of its history, criminology has focused attention on how exclusion from the world of legitimate work motivates criminality. While this remains an important (if unresolved) issue, it is equally important to understand how the organization of the domain of work facilitates or hinders the development of criminal events within this domain. Theories that emphasize the role of social inequality in the generation of crime quite naturally suggest that not having a job may encourage the development of criminal motivations. Victimization risks differ between those who are employed and those who are not. More importantly, particular forms of labour-force participation make crime possible. Relevant here are two factors: (1) the relationship between the jobs people have and the victimization risks they face; and (2) the ways in which jobs provide people with opportunities to behave criminally.

Victimization risk at work is inversely correlated to occupational status, measured by income, with those in lower income occupations being more vulnerable. However, occupation alone is not enough to define victimization risk. Workplace settings can be very important in influencing the opportunity for crime. Risk can be heightened by the fact that money is available to be stolen. Sometimes the nature of the job has a provoking effect on customers, who may vent their anger and frustration at the employee. Crimes that occur in these circumstances are not easy to deter and are underreported. In the aftermath of violent encounters, employees may accept the blame or assume that the employer will blame them for handling the situation poorly. Alternatively, these incidents may be handled informally to avoid the problems associated with police involvement.

Work-related crime may range all the way from pilfering by a disgruntled employee to the gargantuan thefts associated with the American savings and loan scandal. Sutherland (1940) used the term, white-collar crime to refer to "a crime committed by a person of respectability and high status in the course of his [sic] occupation." He saw a need to correct the imbalance in criminological thinking that associated crime almost exclusively with the actions of the poor and the powerless.

Occupational crimes may be distinguished in two important ways. First, they differ with respect to the nature of the offender–victim relationship. Some kinds of crimes are intended to provide direct benefits only for the job-holder, as in the case of the employee who steals. In such instances, the agency or organization is the victim and the employee is the offender. In other cases, the organization may be used to attack those outside of the business or at the bottom of the organizational hierarchy. With respect to these criminal events, the crime may profit the job-holder indirectly in that more direct benefits accrue to the organization itself. Finally, more general patterns of victimization result from crimes that inflict harm on very broad segments of society. Such crimes include political bribery, tax frauds, and industrial pollution.

Occupational crimes differ according to the nature of the organizational settings in which they occur. Some types of occupational crime involve either a lone offender or a small number of offenders, as is exemplified by medical frauds and dishonest household repair services. At the other extreme, corporate crime might involve "large vertical slices" of complex organizations (Snider, 1993). In such cases, it may be difficult to say who did and did not behave criminally, since each individual's actions constitute only a small portion of the criminal event.

Gottfredson and Hirschi argue that the mechanism of self-control is equally applicable to understanding the behaviour of the occupational criminal as it is to understanding the behaviour of the street criminal. What distinguishes occupational crime from street crime is, in Gottfredson and Hirschi's view, not the offender but rather the offence. People who have low self control are likely to engage in a variety of types of crime and deviance, as the opportunities to do so present themselves. Despite the significant financial and physical harm caused by occupational crimes, their low visibility makes them difficult to detect and deter.

Crime may take on the character of a career. As individuals pursue criminal activities, they may follow a career path that is similar to a legitimate one. Research suggests that a disproportionate amount of crime is committed by a small number of individuals; this is particularly true in the case of juveniles. Criminologists do not agree, however, on whether or not it is useful to think about criminal involvement in career terms. The reason for this is that there is no clear evidence that specialization and career progress are typical features of criminality, as they are of other forms of occupational endeavours.

Leaving aside its (debatable) occupational characteristics, we can view crime as operating in a marketplace in which illicit substances and services are traded to customers who know that they are illegal. We reject the notion that there is such a thing as ethnically based organized crime, and instead use the term enterprise crime to refer to this type of criminal activity. Enterprise crime occurs as a result of laws that prohibit certain goods and services. In other words, enterprise crime is made possible when the reach of law creates market opportunities. But more than requiring a definition of illegality, enterprise crime needs the presence of systematic corruption, partnership arrangements between illegal and legal businesses, and favourable market conditions such as a monopoly on the illegal goods.

When we conceptualize the problem of "organized crime" in terms of criminal enterprise rather than in terms of organized crime, it becomes apparent that law-enforcement responses to crime have serious limitations. If enterprise crime functions like other economic markets, removing criminal entrepreneurs (through arrest and imprisonment) will not significantly affect market operation, since it will not reduce the demand for illegal goods.

RESPONSES TO CRIME

10

SUMMARY AND REVIEW OF PUBLIC POLICY RESPONSES TO CRIME

T HE OBJECTIVES OF THIS chapter are (1) to summarize what we have learned in previous chapters about the nature, causes, and consequences of criminal events; and (2) to sketch some of the major policy responses available to us in responding to crime. These objectives are interrelated in that what we can do about criminal events should follow logically from a detailed understanding of their causes and content.

SUMMARY OF FINDINGS ON THE CRIMINAL EVENT

We began in Chapter 1 with a discussion of some important concepts that guide the study of criminal events. Most notably, we emphasized that there are no simple answers to the questions "What is crime?" and "How is crime to be studied?" It is too glib to say that crime is simply behaviour that violates the law. Such an answer obscures our view of the complex social realities that demand our attention. We emphasized a need to recognize that there is more to crime than the behaviour of a lawbreaker. As social events, crimes involve not only offenders, but other participants as well, including victims, the police, witnesses, and bystanders, all of whom act and react within particular social and physical circumstances.

In addition, to view crime simply as behaviour that violates the law is to take the law as a given. We saw that, while we may think about law as a codification of morality, the process of lawmaking is in essence a political process. Sociologists like Joel Best and Joseph Gusfield have located lawmaking in the context of the more general process of claimsmaking. Laws emerge in the political efforts to define social problems and craft their solutions.

Chapter 1 sketched a general picture of crime in Canada. We saw that the amount of crime has increased fourfold in Canada over the last 30 years, and that the majority of crime is directed against property rather than against people. Public views of crime, as articulated in the mass media and day-to-day conversations, influence our views of crime. Unfortunately, media images of crime tend to exaggerate the frequency of serious violent crime and to emphasize the sensationalist character of both crime and the solutions to crime.

Chapters 2, 3, and 4 described the major theoretical orientations that have dominated criminology for the last several decades. We defined criminological theories as generalized explanations of criminal phenomena. We look to theories to make sense out of our observations of the empirical world. Conversely, we look to the empirical world for confirmation, or refutation, of our theoretical views.

Theoretical interest in crime has generally meant theoretical interest in offenders. For this reason, we devoted two chapters to describing alternative conceptualizations of the offender. Chapter 2 focused on theories that derive from "positivist" views of the offender, while in Chapter 3 our attention shifted to explanations that find their origins in "classical" thought. The distinction between positivist and classical views, which we introduced in Chapter 1, has to do with the degree to which human will is thought to dominate social action. Broadly stated, positivist theories seek to understand the factors that cause offenders to do what they do, while classical theories emphasize the significance of rationality and choice in influencing the behaviour of the criminal offender.

Chapter 2 discussed many of the causal theories that have been offered to explain criminal behaviour. While some of these theories emphasize biological, constitutional, or genetic causes of criminal conduct, most emphasize the role of social factors. We examined two major types of social explanations. One of these considers the ways in which socially induced frustration can contribute to the development of criminal motivations. Robert Merton discerned in the gap between the things that people are encouraged by their culture to want and what is actually available to them a major source of frustration that may manifest itself in criminal conduct. Labelling theorists suggest that the societal reaction to minor or petty acts of nonconformity may result in stigmatization, which frustrates the labelled person and thereby contributes indirectly to more serious violations of the law.

Another major social explanation of motivation stresses the role of culture. Subcultural theories suggest that people learn the motivations to behave criminally in the same way that they learn motivations to do anything else. The emphasis here is on the immediate environment in which offenders operate, and on how these environments encourage or facilitate the learning of cultural lessons that support criminal behaviour. The foremost architect of this view was Edwin Sutherland, whose theory of differential association stressed an understanding of crime as a learned behaviour. While Sutherland and the subcultural theorists who followed him encourage us to think about the learning of crime through exposure to criminal cultures, theorists like David Matza and Gresham Sykes have encouraged us to appreciate how lessons that might motivate offending can be learned from mainstream culture.

In Chapter 3, we were concerned with offenders' decision-making processes rather than with their motivations. For theorists who adhere to the classical school, there is little to be gained from attempts to search for unique factors that motivate offending behaviour. Instead, they suggest that such behaviour is more appropriately understood in relation to the formal and informal social controls that might be expected to restrain offending behaviour. When these controls are ineffective, or when individuals are insensitive to them, potential offenders are free to become actual offenders. In such circumstances, people are free to act in ways that, criminal though they may be, also reflect rational self-interest. Social controls that discourage individuals from engaging in the criminal pursuit of self-interest include their social bonds to conformist others, their relationships with their communities, and the sanctions promised by the legal system.

The theoretical explanations discussed in Chapter 4 differ in a fundamental way from those reviewed in previous chapters. Specifically, they do not focus on the behaviour of offenders, but rather on the opportunities to which offenders have access and on the situations in which they find themselves. The position taken by these theories is that an individual who is ready, willing, and able to break the law will not necessarily do so. Other elements must come into play; and depending on how these elements come together, the offender may end up committing one type of crime rather than another.

Opportunity theories suggest that the ways in which people distribute their time and energies over time and across space either increase or decrease the number of opportunities to violate the law that are presented to them. Lifestyle/exposure theory argues that for individuals who pursue lifestyles that bring them into contact with people who have offender characteristics, or that put them in places where crimes frequently occur, the risks of becoming crime victims increase. Similarly, routine activities theory seeks to understand how crimes result when motivated offenders, suitable targets, and an absence of capable guardianship come together in time and space. Other theories reviewed in Chapter 4 focus on the ways in which the interactions between offenders and their victims influence criminal outcomes. Relatively simple theories that speak of "victim precipitation" have been replaced in recent years by theories about crime as a situated transaction that is the product not only of an offender's will or motivation but also of social interaction.

In Chapter 5, we brought together many of the theoretical and empirical issues raised in earlier chapters through an elaboration of the criminal event framework. Most fundamentally, we observed that criminal events are social events in that they involve interaction between human beings. The dynamics of this interaction shape the content of the event and thus the consequences of the event for those involved. We discussed the roles played by the principal protagonists in criminal events—offenders, victims, bystanders, and the police. In examining the social and demographic characteristics of victims and offenders, we were struck by the fact that, for many categories of crime, those who offend and those who are offended against have much in common (a finding contrary to what media reporting sometimes leads us to expect). Victims and offenders tend to be young, socially disadvantaged, and, for many categories of crime, males. There are, of course, important exceptions to this pattern. For obvious reasons, corporate crimes are not typically perpetrated by disadvantaged young males, and many forms of violence uniquely victimize women. We also discussed in this chapter the settings for criminal events, concluding that they do not occur with equal frequency in all types of communities or within communities, or at all types of locations.

Our analysis of criminal events in Chapter 5 led us to conclude that there is value to be derived from investigating these events in the context of particular social domains. Social domains can be defined as the major spheres of life in which we spend most of our time and energy. Three such domains were identified—the family and the household, recreation and leisure, and the workplace—and they provided the organizing themes for the substantive analysis of criminal events presented in Chapters 7, 8, and 9. We argued that a comprehensive examination of criminal events in these domains requires us to focus attention on three important components: precursors, the event, and its aftermath. This approach helps us to understand (1) how social arrangements affect the distribution and timing of criminal events; (2) why some groups in society are more likely than others to be involved in criminal events, whether as offenders or victims; (3) why particular types of criminal events have the content that they have; and (4) how victims and others are affected by these events.

Our analyses of criminal events were grounded in empirical data, the sources of which we investigated in Chapter 6. There we saw that the data on crime derive principally from two types of investigative strategies: observations and reports. Some researchers attempt to gather information about crime through their observations of crime in naturalistic settings and/or experimental and quasi-experimental settings. Most contemporary research, however, focuses on reports of crime made by police, victims, and offenders. While there is much debate about the innate superiority of one type of report over another, we suggest that each type must be appreciated in terms of its own particular strengths and weaknesses. Each type of report provides us with different perspectives on, and data about, criminal events. Their variable nature does not make these data unusable; however, we should be critical and judicious in employing them.

Our discussion of criminal events in specific social domains in Chapters 7 through 9 provided an application of the theoretical and research lessons that emerged from earlier chapters. In Chapter 7, we took up the issue of criminal events in the home. Two general categories of events were discussed. The first involved interpersonal violence in the context of familial relationships. As we saw, such violence emerges from and reflects the social organization of family life. The very factors that lead us to idealize family life—intimacy and privacy—increase the risks of danger to more vulnerable family members. The data clearly indicate that women and children suffer most from violence in the home.

The second major type of criminal event in the family and household domain is property crime. Break and enter and the theft of household goods are very common crimes in Canada, and they result in substantial financial loss. A large number of crimes against the household suggest that much of this crime is opportunistic in nature, involving as they do rational offenders who encounter opportunities for theft. Our discussion of family life and family organization revealed how routine activities create such opportunities.

In Chapter 8, we took up several issues relating to criminal events in the leisure domain. We saw that (particularly in the case of juveniles) leisure is frequently understood as a "cause" of crime. It has been argued that many leisure pursuits in which youth engage promote criminal conduct directly or indirectly. This argument has been made most passionately with respect to television violence, but it also encompasses most other leisure activities pursued by young people. We also saw how leisure pursuits among youth may free them from social controls while at the same time providing them with opportunities for offending. Finally, in Chapter 8, we investigated how particular leisure contexts—the street, bars and taverns, dating, and tourism—provide settings for criminal events.

A final social domain, the workplace, was discussed in Chapter 9. Here we saw that the nature and degree of people's involvement in the work domain has important implications for the kinds of criminal events in which they might find themselves. Two major issues emerged from our discussion of the work domain. The first concerned the relationship between involvement in the legitimate world of work and involvement in criminal events. We saw that particular kinds of work expose employees to particular kinds of victimization and offending risks. In the former case, jobs that involve handling money, travel between remote work sites, or regular exposure to high-risk populations increases the risks people face at work. Highly publicized homicides in the U.S. workplace have brought this issue into sharp relief. The jobs people have may also provide them with unique opportunities to break the law. For instance, corporate criminals have access to highly profitable offending opportunities and very frequently remain insulated from controls that are supposed to deter their behaviour.

The second major issue discussed in Chapter 9 has to do with crime as a form of work. Although we reviewed the shortcomings of attempts to think about crime in career terms, we also pointed out that some types of crime suggest very clear parallels with the world of legitimate work. Enterprise crime is one such example. Like their more legitimate counterparts, criminal entrepreneurs are sensitive to market conditions, endeavour to forge stable partnership arrangements, and attempt to manage their relationships with state agencies that try to control their activities.

Over the course of this book, we have developed an appreciation for the variety and the complexity of criminal events. The fact that these events occur in diverse social domains and involve different categories of actors does not mean that they are not amenable to criminological analysis. Throughout our analysis of criminal events, the same fundamental questions have kept recurring. Why do offenders and victims come together when they do, as they do, and where they do? Why does the event evolve as it does? What are the consequences of what transpired in the event for its participants? Instead of seeking highly specific answers to these questions, we have attempted to link specific concerns to theoretical ones. Moreover, we have been attentive to the pictures of criminal events that are revealed to us by the major criminological data sources. We conclude with a brief consideration of how the criminological understanding of these events helps us to make sense of public attempts to deal with the problem of crime.

RESPONDING TO CRIME

INTRODUCTION

291

*Summary
and Review
of Public
Policy
Responses to
Crime*

Criminal events occur because offenders encounter opportunities to violate the law. Controlling the occurrence of these events might involve attempts to discourage potential offenders. Depending on our theoretical model, we may wish to remove the factors that we believe motivate offending, or we may wish to make crime appear less rewarding to those who regard it as a rational course of action. With respect to the latter strategy, we have commented repeatedly on the role of legal deterrence.

Rather than attempt to prevent criminal events by controlling offenders, we might try instead to empower victims in ways that make them less resistant to victimization. One way of achieving this would be to develop policies that allow potential victims greater access to law, or that teach them about measures, they can take to make themselves less vulnerable to crime. Similarly, we might try to reduce the numbers of criminal opportunities available to offenders by manipulating the physical environments or social situations in which crimes occur.

These preliminary observations suggest several fronts along which any campaign against crime might be conducted. Too often, however, our thinking about crime is less imaginative than it might be. Fed by sensationalist media reporting and political rhetoric, we tend to think of the appropriate response to crime as what some call the "get tough" approach: hire more police, hand down longer sentences, and build more prisons.

In a similar vein, police forces respond to the rising dangers in their jobs with requests for greater firepower. The police in Winnetka, Illinois, have recently proposed the purchase of Uzi submachine guns to replace their aging

BOX 10.1 A PUNITIVE PUBLIC?

It is popularly believed that the Canadian public is very punitive in its reaction to crime. This belief may be used by politicians to justify repressive crime control policies or to justify political opposition to imaginative policies of social prevention.

However, it can be argued that the view of the Canadian public as excessively punitive is based on a narrow reading of public opinion data. Psychologist Edward Zamble (1990), for instance, suggests that when people are asked "global questions" about the criminal justice system, their answers would seem to suggest that they want a harsher system. For instance, if people are asked whether the criminal court is too lenient with offenders, a majority will say "yes," if "yes" and "no" are their only choices. However, Zamble maintains such questions simplify what are actually much more complex views. In other words, these questions require global answers in situations where respondents want to say "it depends."

Through a variety of studies, Zamble and his colleagues have shown that, when respondents are asked highly specific questions about highly specific cases, they judge these cases in pretty much the same way that the criminal justice system judges them.

In one study, for instance, research subjects were asked to assign penalties for hypothetical court cases. The study revealed that the subjects assigned penalties typical of those likely to be assigned by real courts. At the same time, 88 percent of respondents stated that court sentences were too lenient. Zamble suggests that this contradiction can be resolved by recognizing that "[w]hile the public disapproves of what they think the system does, if they were given the choices they would probably do just about what the system actually does."

While there is no doubt support in some quarters for the view that criminals should be locked up and the keys thrown away, it may be that the majority of the public is motivated less by punitiveness than by a desire to deal with crime in a pragmatic and humane manner.

shotguns. These machine guns, which can shoot through walls and fire up to ten rounds a second, are being demanded by a force that patrols a village of 13,000 residents (*The Globe and Mail*, 1989b: A3).

Concerns about police safety have risen in response to changes in the nature of street crimes involving drugs. In the aftermath of a sting operation that went awry, involving the wounding of a police officer, the special narcotics prosecutor in New York City commented, "The rules of engagement in the drug war have changed ... It's getting vicious out there (*The New York Times*, 1989: B2). He attributed this new attitude to the youth of the members of drug-dealing organizations. While experienced drug dealers tend to flee when confronted with a police officer, teenage gunmen seem to believe that they can escape prosecution by killing the officer. This attitude leaves the police more inclined to take strong precautions when dealing with gun-toting offenders, including the option of shooting first. "Deadly force" options probably deter, but they may also heighten feelings of desperation in those who see them as just another risk that goes along with criminal activity.

The use of deadly force raises concerns about breaches in a criminal justice system that ensures fair treatment for all. Still, there appears to be public support for a general get-tough response to crime. Are these responses justified or are they symptomatic of a traumatized society more afraid of the mythology of crime than its reality? This is a difficult question to answer, particularly for people who feel that they have high chances of victimization.

The introduction of mandatory charging and sentencing practices that remove discretion from the police and courts have been implemented in some jurisdictions in the belief that greater certainty of punishment will create greater deterrence. In addition, there has been a determined effort in some American states to implement the death sentence as a severe penalty for capital crimes. The severity of the sentence has not been complemented by swiftness of imposition as the queue on death rows gets longer (in some cases, inmates have waited up to 10 years for a still-to-be-applied punishment).

Some observers have argued that get-tough responses to the problem of crime are inherently limited (European and North American Conference on Urban Safety and Crime Prevention, 1989; Standing Committee on Justice and the Solicitor General, 1993). As they see it, the problem is twofold. First, there seems to be little convincing evidence that we effectively control crime when we simply invest more resources in criminal justice (Graham, 1990). Second, when we view the criminal justice system as the principal social mechanism for responding to crime, we approach the problem in a reactive rather than a proactive manner and thus never really address the "underlying factors associated with crime and criminality" (Standing Committee on Justice and the Solicitor General, 1993: 1).

As with other social problems, it is perhaps more sensible to think about strategies of prevention. We can define crime prevention as "the anticipation, recognition and appraisal of a crime risk and the initiation of some action to reduce or remove it" (National Crime Prevention Institute, 1986: 2). Clearly, the criminal justice system is itself part of an overall crime-prevention strategy in that (1) the threat of legal penalty is meant to deter potential offenders and (2) prison terms, in their capacity to either punish or rehabilitate, are intended to prevent re-offending.

Get-tough approaches to crime tend to involve options that are specifically associated with the criminal justice system. As used by criminologists, the term crime prevention is more broadly based, referring to strategies or tactics that, while they might involve the police (or other criminal justice functionaries), are rooted in the physical and social character of the local community (Lab, 1992; Loree and Walker, 1991; van Dijk and de Waard, 1991). From this perspective, crime prevention involves a range of strategies, including the installation of lights on city streets; the initiation of citizen police patrols; developing Block Watch programs; setting up public information campaigns; locking doors; carrying weapons or alarms; and introducing programs aimed at reducing unemployment or poverty.

PUBLIC HEALTH AND PUBLIC SAFETY

Public policy in the area of health care suggests interesting parallels to the issue of crime prevention. One way society can deal with medical problems is to wait until people get sick and then make health-care services available to them. This is in some ways analogous to the manner in which we think about crime. We can wait until people commit crimes and then take action by using criminal justice resources to catch, confine, or treat them. The use of the word "rehabilitation" in reference to prison programs suggests a quite literal application of the medical model to our thinking about crime and punishment.

In the area of public health, however, it has become evident to most policy planners that it makes sense to use limited resources in a preventive rather than a reactive manner. If we can prevent illness, we won't need to treat it after the fact. It is for this reason that we are advised to get regular medical checkups, exercise, and watch our cholesterol. We might view the problem of crime in a similar way. It is more sensible to take action *before* crimes occur than to take action after harm has been done.

Borrowing from the language of public health, we can think of crime prevention as having primary, secondary, and tertiary dimensions (Brantingham and Faust, 1976; Lab, 1992; van Dijk and de Warrd, 1991).

BOX 10.2 THE CRIME-PREVENTION ARMCHAIR VARIABLES

Sociologist Marcus Felson (1992) has proposed four "armchair variables" that help us to summarize much of what we do, or could do, in the area of crime prevention. He presents these variables as dichotomies, although he indicates that they are better understood as continuous dimensions:

1. *Strategy vs. tactics.* These are military terms that describe the nature of our organizational efforts. A strategy is an overall plan to deal with a problem, while a tactic is a more detailed procedure for carrying out the strategy. Crime-prevention tactics may work at cross-purposes if we lack an overall strategy; and a crime-prevention strategy may fail if our tactics are not part of a strategic plan.

2. *Simple vs. complex.* Strategies or tactics may be simple or complex. Felson advises us that "making automobiles more difficult to steal" is a simple strategy but one that may involve many complex tactics, such as the use of anti-theft computers or policing strategies.

3. *Small area vs. large area.* Some crime-prevention efforts may target a single building or a single neighbourhood. Others may address crime on a city-wide or national basis.

4. *Narrow vs. broad.* Some types of programs might be directed toward a very narrow range of crimes or a single type of crime (e.g., shoplifting), while others (e.g., social development approaches) might be intended to prevent a wide variety of crimes.

295

*Summary
and Review
of Public
Policy
Responses to
Crime*

Primary prevention includes programs aimed at either the entire community or the population at risk. Exemplifying primary prevention are mass-media crime-prevention programs that teach risk-reducing skills to the large audiences (Sacco and Silverman, 1982). Pamphlets, brochures, and posters providing information on family violence are examples of public education (mass media) programming. Secondary prevention refers to programs aimed at those segments of the population that are at particularly high risk (or, in public health language, that show early symptoms of the problem). Examples of secondary prevention include targeting high-crime areas for special treatment (e.g., neighbourhood redevelopment or Neighbourhood Watch programs) and installing security equipment in schools that have experienced problems with intruders.

Finally, tertiary prevention refers to strategies that are intended to prevent the recurrence of crime. Tertiary prevention would include victim–offender mediation, training courses for drunk drivers, treatment programs for wife assaulters, and various forms of diversion and community service.

There have been efforts in the United States to focus on violent crime as one would other forms of disease (Meredith, 1984). James Mason, the head of the Atlanta-based Centres for Disease Control (CDC)—which studies violent crime as a form of life-threatening disease—has stated that public health measures have been successful in treating poverty-related problems (e.g., venereal disease, lead poisoning, and tuberculosis) *in the absence of* attempts to alleviate the social ills associated with them. The campaign against smoking has been particularly successful. Warnings about health hazards, the politization of nonsmokers, demands for nonsmoking areas, and public interest in fitness are all factors that have forced smokers to reconsider their habits (Meredith, 1984: 48).

According to Mason we can do something about violence without first having to come up with solutions to poverty (Meredith, 1984: 45). Among his recommendations for reducing violence are developing programs that teach people how to handle conflict and restricting the availability of handguns.

The gun-control debate is highly contentious. It ranges from the facile observation that "guns don't kill people, people kill people" to evidence that gun-control laws appear to have little effect on the amount of homicide by firearms that we see in Canada (Mundt, 1990; Silverman and Kennedy, 1992) and in the United States (Kleck and Patterson, 1989). Nonetheless, controlling guns is viewed by the CDC as a major factor in the successful eradication of violence in the United States.

Guns are the most popular means of committing homicide in both Canada (Silverman and Kennedy, 1992) and the United States (Meredith, 1984). The issue of gun control is complicated by those who argue that they have a right to use guns for sporting purposes. Despite such protests, guns provide a symbolic as well as real threat to the well-being of societies that are racked by crime. As Silverman and Kennedy (1993) point out, the debate about gun control in Canada intensified in the aftermath of Marc Lepine's murder of fourteen women at the Université de Montréal's École Polytechnique in December 1989. Lepine used a semi-automatic weapon to shoot the women and then turned it on himself. This criminal event generated a storm of public sentiment in favour of restrictions on the availability of multi-shot or assault weapons. Bill C17, which was passed in 1992, allows for the ownership of these guns, but puts strong emphasis on their control. Of particular note is the requirement that the guns be securely stored; there are strong penalties for noncompliance (Silverman and Kennedy, 1993: 245).

A public health approach to reducing violence would emphasize educating members of society about the dangers associated with the improper use of firearms.

Despite the valuable insights of the public health model, its application to crime prevention is problematic (Graham, 1990). First, the model is so wide-ranging that it is unclear where we should draw the boundaries between what is and what is not a crime-prevention practice. Second, the distinctions between primary, secondary, and tertiary prevention are frequently less clear in practice than they are in theory. Third, the attempt to classify crime-prevention practices in this way assumes that our understanding of what causes crime (and, therefore, of how it can be prevented) is more scientifically precise than it really is. Harries (1990) further cautions that public health as an institution has, at the present time, neither the extra resources nor the personnel needed to make a lasting impression on the problem of crime incidence.

In the remainder of this section and in the two sections that follow, we examine three major approaches to crime prevention that extend well beyond traditional get-tough approaches. Each picks up an important theme in the study of criminal events. *Opportunity reduction* focuses on how social and environmental factors might be brought to bear on the reduction of crime opportunities. *Social development* approaches attempt to create social conditions that discourage long-term serious offending and empower potential victims while at the same time contributing to the rebuilding of communities. Finally, *community-based policing* (or, more narrowly defined, problem-oriented policing) considers ways in which the policing role may be expanded beyond the narrow reactive role that brings the police into criminal events when such events are either already underway or finished.

As we have seen, the event conceptualization of crime stresses the importance of opportunity in elucidating where and when crimes occur. It is only when people who are ready, willing, and able to offend encounter conditions favourable to offending that criminal events are likely to develop. From a policy standpoint, it follows that actions that control the appearance or accessibility of opportunities to engage in crime may help to prevent much crime. The important implication of this approach is that we can manage the risks of crime without changing the character of offenders. Because the emphasis in opportunity reduction is on the modification of the situations in which crimes occur, crime prevention through opportunity reduction is sometimes referred to as *situational crime prevention*.

297

*Summary
and Review
of Public
Policy
Responses to
Crime*

BOX 10.3 CASE STUDIES IN SITUATIONAL PREVENTION

Patricia L. Brantingham and Paul J. Brantingham are two Canadian criminologists who are known as international experts in the area of situational crime prevention. Their research (1990) provides the following examples, which clearly illustrate the logic and the value of the approach.

Site/Situation-Specific Examples

Example 1: In a large suburban municipality, there was a brewer's warehouse that experienced repeated problems with people breaking into their delivery vans at night. The vans were empty, but backed up to the loading bay doors and locked up overnight as if they contained merchandise. Offenders, apparently in search of beer, repeatedly cut through a fence on the perimeter of the warehouse lot and broke into the vans. No beer was stolen, since the vans were empty, but there were continuous repair costs to fix the damaged fence and delivery vans. The crime prevention officer convinced the warehouse manager to keep the delivery vans away from the loading bay doors (which were themselves very secure) and unlocked overnight. The vans were opened at night on a few subsequent occasions, but they were not damaged as before.

Example 2: At a convenience store, there was a less serious, but more common problem. A high school was located opposite a church. On the street behind the church there was a convenience store. As might be expected, students from the high school walked through the church parking lot to get to and from the convenience store. Lots of litter was left in the church parking lot, producing calls for police service and complaints. Church members were upset by the mess, but unable to stop either the trespassing teenagers or their littering.

The crime prevention officer found an effective, low cost solution. He convinced the church to dig a ditch across the front of its property (except for an entrance way) and arranged a direct pathway from school to convenience store to be built along one edge of the church property. The new pathway had a tall cedar fence (2.5 metres) on one side to separate it from adjacent houses and a chain link fence to enhance its appearance. The littering on the church grounds stopped and, perhaps surprisingly, the student pathway stayed clear of litter and graffiti. General research on littering and graffiti finds that keeping the area "clean" is a deterrent to further problems.

Example 3: There is a international example of something that has happened in video stores. To eliminate shoplifting, video stores are switching how they display the videos they have for rental. Early on, they tended to place the actual VHS or Beta rental cassettes out on the shelves. People selected a cassette and carried it to a central desk for rental. This is similar to the situation found in many smaller lending libraries. It has the virtue of reducing staff time spent on telling customers whether particular videos are still available for rental: if they are on the shelves they are available; if they are not on the shelves, they are not available.

The situation has now largely changed: most stores display the small empty boxes that the videos originally came in, or they display small plastic display cards with advertising material. The customer must go to a central desk to determine whether a particular video is available and, if so, rent it before actually taking possession of the cassette. This is similar to the controlled stacks situation found in major research libraries: it occupies more staff time, but cuts casual user pilferage.

Situational prevention is based on two important assumptions, the first being that crimes are most effectively prevented when we are attentive to their particular characteristics (Brantingham and Brantingham, 1990). Thus, the first step in opportunity reduction is careful crime analysis. We need to ask who commits these crimes? When are they committed? Where do they most frequently occur? What do offenders hope to achieve by committing crimes? How might certain characteristics of the physical environment contribute to these events? Are there natural forces of guardianship that might be activated in the situations in which crimes typically occur? The answers to such questions help crime-prevention planners tailor specific solutions to specific crime problems.

The second key assumption relates to the nature of the offender. Opportunity-reduction approaches reflect the model of the rational offender (Cornish and Clarke, 1986). In other words, an offender's decisions are based on his or her assessment of the various costs and benefits associated with a particular course of action. How easily can a crime be committed? Is anyone who might take action to prevent the crime standing guard? Are there less risky ways of obtaining the rewards that the commission of the crime promises? Offenders will seek answers to such questions and behave in ways that reflect their best interests. If the opportunities conducive to crime can be made less attractive or less plentiful, many types of crimes (particularly those that are largely opportunistic in nature) may occur much less frequently. According to Clarke (1992), situational prevention involves increasing the risks and decreasing the rewards associated with crime. As offending situations become more difficult, riskier, and less rewarding, rational offenders will be discouraged from offending.

One obvious way in which people increase the difficulties associated with crime is through target hardening; which refers to those measures that decrease the vulnerability of personal or household property. Entry into a house with locked doors and windows is more difficult than entry into a house in which such measures have not been taken. Various forms of access control, such as locked gates and entry phones, also increase the degree of effort needed to commit certain crimes.

The risks involved in the commission of crime may be increased by measures that make it more likely (or, at least, make it *appear* more likely) that the offender will be discovered and apprehended. A high level of surveillance by security guards, citizen patrols, and security cameras is clearly intended to serve this purpose. Perhaps less obvious is the role played by other types of crime prevention measures, such as locks. As Felson (1992) argues,

> *The strategic role of a lock is not to prevent entry! Rather, its strategic role is to force the offender to make a lot of noise, in hope that others will hear that noise. Ideally, the potential offender will take a look at the lock, note the noise it will force him to make, fear the consequences of that noise, and decide against committing the crime (32).*

The role of prevention goes beyond the introduction of defensible space. According to Merry (1981), a neighbourhood may be architecturally designed to discourage crime but still not be adequately defended, because it has little or no social cohesion. Krupat and Kubzansky (1987) note that "[e]ven when buildings are low and the entrances and public spaces focus around a small set of families, people will not react to crime when they believe that they are on someone else's turf, when they do not consider the police effective or when they fear retribution" (61).

Among the most popular measures intended to activate natural surveillance at the local neighbourhood level are Block Watch or Neighbourhood Watch programs that are sponsored by the local police. These programs are supposed to encourage neighbourhood residents to "share information about local crime problems, exchange crime prevention tips, and make plans for engaging in surveillance ("watching") of the neighbourhood and crime-reporting activities" (Rosenbaum, 1987: 104). Surveillance programs increase interaction among neighbours at the same time as they remove opportunities for crime.

In the United States, the Bureau of Justice Statistics reported in 1986 that about one family in five lives in a neighbourhood with a surveillance program, and that, in those areas, 38 percent of residents participate (Garofalo and McLeod, 1988). In Canada, the available data indicate that, while awareness of these programs is high, actual levels of participation are somewhat lower. The Canadian Urban Victimization Survey found that, in the seven cities surveyed in 1981, 42 percent of the respondents had heard of Neighbourhood Watch, but only 15 percent had participated (Solicitor General of Canada, 1984b).

BOX 10.4 VICTIMIZATION PREVENTION ADVICE

Much crime-prevention literature encourages people to reduce their vulnerability to crime by adopting behaviours that make them harder targets. Women, in particular, have been given much advice—in booklets, brochures, and pamphlets—about what they can do to make themselves safer.

Walter DeKeseredy, Hyman Burshtyn, and Charles Gordon (1992), sociologists at Carleton University, provide examples from a government booklet published in 1990:

- Never remain alone in an apartment, laundry room, mailroom, or parking garage.

- Do not put your first name on your mailbox or in the telephone book.

- Do not overburden yourself with packages and a bulky purse.

- Try to avoid isolated bus stops.

- If you babysit, be escorted home after dark.

Such advice has a familiar ring and may even be considered by many to be common sense. But is publishing it good crime-prevention policy? DeKeseredy et al., as well as others (Stanko, 1990a), find this information troubling for several reasons.

First, it focuses women's attention on "stranger danger," despite the fact that women face greater risks from men who are familiar to them. These tips will do little to protect a wife from an abusive husband or a teenager from an assaultive boyfriend. In fact, their effect may be to encourage women to be even more dependent on male protectors from whom they may have more to fear.

Second, it implicitly adopts a "victim blaming" position by telling women that their safety is their own problem; if they become victims, it is because they failed to take appropriate precautions.

Third, long lists of safety tips deny women's experiences. Many women already organize their lives around safety issues. When and where they go, and what kinds of activities they do and do not engage in, are decisions that reflect their awareness of their vulnerability to danger. Such lists tell women that no matter how much they do, they are not doing enough.

Fourth, crime-prevention tips tend to aggravate women's fear of victimization without doing anything that actually makes them any safer.

Feminist writer Elizabeth Stanko suggests that, rather than communicate to women what they have to do to make themselves safer, it makes more sense to discourage men from engaging in behaviour that makes women feel unsafe.

In contrast to the target-hardening advice issued to women, a pamphlet issued by the British Home Office (1989) tells men, for example:

- If you are walking in the same direction as a woman on her own, don't walk behind her. This may worry her. Cross the road and walk on the other side. This may reassure her that you are not following her.

- Don't sit too close to a woman on her own in a railway carriage.

- Remember that a woman on her own may feel threatened by what you think are admiring looks.

While opportunity for crime can be thwarted by the self-help actions of potential victims, individuals who take the law into their own hands may do so in a manner that constitutes vigilantism (Rosenbaum and Sederberg, 1976). Black (1983) describes self-help crime as a potent and frequently used form of punishment and deterrence. The equation of guns with independence and security is evident in the sales pitch for LadySmith, a handgun designed to meet the "physical requirements of women" (*The Globe and Mail*, 1989a: A3). The potential victim is provided the means with which to enact summary justice on her assailant. A National Rifle Association ad that appeared in *USA Today* in 1987, attempted to justify the arming of women by arguing that only 3 percent of rape attempts are completed against victims carrying weapons.

Self-help deterrence can become outright retribution. Bernard Goetz ("the subway vigilante") admitted to having purposely carried a gun when riding on the New York subways in search of trouble. He found trouble when a number of youths carrying screwdrivers, approached him and demanded money. Goetz shot at them, hitting one youth in the back as he was running away. Initially proclaimed a hero for standing up to his "assailants," Goetz's image was badly tarnished by his admission that he had been seeking revenge for an earlier mugging. What had first appeared as a defensive strategy was in fact an offensive act. Goetz had tried to assume the role of police officer, the difference being that the police are normally constrained by professional codes of conduct and due process of the law.

Finally, crime may be made less attractive by reducing the rewards associated with the offence. The requirement that bus riders must use exact change to purchase a fare decreases the amount of money that must be handled by any particular bus driver, and makes the robbery of drivers a less attractive proposition. Similarly, markings that identify the ownership of property may discourage the conspicuous use of stolen merchandise and seriously hurt the chances for resale. As we saw in Chapter 4, reducing the amount of money available in 7-Elevens at any given time is another way in which the rewards for criminality can be curtailed.

There can be little question that opportunity reduction has proven effective in a variety of specific settings. However, this approach is not without its critics. Some have suggested that removing opportunity is more likely to displace crime than to prevent it (Gabor, 1990b). In other words, if we make it difficult for a motivated offender to offend in one situation, he or she might simply find another situation more conducive to offending. If one store takes precautions to prevent theft, can we really be sure that the would-be thief will not simply seek out targets where such precautions are not taken? The evidence suggests that displacement may be a problem with particular types of crime and particular types of offenders. However, it is also the case that many forms of opportunity reduction do in fact prevent crimes rather than just displace them (Brantingham and Brantingham, 1990).

More specific forms of opportunity reduction invite more specific criticisms. Various target-hardening methods, such as installing locks on doors and bars on windows, may be faulted for encouraging a "fortress mentality" that enhances the fear of crime in society (Graham, 1990). Some critics see the use of electronic surveillance as part of a gradual shift toward a "surveillance society" (Clarke, 1992). Critics of Neighbourhood Watch programs argue that, despite the highly favourable publicity they receive and the high regard in which they are held by police and politicians, there seems to be little evidence to suggest that they accomplish what they are supposed to accomplish. According to Rosenbaum (1987),

> *... there is some evidence to suggest (a) if given the opportunity to participate, residents in the majority of high-crime neighbourhoods would not participate, and (b) when citizens do participate, the social interaction that occurs at meetings may lead to increases (rather than decreases) in fear of crime, racial prejudice and other crime-related perceptions or feelings. More important, there is little evidence that these block/neighbourhood meetings cause local residents to engage in neighbourhood surveillance, social interaction, and bystander intervention—behaviours that are posited as the central mechanism for strengthening informal social controls and reducing opportunities for crime (127).*

Perhaps the most frequent and general criticism of opportunity-reduction approaches is that, by placing so much emphasis on reducing opportunities for crime, they ignore the underlying causes of crime (Waller and Weiler, 1984). It has been argued that, because these strategies do not address the root causes of crime, the best they can hope to achieve is short-term solutions. If we wish to consider these root causes, we must turn to another major approach—crime prevention through social development.

Box 10.5 WHO IS THE CRIME-PREVENTION ACTIVIST?

What kinds of individuals take the initiative to organize crime-prevention efforts in their communities? In attempting to answer this question, researcher Stanley Shernock (1986) compared a sample of Neighbourhood Watch leaders with a sample of nonparticipants from the same nonurban area of the United States.

He found that, compared to nonactivists, crime-prevention activists tended to be older, married, and of higher socioeconomic status. No significant differences existed with respect to gender composition or employment status of the two groups. In addition, crime-prevention activists were found to have a larger number of memberships in other voluntary associations.

Activists were no more likely than nonactivists to report having been victimized; nor were they more likely to report having witnessed a crime. Crime-prevention activism was also unrelated to feelings of personal safety. Activists were more likely than nonactivists to perceive the crime rate as increasing, but they were also more inclined to view their own neighbourhoods as less dangerous than the surrounding ones.

Based on this analysis, the author concluded that these crime-prevention activists viewed crime as more of a potential threat than as a present reality. As such, they did not see their activities as directed toward the control of crime that actually occurs, but rather toward the deterrence of crimes that could occur and toward the preservation of neighbourhood stability.

CRIME PREVENTION THROUGH SOCIAL DEVELOPMENT

Crime prevention through social development does not take as its point of departure the criminal act (Gabor, 1990a). Instead, it focuses attention on the serious, repeat offender. As we saw in previous chapters, research suggests that a relatively small number of offenders are responsible for a disproportionately large number of crimes. These offenders begin their criminal careers early in life and end them (if at all) late in life. Over the course of their offending careers, they commit a wide variety of predatory offences. The research also indicates that these individuals tend to come from disadvantaged backgrounds, that they abuse alcohol and other drugs, and that they have experienced serious family problems as well as school- and employment-related problems.

A range of social problems, from family victimization to poverty, and racism, can provide a fertile breeding ground for crime. As we have seen, offenders and victims generally come from the same social and demographic groups. The building of communities is seen by advocates of the social development approach to provide a comprehensive strategy that reduces crime by discouraging potential offenders while at the same time strengthening

BOX 10.6 THE CRIME PREVENTION THROUGH SOCIAL DEVELOPMENT AGENDA

The scope of the social development agenda is illustrated by the following list of recommendations developed by the Canadian Criminal Justice Association (1989).

What Needs to Be Done in Canada?

A. Parents and Families

We recommend that:

1. Governments initiate a comprehensive review of the impact of policies and programs on disadvantaged families, and on their opportunities to escape lives of dependency on the state.

2. Programs be established to help disadvantaged families obtain enriched child care, while encouraging them to take employment training programs that would enhance their self-esteem and improve their opportunities for rising above the poverty line.

3. Family support and crisis intervention services be readily available and expanded to areas where they do not exist.

4. Positive parenting programs be developed, including respite care, parenting information services, toy resource centres, and preventive programs aimed at recognizing and assisting parents at risk of abusing or neglecting their children.

5. High-quality early childhood education programs be established.

6. Increased efforts be made to prevent unwanted pregnancies, particularly among teenagers, through more sex education and provision of family planning in schools, health clinics, and appropriately accessible settings.

7. Special efforts be made by all television networks to provide positive programming for children, particularly targeted to those who are disadvantaged.

B. Schools

We recommend that:

1. Priority be given to the early identification of children likely to have behavioural problems, and to the remedy of these problems through the coordinated work of parents, social services, housing, health, and school officials.

2. Remedial support programs directed to socially and economically disadvantaged children and youth continue to be developed.

3. Curricula be developed which focus on life skills, including parenting, sexual behaviour and other areas of social development, and be implemented for all children.

4. Programs to prevent crime which focus on peer pressure and personal commitment—such as Students Against Drunk Driving—be developed and encouraged.

5. Schools take the initiative in increasing children's chances of successfully finishing school by promoting parent involvement in both home learning and school.

C. Social Housing and Neighbourhoods

We recommend that:

1. Social housing programs continue to emphasize increased integration of public and non-public housing, thereby diminishing the high concentration of disadvantaged young persons in one area.
2. The community and social development of neighbourhoods, including social housing, involve the close participation of all residents, particularly in programs for local environmental improvement, the planning, staffing and development of public services, and local job-creation programs.
3. More challenging and relevant recreational programs be created for disadvantaged young persons, particularly those at high risk of committing crime.
4. Social housing organizations assist in the empowerment of tenants by involving them in the affairs of each housing project through tenants' associations and meetings, and by providing them with full knowledge about how to seek out the services of social agencies.
5. Community agencies give priority to people in social housing by bridging the geographical gap between social housing projects and the agencies, and by acknowledging the mixture of multiple problems faced by social housing tenants.

D. Employment

We recommend that:

1. Through the cooperation of government and the private and voluntary sectors, secondary-school drop-outs be provided with opportunities to acquire the skills necessary to obtain and retain gainful employment.
2. Employment preparation programs available to disadvantaged youth be continued and enhanced.
3. Economic policies be developed to reduce long-term unemployment and to encourage fulfilling alternatives for those who are unemployed.
4. All employers from the private and public sectors put into place within their organizations employment entry programs for disadvantaged youth.

E. Substance Abuse, the Media, and Health

We recommend that:

1. Authorities promote research on and evaluate programs oriented toward children and youth to prevent substance abuse, particularly programs stressing personal commitment and peer pressure.
2. Authorities responsible for regulating mass media monitor the research on crime in the media to reduce the undesirable effects of programming on levels of violence.
3. Research be undertaken to determine the effect of health factors, such as diet, on influencing criminal behaviour.

potential victims. The aim of crime prevention through social development is to correct the criminogenic social conditions that are assumed to be the root causes of crime (Waller and Weiler, 1984). Oriented toward the achievement of long-range prevention, this approach seeks to eliminate the underclass from which serious, repeat offenders typically emerge (Gabor, 1989b; Standing Committee on Justice and the Solicitor General, 1993).

The notion that crime can be prevented by eliminating the social ills that breed crime (particularly teenage crime) is not new. There is a long history of social reformism that argues that we can best fight crime by fighting poverty, racism, unemployment, and other forms of social disadvantage (Graham, 1990; Rosenbaum, 1988). The social development approach differs from these older approaches in its more systematic efforts to identify and attack the root causes of crime (Gabor, 1989a).

Because predatory crime is part of a "tangle of pathologies" (Wilson, 1987), that characterizes the lives of the socially disadvantaged, it is necessary that our policy approaches to crime prevention extend beyond the criminal justice system into the areas of family, educational, housing, and health policy (Canadian Criminal Justice Association, 1989; Graham, 1990, Waller and Weiler, 1984). One important theme emphasizes "resource mobilization," which addresses crime issues in terms of whether or not the law helps people—especially the poor and powerless—protect themselves against victimization. Browne and Williams (1989), in reporting on research done in the United States, observe that the enactment of domestic violence legislation (which makes arrest of offenders more likely), coupled with high levels of resource mobilization (including the provision of shelters for battered women), tended to reduce the rate of female-perpetrated homicide. The more women feel empowered to deal with violence directed against them, the less likely it is that escalation to fatal violence will occur.

Browne and Williams admit that some issues remain unclear. They can not establish the degree of awareness that individuals have of the resources that are being made available. In addition, they have no way of measuring the accessibility that individual women have to the mandated resources. Further, it is not evident how many people actually use the resources that are available; nor it is not clear how effective these resources are in meeting individual needs (Browne and Williams, 1989: 91–92). What *is* clear from this research, however, is that where these resources are available, criminal victimization from fatal assaults are reduced. This finding provides a strong argument for the need to assess the extent to which society can provide alternatives to women that will enable them to avoid becoming victims.

Advocates of the social development approach see crime prevention not as the exclusive domain of any one social or governmental agency. Instead, they place considerable emphasis on the need to establish crime-prevention councils at both the federal and municipal levels. These councils are seen as bringing together those responsible for health, family, employment, and housing policy, as well as the police and those who represent voluntary agencies that are concerned with a broad range of social welfare issues. The idea behind such an arrangement is that by allowing the ownership of the crime problem to be shared, the development of more comprehensive solutions will be facilitated.

While the social development approach has proven more popular in some European countries than in North America, it is clearly gaining momentum in the United States and Canada (Waller, 1989; Waller and Weiler, 1984). Still, some advocates of opportunity reduction maintain that social development as a strategy is too unfocused in that it fails to recognize that crime is not a homogeneous event and that different crimes require different intervention strategies (Brantingham, 1989).

Other critics question whether we have the political will, or whether, in times of fiscal restraint, we are truly prepared to make the financial commitments that a comprehensive social development approach might entail. Hastings and Melcher (1990) point out that, in Canada, despite widespread public concern, crime has never been a major political issue, at either the municipal or the federal level. For this reason, it may not provide the rallying point around which social development programs could be organized. In order to be successfully marketed, these programs should probably be linked to broader social and economic issues that promise benefits to wide segments of the population, even those that are not concerned about crime. We might also ask if the linkages that social development writers draw between factors such as family upbringing, employment, and school experience are as obvious and as straightforward as they are sometimes made out to be. The list of causative factors to which the social development approach draws our attention is long and unwieldy, and as we have seen, there is honest debate among criminologists about the relative importance of these factors (Graham, 1990).

While for the purposes of presentation we have drawn a distinction between opportunity reduction and social development, there is not really an inherent conflict between these two approaches. In the same way that we have borrowed from different theories to explain the criminal event, we can borrow from these different perspectives to create an integrated approach to crime prevention. In fact, many policy-makers have advocated a combination of these strategies in what has come to be known as the "safer cities" approach to crime prevention (Canadian Criminal Justice Association, 1989; Standing Committee on Justice and the Solicitor General, 1993).

How will changes in the nature of our communities condition our ability to implement crime-prevention strategies in the future? Some general trends are apparent. For example, it is clear that the development of new information technologies is transforming the nature of social life, and in so doing is suggesting the possibility of new prevention opportunities. Cellular telephones allow people to intervene anonymously in a variety of situations that would not have been possible before. Computer terminals in patrol cars allow police to tap data bases that provide instant information about known offenders and unsafe locations.

Other trends that bring with them increases in the levels of guardianship and decreases in levels of victimization risk include the growth of remote work sites, which can reduce commuting time (Felson, 1987); the spread of computer technologies, which allow many people to spend part of the working day at home (Cray, 1988); the expansion of part-time work in the service economy (Lindsay, 1990); and the increasing popularity of video and other home-entertainment technologies (Young, 1990). All of these changes may indicate that the shift in routine activities away from the home may be undergoing a reversal. While the long-term impact of such changes on the community remains to be seen, they may allow in the future some forms of community prevention that were not viable in the past.

Felson (1987) provides an interesting example of how our prevention planning must be informed by careful social forecasting. He argues that metropolitan areas in North America are undergoing profound changes that involve the emergence of the "metroquilt" as the new dominant urban form. Within the context of the metroquilt, the city becomes

> *a patchwork of coterminous facilities intervening between homes, business and the larger society. The metroquilt would divide urban space among a large set of corporations, whose facilities managers would be responsible for organizing everyday movements, including security (Felson, 1987: 920).*

This patchwork is apparent in the landscape of any major Canadian or American city. Stores are replaced by malls, single-family dwellings by condominiums and apartment complexes, and businesses and factories by industrial parks. In the metroquilt, Felson maintains, we have a decreasing need to walk or to drive from one address to another and increasing need to drive from the parking lot of one facility to the parking lot of another facility.

In Felson's view, the growth of the metroquilt has far-reaching implications for crime prevention. As facilities develop, the distinction between public urban space and private space becomes increasingly blurred. As people spend increasing amounts of their time shopping in malls, working in office complexes, and visiting friends and relatives in apartments, corporations rather than governments assume greater responsibility for their safety. As a result, the facility could become the major organizational tool for crime prevention. Felson is optimistic about these developments because they seem to suggest the possibility that prevention can be rationalized and that security can be planned. He maintains that safety will become part of the marketing strategy because as facilities compete for customers and tenants there will be a strong incentive for private developers to make environments more crime free (see also Shearing and Stenning, 1983; Walsh and Donovan, 1989).

However, there is a more disturbing side to all of this. If the production of safety is increasingly the domain of the private developer, then safety becomes a commodity accessible only to those who can afford it. The patron of the upscale shopping centre, the resident of the luxurious condo, and people employed in gleaming corporate headquarters may find safety more accessible than those who spend most of their time in facilities where profit motives or government cost cutting mitigate against extensive crime-prevention planning. The risk that safety may become a commodity to be bought and sold, rather than a public good, suggests that issues other than technical effectiveness must inform prevention efforts. The prevention of crime must involve not only logistical matters but also matters of justice and equality. This concern is one that police are now facing as they attempt to adopt crime prevention as a primary focus of their activities.

COMMUNITY POLICING

Gottfredson and Hirschi (1990) argue that the natural limits of law enforcement are set by the spontaneous nature of crime: the offender sees that he or she can get something for nothing and seizes the opportunity. No increases in law enforcement, they suggest, can truly deter this type of behaviour. Research in Canada (Kennedy and Forde, 1992; Koenig, 1991) and elsewhere (Bayley, 1985; Jackson, 1989) has provided strong evidence that there is no relationship between the level of crime in a society and the number of police available to control this crime. (However, according to Liska, Lawrence, and Sanchirico [1982], there is a positive relationship between the level of fear and the number of police officers.) Gottfredson and Hirschi (1990), maintain that, in the overwhelming majority of robberies, burglaries, assaults, homicides, thefts, and drug deals, "the offender does not know or care about the probability of being observed by the police" (270). The primary role of the police, they suggest, is to respond to criminal activity and to maintain social control; they say there is no evidence that increasing police tactical resources has the effect of reducing crime rates.

Unfortunately, police resources have become scarcer, and it has become evident that what the police do primarily is respond to complaints (not crime), maintain visibility in neighbourhoods, and control traffic. In a study of police activity, Lawson (1982) discovered that the police spend only between 10 percent and 15 percent of their time engaged in actual law enforcement; the rest of their time is taken up with order maintenance.

BOX 10.7 COMMUNITY POLICING AND THE FEAR OF CRIME

A broad definition of crime prevention extends well beyond efforts to control crime levels. It may also include attempts to alleviate public worries or anxieties about the problem of crime. This is an important function since many observers have come to recognize the fear of crime—separate and distinct from crime itself—as a social problem that requires attention.

It has been argued that traditional methods of policing, which emphasize motorized patrols, rapid response, and crime investigation have done little to assuage public fears. Some criminologists argue that new styles of community policing may more effectively combat the problem of public fear (Moore and Trojanowicz, 1988; Muir, 1987). In particular, some research studies have shown that, in areas where police use foot patrols, residents exhibit lower levels of concern and worry.

Why should foot patrols and other forms of community policing have this effect? In general, such measures increase the level of contacts between police and residents. These contacts increase communication, which in turn increases trust and the two-way flow of information. As communication between the police and members of the local community improves, confidence in the police may be enhanced. The police may then be better able to deal with problems in a proactive rather than a reactive manner. Police and citizens may inform each other about community problems and solutions. Many of the conditions that give rise to fear may thus be eradicated.

The pressures of order maintenance and restricted resources have forced police agencies to begin to rethink their strategy of law enforcement. The police role has expanded partly as a result of the fact that the police belong to the only 24-hour social agency that is easy to reach and that will make house calls. The police emergency line (911) leaves police overwhelmed with calls that require them to serve not a law-enforcement function, but rather a regulatory or order-maintenance function. In addition, the police are being called upon to become more actively involved in crime prevention, partly as a response to the increased levels of unease that people feel in urban areas.

Given the assumption of routine activities theory that crime is made possible not only by the availability of offenders and victims but also by the absence of visible guardians (such as the police), it is hard to believe, that the police have *no* effect on deterring crime. But, as the research consistently indicates, a direct relationship between policing levels and crime does not exist. Hiring more police does not necessarily lower crime. Many factors intervene to affect this equation. In previous chapters, we examined the police role in defining criminal events. The criteria that the police use in determining whether or not to arrest a person are shaped by a number of factors, including the nature of the police organization and its strategies of policing, differing interpretations of criminal events and differing assessments of the characteristics and motivations of participants in these events, variations in the interpretations of the law, and the cooperation of the public. We will examine how each of these factors can influence the new community strategies (also referred to as problem-oriented policing and compliance-based policing) that are intended to assist the police in dealing with crime. But first we will consider the changes that have taken place in the ways in which the police have functioned over the years.

The original mandate of the police in the 19th century was order maintenance (Wilson, 1983). The order-maintenance or compliance role of the police was coterminous with "community relations." The police were to protect the community from disorderly behaviour—reducing conflict where they found it (Monkkonen, 1983). This role required them to act as "watchmen," keeping track of the comings and goings in the community and looking out for behaviour that might constitute a threat to public order. The compliance role is associated with the "proactive" policing we discussed in Chapter 1. As Klockars (1985: 106–107) has stated, the police are not law-enforcement agencies, but rather regulatory institutions—their job is not to enforce the laws but to regulate relationships between people.

The principal objective of compliance law enforcement is to secure conformity with the law by resorting to means that induce that conformity (Reiss, 1984). Compliance systems return to the original mandate of the police whereby one seeks to create law-abidingness, through preventive or remedial actions. Under these systems, the primary focus of policing shifts from detecting and penalizing violaters to providing incentives to individuals to comply with the law. Compliance-based policing also recognizes the need to include the public in controlling social disorder, beyond merely reporting crime to the police. The public is encouraged to include the police as intermediaries in situations of community conflict (Lawson, 1982).

In the United States, the public has demanded more social order since at least the 1850s (Monkkonen, 1983). In fact, in comparison to crime control, order control as practised by the police has had a long and successful record. As Monkkonen states, Victorian morality has triumphed in most of North America's city streets. We expect, and get, quiet and predictable behaviour from almost everyone. Vice is no longer highly visible. Yet the dramatic rise in crime rates in recent years, and the apparent ineffectiveness of the police in dealing with it and its consequences, have raised concerns again about social order. Monkkonen attributes the increases in crime rates to a number of factors, including urbanization and changes in demographic composition of the population. The effect of these increases early in this century was to narrow the focus of police agencies to crime control alone, leaving the problems of general order to other agencies.

The principal objective of crime control or deterrence law enforcement is to detect violations of the law, identify offenders responsible for violations, and penalize perpetrators. This is done to diminish the chance of future offences both by the offender (specific deterrence) and by others who may contemplate the same criminal act (general deterrence) (Reiss, 1984: 91). Until recently, contemporary policing has had as a stated objective the apprehension of offenders through arrest, which has led to the form of "reactive" policing that dominates the way that police services operate throughout North America (Reiss, 1984: 84).

Police have now begun to realize that crime control, by necessity, requires broadening their mandate once again to include order-maintenance or compliance law enforcement. However, this notion is being resisted by some in police agencies that still regard law enforcement as their principal mandate. The internal workings of police organizations are such that peacekeeping and order-maintenance functions are seen as residual matters. Real

313
*Summary
and Review
of Public
Policy
Responses to
Crime*

policing, some argue, involves arrest. The philosophy of community policing challenges this view, but the problem remains that many compliance-based actions are without legitimation in police organizations, in addition, no training is provided for compliance-based operations. As Mastrofski (1983: 34) notes, the crime-fighting and the noncrime public service functions coexist uneasily in the police profession. The former dominate training curricula, career incentives, and organization evaluations, while the latter dominate the workload.

Notwithstanding this trend, according to Murphy (1988: 178), community policing has replaced professional law-enforcement as the dominant ideology and organizational model of progressive policing in Canada. Bayley (1988: 226) identifies four major features of community-based policing: (1) community-based crime prevention; (2) proactive servicing, as opposed to emergency response; (3) public participation in the planning and supervision of police operations; and (4) the shifting of command responsibility to lower-level ranks. Accompanying these organizational and procedural changes is an emphasis on identifying and solving problems, which are defined not only in terms of breaches of law but also in terms of breaches of social order. Further, the solutions to these problems do not merely reside in the rules and regulations of the police service, they must also acknowledge the concerns and desires of the community in which the problems occur.

According to Goldstein (1990), what he calls problem-oriented policing will require at least five major adjustments in current thinking. First, there must be a recognition of the fact that, to do their job well, police officers must be encouraged to search for alternatives. This encouragement must be reflected in a consistent, agency-wide commitment to improving the quality of police service. Second, the police must not restrict their attention to those problems that have a potential for reducing crime. In some cases, crime is only the final consequence of unresolved noncrime-related problems.

Third, consistent with the acceptance that policing encompasses all of a community's problems, those that do not fit strict law-enforcement criteria must also be addressed. Fourth, there must be some effort to understand the

> **WHAT DOES IT MEAN?**
>
> *Community Policing*
>
> Bayley (1988) argues that community policing includes (1) community-based crime prevention; (2) proactive servicing, as opposed to emergency response; (3) public participation in the planning and supervision of police operations; and (4) the shifting of command responsibility to lower-level ranks.

nature of the problems that are encountered in any given area prior to setting out alternatives. Too often alternatives are prescribed that simply do not work because they are not suited to the area being policed. Like any other large organization, police have difficulty resisting internal pressures to follow established, but rigid, objectives and procedures. Fifth, police must be open to the idea of allowing other agencies to fulfil the job in conjunction with (or in place of) the police. According to Goldstein (1990), this strategy "is intended to dissuade the police from applying a generic response to a generic problem, or to applying a single response haphazardly to a wide range of different types of problems" (104).

Bayley (1988: 226) suggests that, if implemented correctly, community policing will constitute the most fundamental change in policing since the rise in police professionalism early in this century. However, while community policing appears to be gaining acceptance in police circles, there have been few attempts to understand how it actually works or to evaluate its overall performance (Kennedy, 1991). This means that the police may simply be doing the same thing as before but labelling it as something different; or they may be doing something different, but not as well as before.

In fact, community policing has had differing levels of success. At the heart of the concept is neighbourhood team policing, which involves the long-term assignment of officers to a particular area. This strategy allows officers to make a commitment to an area and to assume a broader level of authority in providing policing that is more sensitive to community needs. Neighbourhood team programs have not been embraced by police managers who see the decentralization that is associated with them as limiting their control over their officers (Scheingold, 1984: 134). In addition, aggressive patrol tactics used in crime control may diminish police rapport with the public, thereby undermining the effectiveness of community-based policing (Scheingold, 1984: 135). Finally, their fear of being seen as indecisive may cause many officers to play the role of order restorer rather than that of peacemaker (Palenski, 1984: 35).

Police must look to community members to support them in their efforts to bring about order in the community. This support can take the form of self-help, as discussed earlier, or it can involve a kind of coproduction, whereby the police use members of the community as supporters of police activity (Krahn and Kennedy, 1985). Coproduction can range from passive responses, such as locking doors, to more active responses such as participating in crime-prevention programs or working as an informant (Skolnick, 1966). As Black (1980) points out, since the typical criminal act occurs at an unpredictable time and place, the police must rely upon citizens (most often the victims of a crime) to involve them in the average case.

Providing resources for community policing (outside of community support) has proven to be problematic. Police budgets still depend on case loads of calls for service and crime rates. Community policing activity, directed as it is at problem-solving and referral to outside programs may create an impression of lower activity that would seem to call for lower budgets. The use of alternative programs brings the police into conflict with other agencies, which makes it more difficult for them to define their role in the community and obtain the resources they need to realize their objectives.

Further, it is very difficult for the police to remain apolitical when fighting for budget allocations and arguing for certain policing strategies. The lobbying by communities and by volunteers in community policing programs may make the police appear more politically active than local politicians would wish them to be, thereby making their requests for more funds even more tenuous. Police chiefs in Canada are thus confronted with a plethora of community constraints. These constraints need to be overcome before the chiefs can show that they are fulfilling the objectives of compliance-based policing. In her discussion of policing programs in Britain, Shaffer (1980) argues that improving police–community relations is a crucial first step. The members of a community must get to know the police as individuals who are concerned and sympathetic as well as controlling and disciplining. Without communication and cooperation between the police and the public, she concludes, "[p]olicing in a democratic society is impossible" (38).

SUMMARY AND CONCLUSIONS
■ ■ ■

One response to crime is to see it as a public health problem that is best addressed by removing some of the major instruments that bring about injury (e.g., guns). A second view advocates the mobilization of social institutions and resources as a means of empowering victims to defend themselves against criminal attack. Given the already formidable challenges that public health institutions face in dealing with diseases and injuries that originate from noncrime sources, it is unlikely that there will be much change (at least in the near future) in our heavy reliance on the police to confront the crime problem.

We may look at prevention from the point of view of opportunity reduction or social development. Prevention can include a number of factors, ranging from target hardening to increased surveillance. It can also set as a priority the targeting of violence and offer ways in which violence can be averted. Situational prevention is based on two important assumptions. The first assumption is that crime is most effectively prevented when we attend to the particular characteristics of each crime in question. The second assumption is that, in most cases, we are dealing with a rational offender, who calculates such things as risks, benefits, and ease of accomplishment before committing a crime. It follows from this that raising the costs associated with crimes (which are largely opportunistic in nature) may reduce the frequency with which they occur. Neighbourhood Watch and Block Watch programs assume that crime can be prevented by increasing surveillance and, by extension, the risk of detection and apprehension, as it is perceived by the potential offender.

In contrast to the other prevention strategies, crime prevention through social development is focused on the serious, repeat offender. A relatively small number of offenders might be responsible for a disproportionately large number of crimes. These individuals tend to have in common many social and demographic characteristics. The aim of crime prevention through social development is to correct the criminogenic social conditions that are assumed to be important causes of crime. The focus of the social development approach is on long-range outcomes that enhance social security and reduce crime incidence.

The police are also shifting their attention from crime fighting (i.e., deterrence-based policing) to compliance policing, which is more directly integrated into the community. The principal objective of compliance law enforcement is to secure conformity with law through systems that encourage community participation in defining and solving problems. The exclusive emphasis on the detection and punishment of violators has given way to a mixed approach providing incentives to individuals as a means of encouraging them to comply with the law.

Compliance-based policing recognizes the need to include the public in controlling social disorder, beyond merely reporting crime to the police. Bringing together a number of services within the community, as well as community members, can help to realize a many-pronged attack on crime involving re-education, mediation, opportunity removal, resource mobilization, targeting the roots of crime, and problem-solving. Our success in controlling crime and diminishing the incidence of criminal events depends on our ability to understand where crime comes from and on our commitment to expend resources in broadening our responses to it.

REFERENCES

Abadinsky, H. 1987. *Organized Crime*. 2nd ed. Chicago: Nelson-Hall.

Adams, O., and D. Nagnur. 1990. "Marrying and Divorcing: A Status Report for Canada." In C. McKie and K. Thompson (eds.), *Canadian Social Trends*. Toronto: Thompson Educational Publishing.

Adler, F. 1975. *Sisters in Crime*. New York: McGraw-Hill.

Agnew, R.S. 1990. "The Origins of Delinquent Events: An Examination of Offender Accounts." *Journal of Research in Crime and Delinquency* 27(3): 267–294.

———. 1985a. "A Revised Strain Theory of Delinquency." *Social Forces* 64(1): 151–167.

Agnew, R.S., and A.R. Peters. 1986. "The Techniques of Neutralization." *Criminal Justice and Behavior* 13: 81–97.

Agnew, R.S., and S. Huguley. 1989. "Adolescent Violence Toward Parents." *Journal of Marriage and the Family* 51: 699–711.

Agnew, R.S., and D.M. Peterson. 1989. "Leisure and Delinquency." *Social Problems* 36(4): 332–350.

Akers, R.L. 1985. *Deviant Behavior: A Social Learning Approach*. Belmont, Calif.: Wadsworth.

Albanese, J. 1989. *Organized Crime in America*. 2nd ed. Cincinnati, Ohio: Anderson.

Albini, J.L. 1971. *The American Mafia: Genesis of a Legend*. New York: Irvington.

Allan, E.A., and D.J. Steffensmeier. 1989. "Youth, Underemployment and Property Crime: Differential Effects of Job Availability and Job Quality on Juvenile and Young Adult Arrest Rates." *American Sociological Review* 54: 107–123.

Amir, M. 1971. *Patterns of Forcible Rape*. Chicago: University of Chicago Press.

Anderson, J., and L. Whitten. 1976. "Auto Maker Shuns Safer Gas Tank." *The Washington Post* (December 30), p. B7.

Arnold, B.L., and J. Hagan. 1992. "Careers of Misconduct: Prosecuted Professional Deviance Among Lawyers." *American Sociological Review* 57(6): 771–780.

Auty, S. 1992. *The Safe School Task Force: Resource Kit*. Toronto: The Safe School Task Force.

Bala, N. 1991. "The Young Offenders Act: A Legal Framework." In R.A. Silverman, J.J. Teevan, and V.F. Sacco. *Crime in Canadian Society*. 4th ed. Toronto: Butterworths.

Balkin, S. 1979. "Victimization Rates, Safety and Fear of Crime." Social Problems 26(3): 343–358.

Bandura, A.A., D. Ross, and S.A. Ross. 1963. "Imitation of Film-Mediated Aggressive Models." *Journal of Abnormal and Social Psychology* 66: 3–11.

Barnhorst, R., S. Barnhorst, and K.L. Clarke. 1992. *Criminal Law and the Canadian Criminal Code*. 2nd ed. Toronto: McGraw-Hill Ryerson.

Baron, S. 1989. "The Canadian West Coast Punk Subculture: A Field Study." *Canadian Journal of Sociology* 14(3): 289–316.

Bastian, L.D., and B.M. Taylor. 1991 (September). *School Crime: A National Crime Victimization Survey Report*. Washington, D.C.: U.S. Department of Justice.

Baunach, P.J. 1990. "State Prisons and Inmates: The Census and Survey." In D.L. Mackenzie, P.J. Baunach, and R.R. Roberg (eds.), *Measuring Crime: Large-Scale, Long-Range Efforts*. Albany: State University of New York.

Bayley, D.H. 1988. "Community Policing: A Report from the Devil's Advocate." In J.R. Greene, and D. Mastrofski (eds.), *Community Policing: Rhetoric or Reality*. N.Y.: Praeger.

———. 1986. "The Tactical Choices of Police Patrol Officers." *Journal of Criminal Justice* 14: 329–348.

————. 1985. *Patterns of Policing: A Comparative International Analysis.* New Brunswick, N.J.: Rutgers University Press.

Bechhofer, L., and A. Parrot. 1991. "What Is Acquaintance Rape?" In A. Parrot and L. Bechhofer (eds.), *Acquaintance Rape: The Hidden Crime.* New York: John Wiley.

Becker, H.S. 1963. *Outsiders: Studies in the Sociology of Deviance.* New York: Free Press.

Bell, D. 1953. "Crime as an American Way of Life." *The Antioch Review* 13(June): 131–154.

Bell, D.J. 1987. "The Victim-Offender Relationship: A Determinant Factor in Police Domestic Dispute Dispositions." *Marriage and Family Review* 12(1/2): 87–102.

Bennett, T. 1989. "Burglar's Choice of Targets." In D.J. Evans and D.T. Herbert (eds.), *The Geography of Crime.* London: Routledge.

Bennett, T., and R. Wright. 1984. *Burglars on Burglary.* Brookfield, Vt.: Gower.

Benson, D., C. Charlton, and F. Goodhart. 1992. "Acquaintance Rape on Campus: A Literature Review." *College Health* 40 (January): 157–165.

Benson, M.L. 1985. "Denying the Guilty Mind: Accounting for Involvement in a White-Collar Crime." *Criminology* 23(4): 583–607.

Benson, M.L., and E. Moore. 1992. "Are White Collar and Common Offenders the Same? An Empirical and Theoretical Critique of a Recently Proposed General Theory of Crime." *Journal of Research in Crime and Delinquency* 29(3): 251–272.

Bequai, A. 1987. *Technocrimes.* Lexington, Mass.: D.C. Heath.

Bernard, T.J. 1981. "The Distinction Between Conflict and Radical Criminology." *Journal of Criminal Law and Criminology* 72(1): 362-379.

Best, J. 1990. *Threatened Children.* Chicago: University of Chicago Press.

————. 1988. "Missing Children: Misleading Statistics." *The Public Interest* 92(Summer): 84–92.

Black, D.J. 1983. "Crime as Social Control." *American Sociological Review* 48 (February): 34–45.

————. 1980. *The Manners and Customs of the Police.* New York: Academic Press.

————. 1976. *The Behavior of Law.* New York: Academic Press.

————. 1971. "The Social Organization of Arrest." *Stanford Law Review* 23: 1087–1111.

————. 1970. "Production of Crime Rates." *American Sociological Review* 35: 733–747.

Black, D.J., and A.J. Reiss. 1967. "Patterns of Behavior in Police and Citizen Transactions." In *U.S. President's Commission on Law Enforcement and the Administration of Justice, Studies in Crime and Law Enforcement in Major Metropolitan Areas, Field Surveys III*, Vol. 2. Washington, D.C.: U.S. Government Printing Office.

Blau, J.R., and P.M. Blau. 1982. "The Cost of Inequality: Metropolitan Structure and Violent Crime." *American Sociological Review* 4 (February): 114–129.

Block, C.R., and R.L. Block. 1984. "Crime Definition, Crime Measurement, and Victim Surveys." *Journal of Social Issues* 40(1): 137–160.

Block, R. 1974. "Why Notify the Police?: The Victim's Decision to Notify the Police of an Assault." *Criminology* 11(4): 555–569.

Block, R., M. Felson, and C.R. Block. 1984. "Crime Victimization Rates for Incumbents of 246 Occupations." *Sociology and Social Research* 69(3): 442–451.

Blok, A. 1975. *The Mafia of a Sicilian Village, 1860–1960*. New York: Harper and Row.

Blumstein, A., J. Cohen, and D.P. Farrington. 1988a. "Criminal Career Research: Its Value for Criminology." *Criminology* 26(1): 1–36.

————. 1988b. "Longitudinal and Criminal Career Research: Further Clarifications." *Criminology* 26(1): 57–74.

Blumstein, A., J. Cohen, and R. Rosenfeld. 1992. "The UCR-NCS Relationship Revisited: A Reply to Menard." *Criminology* 30(1): 115–124.

Bockman, L.S. 1991. "Interest, Ideology and Claims-Making Activity." *Sociological Inquiry* 61(4): 452–470.

Bograd, M. 1988. "How Battered Women and Abusive Men Account for Domestic Violence: Excuses, Justifications or Explanations." In G.T. Hotaling, D. Finkelhor, J.T. Kirkpatrick, and M.A. Straus (eds.), *Coping with Family Violence*. Newbury Park, Calif.: Sage.

Booth, A., D.R. Johnson, and H.M. Choldin. 1977. "Correlates of City Crime Rates: Victimization Surveys Versus Official Statistics." *Social Problems* 25(2): 187–197.

Boritch, H. 1992. "Gender and Criminal Court Outcomes: An Historical Analysis." *Criminology* (August), 30(3): 293–325.

Borofsky, G.L., G.E. Stollak, and L.A. Messe. 1971. "Sex Differences in Bystander Reactions to Physical Assault." *Journal of Experimental Social Psychology* 7: 313–318.

Bottomley, A.K., and K. Coleman. 1981. *Understanding Crime Rates: Police and Public Roles in the Production of Official Statistics*. Farnborough, U.K.: Gower.

Bottomley, A.K., and K. Pease. 1986. *Crime and Punishment—Interpreting the Data*. Philadelphia: Open University Press.

Braithwaite, J. 1989. *Crime, Shame and Reintegration*. Cambridge: Cambridge University Press.

———. 1981. "The Myth of Social Class and Criminality Reconsidered." *American Sociological Review* 46 (February): 36–57.

Brannigan, A. 1987. "Is Obscenity Criminogenic?" *Society* 24: 259–284.

Brantingham, P.J. 1991. "Patterns in Canadian Crime." In M.A. Jackson and C.T. Griffiths (eds.), *Canadian Criminology*. Toronto: Harcourt Brace Jovanovich. 371–402.

Brantingham, P.J., and P.L Brantingham. 1984. *Patterns in Crime*. New York: Macmillan.

Brantingham, P.J., and F.L. Faust. 1976. "A Conceptual Model of Crime Prevention." *Crime and Delinquency* 22: 284–296.

Brantingham, P.L. 1989. "Crime Prevention: The North American Experience." In D.J. Evans and D.T. Herbert (eds.), *The Geography of Crime*. London: Routledge.

Brantingham, P.L., and P.J. Brantingham. 1990. "Situational Crime Prevention in Practice." *Canadian Journal of Criminology* 32(1) (January): 17–40.

Brillon, Y. 1985. "Public Opinion About the Penal System: A Cynical View of Criminal Justice." In D. Gibson and J.K. Baldwin (eds.), *Law in a Cynical Society?: Opinion and Law in the 1980s*. Calgary: Carswell.

Brinkerhoff, M.B., and E. Lupri. 1988. "Interspousal Violence." *Canadian Journal of Sociology* 13(4): 407–434.

British Home Office. 1989. *Crime: Together We'll Crack It*. London: The Home Office.

Browne, A., and K Williams. 1989. "Exploring the Effect of Resource Availability and the Likelihood of Female-Perpetrated Homicides." *Law and Society Review*, 23(1): 75–94.

Brunvand, H.J. 1993. *The Baby Train*. New York: W.W. Norton.

———. 1989. *Curses! Broiled Again!* New York: W.W. Norton.

———. 1986. *The Mexican Pet.* New York: W.W. Norton.

———. 1984. *The Choking Doberman and Other "New" Urban Legends.* New York: W.W. Norton.

———. 1981. *The Vanishing Hitchhiker: American Urban Legends and Their Meaning.* New York: W.W. Norton.

Burgess, A.W., L.L. Holmstrom, and M.P. McCausland. 1977. "Child Sexual Assault by a Family Member: Decisions Following Disclosure." *Victimology: An International Journal* 2(2): 236–250.

Cain, Maureen, and Kalman Kulscar. 1981-82. "Thinking Disputes: An Essay on the Origins of the Dispute Industry." *Law and Society Review* 16(3): 375–402.

Calavita, K., and H.N. Pontell. 1991. "'Other People's Money' Revisited: Collective Embezzlement in the Savings and Loan Insurance Industries." *Social Problems* 38(1): 94–112.

Campbell, G. 1990. "Women and Crime." *Juristat Service Bulletin* 10(20). Ottawa. Canadian Centre for Justice Statistics.

Canada. 1982. *The Criminal Law in Canadian Society.* Ottawa: Government of Canada.

Canadian Centre for Justice Statistics. 1992. "Crime Trends in Canada, 1962–1990" *Juristat Service Bulletin* 12(7). Ottawa: Statistics Canada.

———. 1990a. *The Development of Data Quality Assessment Procedures for the Uniform Crime Reporting Survey: A Case Study of Calgary-Edmonton.* Ottawa: Statistics Canada.

———. 1990b. *The Future of Crime Statistics from the UCR Survey.* Ottawa: Statistics Canada.

———. 1990c. "Conjugal Violence Against Women." *Juristat Service Bulletin* 10(7). Ottawa: Statistics Canada.

———. 1988. "Break and Enter in Canada." *Juristat Service Bulletin* 8(1). Ottawa: Statistics Canada.

Canadian Criminal Justice Association. 1989. "Safer Communities: A Social Strategy for Crime Prevention in Canada." *Canadian Journal of Criminology* 31(4): 359–363.

Cantor, D., and K.C. Land. 1985. "Unemployment and Crime Rates in the Post–World War II United States: A Theoretical and Empirical Analysis." *American Sociological Review* 50 (June): 317–332.

Carrigan, D.O. 1991. *Crime and Punishment in Canada: A History.* Toronto: McClelland and Stewart.

Cater, J., and T. Jones. 1989. "Crime and Disorder." In J. Cater and T. Jones (eds.), *Social Geography—An Introduction to Contemporary Issues*. New York: Routledge, Chapman and Hall.

Catlin, G. and S. Murray. 1984. *Report on Canadian Victimization Survey Methodological Pretests*. Ottawa: Ministry of the Solicitor General of Canada, Secretariat.

Chaiken, J., and M. Chaiken. 1982. *Varieties of Criminal Behavior. Rand Report r-2814-NIJ*. Santa Monica, Calif.: Rand Corporation.

Chambliss, W. 1975. "On the Paucity of Original Research on Organized Crime: A Footnote to Galliher and Cain." *The American Sociologist* 10: 36–39.

Chibnall, S. 1977. *Law-and-Order News*. London: Tavistock.

Chilton, R. 1991. "Images of Crime: Crime Statistics and Their Impact." In J.F. Sheley (ed.), *Criminology: A Contemporary Handbook*. Belmont, Calif.: Wadsworth.

Chiricos, T.G. 1987. "Rates of Crime and Unemployment: An Analysis of Aggregate Research Evidence." *Social Problems* 34(2): 187–242.

Clark, R.D. 1988. "Celerity and Specific Deterrence: A Look at the Evidence." *Canadian Journal of Criminology* 30(2): 109–120.

Clarke, R.V. 1992. "Introduction." In R.V. Clarke (ed.), *Situational Crime Prevention*. Albany, N.Y.: Harrow and Heston.

Clarke, R.V., P. Ekblom, M. Hough, and P. Mayhew. 1985. "Elderly Victims of Crime and Exposure to Risk." *Journal of Criminal Justice* 23: 1–9.

Cloward, R.A. 1959. "Illegitimate Means, Anomie, and Deviant Behavior." The Bobbs-Merrill Reprint Series in the Social Science. Reprinted by permission of *American Sociological Review* 24 (April): 164–176.

Cloward, R.A., and L.E. Ohlin. 1960. *Delinquency and Opportunity*. New York: Free Press.

Cohen, A.K. 1955. *Delinquent Boys: The Culture of the Gang*. New York: Free Press.

Cohen, G.L. 1990. "Self-Employment in Canada." In C. McKic and K. Thompson (eds.), *Canadian Social Trends*. Toronto: Thompson Educational Publishing.

Cohen, L.E., and D. Cantor. 1981. "Residential Burglary in the United States: Lifestyle and Demographic Factors Associated with the Probability of Victimization." *Journal of Research in Crime and Delinquency* 18(1) (January): 113–127.

Cohen, L.E., D. Cantor, and J.R. Kleugel. 1981. "Robbery Victimization in the U.S.: An Analysis of a Non-Random Event." *Social Science Quarterly* 62(4): 644-657.

Cohen, L.E., and M. Felson. 1979. "Social Change and Crime Rate Trends: A Routine Activity Approach." *American Sociological Review* 44 (August): 588–608.

Cohen, L.E., J.R. Kleugel, and K.C. Land. 1981. "Social Inequality and Predatory Criminal Victimization: An Exposition and Test of a Formal Theory." *American Sociological Review* 46 (October): 505–524.

Coleman, J.W. 1991. "Respectable Crime." In J.F. Sheley (ed.), *Criminology: A Contemporary Handbook*. Belmont, Calif.: Wadsworth.

———. 1987. "Toward an Integrated Theory of White-Collar Crime." *American Journal of Sociology* 93(2): 406–439.

Collins, J.J., B.G. Cox, and P.A. Langan. 1987. "Job Activities and Personal Crime Victimization: Implications for Theory." *Social Science Research* 16: 345–360.

Conklin, J.E. 1975. *The Impact of Crime*. New York: Macmillan.

Cook, P.J. 1977. "Punishment and Crime: A Critique of Current Findings Concerning the Preventive Effects of Punishment." *Law and Contemporary Problems* 41(1) (Winter): 164–204.

Cooley, D. 1992. "Prison Victimization and the Informal Rules of Social Control." *Forum on Corrections Research* 4(3). Ottawa: Ministry of Supply and Services: 32.

Corcoran, T. 1993. "Media an Accomplice in Pepsi Hoax." *Globe and Mail* (June 18), p. B2.

Cornish, D.B., and R.V. Clarke. 1986. *The Reasoning Criminal*. New York: Springer-Verlag.

Cray, D. 1988. "The Social Impact of Technological Change." In D. Forcese and S. Richer (eds.), *Social Issues–Sociological Views of Canada. 2nd ed.* Scarborough, Ont.: Prentice-Hall.

Cressey, D.R. 1969. *Theft of the Nation*. New York: Harper and Row.

Croall, H. 1987. "Who Is the White-Collar Criminal?" *British Journal of Criminology* 29(2): 157–174.

Cromwell, P.F., J.N. Olson, and D.W. Avary. 1991. *Breaking and Entering: An Ethnographic Analysis of Burglary*. Newbury Park, Calif.: Sage.

Cullen, F.T., B.G. Link, and C.W. Polanzi. 1982. "The Seriousness of Crime Revisited: Have Attitudes Towards White-Collar Crime Changed?" *Criminology* 20(1): 83–102.

Currie, E. 1985. *Confronting Crime: An American Challenge*. New York: Pantheon.

Daly, M., and M. Wilson. 1988. *Homicide*. Chicago: Aldine de Gruyter.

Davis, N.J. 1988. "Battered Women: Implications for Social Control." *Contemporary Crises* 12: 345–372.

Davis, P.W. 1991. "Stranger Intervention into Child Punishment in Public Places." *Social Problems* 38(2): 227–246.

Dechenes, E.P. 1990. "Longitudinal Research Designs." In K.L. Kempf (ed.), *Measurement Issues in Criminology*. New York: Springer-Verlag: 152–166.

DeKeseredy, W.S. 1988. *Woman Abuse in Dating Relationships: A Critical Evaluation of Research and Theory*. Toronto: Canadian Scholar's Press.

DeKeseredy, W.S., H. Burshtyn, and C. Gordon. 1992. "Taking Woman Abuse Seriously: A Critical Response to the Solicitor General of Canada's Crime Prevention Advice." *International Review of Victimology* 2: 1–11

DeKeseredy, W.S., and R. Hinch. 1991. *Woman Abuse: Sociological Perspectives*. Ottawa: Thompson Educational Publishing.

DeKeseredy, W.S., and K. Kelly. 1993. "The Incidence and Prevalence of Woman Abuse in Canadian University and College Dating Relationships." *Canadian Journal of Sociology* 18(2): 152.

Desroches, F.J. 1991. "Tearoom Trade: A Law Enforcement Problem." *Canadian Journal of Criminology* 33(1): 1–21.

———. 1990. "Tearoom Trade: A Research Update." *Qualitative Sociology* 13(1): 39–61.

Deveraux, M.S. 1990a. "Marital Status." In C. McKie and K. Thompson (eds.), *Canadian Social Trends*. Toronto: Thompson Educational Publishing.

———. 1990b. "Changes in Living Arrangements." In C. McKie and K. Thompson (eds.), *Canadian Social Trends*. Toronto: Thompson Educational Publishing.

———. 1990c. "Decline in the Number of Children." *Canadian Social Trends* 18 (Autumn): 32–34.

Dominick, J.R. 1978. "Crime and Law Enforcement in the Mass Media." In C. Winick (ed.), *Deviance and Mass Media*. Beverly Hills, Calif.: Sage.

Dorfman, Andrea. 1984. "The Criminal Mind." *Science Digest* 92(10): 44–47, 98.

Douglas, J.D., and F.C. Waskler. 1982. *The Sociology of Deviance*. Boston, Mass.: Little, Brown.

Dubro, J. 1985. *Mob Rule: Inside the Canadian Mafia*. Toronto: Macmillan.

Durkheim, E. 1964. *The Rules of Sociological Method*. New York: Free Press.

Dutton, Donald G. 1987. "The Criminal Justice Response to Wife Assault." *Law and Human Behavior*, 11(3): 189–206.

Dutton, D., S. Hart, L.W. Kennedy, and K. Williams. 1992. "Arrest and the Reduction of Repeat Wife Assault." In E. Buzawa and C. Buzawa (eds.), *Domestic Violence: The Changing Criminal Justice Response*. Westport, Conn: Greenwood.

Elliott, D.S., and S.S. Ageton. 1980. "Reconciling Race and Class Differences in Self-Reported and Official Estimates of Delinquency." *American Sociological Review* 45 (February): 95–110.

Ellis, D. 1984. "Video Arcades, Youth and Trouble." *Youth and Society* 16(1): 47–65.

Ellis, D., A. Choi, and C. Blaus. 1993. "Injuries to Police Officers Attending Domestic Disturbances: An Empirical Study." *Canadian Journal of Criminology* 35(2): 149–168.

Ericson, R.V. 1991. "Mass Media, Crime, Law, and Justice: An Institutional Approach." *The British Journal of Criminology* 31(3) (Summer): 219–249.

———. 1982. *Reproducing Order: A Study of Police Patrol Work*. Toronto: University of Toronto Press.

———. 1981. *Making Crime: A Study of Detective Work*. Toronto: Butterworths.

Ericson, R.V., P.M. Baranek, and J.B.L. Chan. 1991. *Representing Order: Crime, Law, and Justice in the News Media*. Toronto: University of Toronto Press.

———. 1989. *Negotiating Control: A Study of News Sources*. Toronto: University of Toronto Press.

———. 1987. *Visualizing Deviance*. Toronto: University of Toronto Press.

European and North American Conference on Urban Safety and Crime Prevention. 1989. *Final Declaration*. Montreal.

Evans, D.J. 1989. "Geographical Analyses of Residential Burglary." In D.J. Evans and D.T. Herbert (eds.), *The Geography of Crime*. London: Routledge.

Fagan, J., and S. Wexler. 1987. "Family Origins of Violent Delinquents." *Criminology* 25: 643–669.

Farberman, H.A. 1975. "A Criminogenic Market Structure: The Automobile Industry." *Sociological Quarterly* 16: 438–457.

Farrington, D.P. 1989. "Implications of Longitudinal Studies for Social Prevention." *Canadian Journal of Criminology* 31(4) (October): 453–463.

Fattah, E.A. 1991. *Understanding Criminal Victimization.* Scarborough, Ont.: Prentice-Hall.

Fattah, E.A., and V.F. Sacco. 1989. *Crime and Victimization of the Elderly.* New York: Springer-Verlag.

Fedorowycz, O. 1992. "Break and Enter in Canada." *Juristat Service Bulletin* 12(1). Ottawa: Canadian Centre for Justice Statistics.

Feld, S.L., and M.A. Straus. 1990. "Escalation and Desistance from Wife Assault in Marriage." In M.A. Straus and R.J. Gelles (eds.), *Physical Violence in American Families: Risk Factors and Adaptations to Violence in 8,145 Families.* New Brunswick, N.J.: Transaction.

Felson, M. 1992. "Routine Activities and Crime Prevention." *Studies in Crime and Crime Prevention Annual Review* 1(1): 30–34.

———. 1987. "Routine Activities and Crime Prevention in the Developing Metropolis." *Criminology* 25(4): 911–931.

———. 1986. "Linking Criminal Choices, Routine Activities, Informal Control, and Criminal Outcomes." In D.B. Cornish and R.V. Clarke (eds.), *The Reasoning Criminal.* New York: Springer-Verlag.

Felson, R.B., W.F. Baccaglini, and S.A. Ribner. 1985. "Accounting for Criminal Violence: A Comparison of Official and Offender Versions of the Crime." *Sociology and Social Research* 70(1): 93–101.

Ferraro, K.J. 1989. "Policing Woman Battering." *Social Problems* 36(1): 61–74.

Ferraro, K.J., and J.M. Johnson. 1983. "How Women Experience Battering: The Process of Victimization." *Social Problems* 30: 325–335.

Figlio, R.M. 1990. "Measurement in Criminology and Criminal Justice: A Brief 20-Year Retrospective." In D.L. MacKenzie, D.J. Baunach, and R.R. Roberg (eds.), *Measuring Crime: Large-Scale, Long-Range Efforts.* Albany: State University of New York Press.

Fischer, C.S. 1981. "The Public and Private Worlds of City Life." *American Sociological Review* 46 (June): 306–316.

————. 1976. *The Urban Experience*. New York: Harcourt Brace Jovanovich.

————. 1975. "The Effect of Urban Life on Traditional Values." *Social Forces* 53: 420–432.

Fishman, M. 1981. "Police News: Constructing an Image of Crime." *Urban Life* 9(4) (January): 371–394.

————. 1978. "Crime Waves as Ideology." *Social Problems* 25(5): 631–543.

Flowers, R.B. 1989. *Demographics and Criminality: The Characteristics of Crime in America*. New York: Greenwood Press.

Frank, J. 1992. "Violent Youth Crime." *Canadian Social Trends* 26 (Autumn): 2–9.

Freeman, R.B. 1983. "Crime and Unemployment." In J.Q. Wilson (ed.), *Crime and Public Policy*. San Francisco: ICS Press.

Frieze, I.H., and A. Browne. 1989. "Violence in Marriage." In L. Ohlin and M. Tonry (eds.), *Family Violence*. Chicago: University of Chicago Press.

Frinell, D.E., E. Dahlstrom III, and D.A. Johnson. 1980. "A Public Education Program Designed to Increase the Accuracy and Incidence of Citizens' Reports of Suspicious and Criminal Activities." *Journal of Police Science and Administration* 8(2): 160–165.

Gabor, T. 1990a. "Crime Prevention: The Agenda." *Canadian Journal of Criminology* 32(1): 1–7.

————. 1990b. "Crime Displacement and Situational Prevention: Toward the Development of Some Principles." *Canadian Journal of Criminology* 32(1): 41–73.

Gabor, T., and A. Normandean. 1989. "Armed Robbery: Highlights of a Canadian Study." *Canadian Police College Journal* 13(4): 273–282.

Gabor, T., J. Stream, G. Singh, and D. Varis. 1986. "Public Deviance: An Experimental Study." *Canadian Journal of Criminology* 28(1): 17–29.

Galliher, J.F., and J.A. Cain. 1974. "Citation Support for the Mafia Myth in Criminology Textbooks." *The American Sociologist* 9 (May): 68–74.

Gans, H. 1962. *The Urban Villagers*. New York: Free Press.

Garofalo, J. 1981. "Crime and the Mass Media: A Selective Review of Research." *Journal of Research in Crime and Delinquency* (July): 319–350.

Garofalo, J., and M. McLeod. 1988. *Improving the Use and Effectiveness of Neighborhood Watch Programs*. Washington, D.C.: U.S. Department of Justice.

Garofalo, J., L. Siegel, and J. Laub. 1987. "School-Related Victimizations Among Adolescents: An Analysis of National Crime Survey (NCS) Narratives." *Journal of Quantitative Criminology* 3(4): 321–338.

Garofalo, R. 1914. *Criminology*. Boston: Little, Brown.

Gastil, R.D. 1971. "Homicide and a Regional Culture of Violence." *American Sociological Review* 36 (June): 412–427.

Gelles, R.J., and M.A. Straus. 1990. "The Medical and Psychological Costs of Family Violence." In M.A. Straus and R.J. Gelles (eds.), *Physical Violence in American Families: Risk Factors and Adaptations to Violence in 8,145 Families*. New Brunswick, N.J.: Transaction.

———. 1988. *Intimate Violence*. New York: Simon and Schuster.

Geran, L. 1992. "Occupational Stress." *Canadian Social Trends* 26 (Autumn): 14–17.

Gibbons, D.C. 1988. "Some Critical Observations on Criminal Types and Criminal Careers." *Criminal Justice and Behavior* 15: 8–23.

Gibbs, J.P. 1981. *Norms, Deviance, and Social Control: Conceptual Matters*. New York: Elsevier.

———. 1966. "Conceptions of Deviant Behavior: The Old and the New." *Pacific Sociological Review* 9: 9–14.

Gibbs, J.P., and M.L. Erikson. 1976. "Crime Rates of American Cities in an Ecological Context." *American Journal of Sociology* 82(3): 605–620.

Gilbert, N. 1991. "The Phantom Epidemic of Sexual Assault." *The Public Interest* 103 (Spring): 54–65.

Gillespie, D.L., and A. Leffler. 1987. "The Politics of Research Methodology in Claims-Making Activities: Social Science and Sexual Harassment." *Social Problems* 34(5): 490–501.

Gilsinan, J.F. 1990. *Criminology and Public Policy: An Introduction*. Englewood Cliffs, N.J.: Prentice-Hall.

———. 1989. "They Is Clowning Tough: 911 and the Social Construction of Reality." *Criminology* 27(2): 329–344.

Giordano, P.C., S.A. Cernkovich, and M.D. Pugh. 1986. "Friendships and Delinquency." *American Journal of Sociology* 91(5): 1170–1202.

Glick, P.C. 1990. "American Families: As They Are and Were." *Sociology and Social Research* 74(3): 139–145.

The Globe and Mail. 1993. "Westray Charges Thrown Out" (July 21), p. A1; "Injected with HIV While Asleep, Alberta Man Says" (July 21), p. A4; "Calgary Teen Given Life Sentence for Schoolyard Stabbing of Boy, 13" (July 21), p. A3.

———. 1989a. "Ladylike—and Lethal" (July 4), p. A3.

———. 1989b. "Need Uzis to Do Job, Police in Quiet US Suburb Say" (July 4), p. A3.

Goff, C., and N. Nason-Clark. 1989. "The Seriousness of Crime in Fredericton, New Brunswick: Perceptions Toward White-Collar Crime." *Canadian Journal of Criminology* 31(1): 19–34.

Goffman, E. 1963. *Stigma: Notes on the Management of Spoiled Identity*. Englewood Cliffs, N.J.: Prentice-Hall.

———. 1959. *The Presentation of Self in Everyday Life*. Garden City, N.J.: Doubleday.

Golant, S.M. 1984. "Factors Influencing the Nighttime Activity of Old Persons in their Community." *Journal of Gerontology* 39: 485–491.

Gold, M. 1970. *Delinquent Behavior in an American City*. Belmont, Calif.: Brooks/Cole.

Goldstein, H. 1990. *Problem-Oriented Policing*. Philadelphia: Temple University Press.

Gondolf, E.W., and J.R. McFerron. 1989. "Handling Battering Men and Police Action in Wife Abuse Cases." *Criminal Justice and Behavior* 16: 429–439.

Gordon, M.T., and L. Heath. 1981. "The News Business, Crime and Fear." In D.A. Lewis (ed.), *Reactions to Crime*. Beverly Hills, Calif.: Sage.

Gorelick, S.M. 1989. "'Join Our War': The Construction of Ideology in a Newspaper Crimefighting Campaign." *Crime and Delinquency* 35(3): 421–436.

Gottfredson, M.R. 1984. "Victims of Crime: The Dimensions of Risk." A Home Office Research and Planning Unit Report. London: HMSO Books.

Gottfredson, M.R., and D. Gottfredson. 1988. *Decisionmaking in Criminal Justice*. 2nd ed. New York: Plenum.

Gottfredson, M.R., and T. Hirschi. 1990. *A General Theory of Crime*. Stanford, Calif: Stanford University Press.

———. 1988. "Science, Public Policy and the Career Paradigm." *Criminology* 26: 37–55.

———. 1986. "The True Value of Lambda Would Appear to Be Zero: An Essay on Career Criminals, Criminal Careers, Selective Incapacitation, Cohort Studies, and Related Topics." *Criminology* 24 (2): 213–234.

Gould, L.C. 1989. "Crime, Criminality, and Criminal Events." A paper presented at the Annual Meetings of the American Society of Criminology, Reno, Nevada.

Gove, W.R. 1975. *The Labelling of Deviance: Evaluating a Perspective*. New York: Sage.

Gove, W.R., M. Hughes, and M. Geerken. 1985. "Are Uniform Crime Reports a Valid Indicator of the Index Crimes? An Affirmative Answer with Minor Qualifications." *Criminology* 23(3): 451–501.

Gower, D. 1990. "Labour Force Trends: Canada and the United States." In C. McKie and K. Thompson (eds.), *Canadian Social Trends*. Toronto: Thompson Educational Publishing.

Graber, D.A. 1980. *Crime News and the Public*. New York: Praeger.

Graham, D.F., I. Graham, and M.J. MacLean. 1991. "Going to the Mall: A Leisure Activity of Urban Elderly People." *Canadian Journal on Aging* 10(4): 345–358.

Graham, J. 1990. *Crime Prevention Strategies in Europe and North America*. Helsinki, Fin.: Helsinki Institute for Crime Prevention and Control.

Gramling, R., C. Forsyth, and J. Fewell. 1988. "Crime and Economic Activity: A Research Note." *Sociological Spectrum* 8: 187-195.

Gray, H. 1989. "Popular Music as a Social Problem: A Social History of the Claims Against Popular Music." In J. Best (ed.), *Images of Issues*. New York: Aldine de Gruyter.

Greenberg, D.F. 1992. "Comparing Criminal Career Models." *Criminology* 30(1): 141–147.

Gurr, T.R. 1980. "Development and Decay: Their Impact on Public Order in Western History." In J. Inciardi and C.E. Faupel (eds.), *History and Crime*. Beverly Hills: Sage.

Gusfield, J. 1989. "Constructing the Ownership of Social Problems: Fun and Profit in the Welfare State." *Social Problems* 36(5): 431–441.

———. 1963. *Symbolic Crusade: Status Politics and the American Temperance Movement*. Urbana: University of Illinois Press.

Hackler, J., and K. Don. 1990. "Estimating System Biases: Crime Indices that Permit Comparisons Across Provinces." *Canadian Journal of Criminology* 32(2): 243–264.

Hagan, J. 1992. "White Collar and Corporate Crime." In R. Linden (ed.), *Criminology: A Canadian Perspective*. Toronto: Harcourt Brace Jovanovich.

———. 1989. *Structural Criminology*. New Brunswick, N.J.: Rutgers University Press.

————. 1985. *Modern Criminology*. New York: McGraw-Hill.

————. 1980. "The Legislation of Crime and Delinquency: A Review of Theory, Method and Research." *Law and Society Review* 14(3): 603–628.

Hagan, J., A.R. Gillis, and J.H. Simpson. 1985. "The Class Structure of Gender and Delinquency: Toward a Power-Control Theory of Common Delinquent Behavior." *American Journal of Sociology* 90(6): 1151–1178.

————. 1979. "The Sexual Stratification of Social Control: A Gender-Based Perspective on Crime and Delinquency." *British Journal of Sociology* 30(1): 25–38.

Hagan, J., J. Simpson, and A.R. Gillis. 1988. "Feminist Scholarship, Relational and Instrumental Control, and a Power-Control Theory of Gender and Delinquency." *The British Journal of Sociology* 39(3): 301–336.

————. 1987. "Class in the Household: Deprivation, Liberation and a Power-Control Theory of Gender and Delinquency." *American Journal of Sociology* 92(4): 788–816.

Haller, M.H. 1990. "Illegal Enterprise: A Theoretical and Historical Interpretation." *Criminology* 28(2): 207–235.

Hamlin, J.E. 1988. "The Misplaced Role of Rational Choice in Neutralization Theory." *Criminology* 26: 425–438.

Hanmer, J., and S. Saunders. 1984. *Well-Founded Fear: A Community Study of Violence to Women*. London: Hutchinson in association with The Explorations in Feminism Collective, an affiliation of the Women's Research and Resources Centre.

Hans, V.P. 1990. "Law and the Media: An Overview and Introduction." *Law and Human Behavior* 14(5): 399–407.

Hans, V.P., and D. Ermann. 1989. "Responses to Corporate versus Individual Wrongdoing." *Law and Human Behavior* 13(2): 151–166.

Hansel, M.K. 1987. "Citizen Crime Stereotypes—Normative Consensus Revisited." *Criminology* 25: 455–485.

Harlow, C.W. 1991. *Female Victims of Violent Crime*. Washington, D.C.: U.S. Department of Justice.

————. 1989. *Injuries from Crime*. Washington, D.C.: Bureau of Justice Statistics.

Harney, P.A., and C.L. Muehlenhard. 1991. "Factors that Increase the Likelihood of Victimization." In A. Parrot and L. Bechhofer (eds.), *Acquaintance Rape: The Hidden Crime*. New York: John Wiley.

Harries, K.D. 1990. *Serious Violence*. Springfield, Ill: Charles C. Thomas.

Harris, M.K. 1991. "Moving into the New Millennium: Toward a Feminist Vision of Peace." In H.E. Pepinsky, and R. Quinney (eds.), *Criminology as Peacemaking*. Bloomington: Indiana University Press.

Hartman, D.P., D.M. Gelfand, B. Page, and P. Walder. 1972. "Rates of Bystander Observation and Reporting of Contrived Shoplifting Incidents." *Criminology* (November): 247–267.

Hartnagel, T.F. 1992. "Correlates of Criminal Behaviour." In R. Linden (ed.), *Criminology: A Canadian Perspective*. Toronto: Harcourt Brace Jovanovich.

Hartnagel, T.F., and H. Krahn. 1989. "High School Dropouts, Labor Market Success, and Criminal Behavior." *Youth and Society* 20(4): 416–444.

Hasell, M.J., and F.D. Peatross. 1990. "Exploring Connections Between Women's Changing Roles and House Forms." Environment and Behavior 22(1): 3–26.

Hastings, R., and R. Melcher. 1990. "Municipal Government Involvement in Crime Prevention in Canada." *Canadian Journal of Criminology* 32(1): 107–123.

Hawkins, G. 1969. "God and the Mafia." *The Public Interest* 14 (Winter): 24–51.

Health and Welfare Canada. 1990. "Dating Violence." The National Clearinghouse on Family Violence (Health and Welfare Canada).

———. "Child Abuse and Neglect." The National Clearinghouse on Family Violence (Health and Welfare Canada).

Hennigen, K.M., L. Heath, J.D. Wharton, M.L. Del Resario, T.D. Cook, and B.J. Calder. 1982. "Impact of the Introduction of Television on Crime in the United States: Empirical Findings and Theoretical Implications." *Journal of Personality and Social Psychology* 42(3): 461–477.

Henshel, R.L., and R.A. Silverman. 1975. *Perception in Criminology*. Toronto: Methuen.

Hepburn, J. 1977. "Social Control and the Legal Order: Legitimated Repression in a Capitalist State." *Contemporary Crises* 1(1): 77–90.

Hess, H. 1973. *Mafia and Mafiosi: The Structure of Power*. Farnborough U.K.: Saxon House.

Hindelang, M.J., M.R. Gottfredson, and J. Garofalo. 1978. *Victims of Personal Crime: An Empirical Foundation for a Theory of Personal Victimization*. Cambridge, Mass.: Ballinger.

Hindelang, M.J., T. Hirschi, and J. Weis. 1981. *Measuring Delinquency*. Beverly Hills, Calif.: Sage.

Hirschi, T. 1969. *Causes of Delinquency*. Berkeley: University of California Press.

Hocker, Joyce L., and William W. Wilmot. 1985. *Interpersonal Conflict*. 2nd ed. Dubuque, Iowa: William C. Brown.

Hollinger, R.C., and L. Lanza-Kaduce. 1988. "The Process of Criminalization: The Case of Computer Crime Laws." *Criminology* 26(1): 101–113.

Horowitz, A.V. 1990. *The Logic of Social Control*. New York: Plenum.

Hotaling, G.T., and D. Finkelhor. 1990. "Estimating the Number of Stranger-Abduction Homicides of Children: A Review of Available Evidence." *Journal of Criminal Justice* 18: 385–399.

Hotaling, G.T., and M.A. Straus (with A.J. Lincoln). 1990. "Intrafamily Violence and Crime and Violence Outside the Family." In M.A. Straus and R.J. Gelles (eds.), *Physical Violence in American Families: Risk Factors and Adaptations to Violence in 8,145 Families*. New Brunswick, N.J.: Transaction.

Hough, M. 1987. "Offenders' Choice of Target: Findings from Victim Surveys." *Journal of Quantitative Criminology* 3(4): 355–370.

Humphries, D. 1981. "Serious Crime, News Coverage, and Ideology: A Content Analysis of Crime Coverage in a Metropolitan Paper." *Crime and Delinquency* 27(2) April: 191–205.

Hunt, J. 1985. "Police Accounts of Normal Force." *Urban Life* 13(4): 315–341.

Ianni, F.A.J. 1974. *Black Mafia*. New York: Simon and Schuster.

———. 1971. "The Mafia and the Web of Kinship." *The Public Interest* 16: 78–100.

Ianni, F.A.J., and E. Reuss-Ianni. 1972. *A Family Business: Kinship and Social Control in Organized Crime*. New York: Russell Sage Foundation.

Innes, C.A., and L.A. Greenfeld. 1990. "Violent State Prisoners and Their Victims." *Bureau of Justice Statistics Special Report*. Washington, D.C.: U.S. Department of Justice.

Iso-Ahola, S. 1980. *The Social Psychology of Leisure and Recreation*. Dubuque, Iowa: William C. Brown.

Jackson, M. 1989. "The Clinical Assessment and Prediction of Violent Behaviour: Toward a Scientific Analysis. *Criminal Justice and Behaviour* 16, 1: 114–131.

Jackson, P.G. 1990. "Sources of Data." In K.L. Kempf (ed.), *Measurement Issues in Criminology*. New York: Springer-Verlag.

Jackson, P.I. 1989. *Minority Group Threat, Crime, and Policing*. New York: Praeger.

Jacobs, N. 1965. "The Phantom Slasher of Taipei: Mass Hysteria in a Non-Western Society." *Social Problems* 12: 318–328.

Janoff-Bulman, R., and I.H. Frieze. 1983. "A Theoretical Perspective for Understanding Reactions to Victimization." *Journal of Social Issues* 39(2): 1–17.

Jenkins, P. 1992. *Intimate Enemies: Moral Panic in Great Britain*. New York: Aldine de Gruyter.

Jenkins, P., and G. Potter. 1987. "The Politics and Mythology of Organized Crime: A Philadelphia Case-Study." *Journal of Criminal Justice* 15: 473–484.

Jensen, G.F., and D. Brownfield. 1986. "Gender, Lifestyles, and Victimization: Beyond Routine Activity." *Violence and Victims* 1(2): 85–99.

Johnson, D.M. 1945. "The 'Phantom Anesthetist' of Mattoon: A Field Study of Mass Hysteria." *Journal of Abnormal and Social Psychology* 40: 175–186.

Johnson, H., and V.F. Sacco. 1991. "The Risk of Criminal Victimization: Data from a National Study." In R.A. Silverman, J.J. Teevan, and V.F. Sacco (eds.), *Crime in Canadian Society*, 4th ed. Toronto: Butterworths.

Johnson, G.D., G.J. Palileo, and N.B. Gray. 1992. "Date Rape on a Southern Campus." *Sociology and Social Research* 76(2): 37–41.

Johnson, H., and P. Chisholm. 1990. "Family Homicide" in C. McKie and K. Thompson (eds.), *Canadian Social Trends*. Toronto: Thompson Educational Publishing.

Johnson, H., and G. Lazarus. 1989. "The Impact of Age on Crime Victimization Rates." *Canadian Journal of Criminology* 31(3): 309–317.

Johnson, I.M. 1990. "A Loglinear Analysis of Abused Wives' Decisions to Call the Police in Domestic Violence Disputes." *Journal of Criminal Justice* 18: 147–159.

Jones, M. 1990. "Time Use of the Elderly." *Canadian Social Trends* 17 (Summer): 28–31.

Junger, M. 1987. "Women's Experiences of Sexual Harassment: Some Implications for their Fear of Crime." *British Journal of Criminology* 27(4): 358–383.

Jupp, V. 1989. *Methods of Criminological Research*. London: Unwin Hyman.

Kalmuss, D.S., and M.A. Straus. 1990. "Wife's Marital Dependency and Wife Abuse." In M.A. Straus and R.J. Gelles (eds.), *Physical Violence in American Families: Risk Factors and Adaptations to Violence in 8,145 Families*. New Brunswick, N.J.: Transaction.

Kantor, G.K., and M.A. Straus. 1987. "The Drunken Bum Theory of Wife Beating." *Social Problems* 34(2): 213–230.

Kapferer, J.N. 1989. "A Mass Poisoning Rumor in Europe." *Public Opinion Quarterly* 53: 467–481.

Karmen, A. 1990. *Crime Victims: An Introduction to Victimology*. 2nd ed. Pacific Grove, Calif.: Brooks/Cole.

Katz, J. 1988. *Seductions of Crime: Moral and Sensual Attractions in Doing Evil*. New York: Basic Books.

———. 1987. "What Makes Crime 'News'." *Media, Culture and Society* 9: 47–75.

Keane, C. 1991. "Corporate Crime." In R.A. Silverman, J.J. Teevan, and V.F. Sacco (eds.), *Crime in Canadian Society*. 4th ed. Toronto: Butterworths.

Kelling, G., T. Pate, D. Dieckman, and C.E. Brown. 1974. *The Kansas City Preventive Patrol Experiment: A Summary Report*. Washington, D.C.: The Police Foundation.

Kempf, K.L. 1987. "Specialization and the Criminal Career." *Criminology* 25: 399–420.

Kennedy, L.W. 1991. "Evaluating Community Policing." *Canadian Police College Journal*, 15(4): 275–290.

———. 1990. *On the Borders of Crime: Conflict Management and Criminology*. New York: Longman.

———. 1988. "Going It Alone: Unreported Crime and Individual Self-Help." *Journal of Criminal Justice* 16(5): 403–412.

Kennedy, L.W., and S. Baron. 1993. "Routine Activities and A Subculture of Violence: A Study of Violence on the Street." *Journal of Research in Crime and Delinquency* 30(1): 88–112.

Kennedy, L.W., and D.G. Dutton. 1989. "The Incidence of Wife Assault in Alberta." *Canadian Journal of Behavioral Science* 21(1): 40–54.

Kennedy, L.W., and D.R. Forde. 1992. *Demographic Change and Police Force Growth in Canada: An Analysis of Trends and Future Directions*.

Unpublished manuscript prepared for the Canadian Police College, Ottawa.

———. 1990. "Routine Activities and Crime: An Analysis of Victimization in Canada." *Criminology* 28 (1): 101–15.

Kennedy, L.W., and R.A. Silverman. 1985. "Significant Others and Fear of Crime Among the Elderly." *International Journal of Aging and Human Development* 20(4): 241-256.

Kinderlerher, Jane. 1983. "Delinquent Diets: Partners in Crime." *Prevention* (October): 141–144.

Kirby, C., and T.C. Renner. 1986. *Mafia Assassin: The Inside Story of a Canadian Biker, Hitman and Police Informer.* Toronto: Methuen.

Kitsuse, K.I. 1962. "Societal Reaction to Deviant Behavior: Problems of Theory and Method." *Social Problems* 9: 247–256.

Klaus, P.A., and M.R. Rand. 1984. *Family Violence.* Washington, D.C.: Bureau of Justice Statistics.

Kleck, G., and B. Patterson. 1989. "The Impact of Gun Control and Gun Ownership Levels on City Violence Rates." Paper presented at the annual meetings of the American Society of Criminology, Reno, Nevada (November).

Kleck, G., and S. Sayles. 1990. "Rape and Resistance." *Social Problems* 37(2): 149–162.

Klockars, Carl B. 1985. *The Idea of Police.* Beverly Hills, Calif.: Sage.

Koenig, Daniel J. 1991. *Do Police Cause Crime?: Police Activity, Police Strength, and Crime Rates.* Ottawa: Canadian Police College.

Kornhauser, R. 1978. *Social Sources of Delinquency.* Chicago: University of Chicago Press.

Krahn, H., and Kennedy, L.W. 1985. "Producing Personal Safety: The Effects of Crime Rates, Police Force Size, and Fear of Crime." *Criminology* 23(4) (November): 697–710.

Krohn, M.D., L. Lanza-Kaduce, and R. Akers. 1984. "Community Context and Theories of Deviant Behavior: An Examination of Social Learning and Social Bonding Theories." *The Sociological Quarterly* 25: 353–371.

Krupat, E., and P. Kubzansky. 1987. "Designing to Deter Crime." *Psychology Today* (October): 58–61.

Kurz, D. 1987. "Emergency Department Responses to Battered Women: Resistance to Medicalization." *Social Problems* 34(1): 69–81.

Lab, S.P. 1992. *Crime Prevention: Approaches, Practices and Evaluations*. 2nd ed. Cincinnati, Ohio: Anderson.

Langan, P.A. 1983. "Career Patterns in Crime." *Bureau of Justice Statistics: Special Report*. Washington, D.C.: U.S. Department of Justice.

Lasley, J.R., and J.L. Rosenbaum. 1988. "Routine Activities and Multiple Personal Victimization." *Sociology and Social Research* 73(1): 47–50.

Laub, J.H. 1990. "Patterns of Criminal Victimization in the United States." In A.J. Lurigio, W.G. Skogan, and R.C. Davis (eds.), *Victims of Crime: Problems, Policies and Programs*. Newbury Park, Calif.: Sage.

———. 1987. "Data for Positive Criminology." In M.R. Gottfredson and T. Hirschi (eds.), *Positive Criminology*. Newbury Park, Calif.: Sage.

Lauritsen, J.L., R.J. Sampson, and J.H. Laub. 1991. "The Link Between Offending and Victimization Among Adolescents." *Criminology* 29(2): 265–292.

Lawson, Paul E. 1982. *Solving Somebody Else's Blues*. Latham, Md.: University Press of America.

Lejeune, R., and N. Alex. 1973. "On Being Mugged." *Urban Life and Culture* 2(3): 259–283.

Lemert, E.M. 1951. *Social Pathology*. New York: McGraw-Hill.

Lenton, R.L. 1990. "Techniques of Child Discipline and Abuse by Parents." *Canadian Review of Sociology and Anthropology* 27(2): 157–185.

Leroux, J., and P. Morrison. 1992. "Fraud in Canada." *Juristat Service Bulletin* 12(5). Ottawa: Canadian Centre for Justice Statistics.

Leroux, T.G., and M. Petrunik. 1990. "The Construction of Elder Abuse as a Social Problem: A Canadian Perspective." *International Journal of Health Services* 20(4): 651–663.

Letkemann, P. 1973. *Crime as Work*. Englewood Cliffs, N.J.: Prentice-Hall.

Levi, K. 1981. "Becoming a Hit Man: Neutralization in a Very Deviant Career." *Urban Life* 10: 47–63.

Light, I. 1977. "The Ethnic Vice Industry, 1880–1944." *American Sociological Review* 42 (June): 464–479.

Linder, C., and R.J. Koehler. 1992. "Probation Officer Victimization: An Emerging Concern." *Journal of Criminal Justice* 20(1): 52–62.

Lindquist, J.H., and J.M. Duke. 1982. "The Elderly Victim at Risk." *Criminology* 20(1): 115–126.

Lindsay, C. 1990. "The Service Sector in the 1980s." In C. McKie and K.

Thompson (eds.), *Canadian Social Trends*. Toronto: Thompson Educational Publishing.

Liska, A.E., and W. Baccaglini. 1990. "Feeling Safe by Comparison: Crime in the Newspapers." *Social Problems* 37(3): 360–374.

Liska, A., J. Lawrence, and J. Sanchirico. 1982. "Fear of Crime as a Social Fact." *Social Forces* 60: 760–771.

Lizotte, A.J. 1985. "The Uniqueness of Rape: Reporting Assaultive Violence to the Police." *Crime and Delinquency* 31(2): 169–190.

Lloyd, S.A., J.E. Koval, and R.M. Cale. 1989. "Courtship and Violence in Dating Relationships." In M.A. Pirog-Good and J.E. Stets (eds.), *Violence in Dating Relationships*. New York: Praeger.

Loftus, E.F. 1979. *Eyewitness Testimony*. Cambridge, Mass.: Harvard University Press.

Loree, D.J., and R.W. Walker. 1991. *Community Crime Prevention: Shaping the Future*. Ottawa: The Royal Canadian Mounted Police Public Affairs Directorate.

Loseke, D.R. 1989. "'Violence' Is 'Violence' ... or Is It?: The Social Construction of 'Wife Abuse' and Public Policy." In J. Best (ed.), *Images of Issues: Typifying Contemporary Social Problems*. New York: Aldine de Gruyter.

Lotz, R., E.D. Poole, and R.M. Regoli. 1985. *Juvenile Delinquency and Juvenile Justice*. New York: Random House.

Luckenbill, D.F. 1984. "Murder and Assault." In R.F. Meier (ed.), *Major Forms of Crime*. Beverly Hills, Calif.: Sage.

———. 1977. "Criminal Homicide as a Situated Transaction." *Social Problems* 25(2): 176–186.

Luckenbill, D.F., and J. Best. 1981. "Careers in Deviance and Respectability: The Analogy's Limitation." *Social Problems* 29: 197–206.

Lurigio, A.J., and P.A. Resick. 1990. "Healing the Psychological Wounds of Criminal Victimization: Predicting Postcrime Distress and Recovery." In A.J. Lurigio, W.G. Skogan, and R.C. David (eds.), *Victims of Crime: Problems, Policies and Programs*. Newbury Park, Calif.: Sage.

Luxton, M. 1988. "Thinking About the Future." *Family Matters: Sociology and Contemporary Canadian Families*. Toronto: Methuen.

Lynch, J.P. 1987. "Routine Activity and Victimization at Work." *Journal of Quantitative Criminology* 3(4): 283–300.

Lynch, J.P., and D. Cantor. 1992. "Ecological and Behavioral Influences on Property Victimization at Home: Implications for Opportunity

Theory." *Journal of Research in Crime and Delinquency* 29(3): 335–362.

Maas, P. 1968. *The Valachi Papers*. New York: Putnam.

McCarthy, B., and J. Hagan. 1991. "Homelessness: A Criminogenic Situation?" *British Journal of Criminology* 31(4) (Autumn): 393–410.

MacLean, B.D. 1986. *The Political Economy of Crime: Readings for a Critical Criminology*. Scarborough, Ont.: Prentice-Hall.

McClearly, R.M., B.C. Nienstedt, and J.M. Erven. 1982. "Uniform Crime Reports as Organizational Outcomes: Three Time Series Experiments." *Social Problems* 29(4): 361–372.

McCord, J. 1991. "Family Relationships, Juvenile Delinquency, and Adult Criminality." *Criminology* 29(3): 397–417.

McIntosh, M. 1975. *The Organization of Crime*. London: Macmillan.

Maguire, M., with T. Bennett. 1982. *Burglary in a Dwelling: The Offence, the Offender and the Victim*. London: Heinemann.

Malamuth, N.M. 1983. "Factors Associated with Rape as Predictors of Laboratory Aggression Against Women." *Journal of Personality and Social Psychology* 45: 432–442.

Malamuth, N.M., and E. Donnerstein. 1984. *Pornography and Sexual Aggression*. Orlando, Fla.: Academic Press.

Maltz, M.D. 1976. "On Defining 'Organized Crime': The Development of a Definition and a Typology." *Crime and Delinquency* 22: 338–346.

Martin, R., R.J. Mutchnick, and W.T. Austin. 1990. *Criminological Thought: Pioneers Past and Present*. New York: Macmillan.

Massey, J.L., M.D. Krohn, and L.M. Bonati. 1989. "Property Crime and the Routine Activities of Individuals." *Journal of Research in Crime and Delinquency* 26(4): 378–400.

Mastrofski, S. 1983. "The Police and Noncrime Services." In G. Whitaker, and C. D. Phillips (eds.), *Evaluating Performance of Criminal Justice Agencies*. Beverly Hills, Calif.: Sage.

Matza, D., and G.M. Sykes. 1961. "Juvenile Delinquency and Subterranean Values." *American Sociological Review* 26: 712–719.

Maxfield, M. 1989. "Circumstances in Supplementary Homicide Reports: Variety and Validity." *Criminology* 27(4): 671–695.

Maxfield, M.G. 1990. "Homicide Circumstances, 1976–1985: A Taxonomy Based on Supplementary Homicide Reports." *Criminology* 28.

————. 1987. "Household Composition, Routine Activity, and Victimization: A Comparative Analysis." *Journal of Quantitative Criminology* 3(4): 301–320.

Mayhew, P., D. Elliott, and L. Dowds. 1989. *The 1988 British Crime Survey: A Home Office Research and Planning Unit Report*. London: HMSO Books.

Mednick, S., T. Moffitt, and S. Stack. 1987. *The Causes of Crime: New Biological Approaches*. New York: Cambridge University Press.

Menard, S., and H.C. Covey. 1988. "UCR and NCS: Comparisons Over Space and Time." *Journal of Criminal Justice* 16: 371–384.

Meredith, N. 1984. "The Murder Epidemic." *Science* (December): 41–48.

Merry, S.E. 1981. *Urban Danger*. Philadelphia: Temple University Press.

Merton, R.K. 1938. "Social Structure and Anomie." *American Sociological Review* 3: 672–682.

Messner, S. 1989. "Economic Discrimination and Societal Homicide Rates: Further Evidence on the Cost of Inequality." *American Sociological Review*, 54: 597–611.

Messner, S.F., and J.R. Blau. 1987. "Routine Leisure Activities and Rates of Crime: A Macro-Level Analysis." *Social Forces* 65: 1035–1051.

Michalowski, R.J., and E.W. Bohlander. 1976. "Repression and Criminal Justice in Capitalist America." *Sociological Inquiry* 46(2): 95–106.

Miethe, T.D. 1982. "Public Consensus on Crime Seriousness: Normative Structure of Methodological Artifact." *Criminology* 20: 515–526.

Miethe, T.D., and R.F. Meier. 1990. "Opportunity, Choice and Criminal Victimization: A Test of a Theoretical Model." *Journal of Research in Crime and Delinquency* 27(3): 243–266.

Miethe, T.D., M.C. Stafford, and J.S. Long. 1987. "Social Differentiation in Criminal Victimization: A Test of Routine Activities/ Lifestyle Theories." *American Sociological Review* 52 (April): 184–194.

Miller, D.T., and C.A. Porter. 1983. "Self-Blame in Victims of Violence." *Journal of Social Issues* 39: 139–152.

Miller, G. 1978. *Odd Jobs*. Englewood Cliffs, N.J.: Prentice-Hall.

Miller, L.J. 1990. "Violent Families and the Rhetoric of Harmony." *British Journal of Sociology* 41(2): 263–288.

Miller, J.L., and A.B. Anderson. 1986. "Updating the Deterrence Doctrine." *Journal of Criminal Law and Criminology* 77(2): 418–438.

Minor, W.W. 1981. "Techniques of Neutralization: A Reconceptualization and Empirical Examination." *Journal of Research in Crime and Delinquency* 18: 295–318.

Monkkonen, Eric H. 1983. "The Organized Response to Crime in Nineteenth- and Twentieth-Century America." *Journal of Interdisciplinary History* 14(1): 113–128.

Moore, M. 1990. "Women Parenting Alone." In C. McKie and K. Thompson (eds.), *Canadian Social Trends*. Toronto: Thompson Educational Publishing.

Moore, M.H., and R.C. Trojanowicz. 1988. *Perspectives on Policing: Policing and the Fear of Crime*. Washington, D.C.: U.S. Department of Justice.

Moore, R.J. 1985. "Reflections of Canadians on the Law and the Legal System: Legal Research Institute Survey of Respondents in Montreal, Toronto, and Winnipeg." In D. Gibson and J.K. Baldwin (eds.), *Law in a Cynical Society?: Opinion and Law in the 1980s*. Calgary: Carswell.

Moore, W.H. 1974. *The Kefauver Commission and the Politics of Crime, 1950–1952*. Columbia: University of Missouri Press.

Morash, M. 1984. "Organized Crime." In R.F. Meier (ed.), *Major Forms of Crime*. Beverly Hills, Calif.: Sage.

Morin, E. 1971. *Rumour in Orleans*. New York: Pantheon.

Morris, N., and G. Hawkins. 1970. *The Honest Politician's Guide to Crime Control*. Chicago: University of Chicago Press.

Morrison, P. 1991a. *The Future of Crime Statistics in Canada*. A paper presented at the Meeting of the Canadian Sociology and Anthropology Association, Kingston, Ont.

———. 1991b. "Motor Vehicle Theft and Vehicle Vandalism." *Juristat Service Bulletin* 11(2). Ottawa: Canadian Centre for Justice Statistics.

Moysa, M. 1992. "Crown Backs Off Murder Charge." *Edmonton Journal*, (February 12), p. A1.

Muehlenhard, C.L., and M.A. Linton. 1987. "Date Rape and Sexual Aggression in Dating Situations: Incidence and Risk Factors." *Journal of Counseling Psychology* 34(2): 186–196.

Muir, R.G. 1987. "Fear of Crime: A Community Policing Perspective." Canadian Police College Journal 11(3): 170–196.

Mundt, R.J. 1990. "Gun Control and Dates of Firearm Violence in Canada and the United States." *Canadian Journal of Criminology* 32(1): 137–154.

Murphy, C. 1988. "Community Problems, Problem Communities and Community Policing in Toronto." *Journal of Research in Crime and Delinquency* 25(4): 392–410.

Murray, T. 1987. *Organized Crime: A Comparison Between the Experiences of Canada and the United States*. Ottawa: Ministry of the Solicitor General of Canada. Presented at the Annual Meetings of the American Society of Criminology.

Naffine, N. 1987. *Female Crime: The Construction of Women in Criminology*. Sydney: Allen and Unwin.

National Crime Prevention Institute. 1986. *Understanding Crime Prevention*. Boston: Butterworth.

Nelson, B. 1984. *Making an Issue of Child Abuse*. Chicago: University of Chicago Press.

Nettler, G. 1984. *Explaining Crime*. New York: McGraw-Hill.

Newman, G.R. 1990. "Popular Culture and Criminal Justice: A Preliminary Analysis." *Journal of Criminal Justice* 18: 261–274.

Newman, O. 1972. *Defensible Space: Crime Prevention through Urban Design*. New York: Macmillan.

New York Times. 1989 "Two Men Arrested in Shooting of Officer" (May 7), p. B2.

New York Times Magazine. 1989. "China Erupts: The Reasons Why" (June 4): 26–29.

Normandeau, A. 1987. "Crime on the Montreal Metro." *Sociology and Social Research* 71(4): 289–292.

O'Brien, R.M. 1986. "Rare Events, Sample Sizes and Statistical Problems in the Analysis of the NCS City Surveys." *Journal of Criminal Justice* 14: 441–448.

———. 1985. *Crime and Victimization Data*, Vol 4. Law and Criminal Justice Series. Beverly Hills, Calif.: Sage.

Oderkirk, J., and C. Lochhead. 1992. "Lone Parenthood: Gender Differences." *Canadian Social Trends* 27 (Winter): 16–19.

O'Grady, B. 1989. "Crime Violence and Victimization: A Newfoundland Case." *Canadian Criminology Forum* 10: 1–16.

Ontario Teachers' Federation. 1992. *The Safe School Task Force Resource Kit*, Vol. 1 (June). Toronto: OTF.

Osborne, J.A. 1991. "The Criminal Law." In A. Jackson and C.T. Griffiths (eds.), *Canadian Criminology*. Toronto: Harcourt Brace Jovanovich.

Packer, H.L. 1969. *The Limits of the Criminal Sanction*. Stanford Calif.: Stanford University Press.

Pagelow, M.D. 1989. "The Incidence and Prevalence of Criminal Abuse of Other Family Members." In L. Ohlin and M. Tonry (eds.), *Family Violence*. Chicago: University of Chicago Press.

Palenski, J.E. 1984. "The Use of Mediation By Police." *Mediation Quarterly* 5: 31–38.

Pandiani, J.A. 1978. "Crime Time TV: If all We Know is What We Saw ..." *Contemporary Crises* 2: 437–458.

Parker, G. 1991. "The Structure of Criminal Law." In R.A. Silverman, J.J. Teevan, and V.F. Sacco (eds.), *Crime in Canadian Society*, 4th ed. Toronto and Vancouver: Butterworths.

Parliament, J.B. 1990a. "Women Employed Outside the Home." In C. McKie and K. Thompson (eds.), *Canadian Social Trends*. Toronto: Thompson Educational Publishing.

———. 1990b. "Labour Force Trends: Two Decades In Review." *Canadian Social Trends* 18 (Autumn): 16–19.

Parsons, T. 1951. *The Social System*. Glenroe Ill.: Free Press.

Patterson, G.R., and T.J. Dishion. 1985. "Contributions of Families and Peers to Delinquency." *Criminology* 23: 63–79.

Pearce, F. 1991. *Second Islington Crime Survey: Commercial and Conventional Crime in Islington*. Kingston: Queen's University.

Peek, C.W., J.L. Fischer, and J.S. Kidwell. 1985. "Teenage Violence Toward Parents: A Neglected Dimension of Family Violence." *Journal of Marriage and the Family* 47: 1051–1058.

Pepinsky, H. and P. Jesilow. 1984. *Myths That Cause Crime*. Cabin John, Md.: Seven Locks Press.

Pfohl, S. 1977. "The Discovery of Child Abuse." *Social Problems* 24(3): 315–321.

Pfuhl, E.H. 1986. *The Deviance Process*. 2nd ed. Belmont, Calif.: Wadsworth.

Phelps, T.G. 1983. "The Criminal As Hero in American Fiction." *Wisconsin Law Review* 6: 1427–1454.

Phillips, D.P. 1983. "The Impact of Mass Media Violence on U.S. Homicides." *American Sociological Review* 48 (August): 560–568.

Pileggi, N. 1985. *Wiseguy: Life in a Mafia Family*. New York: Simon and Schuster.

Pillemer, K.A. 1985. "The Dangers of Dependency: New Findings on Domestic Violence Against the Elderly." *Social Problems* 33: 146–158.

Pillemer, K.A., and D. Finkelhor. 1988. "The Prevalence of Elder Abuse: A Random Sample Survey." *The Gerontologist* 28(1): 51–57.

Pitkin, T.M., and F. Cordasco. 1977. *The Black Hand: A Chapter in Ethnic Crime*. Totowa, N.J.: Littlefield, Adams.

Podnieks, E. 1990. *National Survey on Abuse of the Elderly in Canada*. Toronto: Ryerson Polytechnical Institute.

Pound, R. 1943. "A Survey of Social Interests." *Harvard Law Review* 53: 1–39.

Provenzo, E.F. 1991. *Video Kids: Making Sense of Nintendo*. Cambridge, Mass.: Harvard University Press.

Quinn, M.J., and S.K. Tomita. 1986. *Elder Abuse and Neglect: Causes, Diagnosis and Intervention Strategies*. New York: Springer-Verlag.

Quinney, R., and J. Wildeman. 1991. *The Problem of Crime: A Peace and Social Justice Perspective*. Montain View, Calif.: Mayfield.

Randall, D.M., L. Lee-Sammons, and P.H. Hagner. 1988. "Common Versus Elite Crime Coverage in Network News." *Social Science Quarterly* 69(4): 910–929.

Rankin, J.H., and L.E. Wells. 1990. "The Effect of Parental Attachments and Direct Controls on Delinquency." *Journal of Research in Crime and Delinquency* 27(2): 140–165.

Reasons, C.E. 1976. "Images of the Crime and the Criminal: The Dope Fiend Mythology." *Journal of Research in Crime and Delinquency* 13: 133–144.

Reasons, C.E., and D. Chappell. 1985. "Continental Capitalism and Crooked Lawyering." *Crime and Social Justice* 26: 38–59.

Reasons, C.E., L. Ross, and C. Paterson. 1981. *Assault on the Worker: Occupational Health and Safety in Canada*. Toronto: Butterworths.

Reiman, J.H. 1990. *The Rich Get Richer and the Poor Get Prison*. 3rd ed. New York: Macmillan.

Reiss, A.J., Jr. 1986a. "Official and Survey Crime Statistics." In E.A. Fattah (ed.), *From Crime Policy to Victim Policy—Reorienting the Justice System*. London: MacMillan.

———. 1986b. "Policy Implications of Crime Victim Surveys." In E.A. Fattah (ed.), *From Crime Policy to Victim Policy—Reorienting the Justice System*. London: MacMillan.

———. 1984. "Consequences of Compliance and Deterrence Models of Law Enforcement for the Exercise of Police Discretion." *Law and Contemporary Problems* 47(4): 83–122.

Reuter, P. 1984a. "The (Continued) Vitality of Mythical Numbers." *Public Interest* 75: 135–147.

————. 1984b. "Social Control in Illegal Markets." In D. Black (ed.), *Toward a General Theory of Social Control, Volume 2: Selected Problems*. Orlando, Fla.: Academic Press.

Riger, S. 1981. "On Women." In D.A. Lewis (ed.), *Reactions to Crime*. Beverly Hills, Calif.: Sage.

Riley, D. 1987. "Time and Crime: The Link Between Teenager Lifestyle and Delinquency." *Journal of Quantitative Criminology* 3(4): 339–354.

Robbins, L. 1990. "Eating Out." In C. McKie and K. Thompson (eds.), *Canadian Social Trends*. Toronto: Thompson Educational Publishing.

Roberts, K. 1983. *Youth and Leisure*. London: George Allen and Unwin.

Rogers, A.J. 1973. *The Economics of Crime*. Hinsdale, Ill.: Dryden Press.

Roncek, D.W. 1981. "Dangerous Places." *Social Forces* 60: 74–96.

Roncek, D.W., and P.A. Maier. 1991. "Bars, Blocks and Crimes Revisited: Linking the Theory of Routine Activities to the Empiricism of 'Hot Spots.'" *Criminology* 29(4): 725–753.

Roncek, D.W., and M.A. Pravatiner. 1989. "Additional Evidence that Taverns Enhance Nearby Crime." *Sociology and Social Research* 73(4): 185–188.

Rosenbaum, D.P. 1988. "Community Crime Prevention: A Review and Synthesis of the Literature." *Justice Quarterly* 5(3): 323–395.

————. 1987. "The Theory and Research Behind Neighborhood Watch: Is It a Sound Fear and Crime Reduction Strategy?" *Crime and Delinquency* 33(1): 103–134.

Rosenbaum, H.J., and P.C. Sederberg. 1976. "Vigilantism: An Analysis of Establishment Violence." In H.J. Rosenbaum and P.C. Sederberg (eds.), *Vigilante Politics*. Philadelphia: University of Pennsylvania Press.

Rosnow, R.L. 1988. "Rumour As Communication: A Contextual Approach." *Journal of Communication* 38(1): 12–28.

Rosnow, R.L., and G.A. Fine. 1976. *Rumor and Gossip*. New York: Elsevier.

Ross, R., and G.L. Staines. 1972. "The Politics of Analyzing Social Problems." *Social Problems* 20(1): 18–40.

Rossi, P.H., E. Waite, C.E. Bose, and R.E. Berk. 1974. "The Seriousness of Crimes: Normative Structure and Individual Differences." *American Sociological Review* 39: 224–237.

Ruback, R.B., M.S. Greenberg, and D.R. Wescott. 1984. "Social Influence and Crime-Victim Decision Making." *Journal of Social Issues* 40(1): 51–76.

Rubington, C., and M.S. Weinberg. 1987. *Deviance: The Interactionist Perspective*. New York: Macmillan.

Sacco, V.F. 1990. "Gender, Fear and Victimization: A Preliminary Application of Power-Control Theory." *Sociological Spectrum* 10: 485–506.

———. 1980. "An Approach to the Study of Organized Crime." In R.A. Silverman and J.J. Teevan (eds.), *Crime in Canadian Society*. 2nd ed. Toronto: Butterworths.

Sacco, V.F., and B.J. Fair. 1988. "Images of Legal Control: Crime News and the Process of Organizational Legitimation." *Canadian Journal of Communication* 13: 113–122.

Sacco, V.F., and H. Johnson. 1990. *Patterns of Criminal Victimization in Canada*. Ottawa: Minister of Supply and Services.

———. 1990b. "Urbanism and Criminal Victimization." Paper presented at the Annual Meetings of the Canadian Society and Anthropology Association, Victoria, B.C.

Sacco, V.F., and R.A. Silverman. 1982. "Crime Prevention Through Mass Media: Prospects and Problems." *Journal of Criminal Justice* 10: 257–269.

Sacco, V.F., and E. Zureik. 1990. "Correlates of Computer Misuse: Data from a Self-Reporting Sample." *Behaviour and Information Technology* 9(5): 353–369.

Sagarin, E. 1975. *Deviants and Deviance*. New York: Praeger.

Sales, E., M. Baum, and B. Shore. 1984. "Victim Readjustment Following Assault." *Journal of Social Issues* 40(1): 117–136.

Salinger, L.R., P. Jesilow, H.N. Pontell, and G. Geis. 1993. "Assaults Against Airline Flight Attendants: A Victimization Study" in H.N. Pontell (ed.), *Social Deviance*. Englewood Cliffs, N.J.: Prentice-Hall.

Sampson, R.J. 1987. "Urban Black Violence: The Effect of Male Joblessness and Family Disruption." *American Journal of Sociology* 93(2): 348–382.

———. 1985. "Race and Criminal Violence: A Demographically Disaggregated Analysis of Urban Homicide." *Crime and Delinquency* 31(1): 47–82.

Sampson, R.J., and W.B. Groves. 1989. "Community Structure and Crime: Testing Social Disorganization Theory." *American Journal of Sociology* 94: 774–802.

Sampson, R.J., and J.L. Lauritsen. 1990. "Deviant Lifestyles, Proximity Crime, and the Offender Victim Link in Personal Violence." *Journal of Research in Crime and Delinquency* 27(2): 110–139.

Sanger, David E. 1993. "How to Visit America and Get Out Alive." *Globe and Mail* (June 18), p. A9.

Saunders, D.G. 1989. "Who Hits First and Who Hurts Most?: Evidence for the Greater Victimization of Women in Intimate Relationships." Paper presented at the Annual Meeting of the American Society of Criminology, Reno, Nev. (November).

Savitz, L.D. 1978. "Official Police Statistics and Their Limitations." In L.D. Savitz and N. Johnston (eds.), *Crime in Society*. New York: John Wiley.

Scheingold, Stuart A. 1984. *The Politics of Law and Order: Street Crime and Public Policy*. New York: Longman.

Schelling, T.C. 1967. "Economic Analysis of Organized Crime." In *President's Commission on Law Enforcement and Administration of Justice Task Force Report: Organized Crime, Annotations and Consultant's Papers*. Washington, D.C.: U.S. Government Printing Office: 114–126.

Scheppele, K.L., and P.B. Bart. 1983. "Through Women's Eyes: Defining Danger in the Wake of Sexual Assault." *Journal of Social Issues* 39: 63–81.

Schissel, B. 1992. "The Influence of Economic Factors and Social Control Policy on Crime Rate Changes in Canada, 1962-1988." *Canadian Journal of Sociology* 17(4): 405–428.

Schneider, V.W., and B. Wiersema. 1990. "Limits and Use of the Uniform Crime Reports." In D.L. MacKenzie, P.J. Baunach, and R.R. Roberg (eds.), *Measuring Crime: Large-Scale, Long-Range Efforts*. Albany: State University of New York Press.

Schur, E.M. 1979. *Interpreting Deviance*. New York: Harper and Row.

Schwartz, M.D. 1988. "Ain't Got No Class: Universal Risk Theories of Battering." *Contemporary Crises*. 12: 375–392.

Scott, M., and S. Lyman. 1968. "Accounts." *American Sociological Review* 33: 42–62.

Scully, D., and J. Marolla. 1984 "Convicted Rapists' Vocabulary of Motive: Excuses and Justifications." *Social Problems* 31(5): 530–544.

Sedlak, A.J. 1988. "The Effects of Personal Experiences with Couple Violence on Calling It 'Battering' and Allocating Blame." In G.T. Hotaling, D. Finkelhor, J.T. Kirpatrick, and M.A. Straus (eds.), *Coping with Family Violence*. Newbury Park, Calif.: Sage.

Sellin, T. 1938. "Culture Conflict and Crime." *A Report of the Subcommittee on Delinquency of the Committee on Personality and Culture*. Social Science Research Council Bulletin 41.

Selzer, J.A., and D. Kalmus. 1988. "Socialization and Stress Explanations for Spouse Abuse." *Social Forces* 67(2): 473–491.

Servadio, G. 1976. *Mafioso: A History of the Mafia from Its Origins to the Present Day*. New York: Stein and Day.

Shaffer, Evelyn B. 1980. *Community Policing*. London: Croom Helm.

Shaw, C.R., and H.D. McKay. 1942. *Juvenile Delinquency in Urban Areas*. Chicago: University of Chicago Press.

Shearing, C.D., and P.C. Stenning. 1983. "Private Security: Implications for Social Control." *Social Problems* 30: 493–506.

Sheldon, W.H. 1940. *Varieties of Delinquent Youth: An Introduction to Constitutional Psychiatry*. New York: Harper and Brothers.

Sheley, J.F. 1991. "Conflict in Criminal Law." In J.F. Sheley (ed.), *Criminology: A Contemporary Handbook*. Belmont, Calif.: Wadsworth.

Sherman, L. 1992. *Policing Domestic Violence: Experiments and Dilemmas*. New York: Free Press.

Sherman, L., and R. Berk. 1984. "The Specific Deterrent Effects of Arrest for Domestic Assault." *American Sociological Review* 49: 261–72.

Sherman, L., P.R. Gartin, and M.E. Buerger. 1989. "Routine Activities and the Criminology of Place." *Criminology* 27(1): 27–55.

Sherman, L., J. Schmidt, D. Rogan, and C. DeRiso. 1991. "Predicting Domestic Homicide: Prior Police Contact and Gun Threats." In Michael Steinman (ed.), *Woman Battering: Policy Responses*. Cincinnati, Ohio: Anderson.

Shernock, S.K. 1986. "A Profile of the Crime Prevention Activist." *Journal of Criminal Justice* 14: 211–228.

Shibutani, T. 1966. *Improvised News: A Sociological Study of Rumor*. Indianapolis: Bobbs-Merrill.

Shotland, R.L. 1976. "Spontaneous Vigilantism: A Bystander Response to Criminal Behavior." In H.J. Rosenbaum and P.C. Sederberg (eds.), *Vigilante Politics*. Philadelphia: University of Pennsylvania Press.

Shotland, R.L., and L.I. Goodstein. 1984. "The Role of Bystanders in Crime Control." *Journal of Social Issues* 40(1): 9–26.

Shotland, R.L., and M.K. Straw. 1976. "Bystander Response to an Assault: When a Man Attacks a Woman." *Journal of Personality and Social Psychology* 34: 990–999.

Shover, N. 1983. "The Later Stages of Ordinary Property Offender Careers." *Social Problems* 30: 208–218.

————. 1973. "The Social Organization of Burglary." *Social Problems*. 201 (Spring): 499–513.

Sigler, R.T., and M. Johnson. 1986. "Public Perceptions of the Need for Criminalization of Sexual Harassment." *Journal of Criminal Justice* 14: 229–237.

Silverman, I., and S. Dinitz. 1974. "Compulsive Masculinity and Delinquency: An Empirical Investigation." *Criminology* 11: 498.

Silverman, R.A., and L.W. Kennedy. 1993. *Deadly Deeds: Murder in Canada*. Scarborough, Ont.: Nelson Canada.

————. 1992. "Interpersonal Relations and Means of Lethal Violence in Canada." In A. Kuhl (ed.), *Homicide: The Victim-Offender Connection*. Cincinnati, Ohio: Anderson.

Silverman, R.A., and M.O. Nielsen. 1992. *Aboriginal Peoples and Canadian Criminal Justice*. Toronto: Butterworths.

Silverman, R.A., J.J. Teevan, and V.F. Sacco. 1991. *Crime in Canadian Society*. 4th ed. Toronto: Butterworths.

Simon, D.R., and D.S. Eitzen. 1993. *Elite Deviance*. 4th ed. Boston: Allyn and Bacon.

Simpson, S.S. 1989. "Feminist Theory, Crime and Justice." *Criminology* 27(4): 605–631.

Simpson, S.S., and C.S. Koper. 1992. "Deterring Corporate Crime." *Criminology* 30(3): 347–375.

Singer, S.I., and M. Levine. 1988. "Power-Control Theory, Gender and Delinquency: A Partial Replication with Additional Evidence on the Effect of Peers." *Criminology* 26: 627–647.

Skinner, B.F. 1948. *Walden Two*. New York: MacMillan.

Skipper, J.K. 1985. "Nicknames of Notorious American Twentieth Century Deviants: The Decline of the Folk Hero Syndrome." *Deviant Behavior* 6: 99–114.

Skogan, W.G. 1990a. "The National Crime Survey Redesign." *Public Opinion Quarterly* 54: 256–272.

————. 1990b. *Disorder and Decline*. New York: Free Press.

————. 1986. "Methodological Issues in the Study of Victimization." In E.A. Fattah (ed.), *From Crime Policy to Victim Policy—Reorienting the Justice System*. London: MacMillan.

————. 1984. "Reporting Crimes to the Police: The Status of World Research." *Journal of Research in Crime and Delinquency* 21: 113–137.

————. 1977. "Dimensions of the Dark Figure of Unreported Crime." *Crime and Delinquency* 23: 41–50.

————. 1976. "Citizen Reporting of Crime: Some National Panel Data." *Criminology* 13(4): 535–549.

Skogan, W.G., and M.G. Maxfield. 1981. *Coping with Crime: Individual and Neighborhood Reactions.* Beverly Hills, Calif.: Sage.

Skolnick, J. 1966. *Justice Without Trial.* New York: John Wiley.

Smith, D. 1975. *The Mafia Mystique.* New York: Basic Books.

Smith, D.A. 1987. "Police Response to Interpersonal Violence: Defining the Parameters of Legal Control." *Social Forces* 65(3): 767–782.

Smith, D.A., and G.R. Jarjoura. 1989. "Household Characteristics, Neighbourhood Composition and Victimization Risk." *Social Forces* 68(2): 621–640.

————. 1988. "Social Structure and Criminal Victimization." *Journal of Research in Crime and Delinquency* 25: 27–52.

Smith, D.C. 1991. "Wickersham to Sutherland to Katzenbach: Evolving an 'Official' Definition for Organized Crime." *Crime, Law and Social Change* 16: 135–154.

Smith, M.D. 1988. *Woman Abuse in Toronto: Incidence, Prevalence and Demographic Risk Markers.* Toronto: Institute for Social Research and the LaMarsh Research Programme.

————. 1987. "Changes in the Victimization of Women: Is There A 'New' Female Victim?" *Journal of Research in Crime and Delinquency* 24(4): 291–301.

Smith, S.J. 1982. "Victimization in the Inner City." *British Journal of Criminology* 22: 386–401.

Snider, L. 1993. *Bad Business: Corporate Crime in Canada.* Scarborough, Ont.: Nelson Canada.

————. 1992. "Commercial Crime." In V.F. Sacco (ed.), *Deviance: Conformity and Control in Canadian Society.* 2nd ed. Scarborough, Ont.: Prentice-Hall.

Solicitor General of Canada. 1988a. *Canadian Urban Victimization Survey Bulletin 9: Patterns in Property Crime.* Ottawa: Programs Branch/Research and Statistics Group.

————. 1988b. *Canadian Urban Victimization Survey Bulletin 10: Multiple Victimization.* Ottawa: Programs Branch/Research and Statistics Group.

————. 1987. *Canadian Urban Victimization Survey Bulletin 8: Patterns in Violent Crime.* Ottawa: Programs Branch/Research and Statistics Group.

———. 1986. *Canadian Urban Victimization Survey Bulletin 7: Household Property Crimes*. Ottawa: Programs Branch/Research and Statistics Group.

———. 1985a. *Canadian Urban Victimization Survey Bulletin 4: Female Victims of Crime*. Ottawa: Programs Branch/Research and Statistics Group.

———. 1985b. *Canadian Urban Victimization Survey Bulletin 5: Cost of Crime to Victims*. Ottawa: Programs Branch/Research and Statistics Group.

———. 1984a. *Canadian Urban Victimization Survey Bulletin 2: Reported and Unreported Crime*. Ottawa: Programs Branch/Research and Statistics Group.

———. 1984b. *Canadian Urban Victimization Survey Bulletin 3: Crime Prevention: Awareness and Practice*. Ottawa: Programs Branch/Research and Statistics Group.

———. 1983. *Canadian Urban Victimization Survey Bulletin 1: Victims of Crime*. Ottawa: Programs Branch/ Research and Statistics Group.

Spector, M., and J.I. Kitsuse. 1977. *Constructing Social Problems*. Menlo Park, Calif.: Cummings.

Stafford, M.C., and O.R. Galle. 1984. "Victimization Rates, Exposure to Risk, and Fear of Crime." *Criminology* 22(2): 173–185.

Stafford, M.C., and J.P. Gibbs. 1980. "Crime Rates in an Ecological Context: Extension of a Proposition." *Social Science Quarterly* 61(3-4): 653–665.

Stamler, R.T. 1992. "Organized Crime." In R. Linden (ed.), *Criminology: A Canadian Perspective*. Toronto: Harcourt Brace Jovanovich.

Standing Committee on Communications and Culture. 1993. *Television Violence: Fraying Our Social Fabric*. Ottawa: House of Commons

Standing Committee on Justice and the Solicitor General. 1993. *Crime Prevention in Canada: Toward a National Strategy*. Ottawa: Queen's Printer.

Stanko, E. 1990. *Everyday Violence: How Women and Men Experience Sexual and Physical Danger*. London: Pandora.

———. 1990a. "When Precaution Is Normal: A Feminist Critique of Crime Prevention." In L. Gelsthorpe and A. Morris (eds.), *Feminist Perspectives in Criminology*. Philadelphia: Open University Press.

———. 1985. *Intimate Intrusions: Women's Experience of Male Violence*. London: Routledge and Kegan Paul.

Stark, R. 1987. "Deviant Places: A Theory of the Ecology of Crime." *Criminology* 25(4): 893–909.

Statistics Canada. 1985. *Canadian Crime Statistics*. Ottawa: Supply and Services Canada.

Steffensmeier, D.J., and E. Allen. 1991. "Gender, Age, and Crime." In J.F. Sheley (ed.), *Criminology: A Contemporary Handbook*. Belmont, Calif.: Wadsworth.

Steffensmeier, D.J., and R. H. Steffensmeier. 1977. "Who Reports Shoplifters?: Research Continuities and Further Developments." *International Journal of Criminology and Penology* 3: 79–95.

Steffensmeier, D.J., and R.M. Terry. 1973. "Deviance and Respectability: An Observational Study of Reactions to Shoplifting." *Social Forces* 51: 417–426.

Steinman, M. 1992. "Going Beyond Arrest: Police Responses to Domestic Violence." Paper presented at the Annual Meetings of the American Society of Criminology. New Orleans, La. (November).

Steinmetz, S. 1986. "The Violent Family." In M. Lystad (ed.), *Violence in the Home: Interdisciplinary Perspectives*. New York: Brunner/Mazel.

———. 1978. "Battered Parents." *Society* 15(5) (July/August): 54–55.

———. 1977–78. "The Battered Husband Syndrome." *Victimology: An International Journal* 2: 499–509.

Stoddart, K. 1991. "It's Easier for the Bulls Now: Official Statistics and Social Change in a Canadian Heroin-Using Community." In R.A. Silverman, J.J. Teevan, and V.F. Sacco (eds.), *Crime in Canadian Society*. 4th ed. Toronto: Butterworths.

———. 1981. "As Long as I Can't See You Do It: A Case Study of Drug-Related Activities in Public Places." *Canadian Journal of Criminology* 23(4): 391–405.

Stout, C. 1991. "Common Law: A Growing Alternative." *Canadian Social Trends* 23: 18–20.

Straus, M.A. 1991. "Discipline and Deviance: Physical Punishment of Children and Violence and Other Forms of Crime in Adulthood." *Social Problems* 38(2): 133–152.

———. 1990a. "The National Family Violence Surveys." In M.A. Straus and R.J. Gelles (eds.), *Physical Violence in American Families: Risk Factors and Adaptations to Violence in 8,145 Families*. New Brunswick, N.J.: Transaction.

———. 1990b. "Social Stress and Marital Violence in a National sample of American Families." In M.A. Straus and R.J. Gelles (eds.), *Physical*

Violence in American Families: Risk Factors and Adaptations to Violence in 8,145 Families. New Brunswick, N.J.: Transaction.

Strauss, M.A., and R.J. Gelles. 1990. "How Violent Are American Families?: Estimates from the National Family Violence Resurvey and Other Studies." In M.A. Straus and R.J. Gelles (eds.), *Physical Violence in American Families: Risk Factors and Adaptations to Violence in 8,145 Families*. New Brunswick, N.J.: Transaction.

Strauss, M.A., and C. Smith. 1990. "Family Patterns and Child Abuse." In M.A. Straus and R.J. Gelles (eds.), *Physical Violence in American Families: Risk Factors and Adaptations to Violence in 8,145 Families*. New Brunswick, N.J.: Transaction.

Sugarman, D.B., and G.T. Hotaling. 1989. "Dating Violence: Prevalence, Context and Risk Markers." In M.A. Pirog-Good and J.E. Stets (eds.), *Violence in Dating Relationships*. New York: Praeger.

Surette, R. 1992. *Media, Crime, and Criminal Justice: Images and Realities*. Pacific Grove, Calif.: Brooks/Cole.

Sutherland, E.H. 1961. *White Collar Crime*. New York: Holt, Rinehart and Winston.

———. 1947. *Principles of Criminology*. 4th ed. Chicago: J.B. Lippincott.

———. 1940. "White-Collar Criminality." *American Sociological Review* 5: 1–12.

Suttles, G. 1972. *The Social Construction of Communities*. Chicago: University of Chicago Press.

Sykes, G., and D. Matza. 1957. "Techniques of Neutralization: A Theory of Delinquency." *American Sociological Review* 22: 664–670.

Taber, J.K. 1980. "A Survey of Computer Crime Studies." *Computer Law Journal* 2: 275–328,

Tanioka, I. 1986. "Evidence Links Smoking to Violent Crime Victimization." *Sociology and Social Research* 71(1): 58.

Tanner, J. 1992. "Youthful Deviance." In V.F. Sacco (ed.), *Deviance: Control and Conformity in Canadian Society*. 2nd ed. Scarborough, Ont.: Prentice-Hall.

Tanner, J., and H. Krahn. 1991. "Part-time Work and Deviance Among High School Seniors." *Canadian Journal of Sociology* 16(3): 281–302.

Taylor, R.B., and S. Gottfredson. 1986. "Environmental Design, and Prevention: An Examination of Community Dynamics." In A.J. Reiss, Jr. and M. Tonry (eds.), *Communities and Crime*. Chicago: University of Chicago Press.

Taylor, S.E., J.V. Wood, and R.R. Lichtman. 1983. "It Could Be Worse: Selective Evaluation as a Response to Victimization." *Journal of Social Issues* 39: 19–40.

Thompson, W.E. 1986. "Courtship Violence: Toward a Conceptual Understanding." *Youth and Society* 18(2): 162–176.

Thornberry, T.P. 1987. "Toward an Interactional Theory of Delinquency." *Criminology* 25(4): 863–892.

Thornberry, T.P., A.J. Lizotte, M.D. Krohn, M. Farnworth, and S.J. Jang. 1991. "Testing Interactional Theory: An Examination of Reciprocal Casual Relationships Among Family, School, and Delinquency." *Journal of Criminal Law and Criminology* 82(1) Spring: 3–33.

Tierney, K. 1982. "The Battered Women Movement and the Creation of the Wife Beating Problem." *Social Problems* 29: 207–220.

Timmer, D.A., and W.H. Norman. 1984. "The Ideology of Victim Precipitation." *Criminal Justice Review* 9: 63–68.

Timrots, A.D., and M.R. Rand. 1987. *Violent Crime by Strangers and Non-Strangers*. Washington, D.C.: Bureau of Justice Statistics.

Toby, J. 1983 (December). "Violence in Schools." *National Institute of Justice: Research in Brief*. Washington, D.C.: U.S. Department of Justice.

———. 1974. "The Socialization and Control of Deviant Motivation." In Daniel Glaser (ed.), *Handbook of Criminology*. Chicago: Rand McNally.

Tracy, P.E., and J.A. Fox. 1989. "A Field Experiment on Insurance Fraud in Auto Body Repair." *Criminology* 27: 509–603.

Traub, S.H., and C.B. Little (eds.). 1980. *Theories of Deviance*. 2nd. ed. Itasca, Ill.: F.E. Peacock.

Trevethan, S., and S. Tajeshwer, 1992. "Gender Differences Among Violent Crime Victims." *Juristat Service Bulletin* 12(21). Ottawa: Canadian Centre for Justice Statistics.

Turk, A. 1976. "Law As a Weapon in Social Conflict." *Social Problems* 23: 276–292.

Unger, D.G., and A. Wandersman. 1985. "The Importance of Neighbors: The Social, Cognitive, and Affective Components of Neighboring." *American Journal of Community Psychology* 13(2): 139–169.

Ursel, E.J., and D. Farough. 1986. "The Legal and Public Response to the New Wife Abuse Directive in Manitoba." *Canadian Journal of Criminology* 28: 171–183.

U.S. Department of Justice. 1992. *Criminal Victimization in the United States, 1990*. Washington, D.C.

———. 1988. *Report to the Nation on Crime and Justice.* 2nd ed. Washington, D.C.

Van den Haag, E. 1975. *Punishing Criminals: Concerning a Very Old and Painful Question.* New York: Basic Books.

van Dijk, J.J.M., and J. de Waard. 1991. "A Two-Dimensional Typology of Crime Prevention Projects With a Bibliography." *Criminal Justice Abstracts* (September).

Visher, C.A. 1991. "Career Offenders and Selective Incapacitation." In J.F. Sheley (ed.), *Criminology: A Contemporary Handbook.* Belmont, Calif.: Wadsworth.

Voumvakis, S.E., and R.V. Ericson. 1984. *News Accounts of Attacks on Women: A Comparison of Three Toronto Newspapers.* Toronto: Centre of Criminology, University of Toronto.

Wachs, E. 1988. *Crime-Victim Stories: New York City's Urban Folklore.* Bloomington and Indianapolis: Indiana University Press.

Walker, S. 1989. *Sense and Nonsense About Crime: A Policy Guide.* 2nd ed. Pacific Grove, Calif.: Brooks/Cole.

Walklate, S. 1989. *Victimology: The Victim and the Criminal Justice System.* London: Unwin Hyman.

Waller, I. 1989. *Current Trends in European Crime Prevention: Implications for Canada.* Ottawa: Department of Justice Canada.

———. 1982. "Victimization Studies as Guides to Action: Some Cautions and Suggestions." In H.J. Schneider (ed.), *The Victim in International Perspective.* New York: Aldine de Gruyter.

Waller, I., and N. Okihiro. 1978. *Burglary: The Victim and the Public.* Toronto: University of Toronto Press.

Waller, I., and R. Weiler. 1984. *Crime Prevention Through Social Development.* Ottawa: Canadian Council on Social Development.

Walsh, W.F., and E.J. Donovan. 1989. "Private Security and Community Policing: Evaluation and Comment." *Journal of Criminal Justice* 17: 187–197.

Walters, G.D., and T.W. White. 1989. "Heredity and Crime: Bad Genes or Bad Research." *Criminology* 27(3): 455–458.

Warr, M. 1991. "America's Perceptions of Crime and Punishment." In J.F. Sheley (ed.), *Criminology: A Contemporary Handbook.* Belmont, Calif.: Wadsworth.

———. 1989. "What Is the Perceived Seriousness of Crimes?" *Criminology* 27: 795–821.

———. 1988. "Rape, Burglary, and Opportunity." *Journal of Quantitative Criminology* 4(3): 275–288.

Webb, V.J., and I.H. Marshall. 1989. "Response to Criminal Victimization by Older Americans." *Criminal Justice and Behavior* 16(2): 239–258.

Weeks, E.L., J.M. Boles, A.P. Garbin, and J. Blount. 1986. "The Transformation of Sexual Harassment from a Private Trouble to a Public Issue." *Sociological Inquiry* 56: 432–455.

Weis, J.G. 1989. "Family Violence Research Methodology and Design." In L. Ohlin and M. Tonry (eds.), *Family Violence, Crime and Justice—A Review of Research*. Vol. 11. Chicago: University of Chicago Press.

Wellford, C. 1975. "Labelling Theory and Criminology: An Assessment." *Social Problems* 22: 332–345.

Wellman, B., and B. Leighton. 1979. "Networks, Neighborhoods, and Communities: Approaches to the Study of the Community Question." *Urban Affairs Quarterly* 14: 363–390.

Wells, L.E., and J.H. Rankin. 1991. "Families and Delinquency: A Meta-Analysis of the Impact of Broken Homes." *Social Problems* 38(1): 71–93.

———. 1988. "Direct Parental Controls and Delinquency." *Criminology* 26: 263–285.

———. 1986. "The Broken Homes Model of Delinquency: Analytical Issues." *Journal of Research in Crime and Delinquency* 23(1): 68–93.

West, D.J., and D.P. Farrington. 1977. *The Delinquent Way of Life*. London: Heinemann.

Whitaker, C.J., and L.D. Bastian. 1991. *Teenage Victims*. A National Crime Survey Report. Washington, D.C.: U.S. Department of Justice.

Williams, K.R., and R.L. Flewelling. 1988. "The Social Production of Criminal Homicide: A Comparative Study of Disaggregated Rates in American Cities." *American Sociological Review* 53: 421–431.

Williams, K.R., and R. Hawkins. 1986. "Perceptual Research on General Deterrence: A Critical Review." *Law and Society Review* 20: 545–572.

Wilson, J. 1980. "Sociology of Leisure." *Annual Review of Sociology* 6: 21–40.

Wilson, J.Q. 1983. *Thinking About Crime*. New York: Vintage.

Wilson, J.Q., and R.J. Herrnstein. 1985. *Crime and Human Nature*. New York: Simon and Schuster.

Wilson, J.Q., and G.L. Kelling. 1982. "Broken Windows." *Atlantic Monthly* (March): 29–38.

Wilson, N.K. 1985. "Venerable Bedfellows: Women's Liberation and Women's Victimization." *Victimology* 10: 206–220.

Wilson, P.R., R. Lincoln, and D. Chappell. 1986. "Physician Fraud and Abuse in Canada: A Preliminary Examination." *Canadian Journal of Criminology* 28(2): 129–146.

Wilson, W.J. 1987. *The Truly Disadvantaged: The Inner City, The Underclass, and Public Policy*. Chicago: University of Chicago Press.

Wirth, L. 1938. "Urbanism as a Way of Life." *American Journal of Sociology* 44: 3–24.

Wirtz, P.W. and A.V. Harrell. 1987. "Police and Victims of Physical Assault." *Criminal Justice and Behavior* 14: 81–92.

Wolf, D. 1991. *The Rebels: A Brotherhood of Outlaw Bikers*. Toronto: University of Toronto Press.

Wolff, L. 1991. "Drug Crimes" *Canadian Social Trends* 20: 27–29.

Wolfgang, M. 1958. *Patterns in Criminal Homicide*. Philadelphia: University of Pennsylvania Press.

Wolfgang, M., and F. Ferracuti. 1967. *The Subculture of Violence: Towards an Integrated Theory in Criminology*. Beverly Hills, Calif.: Sage.

Wolfgang, M., R.M. Figlio, and T. Sellin. 1972. *Delinquency in a Birth Cohort*. Chicago: University of Chicago Press.

Wright, C., and J-P. Leroux. 1991. "Children as Victims of Violent Crime." *Juristat Service Bulletin* 11(8). Ottawa: Canadian Centre for Justice Statistics.

Wright, J.D., and P. Rossi. 1986. *Armed and Considered Dangerous: A Survey of Felons and Their Firearms*. Hawthorne, N.Y.: Aldine de Gruyter.

Wright, R., and T. Bennett. 1990. "Exploring the Offender's Perspective: Observing and Interviewing Criminals." In K.L. Kempf (ed.), *Measurement Issues in Criminology*. New York: Springer-Verlag.

Young, A. 1990. "Television Viewing." In C. McKie and K. Thompson (eds.), *Canadian Social Trends*. Toronto: Thompson Educational Publishing.

Zamble, E. 1990. "Public Support for Criminal Justice Policies: Some Specific Findings." *Forum on Corrections Research* 2(1): 14–19.

Zatz, M.S. 1987. "Chicago Youth Gangs and Crime: The Creation of a Moral Panic." *Contemporary Crises* 11: 129–158.

Ziegenhagen, E.A., and D. Brosnan. 1985. "Victims' Responses to Robbery and Crime Control Policy." *Criminology* 23: 675–695.

COPYRIGHT ACKNOWLEDGMENTS

Grateful acknowledgment is made to the following for permission to reprint previously published material:

Canadian Journal of Criminology, for three passages: one from P.L. Brantingham and P.J. Brantingham, "Situational Crime Prevention in Practice," *Canadian Journal of Criminology* 32, no. 1 (1990), pp. 17–40; one from the Canadian Criminal Justice Association, "Safer Communities: A Social Strategy for Crime Prevention in Canada," *Canadian Journal of Criminology* 31, no. 4 (1989), pp. 359–363; and one from P.R. Wilson, R. Lincoln, and D. Chappell, "Physician Fraud and Abuse in Canada: A Preliminary Examination," *Canadian Journal of Criminology* 28, no. 2 (1986), p. 129–146. All three passages copyright by the Canadian Criminal Justice Association.

Canadian Journal of Sociology, for material from Walter DeKeseredy and Katharine Kelly, "The Incidence and Prevalence of Woman Abuse in Canadian University and College Dating Relationships," *Canadian Journal of Sociology* 18, no. 2 (Spring 1993).

Canadian Psychological Association, for the table "Husband-to-Wife Violence," from L.W. Kennedy and D.G. Dutton, "The Incidence of Wife Assault in Alberta," *Canadian Journal of Behavioural Science* 21, no. 1, pp. 40–54. Copyright 1989. Canadian Psychological Association. Reprinted with permission.

Correctional Service of Canada, for data from Dennis Cooley, "Prison Victimization and the Informal Rules of Social Control," *Forum on Corrections Research* 4, no. 3

NAME INDEX

SUBJECT INDEX

laboratory experiments and, 218
mass media and, 27, 30, 59, 150, 218, 219, 306
television, 215, 216, 218, 235
times and locations of, 134
victim-offender exchange, 106, 107
victim precipitation of, 104
women and, 21, 27, 58, 59, 87, 168, 190, 191, 219, 220, 224, 227–29, 288, 307
See also Subcultural approach
Violent crime, 23, 24, 26, 27, 28, 34, 76, 117–19, 133, 157, 165, 191, 216, 217, 245, 246, 250, 262, 264, 286, 296

White-collar crime
deterrence of, 61, 136
culture of competition, 59, 122
differential association, 57
media coverage and, 26
myths about, 84
See also Occupational crime
Wife abuse. *See* Family (domestic) violence
Witnesses, 127–29, 140, 147, 148, 166
See also Bystanders; Third parties

Westray coal mine, 3, 10, 260
Women, 19, 21, 27, 33, 58, 86, 87, 117, 124, 127, 130, 140, 168–70, 176, 179, 187, 189–92, 196, 210, 214, 219, 220, 224, 227–29, 233, 288, 301, 307
Workplace domain
crime rates, 245
criminal career, 262–65, 280
employed vs. unemployed, 239–40, 279
labour force changes, 238
occupational and victimization risks, 96, 137, 243–45, 249–50, 279, ·290
reporting of crime, 251, 279
routine activities theory, 240, 241, 248, 252, 254
schools, 225–48, 250
stress, 241–43
violence, 242, 243, 249, 250
work career, 261–62
workplace conditions and victimization risks, 247, 248
work-related crime, 252, 254–60, 266–67, 270–74, 276–81, 289
See also Occupational crime; White-collar crime

To the owner of this book

We hope that you have enjoyed *The Criminal Event,* and we would like to know as much about your experiences as you would care to offer. Only through your comments and those of others can we learn how to make this a better text for future readers.

School _____ Your instructor's name _____

Course _____ Was the text required? _____ Recommended? _____

1. What did you like the most about *The Criminal Event*?

_____

_____

_____

2. How useful was this text for your course?

_____

_____

_____

3. Do you have any recommendations for ways to improve the next edition of this text?

_____

_____

_____

4. In the space below or in a separate letter, please write any other comments you have about the book. (For example, please feel free to comment on reading level, writing style, terminology, design features, and learning aids.)

_____

_____

_____

_____

Optional

Your name _____ Date _____

May Nelson Canada quote you, either in promotion for *The Criminal Event* or in future publishing ventures?

Yes _____   No _____

Thanks!